Research and the Teacher

Research and the Teacher

A qualitative introduction to school-based research

Second edition

Graham Hitchcock and David Hughes

London and New York

First published 1989
by Routledge
11 New Fetter Lane, London EC4P 4EE
Reprinted four times

Second edition published 1995
by Routledge
11 New Fetter Lane, London EC4P 4EE
29 West 35th Street, New York, NY 10001
Reprinted 1997, 1999

Reprinted 2001 by RoutledgeFalmer

RoutledgeFalmer is an imprint of the Taylor & Francis Group

Typeset in Times by Datix International Limited, Broad Street, Bungay, Suffolk
Printed and bound in Great Britain by T.J. International Ltd, Padstow, Cornwal

British Library Cataloguing in Publication Data
A catalogue record for this book is available from the British Library

Library of Congress Cataloguing in Publication Data
A catalogue record for this book has been requested

ISBN 0-415-10102-6

Contents

Figures

Preface

Much has happened in the worlds of education and research since we first wrote this book. This second revised edition is an attempt to take into account some of these important changes and reflect more accurately the contemporary practice of qualitative research. The audience we have in mind remains largely the same: practising teachers at all levels of the education system as well as those engaged in research for formal qualifications at both undergraduate and postgraduate levels. However, increasingly those engaged in 'teaching' in the health and caring professions are becoming actively involved in qualitative research and we hope that there will be something of interest to them here. Theoretically, whilst the divisions between quantitative research and qualitative research remain and the debates between positivism and interpretivism continue we are no longer concerned to justify qualitative, interpretive and naturalistic approaches in the human sciences via an extended critique of other positions. Instead we believe that it is much more profitable to confront the contemporary diversity of qualitative traditions and explore the value of these approaches for practitioner research.

Since we first wrote this book, and indeed for some time before that, the impact of feminist scholarship and a consideration of the significance of gender on all aspects of social research has had far reaching consequences. Chapter 4 therefore explores this area in some detail. Second, qualitative research and teacher research has not escaped the influence of broader intellectual currents. Feminism is one; the notion of reflection in professional practice and postmodernist thinking are two other trends we have attempted to engage. Much higher profile is also given early on to the significance of ethical issues and the challenge this poses for school-based research.

Whilst these theoretical concerns are significant it is important to have a sound practical and operational understanding of the research process. We have therefore provided, in Chapter 5, a pathway through the research process which covers all of the major aspects of the research enterprise likely to be encountered by anyone doing any kind of research. Our comments and guidance, however, has qualitative research specifically in mind. We have also paid much more attention to the complex issues surrounding qualitative data analysis, devoting the whole of Chapter 12 to a synthesis of current practice. Since many students in a variety of contexts we have worked with have been dealing with visual data sources we have attempted to unravel some of the analytical issues in Chapter 12.

Similarly, the growth in the use of documents has meant focusing in some detail on the issues raised with these materials. Chapter 9 seeks to maintain a balance between recent thinking on the primacy of language and more traditional approaches to the establishment of meaning and the interpretation of documents in looking at documents as sources of data in qualitative research. One of the most promising and significant developments in research on teaching and learning has been the focus, via life history work, on individual biography. The 'biographic move' is discussed extensively in Chapter 8. In order to attempt some kind of coherence we have suggested that the case study format is the most appropriate framework for small-scale qualitative school-based research. Finally, one of the most profound influences on the changes we discuss throughout the book, with the contemporary diversity of qualitative research, has been a renewed concern with writing and the writing/communication process. This has particular relevance for practitioner research and we explore conventions, narrative and stories in the final chapter. We raise questions about research, the ownership of knowledge and the most appropriate ways of presenting research.

We can only hope to offer a broad framework and raise questions as well as give advice. Those involved in research will have to engage directly with the literature. To this end we have revised, extended and updated our examples, illustrations and suggestions for further reading. In particular, we have drawn examples and highlighted work from both the USA and Canada. In doing so we feel exempt from the kinds of criticism applied to much North American research, that it systematically ignores work in the British tradition, by deliberately taking on North American developments.

Whilst we believe that this is a fairly comprehensive selection, the suggestions for further reading are *suggestions*, the reader can and should pursue her own list. We hope they highlight the best of the past and the best of the contemporary dealing with the most appropriate ways of exploring the world of teaching and learning, with the continuing debate over professional development. This it is hoped will lead to a better understanding of our work with each other, and with children, young people and adults.

As with the first edition this second revised edition is not intended as a simplistic 'how to do it' text. There are plenty of such unreconstructed text books about. We did not want to add to this list, believing that our readers, our colleagues and students and our friends deserved more. The issues are complex and controversial. We have not attempted to gloss over this. The role of the teacher in contemporary society is constantly changing and being contested. Issues of power, knowledge and ownership abound. We need to look very closely at the nature of evidence and the claims made about school and classroom processes. We hope to have addressed some of these and other issues in writing a book not just for the 1990s but beyond.

We wish to acknowledge the secretarial support of the following people: Eileen Stables, Jackie Wells, Thea Boulton, Lynn Molloy, Lorraine Walker and Carolyn Beardsmore who have struggled with our manuscripts and their wordprocessors.

Acknowledgements

The authors and publishers would like to thank the following for permission to reproduce copyright materials: Routledge & Kegan Paul, for the observation categories of the teacher record, p. 17, from M. Galton and B. Simon (eds) (1980) *Progress and Performance in the Primary School*; Falmer Press, The Taylor and Francis Group, for floor plan of Harmony Pre-school, p. 84, and for flowchart for 'Sue', Harmony Pre-school, p. 47, from S. Lubeck (1985) *Sandbox Society: Early Education in Black and White America - A Comparative Ethnography*.

Part I

Designs and approaches

1 Introduction

AIMS

We aim to try and do a number of things in this book which we hope will be of value and significance to teachers working in a variety of contexts. Essentially, our aim is to provide teachers, from those working with reception classes to those in further and higher education, with a knowledge and understanding of just how they might go about researching their own practice. However, this is not a simple 'how to do it' text. Many complex issues surround, for example, the nature of particular research strategies; what, in fact, to research in the first place, or even what counts as acceptable evidence. These and other questions will all need to be explored and some kind of answers provided. In this book we aim to:

- Provide an understanding of the kinds of relationships which can exist between teaching, teachers and research.
- Develop skills for the critical assessment of evidence about school/college educational processes.
- Present an account of some of the main methodological orientations in social and educational research in general and qualitative research in particular.
- Provide a 'hands on' appreciation of major qualitative research techniques.
- Emphasize the socially situated nature of research, and
- Enable teachers to design, conduct and evaluate small-scale research into teaching and learning by use of a variety of qualitative research techniques.

This book is written from a firm commitment that there is an important relationship between teaching, teacher research and reflection. We are not arguing that all teachers must become social/educational researchers. We are arguing that a knowledge and understanding of research and critical inquiry will help teachers to assess more effectively the quality and significance of evidence and claims about teaching and learning. We are arguing, and many initial and in-service and post-graduate courses back this up, that teachers can develop the kinds of skills needed to engage in small-scale research into their own practice and that this is an integral aspect of professional self- and critical reflection and development. A number of ideas and questions are tangled up here. These include:

- What constitutes teaching?
- What is a teacher?
- What counts as research?
- What is reflection and how can it be developed?

We will take each of these in turn and unravel the ideas and assumptions entailed in them, thus setting the scene for our vision of teachers as researchers.

TEACHING

What might constitute an all-encompassing definition of teaching in the 1990s is certainly debatable. Obviously, teaching is that which goes on between teachers and learners in classrooms, but it is also an activity which can take place in a variety of settings and with markedly different groups of learners. What then seems essential to the notion of teaching? Teaching involves the application of technical and professional skills and knowledge to particular situations. It must necessarily involve teachers making judgements in the light of these skills and knowledge. Teachers will, therefore, have to have certain levels of underpinning knowledge, whether it be technical or traditional academic subject knowledge, as well as the skills and competencies required for delivery of that knowledge, and the management of the learning environment. Since teaching and learning are social activities it is reasonable to assume that teaching will be based upon an understanding of the learning process and the specifics of child development and adult learning, for example.

Whilst no one would, we feel, disagree with the above description in broad terms, the particular configurations of these elements which may be regarded as producing effective teaching, is a controversial matter indeed. Most notable are the debates over 'formal' versus 'informal' teaching styles or the need to get 'back to basics'. The evaluation of policies, curricula and pedagogic practices is an important aspect of educational research. Hence, whilst on the one hand the notion of teaching is self-evident, on the other hand, it is clearly not.

TEACHERS

Although teachers are professionals, they are also individual human beings. Many reforms over the last few years have failed to grasp the important factor that changes in education also involves changes in teachers' lives. We regard this as so important that we have devoted a whole chapter to the significance of individual biography in understanding the teaching and learning process. Teaching is made up of individual teachers and these individuals all have their own personal and career histories, their own personalities, their own attitudes, values and experiences. Their views and experiences are shaped by their past, their gender, age and ethnicity. All these factors, or variables have a role to play. Most teachers nowadays will have come into direct contact with 'research' either in the form of accepted wisdoms, evidence and information gained through training, or from further study or in-service courses.

Unlike, for example, the education of nurses, teaching has never been wholly 'research based'. Yet, research has often been referred to as providing the evidence for preferred curricular, classroom or pedagogic options. What individual teachers choose to do with, or make of, research is what concerns us. Research and reflection, as we will define them shortly, are regarded by us as central ingredients in the individual professional development of teachers. The skills of either conducting research or being able to assess research evidence, and the ability to engage in critical self-reflection, have major advantages for professional development. Teaching can become more than simply the application of technical and professional skills and knowledge, and teachers become more than simply practitioners. This, of course, begs the question of what we mean by research and reflection.

RESEARCH

As we use the term here, 'research' refers to 'systematic inquiry', inquiry that is characterized by sets of principles, guidelines for procedures and which is subject to evaluation in terms of criteria such as validity, reliability and representativeness. In this sense, 'social research' refers both to the collection and analysis of information on the social world, in order to understand and explain that world better. 'Educational research' or 'classroom research' is based on the world of education. Research, therefore, refers to the process of obtaining and analysing information and data. 'Research finding' refers to the products of that research. Both the process of researching and research findings must be looked at critically and with a fair degree of caution. We will try to show how this can be done.

The link between teaching and research is a complex one. It is our view that research has and continues to contribute much of significance to our understanding of the educational process. Research can function to generate questions about teaching and learning. It can explore and test existing theories and explanations. Research can be used to open up difficult and problematic areas, providing descriptions of them and through evaluation studies, research can focus upon the effectiveness of existing curricular and pedagogic policies and processes.

Definitions of kinds of research

Research is often prefixed by words such as 'pure', 'basic', 'applied' or 'action'. What do each of these terms mean, and what are the connections, if any, between them? A distinction is often drawn between 'pure' and 'applied' research. It is often argued that pure research is not primarily concerned to develop understanding of practical problems but rather to advance knowledge within a particular area of human life or one academic discipline. Whereas applied research is in no way less rigorous in its approach, its attention is focused on certain issues from the beginning. An example is modern research into learning theory which, while extending general knowledge, has as one of its objectives the application of its findings to a number of areas. The point is that applied research seeks generalizations from a large number of cases and the link between the research findings and their application need not be immediate. Another feature of applied research is that the link between those who do the research and those who apply it need not normally be a close one. The dissemination of information is often secondhand, via books, articles and teaching.

Action research, on the other hand, which has often been put forward as the model for teacher–researchers to adopt, might be described as inquiry conducted on a particular issue of current concern, usually undertaken by those directly involved, with the aim of implementing a change in a specific situation. Cohen and Manion (1986) have drawn the distinctions between action research and applied research by suggesting that the conditions which usually govern applied research are somewhat more relaxed in action research since the latter focuses upon a specific situation or problem in a specific setting (Cohen and Manion 1986: 209).

In contrast, by 'evaluation' we mean the systematic study of a particular programme or set of events over a period of time in order to assess effectiveness. This kind of research may be a case of simple appraisal carried out by an individual teacher into an aspect of curriculum, or a nationally conducted survey, such as that currently being undertaken by the National Foundation for Education Research into the Technical and Vocational Education Initiative (TVEI). The emphasis in evaluation is on the assessment of the effectiveness of a particular programme or how well it has worked in terms of its aims.

Underlying these various definitions of research are debates about the relationship between research and practice. Nowhere is this more crucial than in research undertaken by the teachers' research movement:

- Is the role of educational or teacher research to provide tips for teachers?
- Is the goal of research the development of more effective teaching strategies?
- Alternatively, ought research to throw light on the social and cultural processes which affect a student's learning or help teachers and policy-makers

obtain a better understanding of the context in which teaching and learning takes place?

It is clear that teacher research can embrace any of these aims. Teachers may find themselves engaged at different times in a variety of types of research, each having rather different aims.

Teacher research refers to the research that the practising teacher is able to conduct in the context of immediate professional practice. This utilizes and modifies the insights and procedures of social and educational research in applying them to school or college circumstances.

In this sense, research will have a number of benefits. Carrying out research will encourage a systematic approach to the collection of information and, furthermore, will help to develop a respect for evidence which, in turn, will lead to more critically informed opinions. Those involved in research will have the opportunity to rethink assumptions. A distinction may instantly be drawn between professional researchers and teacher–researchers.

Despite the fact that the number of teachers with research experience has grown over recent years, teachers are not professional academic researchers they are teachers. For many, the terms 'teacher' and 'research' are mutually exclusive. Doubts are raised about the knowledge base from which teachers might carry out research. Their jobs are so demanding, it is argued, that they simply have no time in which to do any research. Furthermore, they have not received any training in the skills required and lack the appropriate objectivity or distance from the subject of their research. Although many argue, quite rightly, that teachers should be made more familiar with the assumptions and methods of educational research so that they might better evaluate its products, the process of researching itself is best left to professional researchers.

In contrast, we have taken a rather different view of the relationship between teaching and research. Whilst not underestimating the difficulties involved in teachers undertaking research, we emphasize the importance, positive value and excitement of teacher school-based research. There is also an important sense in which teacher research, viewed as a critical, reflexive and professionally oriented activity, might be regarded as a crucial ingredient in the teacher's professional role. This ought to have the effect not only of enhancing the teacher's professional status but also of generating self-knowledge and personal development in such a way that practice of teaching can be improved. It should also have the additional advantage of enhancing the intellectual status of teachers as they demonstrate these skills in numerous aspects of their work. However, we are not saying that teachers *must* become researchers, but, rather, that engagement with the process and products of research can enhance professional development.

Another view which is often expressed is that teachers themselves have little regard for the findings of conventional educational research, seeing it as having limited, if any, practical value. They are especially critical, it is contended, of the divorce (as they perceive it) between theory and practice, and to the abstract and alien language of the social sciences of which conventional educational research is part. The obscurity of the language and the high level of generality implied in much research has often resulted in teachers perceiving this work as being remote and divorced from their needs and situations. This has led some to argue that, whereas teachers should engage in systematic inquiry into their practice, such research should have a strictly pedagogic intent, and teachers need not become over-involved in the methodological issues of social science.

Here again, we will argue a different viewpoint. Although research into education, especially that undertaken by teachers, has its own individual focus, schools inhabit the same world that is explored by all social scientists. That being the case, educational research cannot divorce itself completely from the methodological issues which social science research raises, nor from understanding the language in which such research is conducted. As such, it is important for teachers considering undertaking research into their own practice (at whatever level) to acquire an appreciation of the frameworks within which research has been discussed and practised in the social sciences. Any piece of social or educational research is informed by some basic underlying assumptions and employs certain procedures. It is vital, therefore, to know what these are in order to carry out research and to assess in any meaningful way the products of such research. Our ideas are reinforced by the increasing amount of research which is now being conducted by teachers, some of it being published, and by the enthusiastic way in which some of the teachers we have worked with have tackled the methodological and substantive issues raised by investigations of topics such as gender and schooling, multicultural issues, parental involvement, and mainstreaming children with special educational needs. An understanding of models of research design in education and the human sciences is important since both conventional educational research and that which is applied to the solution of particular problems undertaken by professional academics and others has always been closely linked to educational policy and training. The modern teacher needs, in our view, to be equipped to understand the methodologies and language that underpin research not only to make sense of both current policy and initial and in-service training approaches but also to be able to apply a selective and critical attitude towards its relevance and application in practice.

A common response by teachers who have undertaken a course with a methodological or research component is that it has improved their ability to contribute to discussions on school policy in a more critical and effective manner and to assess the evidence and claims of educational research more effectively.

It has, perhaps, never been more important to challenge the findings of research and the nature of claims made than in periods of rapid educational reform. One of the research skills we wish to develop in teachers is their ability to scrutinize and assess research findings. A number of examples are provided throughout the book. However, an important recent example of the need to be critical about the nature and function of research findings is identified by Hammersley and Scarth (1993).

Hammersley and Scarth (1993) subject one of the most influential recent reports in education to serious scrutiny. The report of the so-called 'three wise men' *Curriculum Organisation and Practice in Primary Schools: A Discussion Document*, (DES, 1992) raised many issues about the nature of primary school practice and the implications to be drawn from educational research in this area. The unprecedented media coverage and clear political nature of the debate meant that this report and its findings were given an unusually high profile. Martyn Hammersley and John Scarth, experienced researchers, explore the background to the report and examine and assess its key arguments. Briefly, they argue that the research evidence cited does not offer any kind of convincing support for the claims made (see also Alexander 1992).

Robin Alexander, Jim Rose and Chris Woodhead (the 'three wise men') were charged by Kenneth Clarke (then Secretary of State for Education) with the task of reviewing evidence about the current state of primary education. After reminding us of the significance of the historical/political context of any report such as this, Hammersley and Scarth (1993) concentrate their attention upon those aspects of the report which focus upon educational standards and the quality of teaching.

Basically, the 'three wise men' argued that there were unsatisfactory levels of pupil progress, in particular in literacy and numeracy, and that this was the product of poor quality teaching which, in turn, was the result of many teachers' adherence to a 'progressive' dogma. In contrast, the report encourages the use of greater whole-class teaching approaches and more subject specialization (DES 1992: para 2, 3, and 50). The authors themselves claim the research on this is itself inadequate. On these grounds alone, it is not possible then to draw conclusions about particular trends.

On the question of possible cause for this (as yet, a situation which is confused and only partly understood), the now-familiar strategy of blaming teachers is appealed to by the report. The reason, of course, is the old chestnut of 'progressivism'. This dogma, it is argued, has made classroom practices, on the one hand, overly complex and, on the other, lacking structure. Hammersley and Scarth (1993: 493) point out that the beliefs which are supposedly held by teachers and which are responsible for these shortcomings are complex, diverse and sometimes contradictory. In any case, the research on documenting teachers' pedagogical orientations is not conclusive. Such research poses special methodological problems and, anyway, there may be other important causal factors.

It appears very much as if these 'three wise men' are doing no more than simply 'passing off their own opinions as established facts, and doing so on the basis of a spurious appeal to the findings of educational research' (Hammersley and Scarth 1993: 495).

We have drawn attention to the DES (1992) report and to Hammersley and Scarth's (1993) critique of the basis of this report for a number of reasons. First, it is essential to unravel the ambiguity which surrounds assumptions about the relationship between research and practice. Second, it is important to be able to make sound judgements about the nature of claims and their relationship to evidence and, third, in our encouragement of reflection, dialogue and critical self-development, it is necessary to challenge the contemporary orthodoxy that views teachers as unthinking, mechanical beings. We hope to make a contribution to the development of this understanding among practising teachers.

In addition to the development of a critical stance to educational research and its findings, it is important to become familiar with the advantages and disadvantages, and the potential and limitations of particular research techniques. There are a number of practical constraints which stem from the nature of the teacher's role that will also affect both the choice of a particular technique and the way in which it can be used. We place each of the techniques we discuss in the context of school and classroom life and provide guidelines on the choice of technique. Perhaps the most often heard reservations about teacher research is that teachers invariably possess neither the skills nor the resources to carry out satisfactory and acceptable research. Although this book cannot do anything to change the resources available to teachers, it can help to provide knowledge of the contemporary situation and the ways in which these resources may be used. It is to be hoped that having worked through the sections on techniques, teachers will develop an appreciation of the skills involved in researching. Our experience of working with teachers who have conducted small-scale, school-based research, and the products of teacher research now emerging (Hustler, Cassidy and Cuff 1986) suggests that teacher research can generate rich, illuminating and important insights into the way in which we teach and learn in our society. Such insights ought to have a crucial place in the formulation of policy and practice. Furthermore, qualitative research traditions, which are the major focus of this book, provide an important alternative to the quantitative statistical–experimental paradigm which has been the major influence in informing UK educational policy.

So far, we have considered the nature of teaching, teacher research and the notion of teacher research. We believe that there is another important aspect. Reflection is an essential aspect of teacher development. It can be encouraged and fostered by involvement in and understanding of the process and products of research.

REFLECTION AND REFLECTIVE PRACTITIONERS

The notion of reflection entails the idea that an individual can move up and beyond the immediate unique situation, usually defined in commonsense terms, to a more reflective one, looking again at a situation from a different perspective. Reflective teaching, therefore, is teaching which is capable of moving beyond the logic of common sense, often expressed in anecdotal terms, and practical reasoning, to action which stems from critical, professional thinking based upon 'a looking again', 'around and about' phenomenon and, maybe, applying the 'researcher's eye', making the familiar strange, not taking for granted what is characteristically taken for granted and so on. Stemming from Dewey (1933) who contrasted 'routine action' with 'reflective action' and articulated by Schon (1983) in terms of the reflective practitioner, reflection involves moving beyond commonsense routine and habitual action to action which is characterized by self-appraisal, flexibility, creativity, social, cultural and political awareness. These are precisely the kinds of skills and attitudes which engagement with 'research' is likely to develop.

It is instructive, therefore, to contrast the characteristics of research which we have identified with what two leading proponents of 'reflective teaching' in an excellent text have identified as key characteristics of reflective action in teaching:

> Dewey's notion of reflective action, when developed and applied to teaching, is very challenging. In this section, we review its implication by identifying and discussing what we have identified as six key characteristics. These are:
>
> 1 Reflective teaching implies an active concern with aims and consequences, as well as means and technical efficiency.
> 2 Reflective teaching is applied in a cyclical or spiralling process, in which teachers monitor, evaluate and revise their own practice continuously.
> 3 Reflective teaching requires competence in methods of classroom enquiry, to support the development of teaching competence.
> 4 Reflective teaching requires attitudes of open-mindedness, responsibility and wholeheartedness.
> 5 Reflective teaching is based on teacher judgement which is informed partly by self-reflection and partly by insights from educational disciplines.
> 6 Reflective teaching, professional learning and personal fulfilment are enhanced through collaboration and dialogue with colleagues.
>
> (Pollard and Tann 1993: 9)

The links between reflection and the kinds of research activity we are proposing here are quite clear. Reflective teaching and inquiry involve similar sets of skills. One of the best ways of developing reflective skills is to develop research skills, but research skills are, on the one hand, generic, yet, on the other, will relate to different styles and forms of research. We may have given the impression that 'research' is an activity which is understood by most people in much the same way. This is evidently not true.

A QUALITATIVE APPROACH

There are major divisions in the human sciences concerning the relative merits of differing models of research, and about the strengths and weaknesses of particular data collection techniques. The nature of these debates will be briefly touched upon in Chapter 2. At this point, we need to identify the methodological orientation which underpins our thinking.

A clear and respected tradition can be traced across all the human sciences which stresses the need for research to be commensurate with the nature of the social world. This involved the abandonment of the natural science model for social and educational research and the replacement of this with an interpretative, ethnographic or, more broadly, a *qualitative* model of social research. By qualitative methodology, we mean approaches that enable researchers to learn at first hand, about the social world they are investigating by means of involvement and participation in that world through a focus upon what individual actors say and do. This approach offers a new and considerable potential for teachers yet also brings with it fresh problems. Qualitative as opposed to quantitative research is more amenable and accessible to teachers and has the considerable advantage of drawing both the researcher and the subjects of the research closer together. This approach focuses upon investigating social behaviour in natural settings and in terms of school-based research requires that close attention be paid to what ordinarily and routinely happens in schools and classrooms. The products of such research therefore are firmly based within the areas of educational thought and practice.

Over the years, considerable work has been done on developing and refining the qualitative research techniques on which this approach is based and there is now a growing body of studies which demonstrate the applicability and value of these approaches to the study of education. One of the aims of this book is, therefore, to provide teachers with an introduction to the use of these techniques in school-based research.

SUMMARY

From what has been said, we clearly aim to achieve a lot, and to cover a broad field. The book is, therefore, organized into three interrelated parts, each dealing in the main with different aspects of the research process. Part I looks at the relationship between teaching, teachers, research and reflection by a focus upon designs and approaches. Chapter 2 overviews the main strands of research in the human sciences and argues a case for the appropriateness of a qualitative approach to school-based teacher research. Since questions of access and ethics are of such fundamental significance, we have placed our discussion of this in Chapter 3. From our vantage point of the 1990s, it is difficult to conceive of a time when gender issues, equal opportunities and related concerns were not high profile. Chapter 4 looks at the significance of gender as a key variable in the research process. This will further help to identify the socially situated nature of research and the significance of socio-cultural factors for both teaching and learning and doing research. Part I concludes with an overview account of the research process which will act as a guide to the generation, development and conduct of a research project from design stages, choice of topic to analysis and the presentation of findings. Whilst Part I focuses upon designs and approaches, Parts II and III, respectively, deal with qualitative research techniques and qualitative data analysis and case study and writing.

The nature of qualitative methodologies can be opened up by exploring the notion of ethnography. Chapter 6, therefore explores ethnography, field-work and the possibilities for teacher research. Chapters 7, 8 and 9 deal, respectively, with the most widely used techniques and sources of data, namely interviewing, a focus upon biographies and documentary sources. Part II concludes by offering accounts of the ways in which classroom interaction, and spatial arrangements in school and classrooms, can be investigated.

Finally, Part III attempts to draw what we have said together by looking at qualitative data analysis and suggesting that the case study framework is an appropriate one for teachers as researchers to employ. In Chapter 12 the possibilities and complexities of qualitative data analysis are opened up. Finally, Chapter 14 deals with the complexities of the writing process. We have provided suggestions for further reading at the end of each chapter which, as far as possible, offer intending researchers a firm basis from which to proceed after working through the chapters here. We have referred to literature from both this country, North America and Canada.

Teaching and research are exciting endeavours. We hope that, despite the very many constraints under which we all work, we are able to convey a sense of this excitement and encourage a greater awareness of the fundamental significance of these activities as a basis for professional development.

SUGGESTED FURTHER READING

There is now a growing literature in the area of teacher/practitioner research and the development of a reflective stance. A general guide to the whole area of teacher research worth considering is *Applying Educational Research: A Practical Guide for Teachers* (Borg 1981).

A Teacher's Guide to Action Research (Nixon 1981) is a collection of articles focusing upon key questions explored by teachers in a practical school-based inquiry. The line between research and evaluation is sometimes not clear but the contributions all throw light on methods of working and on what can be achieved. In particular, Lee Enright's chapter on the 'diary' of a classroom and Alan Root's contribution on working with a colleague are revealing. *The Enquiring Teacher: Supporting and Sustaining Teacher Research* (Nias and Groundwater-Smith 1988) contains a collection of papers deriving from a conference in 1986 on the teaching of inquiry-based courses, i.e. those courses where students undertake inquiry and investigation into their own or others' practice. The papers demonstrate well the possibilities and problems of teacher research, and attempt to link theory with practice. Of special interest is the chapter by Winter on writing. *A Teacher's Guide to Classroom Research* (Hopkins 1985) offers a clear and straightforward account of the rationale underlying teacher research and how to go about it, focusing upon the applicability of various types of research to practitioner problems and circumstances. The book makes use of examples of research done by teachers and has a useful section on the ethics of classroom research, whereas *Action Research in Classrooms and Schools* (Hustler, Cassidy and Cuff 1986) contains contributions from teachers on their own 'action research' in schools on a number of topics.

The best account to date of the notion of the reflective practitioner is contained in *Educating the Reflective Practitioner: Towards a New Design for Teaching and Learning in the Profession* (Schon 1987). Increasingly, the idea of focusing upon a critical incident as a means of developing reflection and personal professional development is seen as being of value. It is instructive to see how this is being used in management – for example, *Critical Incidents in Management* (Champion and James 1980), and teaching *Critical Incidents in Teaching* (Tripp 1993) provide excellent accounts with numerous examples to show the benefit of a critical incident approach.

Research and management issues

A key phrase at the moment seems to be 'the management of change'. Many students will be doing projects which will touch on management issues to a greater or lesser extent. What is the relationship between research and management? How can research influence management in schools? How does evaluation relate to management and improve practice? Some of these areas can be approached by looking at the following works.

Education and Care (Best, Ribbins, Jarvis and Oddy 1983) is an interpretative study of 'pastoral care' at 'Rivendale'. The study shows how a number of school management issues can be explored by considering the role of middle managers. *Experiencing Comprehensive Education* (Burgess 1983), a study of Bishop McGregor's Comprehensive School, like that of Best *et al.* (1983) on 'Rivendale', throws light upon a number of aspects of middle management activity and how it can be explored. *The Meaning of Educational Change* (Fullan 1982) provides an accessible account of the ways in which change can be brought about and the processes involved. Michael Fullan is regarded as being a key figure here. *Managing Education: The System and the Institution* (Hughes, Ribbins and Thomas 1987) offers a very important collection of articles. In particular, the contributions by Ribbins 'Organisational theory and the study of educational institutions' and Thomas 'Perspectives on evaluation' are relevant. *Research in Educational*

Management and Administration (Ribbins and Thomas 1981) is an important collection of papers which provides a good perspective on researching management and administration issues. The contribution by Ribbins, Best, Jarvis and Oddy, 'Meanings and contexts: the problem of interpretation in the study of a school' is sensitive and revealing. In conclusion, *The Man in the Principal's Office: An Ethnography* (Wolcott 1973) is an early, neglected classic which has much to say on researching principals, heads and other managers and deserves to be more widely read. Finally, *The Management of Change: Increasing School Effectiveness and Facilitating Staff Development Through Action Research* (Lomax 1989) contains an interesting collection of articles which show how teacher-initiated action research can help to improve the organization and management of schools. As well as documenting significant pieces of research the articles also reveal quite clearly the stages through which such research moves, and the methodological principles involved. Many of the contributors are practising teachers and the book gives a realistic sense of the nature of action research in schools and classrooms.

Recently a very strong case has been put forward for the use of qualitative research approaches in the further education sector in the UK. 'Qualitative research, educational management and the incorporation of the further education sector' (Elliott and Crossley 1994) strikes a resounding blow at the way in which the management of this sector of education is informed by quantitative, statistical information. Elliott and Crossley argue a logical rationale for the value of qualitative research methodologies when exploring the reality of the world of colleges. Their article ought to be compulsory reading for all managers in the newly incorporated further education section and offers some suggestions for research topics.

2 Research approaches

INTRODUCTION

Social research depends upon some basic principles and foundations which have developed and evolved over a long period of time. These background assumptions have come together to create different models of social and educational research. These models of research design act as plans and blueprints for the researcher to follow. They supply sets of concepts and ideas, and preferred tools and techniques for the conduct of research. As such, these models of research design will exercise a considerable influence over the whole of a study or project. There has been an enormous amount of controversy over the most appropriate models for researching the social world and, subsequently, the best techniques to employ.

Research as we describe it is concerned with systematic inquiry. A major assumption has been that this systematic inquiry must also be scientific in the same way in which we see physics or biology as being scientific. Some researchers, described as 'positivists', argue that social research must use the methods and procedures of the natural/physical sciences. Others, described as 'anti-positivistic', or adopting a naturalistic stance, or post-positivist position, have argued that the nature of the social world is such that its investigation must be, in principle, different from investigation of the physical world. These researchers argued for the importance of discovering the meanings and interpretation of events and actions. They are described as adopting an interpretative or qualitative approach. We know also that evaluation studies and action research models have been widely used in educational research over recent years. Furthermore, increasing concern with the biographical aspects of teachers' lives, equal opportunities and gender issues has not only shaped the kind of studies of schools and classrooms but also the ways in which those studies have been conducted.

In the following sections we aim to provide a general introduction to the major approaches to educational research and, in particular, to articulate a rationale for the qualitative research approaches which underpin our thinking. This will inevitably involve some philosophical debate. Our main concern here is with the nature of research approaches and the way in which this shapes and determines the conduct of research. Certainly, research design (albeit a crucial element) is only one aspect of the research process. Parts II and III of this book deal, respectively, with data collection and data analysis, presentation and writing up.

Research in education has had strong links with the research traditions of the social sciences. Indeed, psychologists, sociologists and anthropologists have all contributed to research into educational processes and practices. In many important more general respects, educational research is not distinct from social research. Educational research and education as a discipline both rely upon the tools, techniques and insights of the social sciences. In turn, prospective teacher–researchers need to be aware of the complex and complicated themes of social research as well as being responsive to the teaching situation. Ultimately, the object of inquiry, the social world, is the same for both professional social science researchers and teachers. The major difference lies in *why* one wants to do the research in the first place. Research and its products should facilitate reflection, criticism and a more informed view of the educational process which will, in turn, help to improve professional practice.

Unfortunately, social research is neither simple nor uncontroversial. Social research, individual tools and techniques and particular models of research have been the subject of many heated debates. These debates are not new and go back to the writings of the great philosophers. The problem concerns the ways in which we can produce knowledge of the social world, and the appropriate methods and procedures for the delivery of this knowledge. We will describe these issues in this chapter so that teacher–researchers may consider the particular aspects of individual research techniques, which are the subject of Part II, and the practice of carrying out school-based research, the subject of Part III. We need to begin by briefly contrasting the two predominant opposing research traditions.

PETROLEUM ENGINEERS AND EXPLORERS – POSITIVISTS AND INTERPRETIVISTS

Spradley (1980) accepts the existence of the two predominant models of social research which we earlier described as positivistic and interpretative. He likens the differences between positivists and interpretative researchers to those between petroleum engineers and explorers. Spradley (1980) argues that most social scientists operate in a fashion that is not unlike the way in which petroleum engineers work. These people are already in possession of some detailed knowledge of a geographical location in which they expect to find oil. In this analogy the social scientist, like the petroleum engineer, knows what he is looking for, how to look for it, and what to expect. Like the petroleum engineer the social scientist works in a linear, sequential, or step-by-step fashion. In contrast to the petroleum engineers, Spradley (1980) describes the explorer who is trying to map an uncharted wilderness, with little or no prior knowledge of the area. Whereas the main aim of the petroleum engineer's work is the discovery of oil, the explorer's main task is the description of what is found. Spradley (1980) likens the positivistic researcher to the petroleum engineer and the ethnographer to the explorer:

> The ethnographer has much in common with the explorer trying to map a wilderness area. The explorer begins with a general problem, to identify the major features of the terrain; the ethnographer wants to describe the cultural terrain. Then the explorer begins gathering information, going first in one direction, then perhaps retracing that route, then starting out in a new direction. On discovering a lake in the middle of a large wooded area, the explorer would take frequent compass readings, check the angle of the sun, take notes about prominent landmarks, and use feedback from each observation to modify earlier information. After weeks of investigation, the explorer would probably find it difficult to answer the question, 'What did you find?' Like an ethnographer, the explorer is seeking to describe a wilderness area rather than trying to 'find' something.
>
> Most social science research has more in common with the petroleum engineer who already has some detailed maps of the same wilderness area. The engineer has a specific goal in mind; to find oil or gas buried far below the surface. Before the engineer even begins an investigation, a careful study will be made of the maps which show geological features of the area. Then, knowing ahead of the time the kinds of features that suggest oil or gas beneath the surface, the engineer will go out to 'find' something quite specific. A great deal of social science research begins with a similar clear idea of something to find; investigators usually know what they are looking for.
>
> (Spradley 1980: 26)

The debates between 'petroleum engineers' and 'explorers' or positivist and interpretative researchers are far too important to be ignored by the prospective teacher–researcher. These debates and controversies while clearly philosophical in nature, and hence for many people suitably obscure and often irrelevant, do have important consequences for educational research. So much so that we have had to state on which side of the divide we are in writing this book. At a time when the functions and organization of schooling are changing at a pace that has rarely been seen before and when dissent is rife, the researcher must be sure about the philosophical basis of her school-based research.

In terms of social research these philosophical themes may be translated into a series of questions:

- How do different propositions about social reality influence the investigation of the world?
- How might researchers establish the truth of their claims?

- How do different propositions about the social world and views about truth influence methods of data collection?

The answers to these questions have resulted in social researchers employing different logics, models and techniques to investigate the world. Ultimately, these differences are based upon different background assumptions. The literature makes use of a number of key concepts and ideas in handling these debates and it is worth unravelling the ways in which they are used.

SOME KEY TERMS DEFINED

Frequently, writers employ terms such as 'method' to apply to all aspects of social research, for example. Other writers distinguish between 'theory' and 'methodology' and there is certainly some confusion. In the context of most discussions of the philosophy of social research a number of key terms are used and it is important to understand and appreciate the ways in which they are employed. These terms include ontology, epistemology, philosophy, method, methodology and theory. We offer below some simple definitions and explanations of these terms which might help to avoid confusion.

Ontology

When the word ontology is used it refers to issues concerning *being*. As far as social research is concerned ontological questions and assumptions are those which surround the nature of the subject matter namely, the social world. How is the social world perceived and understood? What is a human being? These are ontological questions.

Epistemology

Epistemological questions surround the question of *knowing* and the nature of knowledge. The history of the human sciences entails many theoretical debates about the sources of knowledge. They include assumptions about the form knowledge takes, the ways in which knowledge can be attained and communicated to others, and ultimately who can be a knower, and what tests and criteria must be involved in order to establish knowledge. It follows therefore that epistemological questions will also involve discussion of what can be known. One can ask questions about the spiritual or religious basis of knowledge and about whether knowledge can be obtained only directly from personal experience or indirectly by other means. An epistemology is therefore a theory of knowledge and writers refer to conventional epistemology, feminist epistemology or Marxist epistemology, for example, as ways of justifying beliefs. The ways in which different sociologists, for example, have resolved these epistemological questions has given rise to a range of different perspectives in sociology. Clearly, epistemological assumptions will have a major impact upon the kinds of data-gathering choices made (methods) and the general view of the research process (methodology) and how theories and theoretical structures may be applied.

Philosophy

This term is here used to refer to questions of our knowledge, understanding and the meaning we give to the structure, order and organization of the world in which we live so as to provide a rationale for the ways we investigate the world (methodology), how we explain, and what we do with that knowledge of the world (theory).

Method

Methods in social research are ways of proceeding in the gathering and collection of data, a method is therefore a technique employed to gather data. Methods consist either of listening to subjects, observing what people do and say or collecting and examining documents which human beings construct. Methods are the tools and techniques of social research and involve technical, practical and ethical dimensions.

Methodology

Methodology refers to the whole range of questions about the assumed appropriate ways of going about social research. Methodology is, therefore, a theory or an analysis of how research should operate. As such, methodology refers to the ways in which general scientific statements or procedures of disciplines or perspectives are acted out in research situations. Hence, a methodology is a broad yet complex array of ideas, concepts, frameworks and theories which surround the use of various methods or techniques employed to generate data on the social world. Questions about the collection of quantitative data via surveys or questionnaires, or qualitative data via participation and involvement are methodological questions. In this way, for example, cognitive psychology, ethnosemantics, functionalism, Marxist political economy approaches, hermeneutics, feminism or phenomenology all entail methodological questions and analyses.

Theory

Theory is seen as being concerned with the development of systematic construction of knowledge of the social world. In doing this theory employs the use of concepts, systems, models, structures, beliefs and ideas, hypotheses (theories) in order to make statements about particular types of actions, events or activities, so as to make analyses of their causes, consequences and process. That is, to explain events in ways which are consistent with a particular philosophical rationale or, for example, a particular sociological or psychological perspective. Theories therefore aim to both propose and analyse sets of relations existing between a number of variables when certain regularities and continuities can be demonstrated via empirical inquiry.

It follows that ontological assumptions will give rise to epistemological assumptions which have methodological implications for the choice of particular data collection techniques. The significance of the interplay of all these aspects cannot be over-estimated. However, as we shall point out later, it is not our intention in this book to rehearse these debates in the philosophy of social research.

These background assumptions are so important yet so complex that responses to questions of an ontological, epistemological, and methodological nature have resulted in two quite distinct perspectives or traditions in social research. This distinction has important implications for educational research because it has meant that not only have schools and classrooms been investigated in different ways but also what is seen to count as valid and appropriate data on schools and classrooms has varied also. In the following sections we will briefly outline the major elements of these two contrasting ways of making sense of social reality in the shape of the two traditions which are readily seen in most of the social sciences. It will become clear that understanding the differences between the two traditions is neither simple nor straightforward.

THE POSITIVISTIC SCIENTIFIC MODEL OF SOCIAL RESEARCH

What follows is, first, a comparison of the two major research paradigms in social research: the positivistic and qualitative and, second, an account of action research which has been advanced as the ideal research approach for undertaking quantitative school-based studies and, third, a look at research and evaluation.

From about the late nineteenth century onwards the scientific model employed by the natural and physical sciences, such as biology, physics and chemistry, quickly became defined as the most appropriate model for investigating the social world. This may be described as an empiricist position. 'Empiricism' suggests that the only reliable source of knowledge is through experience, by literally seeing and hearing, which usually took the form of some kind of observation or controlled experimental situation where the researcher could effectively exercise some authority over what was being experienced.

Most people would accept that positivism is based upon the view that the natural sciences provide the only foundation for true knowledge and that the methods, techniques and modes of operation of the natural sciences offer the best framework for investigation of the social world. Thus, a definition of positivism would be the position in the social sciences which aims at objectivity in social inquiry by means of adopting the methods and procedures of the natural or physical sciences. Clearly, for this view to be tenable certain propositions and assumptions would have to be made.

Key assumptions are made by positivists about human behaviour. First, and most important from this viewpoint, human behaviour is predictable, caused and subject to both internal pressures (for behaviourist psychologists) and external forces (for positivistic sociologists). Second, these aspects can be observed and measured. The notion of causality in human affairs suggests that human actions can, once correctly observed and identified, be predicted. Ultimately, positivism assumes therefore that there is no qualitative difference between the natural and social world. As positivism developed in the social sciences two central principles of social research began to emerge and it is worth defining and describing these briefly here. The principles of 'deductive reasoning' and 'falsifiability' became the hallmarks of what is described as the scientific method.

Deductive reasoning suggests that it is possible to move, following the scientific method, from general kinds of statements to particular statements which can, in fact, be objective and independent of experience. One of the key figures in the philosophy of science is Karl Popper; his book *The Logic of Scientific Discovery* (Popper, 1959) has been immensely influential. He argued that theories and subsequently explanations cannot be regarded as being scientific in the true sense, unless they are falsifiable; hence it can be argued that the main criterion of whether a statement has any scientific status resides in its testability. This means that scientists must do two things: (1) they must frame their theories in a way that leaves them open to falsification, and (2) they must be prepared to disregard such theories if either they are not open to falsification *per se*, or they prove wrong in the light of falsifying evidence. Popper's ideas have been highly influential and the testing of falsification procedures he describes has been widely accepted as the basis of good scientific practice.

Those social scientists who hold this positivistic tradition are for many reasons likely to concentrate upon the collection of large amounts of data since the concern is with establishing patterns and regularities in that data and testing theories about that data by means of falsification procedures. As a consequence, this approach is likely to be quantitative in orientation.

From what we have said so far it is now possible to identify the major assumptions of science and how the scientific method provides the most widely used model for social research. It is fair to say that a large proportion of research in both education and the social sciences has adopted, to a greater or lesser extent this scientific method as the model for its research design. It is also fair to say that the driving force for much of this research was the desire to emulate in social research the precision and level of understanding characterized by the physical sciences. The general principles underlying positivism then come together in the scientific method. The concern to measure and quantify social behaviour in order to explain the regularities of such phenomena and the relationships that may be observed between them by matching the sophistication and rigour of the physical sciences in order to develop general, universal law-like statements is what the scientific method is all about. This is where we find Spradley's (1980) petroleum engineers.

We can now approach the operation of this scientific model of social research in a bit more detail. Figure 2.1 outlines the kinds of stages which a typical piece of social research based upon this scientific model would take. What stands out most clearly here is the linear or sequential pattern of this research and the reliance upon hypotheses. Before we move on to discuss some of the problems with this model, the kinds of criticisms which have been made of it, and the development of an alternative tradition, we will pause to consider this framework.

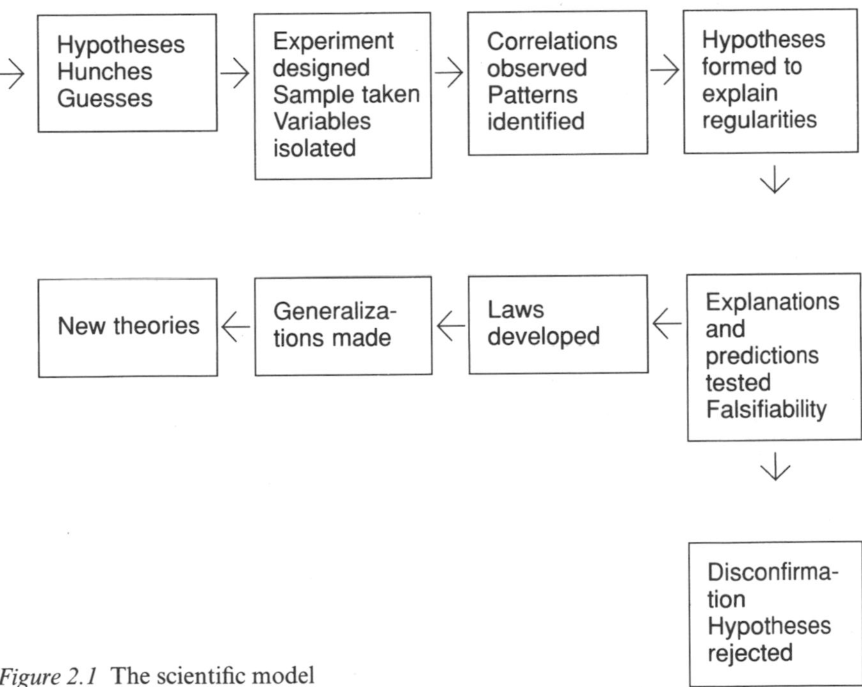

Figure 2.1 The scientific model

The assumptions of science and the background ideas which direct scientific inquiry have resulted in a model of research for the investigation of the social world. However, whereas these general assumptions are accepted by natural scientists and social scientists working within the positivistic tradition, the subject matter of the natural sciences and that of the social sciences obviously varies fundamentally. This observation has formed the basis for the main criticisms of positivism in social science. The scientific method might be said to involve a set of widely accepted procedures which if followed, it is claimed, will produce knowledge of certain phenomena and theories which can explain them. If we take a closer look at Figure 2.1 we will see how these procedures take the form of a series of fairly well-defined stages which follow a sequential and ordered pattern. All the features and assumptions we have discussed so far come together within the framework of this scientific model.

Sometimes this model is described as employing the 'hypothetico-deductive' technique, HD for short.

EVALUATION OF POSITIVISM AND THE SCIENTIFIC METHOD

As a result of the importance and widespread acceptance of the scientific method and the positivistic assumptions which underpin it we have spent some time unravelling this tradition. This is only one, albeit the most influential, model of social research and has played a crucial role in providing a basis for much educational research. One of the features of the social sciences over the last few years has been an ongoing and often acrimonious debate between those who argue that positivism and the scientific method provide the only acceptable route to knowledge of the social world and those who reject all or part of this claim.

Some important question marks hang over the scientific method as we have described it. These criticisms have developed from within other perspectives or traditions in the social sciences, educational research and the teacher–researcher movement. Some of these criticisms appear so far reaching that the term 'anti-positivists' is applied to some of these researchers.

Although we do not wish to rehearse these debates here it is important to have a feel for the issues raised. These are usually treated under the following headings.

- The nature of the social scientists' subject matter.
- Forms of explanation and the appropriateness of positivistic methodology.
- Causes and meanings.
- Quantitative and qualitative data.
- Generalizations.

The assumptions of positivism as a philosophy of social research are based on the idea that:

> There is an external world, but (also) that the external world itself determines absolutely the one and only correct view that can be taken of it, independent of the processes or our circumstances of viewing.
>
> (Kirk and Miller 1986: 14)

In contrast, we would argue that the whole foundation upon which any claims mounted in favour of teacher research must be firmly based on the rejection of such a position. This is not the place to rehearse the complex and by now fairly well known debates within the philosophy of science. A good account is provided by Anderson, Hughes and Sharrock (1986).

Instead it is our view that the battle between positivism and anti-positivism has been neither won nor lost. Rather than exploring these lengthy debates yet again, a more constructive and purposeful way to work is to explore the nature of qualitative approaches and contemporary methodological debates rather than waste time on those in the past. Those wishing a fuller account of these issues should consult Hitchcock and Hughes (1989: 12–37).

QUALITATIVE APPROACHES IN SOCIAL AND EDUCATIONAL RESEARCH

A qualitative orientation to both social and educational research underpins the thinking behind this book. The move towards employing qualitative research techniques in school-based research over the past two decades has, we believe, been instrumental in moving the focus of much educational research back into the classrooms, staffrooms and offices of schools. This has replaced the emphasis of an over-reliance on quantitative methods, with the use of large samples and statistical analysis as the main sources of information on how schools worked and learning takes place. Instead, the context of teaching and learning itself becomes the focus. It is important to outline briefly what is meant by *qualitative* in this context. It has been our view for some time that the processes of education, teaching and learning are so complex and multifaceted that to focus only upon cause and effect, products, outcomes or correlations in research on schools is of limited value. The complexity of education demands the use of very many different research techniques and models. The most productive approach we believe is a qualitative one.

Qualitative, and more generally ethnographic approaches we believe offer school-based research unique opportunities. A qualitative research orientation places individual actors at its centre, it will focus upon context, meaning, culture, history and biography. The life history approach is one such qualitative technique, whereas ethnography provides an overall holistic framework for such an approach in terms of the kinds of data collected and the procedures employed to collect them (Lutz 1981: 51–64). The application of ethnographic approaches to education is now well known and constitutes the major alternative research tradition to that of projective, correlational, quantitative techniques (Bogdan and Biklen 1982; Dobbert 1982). Ethnography *in* education might therefore involve a focus upon individual biography in the form of life histories of teachers and pupils, and attention to features such as the historical background, cultural and neighbourhood contexts as well as socio-linguistic investigations (Erickson 1987: 119–61; Delamont and Atkinson 1980: 139–52). It could include a focus upon school and classroom processes, organization and culture, or about the ways in which teacher and pupil expectations shape the learning environment.

Qualitative research is often misunderstood as being one single, clearly defined approach. As Jacob (1987) points out, there are a number of different 'traditions'. She identifies six major domains: human ethnology; ecological psychology; holistic ethnography; cognitive anthropology; ethnography of communication, and symbolic interactionism, as a way of capturing the vast range of qualitatively oriented research, (Jacob 1987: 1–50). However, Atkinson, Delamont and Hammersley (1988) are critical of the notion of 'traditions', here pointing out that Jacobs (1987) neglects important British work. Another term often used here is 'naturalistic'. A naturalistic paradigm has been known under a number of different headings. Guba and Lincoln (1985: 7) has pointed to at least eight different terms for naturalistic enquiry: post-positivist; ethnographic; phenomenological; subjective; case study; qualitative; hermeneutic; and humanistic. Much confusion can arise from a crude quantitative–qualitative distinction, or, as we noted earlier, from assuming qualitative research to be all the same. Applied to educational contexts qualitative or naturalistic research recognizes that what goes on in our schools and classrooms is made up of complex layers of meanings, interpretations, values and attitudes. Schools, classrooms and their participants have histories and careers, teachers and pupils have their own educational and life histories, departmental members engage in interpersonal relations, conflicts and alliances emerge, responses to innovation and institutionalization ensure that schools and classrooms have cultures and an ethos. A firm understanding of these variables and the ways in which they interact to create the politics and dynamics of educational change requires a qualitative appreciation of these factors. *That is, qualification of actions, ideas, values and meanings through the eyes of participants rather than quantification through the eyes of an outside observer.*

In the introduction to a major new handbook on qualitative research traditions Norman Denzin (Denzin and Lincoln, 1994) has tried to characterize the nature, scope and variety of qualitative research as a site of multiple methodologies and research practices. Denzin highlights the contemporary diversity of qualitative methodologies:

> Qualitative research, as a set of interpretative practices, privileges no single methodology over any other. As a site of discussion, or discourse, qualitative research is difficult to define clearly. It has no theory, or paradigm, that is distinctly its own. As Part II of this volume reveals, multiple theoretical paradigms claim use of qualitative research methods and strategies, from constructivism to cultural studies, feminism, Marxism, and ethnic models of study. Qualitative research is used in many separate disciplines, as we will discuss below. It does not belong to a single discipline.
>
> Nor does qualitative research have a distinct set of methods that are entirely its own. Qualitative researchers use semiotics, narrative, content, discourse, archival, and phonemic analysis, even statistics. They also draw

> upon and utilize the approaches, methods, and techniques of ethnomethodology, phenomenology, hermeneutics, feminism, rhizomatics, deconstructionism, ethnographies, interviews, psychoanalysis, cultural studies, survey research, and participant observation, among others.
>
> (Denzin and Lincoln 1994: 3)

We are not concerned to be prescriptive, major debates are now opening up in this tradition. Qualitative research then is ultimately a frame of mind, it is an orientation and commitment to studying the social world in certain kinds of ways. Part II concentrates upon the nature of the range of techniques and approaches Denzin highlights. Part III unravels the nature of styles of qualitative data analysis. One of the problems with educational research is that a number of different research designs have made use of qualitative, naturalistic techniques to assemble data and information. Two of these stand out for consideration: action research and evaluation. We will attempt to unravel each of these approaches and identify their relationship to qualitative data and qualitative research techniques.

ACTION RESEARCH

It is important to locate action research as a strategy of educational research in the 'Teacher as Researcher' movement headed by Lawrence Stenhouse, but the approach can also be used in the higher education setting (Zuber-Skerritt 1992). This was associated in particular with the Humanities Curriculum Project (Stenhouse 1975). The principal features of an action research approach are *change* (action) or *collaboration* between researchers and researched. Action researchers are concerned to improve a situation through active intervention and in collaboration with the parties involved. This gives action research a very particular character. Since the end of such research is not simply the contribution to knowledge, but practitioner-relevant information, action research has a different audience and is likely to be presented differently to other kinds of research. It is argued that action research is underpinned by a democratic principle (see also Wakeman 1986). The ownership of knowledge and control over research are therefore important questions for action researchers. Action research can be said therefore to constitute a paradigm in its own right (Kemmis and Henry 1984; see also Kincheloe 1991).

Action researchers can use a variety of research techniques and both quantitative and qualitative data. The differences and similarities between action research and other approaches are neatly summarized in the following quotation:

> The model of research that was used in this project is 'action research'. This method of research is usefully distinguished from a range of other kinds of social science research by its emphasis on action. It is different from 'positivist' research, which uses the physical sciences as a model.

> Action research is not trying to identify large scale causal laws. Instead it focuses on the rigorous examination of a single situation, using knowledge drawn from experience and research findings to illuminate it, in order to improve it. The differences from 'positivist' models are the most obvious, but it is important to note that it may make use of 'qualitative' or 'ethnographic' research techniques, it is different from other qualitative or ethnographic research in that it is not seeking to contribute to large scale explanations of events. Nor is it seeking to discover grounded theory by the meticulous analysis of data. The purpose is always to improve practice, rather than to find truths, universal or particular.
>
> (Griffiths and Davies 1993: 45)

Generally speaking, action research involves a cyclical approach. The research of Griffiths and Davies (1993) into pupils' learning in years five and six of a primary school in order to consider the possibility of improving equality of opportunity involved four cycles of action research. The cycles of an action research project will involve identification of a problem, collecting information, analysing, planning action/intervention and implementing and monitoring the outcomes. The writing up of action research is also likely to be much less impersonal than in traditional scientific research, offering a wider potential for making use of different writing styles.

This rather simple sketch of action research disguises the controversies, conflicts and debates which the approach has generated. Above all, the essential ingredient of action research is that it combines action with theorizing. For Kemmis and McTaggert (1982) in *The Action Research Planner*, the process includes trying out particular ideas in practice as a means of improvement and increasing our knowledge of the curriculum as both form and content. Those involved in the studies themselves have the responsibility for planning any changes and carrying out any evaluation. In this sense it is fundamentally 'grass roots practice'.

The most salient underlying feature of action research is, of course, reflection (see also Webb 1990). The idea of reflection and a reflective practitioner has almost become the *sine qua non* of the action research movement. Whilst we accept and support the idea of reflection, seeing it as a crucial aspect of professional development, it is equally clear that acquiring, developing and using reflection is something of a different matter. This is further confused by the diversity of meanings and intentions found in the literature on reflection (Adler 1991).

Collaboration also seems to be a significant feature of the action research movement including collaboration between practitioners within and outside of the organization, and collaboration between organizations. It is assumed that through collaboration action research can personalize public debates in education and begin to relate more directly to concrete situations. This assumes that the organizational culture or ethos of an institution will be supportive of such activity. This is certainly problematic, not just for action research but for most educational research activities. However, organizational culture and ethos take on a major significance with action research. A direct consequence of the very nature of action research is that it is assumed to be collaborative, supportive, democratic and even critical. At this point we see the emergence of some very problematic questions for action research. The challenge for action research is to demonstrate how these problems may be overcome.

To summarize then action research, originally developed by Lewin (1946) and developed by Schon (1983) and Carr and Kemmis (1986) amongst others, is clearly a *cyclical* process involving stages of action and research followed by action. This often takes the design form illustrated below (Figure 2.2):

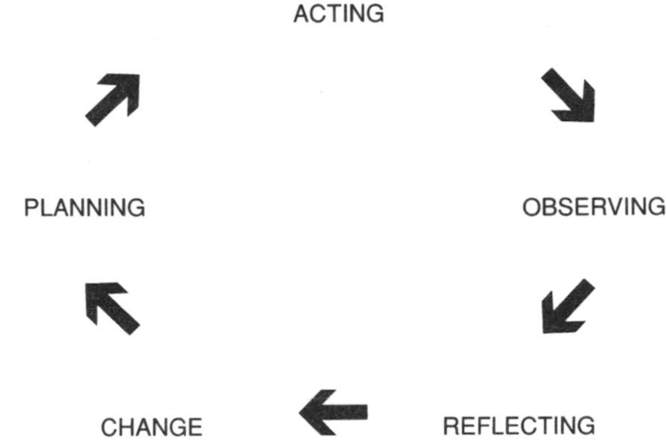

Figure 2.2 An action research cycle

The actual details of the ways in which these action research cycles work out in practice will vary, depending on the scale, character and substantive focus of the research.

ACTION RESEARCH AND 'RESEARCH PARADIGMS'

It is important to place action research within the broad scheme and continuum of research paradigms we identified earlier in this chapter. It is clear that the action research movement, with its emphasis upon practice, participation/collaboration, reflection, interpretation and, often, emancipation, puts it squarely in opposition to positive social research. Indeed, action research most frequently uses qualitative methodologies and techniques, the most notable of which is the case study. The anti-positivistic stance of action researchers is also often coupled with a radical socialist or Marxist imperative. This is contained in the idea of 'becoming critical'. As a research approach, action research clearly sits most happily with qualitative, interpretative or phenomenological research designs. Whereas there are clearly shared assumptions, the most significant of which is a common critique of positivism, there are also differences of emphasis and orientation. However, an orientation to action research must be seen as challenging many of the founding assumptions of conventional social research.

SOME POTENTIAL CRITICISMS OF ACTION RESEARCH

Action research has been criticized both in terms of its general approach and the products of that approach. The following statements might serve as a useful starting point in evaluating the nature of action research in education (some of these issues are taken up in the suggestions for further reading at the end of the chapter):

- Action research needs to clarify the distinction between the nature of 'action' and 'research'. The two terms are not interchangeable. If this is not carefully done then all the old confusions surrounding the apparent distinctions between practice and theory are likely to re-emerge.
- Reflection is a current vogue term used widely and often loosely. There is certainly greater need for clarity and precision in the use of this term in teacher education and research more broadly. The distinction between reflection and description is often not fully understood. Reflection can degenerate into anecdotal description. Furthermore, there are fundamental questions surrounding the capacity to reflect. For example, a newly started young teacher and an experienced mature head of a department may be differentially placed to reflect. This is but one example of a potentially highly problematic aspect of action research methods.
- Emancipation is seen as a key element of action research enquiries. The question here surrounds the issue of emancipatory for whom? The political agenda of many promoting the action research model has to be seen in the current educational and political context. This may mean taking a longer, colder and much more dispassionate view of emancipation.
- In its often avid anti-positivistic stance action research can fall prey to criticisms of 'soft science'. The preference for interpretative style action research cycles or spirals has prompted some to question the potential lack of rigour of such enquiries, or worse still that it is not proper research conducted by proper researchers. Although different in orientation and kind it is vital that such research provides criteria for, and demonstrates degrees of, rigour.
- Collaboration is seen as a central ingredient in action research. How is this to be achieved and at what degrees or levels? A body of literature is now emerging which clearly demonstrates the potential and problems of collaboration (Griffiths and Davies 1993). It is likely that collaboration will continue to attract attention in the future as an issue in its own right.
- The contribution of action research to educational theory and practice needs to be seen within the overall cultural and political context of education in

Western societies. These societies have different structural arrangements, different patterns of legislation and differing views on the role of teachers. Any assessment of the contribution of action research to change will need to take these factors into account.

- A number of question marks hang over the ethics and accountability issues associated with action research. There does seem to be confusion and in some cases the ethical position is quite simply untenable. Some of these concerns are raised in the discussion of ethics and school-based research in subsequent chapters.

EVALUATION

Evaluation is big business. Evaluation is complex. Evaluation has become one of the most significant developments across a range of professions from health care to education over recent years. Professional evaluators, quality auditors and the like have appeared. Evaluation provides a distinct research approach and, given the significance of educational evaluation over recent years, it is important that we consider this approach briefly here. Evaluation involves examining a set of practices with regard to their functioning, efficiency and quality. It implies some form of systematic examination of events in order to be able to make more informed decisions about a particular programme. Clearly, evaluation will involve making value judgements about situations. In the field of health care and education the increasing emphasis placed upon professional development has meant that there is now an increase in the formalization of 'evaluation activities'. Certainly, evaluation can point up good practice and it can highlight weaknesses and problems. In this sense evaluation is not neutral. As a research approach evaluation exhibits particular research design features. As with any other kind of research, evaluation researchers will collect data in much the same ways as other researchers, via observations, interviewing, the use of questionnaires, testing and interrogating documentary evidence. However, the presentation of findings and the analysis of information in evaluation research is intimately geared up to the purposes of the research and this is where evaluation research differs markedly from other forms.

It is possible to summarize a range of features associated with and often regarded as being central to evaluation approaches:

- Evaluation is *not neutral*.
- Evaluation is *systematic*.
- Evaluation is about both *products and processes*.
- Evaluation is concerned with *policy and practice*.
- Evaluation defines and explores *effectiveness*.
- Evaluation can be a process of *curriculum inquiry*.
- Evaluation may be central to *professional development*.
- Evaluation is part of the *quality assurance* process.

- Educational evaluation is a process of *systematic description of educational objects*.
- Evaluation and improvements are linked.
- The *evaluation process* will include (i) *the focus upon a problem*; (ii) *collecting and analysing relevant data*, and (iii) *communicating findings and making recommendations*.
- Evaluation can be *autocratic, democratic* or *bureaucratic*.
- Evaluation can be open or closed.
- The nature of an evaluation inquiry will be linked to the purposes of the evaluation.
- Evaluators *make judgements*.

This list of key features of evaluation hardly does justice to the complex and controversial debates surrounding this approach. One of the first problems concerns the distinction between so-called pure educational research and applied research mentioned earlier. Another set of questions surround the most appropriate form of data collection for evaluation studies. Clearly, many approaches may be adopted under the broad heading of 'evaluation'. We regard the research process as involving, though not in a sequential form, various stages, including design data collection, analysis and reporting. We explore this more fully in Chapter 5. It is possible, using ideas developed by Hopkins (1989: 32–8) to map approaches to evaluation into our overview of social and education research. Figure 2.3 attempts to do this.

Stake (1986: 252–3) has provided a comprehensive matrix describing nine approaches to educational evaluation with reference to purpose, key elements, key players and protagonists, the likely risks and potential pay-offs. Certainly, these are crucial underlying assumptions which underpin these approaches and the methodology and data-collection techniques employed must have a 'fitness for purpose' in relation to the task at hand. Two questions remain for us. First, 'What is the relationship between evaluation and teacher research?' and second, 'What is the relationship between qualitative, naturalistic approaches and evaluation?' We will briefly attempt to provide some answers to these questions.

EVALUATION AND TEACHER RESEARCH

Evaluating curriculum programmes has been seen as one of the main areas where teachers can undertake school-based inquiry. Stenhouse's (1975) critique of the objectives model of curriculum evaluation in the 1970s can be seen in retrospect as an important milestone in encouraging teacher research. One of the most telling points was that teachers were the main audience for the conclusions of evaluation research and that such research should be 'relatively non-technical and accessible' (Stenhouse 1975: 120). Indeed, Stenhouse (1975) argued vigorously for not distinguishing between the roles of the developer and the evaluator and so opening up the way for

RESEARCH DESIGN	DATA COLLECTION METHODOLOGY	DATA ANALYSIS	FINDINGS REPORT RECOMMENDATIONS
EVALUATION			
TYPES OF EVALUATION INQUIRY			
AUTOCRATIC Evaluator as external validator	Non-participatory Imposed External Systematic	Closed variables Often quantitative	Clear statements of revised practice Implementation
BUREAUCRATIC Consultant/client relationship	Clear definition of researchers Non-reactive	In relation to practice Achievement of goals	Organization Systems reported to
DEMOCRATIC Confidential Negotiated Accessible	Participatory Collaborative Democratic	Open Often qualitative	Non-recommendatory Illuminative

Figure 2.3 Evaluation as a mode of inquiry
Source: Hopkins (1989: 32–8)

teacher-led and researched evaluation. This is an important point because much evaluation is undertaken in the interests of management or policy makers and is conducted by means of outside evaluators and consultants who may or may not take into account teachers' views and who are not directly addressing them as an audience. MacDonald (1974), for example, has pointed to the inherently political nature of evaluation and advocated in consequence a more democratic and open stance by evaluators towards the dissemination of their findings both to a professional and non-professional audience. However, Elliot (1986: 228–37) has argued that one needs to draw a distinction between educational evaluation, which is aimed at an educational–professional audience, and social evaluation, which is the general public's 'right to know'. As 'telling the truth' is not context free one may need, for ethical and other reasons, to provide different versions for each audience. These comments were meant for professional researchers and were about their responsibilities both to those who might be funding their evaluation and to the wider audience both of teachers and the public. The point here is that evaluation, whether undertaken by external evaluators or by school senior management teams or individual teachers evaluating their own practice, is seldom possible without involving other people. Because it is about effectiveness it can affect others and be a sensitive issue, raising questions of confidentiality and negotiation. So, the key factors here are: who is undertaking the evaluation; for what purpose; and with what aim(s) in view. This is why the view of Stenhouse (1975) that the evaluation or case study should be undertaken by teachers in both roles, as evaluators and agents of change, is such an important one.

We can define evaluation for our purposes as the systematic study of a particular programme or a set of events covering a given period of time. One may make an initial distinction between what Scriven (1987) called 'formative evaluation' and 'summative evaluation'. In the former the aim is the study of a programme or curriculum scheme through its developmental stage and, in the latter, the aim is the appraisal of the completed programme or curriculum scheme when it is in operation. Evaluation is similar to other research in that it is a systematic investigation of an issue and needs to be conducted with rigour and through empirical inquiry methods. One difference between evaluation and other kinds of research concerns the audience at whom the research is aimed. Another concerns whether it is possible to draw a distinction between 'pure research', the primary aim of which is to advance knowledge, and evaluation, the aim of which is to understand a process so as to improve decision-making. However, as most research in education has an applied aim this distinction loses its force. Evaluation should be seen as being central to making schools more effective and setting an agenda for staff development. Evaluation has links with both case study research and with action research in the sense both of research design and data collection. Action research, of course, is intended to intervene in the actual teaching process to facilitate change. It is on questions such as the audience at whom the research is directed, and the emphasis on change and developing judgement that are the principle distinguishing features.

EVALUATION AND QUALITATIVE APPROACHES

The use and design of evaluation is part of the continuing debate about the form that educational research should take. Evaluation can be purely qualitative in the way it is designed and the data collected and analysed, or it can be a mixture of quantitative and qualitative approaches, or it can be purely quantitative, though here we shall be concerned with the contribution that qualitative methods can make. As Fink has argued:

> Qualitative evaluations collect data from in-person interviews, direct observations, written documents (such as private diaries). These evaluations aim to provide personalized information on the dynamics of a programme and on participants' perceptions of their outcomes and impact. Qualitative evaluation methods are useful for a programme whose goals are in the process of being defined and to test out the workability of the evaluation's methods. Because they are 'personalized', qualitative methods may add emotion and tone to purely statistical findings and provide a means of gauging outcomes when reliable and valid measures of those outcomes are unlikely to become available in time for the evaluation report.
>
> (Fink 1993: 11)

The most systematic attempt to develop a naturalistic approach to evaluation is that provided by Worthen and Sanders who argue that:

> The major role of evaluation is one of responding to an audience's requirements for information in ways that take account of the different value perspectives of its members. By taking a naturalistic approach to evaluation, the evaluator is studying an educational activity *in situ*, or as it occurs naturally, without constraining, manipulating, or controlling it. They are seeing it from the informant's (teacher's) point of view.
>
> (Worthen and Sanders 1987: 138–9)

One can see how such an approach can be adopted by teachers themselves undertaking naturalistic evaluation case studies of practice.

What is important to remember is that evaluation by whatever means, quantitative, qualitative or a mixture of the two, is both a political and a scientific activity and the aims and ownership of the results are crucial issues. MacDonald's (1974) much quoted typology of three evaluation models namely bureaucratic, autocratic and democratic highlighted this fact and led Walker (1985) to conclude that the adoption of a participant observer role may in part be a political one on the part of the researcher and 'relates to a decision to report sideways and downwards rather than upwards' (MacDonald and Walker 1974: 17–18) and Walker (1985: 86). The

Research questions stage	POSING QUESTIONS ABOUT THE PROGRAMME
Criteria establishment stage	SETTING STANDARDS OF EFFECTIVENESS
Research design stage	DESIGNING THE EVALUATION AND SELECTING PARTICIPANTS
Data collection stage	COLLECTION OF DATA
Data analysis stage	ANALYSING DATA
Findings Presentation	REPORTING RESULTS

Figure 2.4 A programme evaluation
Source: Fink (1993)

following diagram (after Fink 1993) identifies the main stages in a programme evaluation and how these relate to conventional research stages and phases (Figure 2.4).

Since many teacher–researchers are engaged in evaluation of one sort or another we hope these comments are instructive. There is a relationship between evaluation and qualitative approaches and we have attempted to show what this is. For further consideration of this issue it is instructive to consult the work of Patton (1980).

CONCLUSION

In may respects this chapter probably contains some of the most crucial debates and discussions currently occupying educational research. We have tried to identify different underlying philosophies of social research and to unravel the nature of action research models and evaluation models which have recently dominated research and educational processes. We have concentrated upon the underlying assumptions which inform social and educational research. For a long time social and educational researchers have been stuck at the level of debate between paradigms or traditions. Far too much emphasis has been given to theoretical differences and not enough to substantive and methodological debates. We wish to leave the high theoretical controversies behind and instead concentrate upon what it is that qualitative, naturalistic methodologies have to offer the teacher–researcher and, indeed, other groups. For us, the battles at one level have been fought and won. The contemporary diversity of qualitative research suggests that a wider new set of questions and debates will ensue within the qualitative, naturalistic tradition. Parts II and III of the book take these up in some detail.

The following two chapters deal with crucial aspects of social and educational research: access ethics and objectivity, and the pervasive influence of gender. Both these discussion are informed by what we have been considering here.

SUGGESTED FURTHER READING

The term 'methodology' refers to a range of issues about the assumed ways of conducting social and educational research. As such, methodology will involve a broad set of ideas, concepts, frameworks and theories which surround the use of particular methods or techniques. Lying behind these methods and techniques are complicated assumptions of a philosophical and theoretical nature about the most appropriate ways of exploring and investigating the social world. Any particular research strategy, as well as being guided by practical concerns and the nature of the areas being investigated, will also be heavily influenced by these theoretical and philosophical issues. The following works provide discussion of these complex debates. *Becoming Critical: Education, Knowledge and Action Research* (Carr and Kemmis 1986) is one of the most important and influential recent texts in this area. It grounds the theoretical and philosophical aspects of research in the debate on teacher, curriculum and action research. The book draws out the relationships and interrelationships of teachers' research and the curriculum, comparing natural scientific positivist approaches with interpretative views. The authors stress the way in which education and educational research should become critical, arguing that an action research model will help to link theory with practice. *Feminism and Methodology* (Harding 1988) is an important collection of articles which highlights the contribution feminist researchers are making to the debate on epistemology, theory and methodology. In particular, although fairly advanced, Sandra Harding's introductory essay 'Is there a feminist method?' poses a number of serious questions about whether feminist research is distinguished by method or by the shaping of the research and the questions asked. Although the essays cover the fields of sociology, psychology, literature and history, there is much of direct relevance to educational research on, for and by women. The collection poses questions about the nature of our knowledge of women's experiences and the types of bias encountered by them. Those readers unfamiliar with the background to contemporary debates on the nature of the human sciences might consider *Philosophy and the Human Sciences* (Anderson, Hughes and Sharrock 1986) which has the rare quality of dealing with some extremely complex issues in a clear, straightforward way. In addition, a number of dictionaries of education and the social sciences are appearing which contain entries on particular methodological issues or individual techniques and are worth consulting. A collection of classic studies in classroom research can be found in *Case Studies in Classroom Research* (Hammersley 1986).

Increasing numbers of 'evaluation studies' or studies involving a degree of evaluation are appearing. *Researching into the Curriculum* (Bastiani and Tolley 1989) is a short 'rediguide' outlining the curriculum as a field of study. The authors discuss the organization and range of curriculum research and evaluation studies. *Evaluation for School Development* (Hopkins 1989) is a very readable account of the process of evaluation which will be of help to those engaged on programmes of school-based evaluation for part or all of their dissertation. *Evaluating Education: Issues and Methods* (Murphy and Torrance 1987) brings together a number of key articles in the field of evaluation research as applied to education. The introduction and various articles highlight the importance of evaluation research as a means to improving practice, focusing on theoretical, methodological, ethical and practical issues. *Education, Training and the New Vocationalism* (Pollard, Purvis and Walford 1988) will be of considerable value to those students doing projects based around the post-16 group of students either in school or the further education context. The impact of the 'New Vocationalism' has been felt throughout the educational world, but most research and analysis of these initiatives has been through examining outputs, effects and numbers. This collection of articles shows how ethnographic research orientations can be used to explore applied fields and the influence of educational policies. These studies are useful in demonstrating how a qualitative, ethnographic orientation can help to provide an appreciation of the ways policy works out in practice.

3 Access, ethics and objectivity

The challenge for school-based research

INTRODUCTION

We have been concerned so far with unravelling the nature of teacher research, providing a justification for qualitative approaches and outlining and introducing issues of research design and methodology. Research does not take place in a vacuum, it always has a context. Social and educational research is conducted by thinking, feeling human beings and in qualitative approaches the researcher takes on a highly-interactive profile. Qualitative techniques are regarded as being highly reactive techniques. When the nature of the research is so intimately linked to professional practice, a whole series of fundamental questions are raised. These questions need to be explored under the related headings of access, ethics and objectivity. With the increasing numbers of teachers taking responsibility for research into their own and others' practice, and their own professional development, it is important to be clear about the nature of the problems and the individual stance one is to take. We will try to do this by focusing upon the nature of access and entry questions, ethical issues and the notion of objectivity as these have been dealt with in social research, highlighting their significance for the teacher–researcher. Taken together, issues of access, ethics and objectivity pose philosophical, practical, methodological, theoretical and personal problems for the researcher. We now consider these questions to be of such significance that we feel it is important to try and unravel them prior to consideration of research techniques in detail.

ACCESS TO RESEARCH SITUATIONS AND NEGOTIATING ENTRY

On the surface, access and entry are not problems which immediately appear as problems teacher–researchers will face. The field is, so to speak, immediately there, therefore access ought not to be a problem. All that needs to be done can be done in familiar environments with familiar others. This is, of course, not always that easy. Schools, are organizations which have a power structure. Knowledge is not equally distributed but is socially constructed. There are changing relationships both inside and outside schools and colleges. All these factors go towards making what might appear, on the surface, to be the relatively easy tasks of access and entry to the research

situation, much more complex. As the world of education becomes increasingly politically contested, the potential for conflict between professional integrity and the demands of policy become more acute. Why does a teacher want to do a particular piece of research in a particular setting?

We will emphasize the importance of entry to a field situation in ethnographic naturalistic research and the need for the researcher to develop a credible role in the field. The problem will surround the ability of the researcher to develop a reasonable argument for doing a particular piece of research and gaining acceptance and co-operation from the parties concerned. Of course, in school-based research, a distinction would need to be drawn between those teachers who are already in the situations they wish to explore and those who are outside the immediate settings they want to focus upon. The further away from the research area the teacher is, the greater the problem of access.

Until fairly recently most research in schools has been carried out by outside professional researchers. In many ways, these researchers were able to control the research process and, unlike many teachers, left the scene of the research once the data had been collected. Even in qualitative orientated research there was much of this 'smash and grab ethnography'. However, teacher research raises quite different problems of access which can be so basic that the teacher will have to consider them at the research design and initial preparatory stages of the project. To begin with, the teacher will need to identify at an early point the relevant persons from whom permission will need to be obtained. A lot of work in the past has been held up or even had to be abandoned because an initial consideration of the question of access was not properly thought through. There may be said to be some fairly simple rules which are worth following in these matters:

- The researcher must establish points of contact and individuals from whom it is necessary to gain permission. At this stage it is important to establish exactly what activities are going to be observed and what documents will be examined. It may be necessary to obtain the support of immediate superiors in order to facilitate this.
- The researcher must be as clear and as straightforward as possible in articulating the nature and scope of the projected study. This will clarify the demands which are likely to be made on the individuals or groups involved. Large complicated questionnaires can lie uncompleted on teachers' desks for some time, or an expected interview does not take place because it has been arranged at a particularly busy time. If the demands of the research are clearly established in the beginning, then some of these problems may be offset.
- It is worthwhile trying to anticipate any potentially sensitive areas or issues the research may focus upon and explain in advance how these are likely to be dealt with in the research.
- The teacher–researcher must be sensitive to the hierarchy of the school or

organization concerned, even if this is his or her own. Experience has shown that research projects have met problems when their aims and methods of data collection have conflicted with a superior's perceived area of jurisdiction and responsibility. As Holly (1984: 100–3) has observed, there may, in fact, be an in-built opposition between democratically conceived research and hierarchically structured schools! This may be a particular issue for research concerned directly with the relationship between practice and policy. The aim must be to resolve any such conflicts before the research begins or as soon as potential areas of conflict arise during the course of the work. Let us take the example of a headteacher researching into an aspect of her school policy. The problem here might surround the difficulty of separating one's role as a head and, therefore, manager, from that of participant observer where certain kinds of field relationships need to be developed.

- The teacher–researcher must also be aware that the aims and objectives of 'applied' or 'action' research are often to change practice in a particular direction. Such research may, whatever its good intention, appear to other colleagues to threaten their own professional practice.
- Researchers, whether teachers or not, must therefore take account of the fact that their activities take place within special social, political and cultural contexts. Even if the object of the research may be restricted to helping the researcher's own practice, the above considerations need addressing at an early stage; even more so if the research design and conclusions have implications for other colleagues.
- Teacher–researchers may experience conflict between their own perceived, professional and personal development and those of the school, local education authorities, or, in the future, school governors. These differences may be difficult to reconcile. However, they will all influence access to the situations under study and the responses and feedback the teacher–researcher is likely to obtain.

As we stated earlier, these rules are not hard and fast. Individual circumstances must be the final arbiter. As far as possible, it is better if a researcher can discuss her research with all the parties involved. On other occasions, it may be better for the teacher to develop a pilot study and uncover some of the problems in advance of the research proper. If it appears that the research is going to come into conflict with aspects of school policy, management styles or individual personalities, it is better to confront the issues head on, consult the relevant parties and make arrangements in the research design where possible or necessary. It should by now be clear to everyone that, in the future, one will have to argue clearly and with conviction about the positive values of school-based research.

Skeggs (1992) has highlighted the social dimension of access issues in relation to gender and sexuality:

> Access is not just a matter of getting into the right localities to speak to

people. It usually makes you confront the nuances of power. It also makes you aware of how morality is underpinned with assumptions about gender and sexuality. For instance, I have recently spent over a year with a colleague trying to gain access to a further education college to ask students questions on attitudes to sexuality and sexual practice in order to be able to develop educational materials on HIV and AIDS. After 10 months of creative delaying strategies, we have had to give up. The person in the college who was able to give us access believed that what we were doing was morally wrong. He believed that young people either did not or should not have sex, and that we should not encourage irresponsible behaviour by discussing it. He was offended by our questions on female sexuality. He also believed that, as a result of Clause 28, undue publicity would be given to the college. His morality operated with the support of the institutional power of the college and of the state. He was able to enforce it. As other researchers have found, any work on sexuality has to find ways of getting round the assumptions inherent within the dominant moral order.

(Skeggs 1992: 15)

FUNDING AND RELATIONS WITH SPONSORS AND CLIENTS

Although conflicts about funding and sponsors will be considerably less acute if the individual teacher–researcher is responsible for her own research, its design, execution and dissemination, they take on a higher profile when the research is 'funded' or 'sponsored' or is in any sense under the direct control of some other person or agency. Even if the teacher–researcher is entirely responsible for her own research it will still be difficult to avoid 'gate-keepers' altogether and the issues involved in researching 'one's own patch' can arise.

The main problems concern a series of interrelated questions. How is the research to be funded? What are its aims and objectives? How will the data be collected and the information used? Within social science, these questions became more pressing as funding for research became more a tool used by governments and business to pursue ends which run counter to the perceived values of the researcher, as the infamous example of 'Project Camelot' revealed (Horowitz 1967). This US military-funded research project not only showed the dangers inherent in research sponsorship and the need for researchers to direct and control as much as possible not only their research but also its outcome, but showed also that researchers can be deceived by their own research assumptions. Here, a failure to understand the nature of power and the limitations of the 'scientific-positivist' research model adopted to preserve objectivity and independence showed the need for codes of practice to be evolved in order to deal with such cases. It was such instances which produced, via the American Anthropological Association

(1971 and 1973) and the Society for Applied Anthropology, some of the first social science codes of practice. In 1973, the British Sociological Association followed with its own code, as did, later, the British Psychological Society, the Market Research Society (1986) and the Economic and Social Research Council (1984).

The key issue with funding is 'who pays for the work'? The more independent the funding the more open the outcome is likely to be. If funding for 'outside or award bearing' in-service research is conducted 'in-house' (as is currently happening in the English education service) then this will affect not only the amount but also the control and uses of any inquiry/research undertaken by teachers. Teacher–researchers will face the same sort of pressures that all who work in more applied or pedagogic fields have – of trying to convince others of the value of their work and how it may forward the aims of school or college policy. This will enable them to argue for the value of research as one of the necessary bedrocks of effective management but it will also mean that an individual teacher–researcher may have less independence in choice of project and control over the dissemination of their findings.

Many interview schedules are specifically designed to break into a subject's private space and breach their defences. Life history interviews, which attempt to get close to the subject's perceptions of the world, will do this whether intentionally or not. The teacher–researcher should be sensitive, therefore, to the intrusive potential of the life history interview and its uses. The life history interview can be therapeutic, cathartic, or even uncomfortable and unnerving. It will be necessary to keep control of any tapes or transcripts which may contain sensitive information, especially if permission has not been obtained from the subject. Special problems can arise if, during the course of an interview, opinions are obtained about other subjects who may not have the opportunity to give or withhold consent. Here, the first interviewees are being used as surrogate informants and one has to be especially careful in controlling access by others to this information, especially if they have power over the subjects.

THE MEANING OF 'ETHICS'

The relationship between ethics and the conduct of qualitative school-based teacher–researcher inquiry is a complex one. Considerable conceptual and philosophical spade-work is needed. Here we propose to tackle the issue, first, by trying to come to terms with the notion of ethics and the nature of ethical conduct and, second, by remembering what it was that we said was integral to the nature of qualitative research. Finally, we will try to draw all this together by considering ethical issues as they relate to forms of educational inquiry which are predominantly qualitative in nature, namely, evaluation inquiry, action research inquiry and feminist research. This will lead on to some specific problems relating to the use of certain research techniques.

It is clear that the very nature of qualitative research itself will give rise to certain kinds of ethical issues. It is the responsibility of the teacher–researcher to have a clear grasp of what they are. The resolution of these issues is, of course, another matter.

It is easy to forget that the very subject matter of educational inquiry, namely education, is itself fundamentally a moral enterprise. That is, education is regarded by everyone, though obviously not in the same way, as having to do more or less with the good of society and the good of the individual. Whilst there is heated debate at present over the purposes and functions of education this serves only to confirm that. Education takes place in a socio-cultural, historical, political and economic context. The educational sphere of society is par excellence a moral sphere where judgements, assumptions, values and beliefs are held about what is right and wrong, good and bad, appropriate and inappropriate, justifiable and non-justifiable. This is clear and obvious but gets eschewed if one believes that research in education can be value free, or without any moral or political predilections. If we accept that education operates in the moral sphere what do we precisely mean by 'ethics' and subsequently 'ethical conduct' or 'unethical conduct'?

Ethics refers to questions of values, that is, of beliefs, judgements and personal viewpoints. Central here is the question of responsibility. Responsibilities relate to the individual researcher, the participants in the research, professional colleagues and the teaching community and towards the sponsors of the research. In this sense, the ethics of research concern the criteria which, on being met, enable the researcher to do what is right and correct and which facilitate the adequate discharge of the kinds of responsibilities outlined above.

Whilst all this may seem fairly straightforward we need to consider the questions in relation to the nature of qualitative and naturalistic research traditions. As we have noted, qualitative research is all about capturing the reality of life in colleges, schools and classrooms, that is in educational contexts and the immediate cultural milieu which surrounds that reality. Qualitative research methodology is the systematic attempt to generate and use non-quantitative techniques and methodologies which will facilitate understanding and conceptualization of the face-to-face routine, everyday socio-cultural context of educational processes and institutions. Indeed, one of the major claims of qualitative research is that it can provide deep, rich 'thick' (Geertz 1973) descriptions unavailable to quantitative research. The very stuff of qualitative research then is ideas, ideas entail values, values involve assumptions about right and wrong, good and bad. Inevitably, qualitative research will be concerned with first-hand involvement in this moral sphere. Furthermore, the centrality of the teacher–researcher in qualitative research and the highly reactive nature of the techniques employed and the stance developed means that qualitative researchers are certainly unable to retain a 'value free' position and would find it very difficult to maintain a stance of ethical neutrality. We will follow these questions up in more detail as we look at the concept of objectivity.

THE ETHICAL CONDUCT OF SCHOOL-BASED RESEARCH

The teacher–researcher, like all other social researchers, is a moral agent with views, opinions, values, and attitudes. It follows that the teacher conducting research in schools will be faced with ethical and moral dilemmas. What lengths can research go to in investigating its subjects? What rights do the subjects of a piece of research have? How can trust be established or confidentiality and anonymity be guaranteed? These and other questions will all emerge when considering the ethical conduct of school-based research.

It is generally recognized that specific ethical problems will emerge from the use of one or other research strategy or data-collection technique. The thrust of this book has been to explore the potential of qualitative research methodologies for school-based research. Since the researcher in such approaches is the major instrument or funnel through which data are obtained, it follows that qualitative research will pose special ethical questions for such a researcher. Because the researcher is so close to the subjects of the research it follows that one of the main ethical questions posed by qualitative educational or teacher research is the researcher's responsibilities towards the subjects themselves, in our case teachers and pupils.

OPEN OR CLOSED RESEARCH?

A major starting point for researchers using qualitative approaches is the degree to which the investigation is conducted overtly or covertly. Erikson (1967) discussing in particular, participant observation, argued that to disguise one's intentions compromised both the researcher and the subject and amounted to the same thing as a doctor carrying out surgery without the patient's permission. For Erikson disguised observation was, ultimately, simply bad science. Douglas (1976), on the other hand, maintained that what he described as 'investigative social research' was necessary at times and in any way turned out in the end to be relatively harmless. Our point, as Platt (1981a,b,c) and others have pointed out, is that both ethical and methodological issues are inextricably linked in qualitative work whether using observation or interviews. The 'insider' doing research is not immune from these issues; in fact, they can be more difficult to reconcile because of the simple fact that one is part of the situation one is investigating. An outside researcher can maintain greater distance from the inquiry and at the end of the research will leave the scene.

The significance and value of qualitative research methods for teacher–researchers lies in their ability to reconstruct faithfully the realities of the school or college from the participants' viewpoint by both formal and informal means. It is very likely that life history interviews, for example, will form part of a wider research approach to an issue that will involve some sort of observation as well. The particular ethical issues raised by life history interviews cannot therefore be separated initially from those generally raised by qualitative approaches. When, for example, does formal observation end and informal observation begin? Is it justifiable to be open with some colleagues and closed with others? (Hitchcock 1983a: 19–35; Burgess 1984a; 1984b). This question could apply even more to the use of pupils as subjects (Pollard 1984: 95–118) where the issue might involve how much to tell pupils and how far to involve them in the study? When is an overheard casual conversation part of the research data and when is it not? This latter issue is especially relevant to school-based evaluation work (Simmons 1984). Is gossip legitimate data and can the researcher ethically use material that has been passed on to her in confidence? The list of issues is endless since the range and scope of methods employed and sources of data used in ethnographic or qualitative research is bound to place the teacher–researcher in many different situations, so that she will certainly become party to more than one version of any given situation or phenomenon. The same issues arise before, during and after an interview when off-the-record comments and casual conversations can be particularly insightful. Indeed, we know of a number of situations where a formal interview with a teacher has ended only to be followed by a series of very revealing and insightful comments which did not feature in the interview. Hearsay, gossip, asides and so on, the informal lines of communication, constitute as much a part of the way organizations work as the formal structures. They are particularly important sources of data about the working 'culture' of an organization and of the people who work there. But how does the researcher handle such often potentially explosive information?

A central element of the qualitative research tradition has been the establishment and development of field relations. Part of this process entails the development of rapport, trust and confidence between subject and the researcher as we will explore more fully in Chapter 6. This a useful example for us to consider here. The teacher–researcher has to start from the position that as a researcher one's first responsibility is to the subject(s) and that this is the bottom line as far as confidentiality is concerned. It is all too easy to assume that it is possible to reconcile one's personal research agenda with those of the organization for which one works or is working. It really comes down to a question of who is sponsoring and/or overseeing the work. If the researcher is free from these pressures and is working independently, the problem may not arise, but if not, it can.

Many of these issues are dependent upon the individual researcher's own place in the organization. Let us first take the example of a head teacher researching into an aspect of her school policy. In the course of collecting data a series of life interviews are used and analysed. The issue that arises here is the near impossibility of completely separating one's role as a head and therefore a manager and that of an observer. One is bound to obtain information that then or in the future could colour a decision about an individual: perhaps to do with a promotion. The increased powers and access to information given in recent Government legislation concerning the role and power of school governing bodies might also be a crucial factor here. Again, an example drawn from our own experience may illustrate this point more clearly. A head teacher of a primary school was undertaking research into an aspect of the school curriculum, the aim of which was to evaluate a new approach to reading. In the course of this research a series of interviews were conducted with certain members of staff in which they expressed their views about the new approaches. The head later in the completed study revealed that the interviews had been used by her as a means of assessing the suitability of those interviewed for an allowance post within the school.

Here is a good example of means and ends and of the tension which exists between the demands of research and the demands of management. Heads cannot abrogate their managerial functions and are bound in the course of their work to have access to sensitive information. It also highlights the need for institutions to which teacher–researchers may be attached to have clear policies and monitoring processes on ethical and practical issues when undertaking school-based research. The question remains as to whether in this case ethical considerations and responsibilities had been overtaken by managerial concerns?

It could be argued here that to have told the interviewee of the possibility that the data collected could be used in this way would have resulted in the interviews lacking the flexibility and intimacy claimed as one of the chief advantages of this approach. In the introduction and development of new curriculum ideas it is natural to seek those who have sympathy with the approach rather than those who have not. Here, it is clear that the life history interview should not have been used as a partial appraisal interview yet it also shows that one cannot easily separate research responsibilities from managerial ones. If, as we have pointed out earlier, the research becomes more applied and more pedagogical in its claims these questions assume more significance. What the researcher must do is be clear about the possible consequences of actions and attempt to balance the information gained by other criteria. One has also to hold on very firmly to the confidentiality aspect by not revealing the data to others in normal circumstances. Eventually, it is a matter of individual personal integrity and consideration of the feelings and professional needs of colleagues and pupils. It is also clear that there may be limits to the amount of confidentiality it is possible to guarantee.

Given the issues raised above about the ethical problems that arise from participant observation and allied qualitative techniques, what is the correct role for the teacher–researcher? A teacher–researcher cannot, in investigating her own or her colleagues' practice, achieve the role of 'non-participant observation' that King (1978) adopted in his study of infant classrooms.

Unlike a researcher such as King, the teacher–researcher is normally always an active participant in a given situation. Nor are teacher–researchers likely to be able to achieve the role of 'participant as observer' that researchers into school practice, such as Hargreaves (1967) and Lacey (1970), adopted. The teacher is normally a researcher and an informant at the same time.

In a sense the nearest model or ideal type in qualitative research to that of teacher–researcher is that of the complete participant. Here the researcher disguises her aim and opts for a covert operation to secure the necessary data. Now it would be possible though not desirable for teachers to adopt this model. Apart from some of the ethical issues already raised, the adoption of such a role would limit severely the scope of the research. For example, it would make interviewing other subjects virtually impossible. Again, access to certain kinds of data may be difficult to obtain unless an explanation is given. Of course, the question of openness can be taken to absurd lengths and being an active participant means that one is bound to observe relevant material for data collection all the time. The key question here is 'Would being covert compromise the researcher in her professional duties?' Another way of looking at this is 'Would the data collected and results have been different if the research had been open, not secret?'

The normal relationship between the roles of 'insider' (observation) and 'outsider' (analysing data) with the researcher stepping into one role and then out into another is also difficult for the teacher investigating practice. The sharp distinction between the two roles is considered crucial to avoid the researcher becoming over-identified with the group she is studying and to assist data collection.

Teachers must, however, be identified in given situations with fellow subjects by the very nature of their work and culture. Yet it can be argued that the role of participant observer involves a clash of roles that can be resolved only if that of the 'outsider' is emphasized. Teacher–researchers need therefore to be aware of the two roles that participant observation involves and be able to overcome any conflict during the research process by adopting as open an approach as possible.

Participant observation is a good example to begin with. Participant observation can take two forms. Although we would encourage teachers to be as open as possible about their research and observation there are occasions and situations, even within overt observational research, when the teacher–researcher will be involved in covert participant observation. This refers to a situation where, as Bulmer describes it:

> The researcher spends an extended period of time in a particular research setting concealing the fact that he is a researcher and pretending to play some other role. In such a situation, the identity of the researcher and knowledge of his work is kept from those who are being studied, who have no knowledge that they are being studied.
>
> (Bulmer 1982: 4)

There are arguably many situations in the course of ordinary school life where pupils are observed by teachers without their knowledge. Covert or overt participation as a research strategy will place the teacher in very different circumstances and therefore raises different ethical issues (Bulmer 1980). These questions are not unique to educational research or school-based teacher research and over the years an important debate has emerged about the limits to deception in social research and the ethics of covert participation as we earlier indicated in this chapter.

These problems generated some heated discussion in the social sciences and studies by Festinger, Riecken and Schochter (1956), Humphreys (1970), and Milgram's (1974) famous study of obedience all point to the limits of deception in social research. Even if prospective teacher–researchers follow Erikson (1967) and reject disguised research as both unethical and not applicable to their own very different relationship with the subjects of their research, problems of responsibilities will not go away. Ultimately, these questions come down to trust, confidentiality, and anonymity.

As we will argue in Chapter 6, an essential ingredient for the successful completion of ethnographic research is the establishment of good and effective field relations. This involves the development of a sense of rapport between the researcher and subjects leading to feelings of trust and confidence. Inevitably, the researcher will receive much information on trust from subjects and the teacher–researcher will have to develop some way of safeguarding the anonymity of the subject by, for example, the use of pseudonyms. It may even be necessary for the teacher–researcher to assure the subjects that pseudonyms will be used in any subsequent written material. Where records or reports of individual children are concerned it is, of course, absolutely essential to maintain anonymity thereby safeguarding the pupils involved. It is quite important for the teacher to step back from the research situation and to analyse carefully what the appropriate ethical response to a situation might be. The principles of confidentiality and anonymity can, however, resolve many of the ethical dilemmas the teacher–researcher may find herself in. If the researcher has built up a good trusting relationship with the subjects this will carry with it certain rights, obligations, and responsibilities. But, the researcher might have more power, status, or authority than the subjects or might even hold widely differing values. Special problems can result from particular techniques employed in qualitative research and we will point to some of these as we approach each of them in detail. We have also pointed out the general ethical issues involved in qualitative approaches. Research design will also have a significance here. Most notable have been the claims for a distinct feminist research ethic as a result of the implications of feminism for research design.

A FEMINIST RESEARCH ETHIC?

The feminist critique of conventional social science, its epistemology and practice, with a commitment to the liberation of women, pushes a feminist method in particular directions. Acker, Barry and Esseveld have outlined what they consider to be the three central principles of feminist research:

> Research should contribute to women's liberation through producing knowledge that can be used by women themselves; should use methods of gaining knowledge that are not aggressive; should continually develop a feminist critical perspective that questions dominant intellectual traditions and can reflect on its own development.
>
> (Acker, Barry and Esseveld 1983: 42)

It is of course logical to assume that a distinct feminist method will entail a feminist ethic for carrying out social and educational research. Since qualitative methodologies rely so heavily upon close involvement, subjective and personal materials, and are frequently used by feminists the ethical questions we have been raising will loom large.

The Nebraska Feminist Collective consists of a group of *wimmin* (their own spelling) concerned initially with sexism, racism, classism and heterosexism within the field of sociology. This interest quickly spread to embrace the question of ethics, which is transformed when prefixed by 'feminist'. The Nebraska Feminist Collective (1983) base their discussion of a feminist ethic for social research upon the epistemological arguments we have in part alluded to in Chapter 2, in particular the problems surrounding the separation of knower and known in objectivist research. Their account is based upon three sets of interrelated assumptions: first, the idea of women solely as research objects; second, the use and abuse of language in sociology; and third, the gatekeeping processes in employment, funding and research. Their conclusion is uncompromising:

> A feminist ethic differs from the traditional sociological ethic in several fundamental ways. While the goal of traditional social science is to gain knowledge for the 'advancement/enlightenment' of the discipline, the feminist analyses social aggression to empower herself, wimmin and minorities. Whereas the traditional scientist is accountable to the profession, the feminist is accountable to the wimmin's movement, a feminist ethic, and women in general.
>
> (The Nebraska Feminist Collective 1983: 541)

Certainly, these comments move away from the cosy liberal treatment of ethical issues commonly found in the social sciences and highlight the ways in which the aims of a feminist social science are inextricably bound up with the processes of carrying out feminist research. This brings us back to a discussion of the very processes involved in researching.

THE IMPORTANCE OF ANONYMITY

In qualitative research, such as life history, oral history and documentary research, the actual accounts, words, stories and narratives of participants often feature heavily in the finished written account. In order to retain this essential ingredient of qualitative research while safeguarding the rights and confidence of the subjects the researcher must use pseudonyms to protect the anonymity of the school, parents, teachers and pupils involved. This procedure can save much unnecessary embarrassment and it really should be seen as an essential aspect of the presentation of much, though not all, school-based research. It is possible to be quite ingenious in the use of pseudonyms in order to retain some of the character of the settings, classrooms and issues explored. Confidentiality and anonymity are important since, as has been pointed out earlier in this chapter, the world of schools and classrooms are full of values and perceived conflicts of interest, perhaps never more so than today. The researcher, as we have also indicated earlier, may have more 'power', authority and status than the subject, or the researcher may hold very different values to the subject.

Balancing these responsibilities is hardly ever achieved with total satisfaction. It can be a complicated juggling act. One set of responsibilities can be met only to discover that they conflict with others. This has led many of the professional social science associations to attempt to develop acceptable 'codes of conduct' for their members to follow. The *Statement of Ethical Principles and Their Application to Sociological Practice,* (British Sociological Association 1973) are possibly the most relevant to the kinds of situations the teacher–researcher is likely to encounter and we have formulated a series of ethical rules for school-based research based upon this statement. Although these 'rules' cannot cover every situation the teacher might encounter they will go some way towards resolving ethical problems of school-based research.

SOME ETHICAL RULES FOR SCHOOL-BASED RESEARCH

Professional integrity

1 Ensure that the research you propose is viable, that an adequate research design has been established, and appropriate data-collection techniques chosen.
2 Explain as clearly as possible the aims, objectives, and methods of the research to all of the parties involved.
3 If using confidential documents ensure that anonymity is maintained by eliminating any kinds of material or information that could lead others to identify the subject or subjects involved.

Interests of the subjects

1 The researcher must allow subjects the right to refuse to take part in the research.
2 The researcher must demonstrate how confidentiality is to be built into the research.
3 If any or part of the research is to be published the teacher may need to gain the permission of the parties involved.
4 If the teacher is involved in joint or collaborative research then it is important to ensure that all researchers adhere to the same set of ethical principles.

Responsibilities and relationships with sponsors, outside agencies, academic institutions, or management

1 If the research is 'sponsored', the researcher must be clear on the terms of reference and their own and their subjects' rights in relation to the finished research.
2 The teacher must be aware of the possible uses to which the research may be put.

(after British Sociological Association 1973)

TAKING SIDES?

> The question is not whether we should take sides, since we inevitably will, but rather whose side are we on?
>
> (Becker 1967: 239)

In the issues raised by the above discussion there is one that we have not yet explored in any depth, though we have touched upon it in the discussion on access and the funding of research, namely the question of objectivity and truth. Whose side are we really on? For example, our colleagues, management, the children or the students? Many of the important issues relating to the ethics of research in the social field and the involvement and stance of the researcher are contained within the various debates on objectivity in the human sciences. The debates are complex, rooted as they are in some difficult philosophical puzzles. Here we will take the position adopted by those social scientists working within the phenomenological and interpretative traditions. The question of whether or not the researcher should, or indeed could, be objective has received considerable discussion within sociology and allied disciplines under the heading of objectivity and value freedom. An essential feature of science and the 'scientific method' as practised in the Western world over the past three centuries or so has been the claims of its practitioners about the objectivity and freedom from bias which may be achieved by emulating and following the procedures of the natural, physical sciences in the human sciences.

In this discussion objectivity was defined as a special way of looking at a situation from the outside, that is, without making prescriptive, value-laden judgements or moral assumptions about the phenomena. Facts were seen as statements concerning what 'is' the case and values were statements concerning what 'ought' and 'should' be the case.

Science, namely the natural sciences and especially physics, dealt with 'facts' since it was argued that you cannot derive a statement of 'fact' from a statement on 'values'. Yet the problem of objectivity in the sciences and hence in social, educational and school-based research is essentially that of values and of achieving value freedom and value neutrality. School-based research, therefore, is vulnerable in these debates since its subject matter very often involves values, opinions, beliefs and attitudes. Values can enter a piece of social and educational research at a number of points: in choice of subject; choice of research design; choice of data-collection techniques; unravelling the policy implications of a study, as well as a number of other areas.

But, to the social scientists of the nineteenth and early twentieth century the appeal of objectivity and value freedom was attractive and its appeal clearly lay in its ability to make their research seem reliable. In accepting the essential similarity of the social and physical worlds for research purposes, society could be studied in the same way as the natural world. In this view, called *positivism*, the 'facts' spoke for themselves and the task of the social researcher was to discover these true facts without letting personal, political, moral or religious judgements enter into research, thereby 'distorting' the 'truth'. Theories in this view are verified by facts and they stand or fall by means of a process of verification. Objectivity, in this view, was both desirable and a necessary condition of good research. This is the pursuit of knowledge for its own sake and one which rejects political partisanship. We have, however, seen earlier in a discussion of the Operation Camelot affair that adopting a positivist approach is no guarantee of value freedom and neutrality (Horowitz 1967).

Indeed, as Denzin (1970) has argued, any 'myth' about the value freedom of the researcher is called into question equally by the social and political environment in which the researcher operates. Perhaps more pertinent for teacher–researchers is the tendency of organizations studied to expect some 'pay back' in the form of value-free and quantifiable 'facts' or 'remedies' often to support their existing or future policies.

Max Weber, in the early part of this century, pointed out that all research was to some degree contaminated by the values of the researcher. Indeed, Weber (1949) argued, it was through these values that particular issues are defined and studied. Actually, the 'scientific method' with its emphasis on neutrality was itself a held value. Equally, the conclusions which the researcher drew were influenced by her own moral and political values.

Two famous lectures given during the First World War laid down what we can call the liberal position which places emphasis on the individual conscience of the researcher as the basis of action. As Silverman later observed:

> Taking the classic Kantian position, Weber argued that values could not be derived facts. However, this was not because values were less important than facts (as logical positivists were soon to argue) rather, precisely because 'ultimate evaluations' (or value choices) were so important, they were not to be reduced to purely factual judgements. The facts could only tell you about the likely consequences of given actions but they could not tell you which action to choose.
>
> (Silverman 1985: 180)

According to Silverman (1985), Weber therefore appealed to the scholar's individual conscience as the sole basis for conferring meaning and significance upon events.

Both the position of Weber and, over fifty years later, that of Denzin (1970), emphasized the absolute freedom of the researcher/scholar to 'pursue one's activities as one sees fit'. One could add that this was allied to rigorous scholarly method and an understanding of the need for the researcher's own values and judgements to be made clear at the end of the research. The work was also open to scrutiny by fellow scholars which acted as a check on both reliability and validity.

But this enlightenment model has not found universal acceptance and later social scientists have argued that such a position underplays the social and political power relationships within the world in which the researcher/scholar operates. This is at the centre of Silverman's (1985) critique of Bulmer's (1982) version of the 'enlightenment' model which on the surface seems to offer the applied researcher a degree of 'professional freedom' while influencing social policy. This model saw the applied researcher as providing new problems and new concepts to aid the policy maker in her decision-making. This model, according to Silverman (1985), 'offers a purely bureaucratic version of politics; as such it totally fails to address the political and moral issues of research which is at anything other than arm's length from the state' (Silverman 1985: 183). Research is bound to a political activity however defined as Hammersley and Scarth's (1993) critique of the 'Three Wise Men' shows.

A quite different line on these questions has been taken by those social scientists from within the phenomenological and interpretative traditions. A central tenet of this position been a commitment to documenting the way in which individuals and groups of individuals define and perceive their worlds. Hence the concern of those researchers with subjective experience. Positivist researchers, in their efforts to maintain objectivity, by the use of pre-coded questionnaires, surveys or structured interviews, for example, actually define themselves what they perceive to be important, relevant, worthy of investigation and so on. This may lead them to ignore or play down the real feelings and attitudes of the subjects of their research. It is in this sense that the phenomenological and interpretative sociologists argue that whereas positivistic research claims to be objective it actually turns out in practice very often to be reinforcing the sociologists' (and policy makers') viewpoint.

Researchers in the qualitative mould stress, therefore, the inevitability and indeed, necessary, involvement of the researcher in the social world. They also argue that in such research complete objectivity is unobtainable and that value-free knowledge does not exist as such. As Gouldner (1968) has argued, the only sure course for a qualitative and, indeed, a quantitative researcher is to express their values, openly and honestly, and reject the myth of a moral neutrality. Gouldner (1968) has also cautioned qualitative researchers from adopting what he terms 'ombudsman sociology' in an attempt to justify investigating the social worlds of deviant, marginal or underdog groups such as pupil sub-cultures in schools and colleges. To attempt to keep a distance from the group by abrogating 'sentimentality' as advocated by Howard Becker is in Gouldner's eyes, tantamount to throwing out the baby with the bath water. To him giving in to sentimentality means intellectual sterility and moral irresponsibility. As Myrdal (1944) pointed out, his massive study on race relations in America was bound to be influenced by his own anti-racist stance. As with Gouldner (1968), he argued that researchers should make their values explicit so that those who read the outcome of the research can make up their own mind. We might note here the recent feminist critique of action research (Chisholm 1990). Certainly, the notion of an 'entitlement' curriculum or the concept of empowerment frames the ethical conduct of teacher research in a somewhat different light.

The problem might therefore be conceived not as one of objectivity, value-freedom, ethical neutrality or stating whose side you are on, but rather of making explicit in the research the assumptions, starting points, premises and values of the researcher. Put another way, who should know what? (Barnes 1979). Indeed, as those practitioners adopting a qualitative–ethnographic approach have long argued it is only when you as a researcher suspend your own judgements and values and cease to take the world for granted, that you can approach 'the life world' and the subjective experiences and interpretations of the actors themselves; teachers, pupils or whoever.

CONCLUSION

The philosopher of education, Jonas Soltis (1989), has provided a broad overview of the ethics of social research relevant to us here. In this part of the book we have discussed some of the varying purposes to which qualitative research in education may be put. These included action research, evaluation enquiry, and feminism. Soltis (1989) focuses upon four major purposes to which qualitative research in education may be put showing how each of these positions gives rise to both generic and specific research setting types of ethical issues. He identifies *descriptive qualitative research, qualitative educational evaluation research, intervention qualitative research* and finally *critique, (critical ethnography),* of areas such as gender race and class (Soltis 1989: 125). These purposes correspond to general qualitative interpretative research, evaluation inquiry, action research and, for example, feminist research which we discuss in Chapter 4. His point is that whilst some ethical issues cut across all these purposes others seem to be more specific to one or other of them. Furthermore, Soltis (1989) importantly highlights three different parts of 'philosophical–ethical–educational perspectives'. As he points out:

> Sometimes ethical issues are seen differently because they take on different quality tones for individuals depending upon which perspective they have assumed. I call these the personal, the professional, and the public perspectives.
>
> (Soltis 1989: 125)

Ethics is certainly a highly personal matter and dilemmas will appear in interpersonal contexts. We must never underplay the significance of ethical problems at the level of personal perspective. A professional perspective will involve moving from a personal to a communal point of view. Here the collective, shared viewpoints and obligations of a community of practitioners will hold sway. Frequently, this results in professional codes of conduct. Recognizing that research operates in the broader wider public domain Soltis's ethical obligations and issues will apply in a particular historical and socio-political, cultural context. Soltis (1989) offers a particularly useful framework here since he breaks down a number of complex interrelated aspects.

Soltis (1989) goes on to give some examples of typical ethical problems encountered in each of the four main qualitative research traditions in education. The emphasis on 'thick description' in descriptive research may, for example, mean that privacy, confidentiality and so on pose the researcher particular personal ethical problems. Since qualitative descriptive research places the researcher in face-to-face interactional encounters these problems are bound to arise. Evaluative research raises contract obligations. The development of measures of effectiveness may introduce personal bias and, above all, evaluation raises the use to which the findings of such work are put. In a similar way intervention research raises the fundamental question of the right to intervene and or change. Many of these questions were raised by us in our critique of action research in Chapter 2. There is the dangerous suggestion implied in some action research and intervention research that the 'researcher knows best'. Finally, those researchers in the qualitative tradition committed also to political, social, cultural or ideological critique will experience different kinds of ethical problems. In a sense the reverse problem for evaluation research is observable here. Knowing what is 'right', 'good', or 'effective' in evaluation research poses the same ethical question as knowing what is wrong, bad or ineffective in critical research. As Soltis (1989) argues the basic ethical question is how you know and establish either.

We have attempted to approach the issues of access, ethics and objectivity at an early point in this book because they are crucial. Since qualitative researchers have often been criticized for having a minimally developed critical awareness, we have demonstrated how this is not, in fact, the case. The politics of social research pose general questions; the politics of qualitative school-based practitioner research pose some quite distinct problems and we have tried to approach these here. The personal responsibilities of the teacher–researcher will eventually dictate the way she faces access, ethical and other related issues. Before we begin to look at some pathways through research we need to consider another major fundamental issue. Chapter 4 explores the impact of gender as a key variable in social and educational reasearch highlighting the consequences of this standpoint exploring the contribution of feminist research, and examining some of the pioneering research on gender and education from a broadly qualitative standpoint.

SUGGESTED FURTHER READING

The whole issue of the ethical conduct of social and educational research is a complex one. Some key methodology texts that make reference to ethics worth consulting include *Ethics and Anthropology: Dilemmas in Fieldwork* (Rynkiewich and Spradley 1976) and *Doing Anthropology: Warnings and Advice* (Wax 1971). Works relating to ethical issues arising from general ethnographic, qualitative research techniques include *Social Research Ethics: An Examination of the Merits of Covert Participant Observation* (Bulmer 1982) which contains many of the classic articles in the debate; and 'Ethical problems, ethical principles and field research practice' in *In The Field: An Introduction to Field Research* (Burgess 1984a). An updated view of the politics of fieldwork and the ethical features of qualitative research are extensively considered by Punch (1994) in 'Politics and ethics in qualitative research' in the *Handbook of Qualitative Research* (Denzin and Lincoln). Qualitative research covers a broad spectrum of techniques in particular research strategies, and raises special ethical issues. 'Reporting interviews: a code of good practice' (Powney and Watts 1984) contains some sound practical advice. On the other hand, 'On interviewing one's peers' (Platt 1981c) has some sobering thoughts. Plummer (1983) has approached the ethical questions raised by the use of personal documents in *Documents of Life: An Introduction to the Problems and Literature of a Humanistic Method*. Increasingly, the ethics of school-based research and the subsequent 'ownership' of knowledge has featured in many reports: the accounts by Ball (1985), 'Participant observation with pupils' in *Strategies of Educational Research: Qualitative Methods* (Burgess 1985b); 'The whole truth: some ethical problems in the study of a comprehensive school' in

Field Methods in the Study of Education (Burgess 1984b) and Pollard (1985a) 'Opportunities and difficulties of a teacher–ethnographer: a personal account'. The debate via case studies is contained in *The Ethics of Education Research* (Burgess 1989). Over recent years the sustained feminist critique has raised fundamental questions about politically engaged research. In particular, the personal and affective dimension of research has been explored by feminist researchers such as Skeggs (1992) 'Confessions of a feminist researcher'. Some of these questions are followed up in 'Feminism and research' (Kelly 1978). For an account of the politics of research in reaction to the patriarchal nature of the research community see *Beyond Methodology: Feminist Scholarship as Lived Experience* (Fonow and Cook 1991) and the whole of Chapter 4 in this book. It is good for those working in education to compare their access and ethical problems with those of researchers working in other fields. Here two studies are worth looking at: 'Observations of research on the national front' (Fielding 1982) and '"An inside job": a case study of covert research on the police' (Holdoway 1992) both in *Social Research Ethics: An Examination of the Merits of Covert Participant Observation* (Bulmer 1982).

4 Gender, research and education

INTRODUCTION

From the vantage point of the 1990s it is difficult to remember a time when questions of equal opportunities and the complex relationship between gender and education were not high profile. This has not always been the case and there are certainly no grounds for complacency since major inequalities and differences of experience still exist in our educational system between girls and boys and women and men and, indeed, between a number of other groupings; many of these are mirrored in other areas of society. One of the main social science associations in Great Britain, for example, the British Sociological Association, only formally began to take seriously sexual divisions by setting up study groups as late as 1976. There is now a clear and strong interest in the relationship between gender and education at a variety of levels. From national government initiatives through to the Equal Opportunities Commission down to LEAs and school and classroom level initiatives, the interest in gender and education is quite rightly extensive.

We aim in this chapter, first, to provide an understanding of some of the key issues in the debate on gender and education by developing an appreciation of certain ideas and theories and second, to provide some frameworks for studying gender in the context of teacher research. We will explore theoretical and conceptual ideas, methodological issues and some of the substantive work done on the interaction of gender and education. We are writing from a perspective which is committed to the principle of equal opportunities but which sees the issue of gender as raising some crucial questions for the research process in general and qualitative research in particular. In other words gender is regarded as a crucial variable in the teaching and learning process as well as significantly influencing the research process itself.

SOME KEY CONCEPTS AND IDEAS

The emergence of a scientific focus upon gender as a key variable in social life and more recently as a key factor in the educational process itself needs to be placed in some kind of context. This context is complex but it is important to have an appreciation of this since it has been responsible for shaping our vocabulary and way of thinking about both gender, and gender and education. This context is historical and political and relates to changes in our way of thinking about the world we live in. In particular, changes in post-World War Two society brought about a number of different patterns of social relationships in both the home and at work. People began to reappraise their lives and goals, particularly in terms of the relationship between the sexes. Official educational policy was also clearly affected and this can be seen in the recognition of inequality by the 1944 *Education Act* in proposing the concept of equality of educational opportunity. In the meantime the development of the women's movement and civil rights campaigners in both Great Britain and the USA highlighted the question still further, extending the discussion from straightforward inequalities between the sexes to broader socio-cultural questions, such as motherhood, housework, reproduction, sexuality, male violence, health and education and definitions of masculinity and femininity.

From the 1970s onwards in Great Britain key pieces of legislation, including the *Sex Discrimination Act* (1975), the *Race Relations Act* (1976) and the setting up of the *Equal Opportunities Commission* (EOC) and the *Commission for Racial Equality* (CRE) meant that questions of discrimination on grounds of sex or race would be in principle at least seriously explored. As a result, researchers began to focus in much more detail upon both the gender, racial and ethnic aspects of life in Great Britain. Trends and developments described as multicultural or multi-ethnic and anti-racist, anti-sexist strategies and policies also began to emerge. The social sciences were characteristically slow to take on these new ways of thinking but once they did the disciplines of anthropology, psychology and sociology began to make major contributions towards our understanding of gender and gender and education.

WOMEN, GENDER AND KNOWLEDGE

Many commentators have spoken about the so-called *invisibility* of women in the social sciences. That is, as a focus of inquiry and as a source of data and information women have characteristically been relegated to certain areas only. For example, in sociology Smith (1989) has developed a sustained critique of the ways in which sociology has handled gender issues and, in particular, women. This invisibility must be seen as an important starting point and we will take sociology as an example.

This absence and invisibility of women in key areas of social life, or reference to them within specified areas only, is a legacy of male-dominated sociological world views. For example, many of the 'founding fathers' in sociology had specific views on women which, in turn, had implications for the generation of a male-dominated sociology. Durkheim's study of suicide is based upon explicit sexist assumptions when he writes that 'Women's sexual needs have less of a mental character because, generally speaking, her mental life is less developed' (Durkheim 1952: 272). Parsons' (1952) well-known discussion of the family is equally based upon overt sexist assumptions. Women, for Parsons, were more 'emotional', whereas men were more 'instrumental' and 'task oriented'. Parsons even spoke about women fulfilling the glamour role. Such viewpoints have provided the basis for the development of a sociology which is primarily 'about men for men'. It is not surprising therefore that women are absent or invisible in much early sociology. For example, the study of stratification turns out more often than not to be the study of the stratification of men because the male is assumed to be the head of the household and women's work is treated as insignificant (Goldthorpe 1983; Stanworth 1984). Where women are discussed it is often in terms of their involvement in traditional roles of, for example, the family. Areas such as deviance and crime are remarkable for the ways in which women have been virtually ignored. One of the responses to this situation has been the development of a focus upon new areas and aspects of women's experience and amongst these we would point to a focus upon housework and the nature of women's 'paid' and 'unpaid work' (Oakley 1974; Delphy 1984): motherhood, childbirth, pregnancy (Chodorow 1978); women, gender and education (Deem 1980; Stanworth 1981); women and health issues; women and crime; girls' subculture.

Although work in these areas continues it is clear that a focus upon women's experience must get over the dominating male view of society and consequent male hold on many of the disciplines of the social sciences. There are now more women sociologists than before, seeking to develop a sociology which does not simply add women to the agenda but seeks to incorporate women's perspectives as a fundamental aspect of the social world. However, in order to achieve this re-definition considerable conceptual reorientation has had to take place. For example, the concept of 'work' has been extended to include the whole range of 'unpaid' work done by women. It is in this sense that 'housework' may be regarded as significant work. Certainly, more people are paying reference to gender relations in their study of society. Now, sociologists tend to speak more appropriately about the household rather than the family. Focus upon gender relations in this way is responsible for reorienting much sociological research. As we shall see some of these changes in focus have considerable implications for research.

Anthropological theory, on the other hand, has been justly criticized for its implicit equation of man = human = male, resulting in stereotypes of men such as 'man-the-hunter' and women as 'woman-the-gatherer' (Slocum 1975: 36–50). Neither has psychology escaped such charges of sexism. Generalizations about both men and women have abounded in psychology in the past. In particular, it seemed to be commonly accepted that generalizations about the psychology of men and women could be made on the basis of studies on men alone or very limited studies on women. The typical focus of psychological research on differences in attitudes and achievement, for example, may eschew identification of the causes of these differences and their possible social origins.

The work of Smith (1989) is important here since she asks us to think about the everyday world we live in as being problematic rather than taken for granted, a world that is shaped, created and known by women. The researcher needs therefore to be sufficiently reflexive to 'view the world' from a woman's point of view.

It is important, however, to have a reasonable grasp of the concepts, terminology and ideas which are now in common use and to be clear about what is meant by the use of terms such as sex, gender, feminism, patriarchy and so on. A consideration of this vocabulary sets the scene for the subsequent discussion of gender and education and frameworks for studying gender. Certainly, we need to ask not only about the relationship between gender and education but also about the ways in which gender acts as a key variable in the research process in general and qualitative research in particular. There is no better place to begin than by an examination of the concept of gender itself.

THE SEX–GENDER DEBATE

There has been a long and considerably protracted debate about the relative importance of genetic, hereditary or biological factors over social, cultural and environmental factors in shaping human behaviour. This can be seen in the IQ debate and, more recently, in the debate over the differences, in particular in achievement, between girls and boys and women and men. It is important to have a clear idea of what the various terms actually mean and a knowledge of how they are employed. *Gender* as we use the term here refers to the socially and culturally structured and constructed attitudes and behaviours designated as female or male, in any particular society. As a consequence, sociologists and anthropologists focus upon gender and gender relations as an organizing principle of human social life. Gender is therefore distinguished from *sex*, sex being a biological concept which describes genetic differences. Sex must be distinguished from *sexuality* which we might like to refer to as the social processes that create, organize and express *desire*. Whereas the terms *gender* and *sex* are relatively uncontroversial and these definitions are now largely accepted, there is still a continuing debate about the nature of female sexuality within feminist theory.

What is in question for some people is the relative importance of sex and biology as opposed to gender as defined above. We use the word gender explicitly here to emphasize the socially structured and constructional aspects of human behaviour. However, traditionally, gender differences have been described and accounted for in terms of biological and genetic differences. This view holds that the biological tends to determine or cause the social to a considerable extent setting fairly rigid limits upon what people can and cannot do. Often referred to as a biological reductionist or determinist position the fundamental idea is that 'biology is destiny'. We are what we are because of our biological make up. Hence, the typically subordinate position many women find themselves in in our society could be explained as being the result of biological factors which generate certain psychological traits and emotional states, resulting in tendencies towards passivity and dependency.

There is, in fact, very little evidence to support such a viewpoint. On the contrary there is much evidence, particularly anthropological and cross-cultural, to suggest that biology plays a very limited part in shaping behaviour. Notable here is the writing of Mead (1971). Social scientists have looked elsewhere for explanations using the concept of gender as a guiding principle and an all-encompassing phrase which relates to the social organization of the sexes in society, the social construction of masculinity and femininity and the role of power and status in these circumstances.

The concepts of gender and gender differences have been used to argue that the differences between men and women are due to social and cultural differences. The differences result, above all, from differences in status, prestige and power and are ultimately based upon male domination. Whilst recourse to the notions of sex and biology would seem to presuppose that sex-related behaviour is fixed and to a large extent innate, gender assumes a social-constructional dynamic in human behaviour. This view holds that as a result of a number of complex factors human beings construct and reconstruct 'appropriate' expectations of men and women which are in keeping with and justified by the prevailing ethos of their group, culture or society. Furthermore, the society will organize itself along these gender expectations so that for example a sexual division of labour will emerge, or a distinct cultural understanding of femininity or masculinity will be visible at any particular historical period. The use of the concept of gender therefore has been one of the most significant aspects of the study of society and of education. This has led researchers to focus upon, for example, the development of gender identity, gender stereotyping, sexism, and equal opportunities policies. One important social and intellectual movement (though it is actually a series of related movements) which has been responsible for extending our knowledge of these questions is, of course, feminism.

Feminism as a term defies any kind of conventional, bourgeois, liberal academic definition. Feminist thought has gone through a series of changes each often designated by one label or another, for example, 'liberal feminism', 'Marxist feminism', 'Radical feminism', etc. There are many feminisms, some often conflicting. All the same there are some fundamental, shared assumptions amongst the main characteristics of this way of looking at the social world, we could say that feminism embodies simultaneously a commitment to equal rights for women, and a theory of women's points of view. As such, feminism is committed to exposing all aspects of inequality and oppression and highlighting the shared nature of women's experience. Feminism embodies a political theory which is determined to unravel the ideology of male supremacy and to replace this by the emancipation and liberation of women primarily through the processes of consciousness raising and ultimately by changing the structural dynamics of society. As noted already, there are a number of different epistemological standpoints within the broad theoretical orientation. Radical feminists focus their ideas upon the sex–class system, arguing that *patriarchy* is the central feature of society; others hold an essentialist view of women, arguing that this must be celebrated as, for example, 'sisterhood', or 'womanhood'. Feminism in general has been responsible for the development of a radical critique of the ungendered accepted orthodoxy of much social science. This manifested itself in the emergence of a special field of study, namely Women's Studies.

Despite the lack of unity in feminist thought it seems clear that a fundamental objective of feminist research is the analysis of gender relations. This not only involves describing the ways in which gender relations are constituted and reconstituted in society and social institutions but also challenges many of our conventional ways of viewing society and our social institutions. Central here is the concept of patriarchy.

Patriarchy is seen as being the basis of society which creates and recreates gender divisions and sexual inequality. Patriarchy refers to the extensive and embedded nature of male power and authority which oppresses women through the whole range of social, political and economic relations in society. Patriarchy results therefore from the greater access to and power over the resources and rewards found in any society, by men. In this sense, patriarchy is a crucial concept for feminism since it refers to the totality of male oppression and exploitation. However, different writers focus upon different aspects of patriarchy in order to expose the basis of female oppression. Some attempt to relate patriarchy to the capitalist mode of production, and to a materialist basis, others relate patriarchy to the male sexual devaluation of women. Despite the fact that there are many different strands of feminism it is possible to identify some key elements and tendencies in feminist social research. The following provides an overview of what seem to be the salient features of a feminist approach. You may wish to consider the implications of each of these areas/statements for the formulation and conduct of school-based enquiry.

Key elements of a feminist viewpoint in social research

- Commitment to revealing core social processes and recurring features of women's oppression.
- Insistence on the inseparability of theory and practice.
- Insistence upon the connections between the private and the public, between

the domestic and the political (the personal is political, especially sexual, relationships).

- Concern with the construction and reproduction of gender and sexual difference.
- Rejection of narrow disciplinary boundaries.
- Rejection of the artificial subject researcher dualism.
- Rejection of positivism and objectivity as male mythology.
- Increased use of qualitative, introspective biographical research techniques.
- Recognition of the gendered nature of social research and the development of anti-sexist research strategies.
- Review of the research process as consciousness and awareness raising and as fundamentally participatory.

A focus upon gender issues mainly generated by feminism and the women's movement certainly opened up new areas for research. The initial focus was upon women's experience, later research began to consider masculinity also. Such a focus brought about some very significant methodological and theoretical discussions that are relevant to the practice of school-based research. As we describe it, methodology refers to the whole array of concepts, ideas, practices, and frameworks which surround the use of various methods or techniques employed to generate data on the social world. Much discussion has taken place on the implications of a focus upon gender, together with the insights of feminist writers, for carrying out social and educational research. We will examine this later. In methodological terms, a recognition of the significance of gender in social life will have far reaching effects on how and in what ways social and educational research is to be conducted. Some feminists, for example, have argued that the nature of women's experience is such that a special methodological orientation is required (Bowles and Duelli-Klein 1983; Harding 1988; Stanley and Wise 1983).

There are some very important theoretical implications which may be drawn from what we have been saying so far. As outlined earlier, theory may be said to be concerned with the production of *knowledge* of the social world. Why and how an event happens is understood by reference to concepts, systems, models, structures, beliefs, ideas and hypotheses. Statements based upon observation of data can therefore be made in order to generate analyses of their causes, consequences and processes. That is to explain events in ways which are consistent with a particular philosophical rationale. Theories therefore aim both to propose and analyse sets of relations existing between a number of variables where certain regularities and continuities can be demonstrated via empirical inquiry. Feminists challenge the ungendered orthodoxy which they claim has underpinned much social and educational theory and highlight the ways in which many concepts entail an implicit and often explicit male bias. In particular, the reliance of conventional social research upon natural scientific frameworks is not only misplaced but its objectivity is merely a disguise for male subjectivity, it is claimed.

We have so far tried to provide some general background and a context for the ways in which a focus upon gender and the issues raised by feminists will have an impact on the conduct of research. The prospective researcher will need to have a deeper appreciation of some of the technical aspects involved. We will approach this by trying to develop some frameworks for studying gender issues.

FRAMEWORKS FOR STUDYING GENDER ISSUES

There are a number of ways in which the researcher concerned to recognize the significance of gender in social and education research, or even to explore specifically gender issues, might look at the question. Gender shapes and influences research in at least three distinct yet interrelated ways:

1 Choice of topic/focus.
2 Choice of data collection techniques.
3 The practice of research and researcher/subject relations.

We will try to unravel each of these areas in general terms but will be concerned in more detail with the significance of gender in qualitative research. Some feminists have argued that the pervasiveness of gender justifies claims for a distinct feminist methodology and we will have a look at this argument shortly.

Choice of topic/focus

There are many factors which influence the choice of an area, topic or problem to investigate. Professional researchers may have a different agenda to those of practitioners. Whatever the motive of the researcher, recognition of the significance of gender will influence and direct that investigation. The main point here is the notion of differentiation. Recognizing gender as a key variable in social life, thereby giving rise to sets of gender relations, directs the researcher's attention to the differential nature of boys' and girls' and women's and men's experiences, attitudes and expectations. Further, the pervasive significance of gender suggests that the way we perceive the world and the knowledge so produced is, in fact, 'gendered knowledge', that is knowledge which is constructed and reconstructed through the eyes of men and of women. This idea suggests that who should know what is ambiguous. As Foucault reminds us, knowledge is power and the way in which knowledge is mediated via gender relations is important. The impact of gender on the choice of a research topic or focus then is to highlight differentiation, the socially constructed nature of knowledge and the existence of inequalities. This can clearly be seen in the kinds of research and topics of investigation which have been carried out in the field of gender and education. Research has focused upon the way in which curriculum knowledge, even the development of subjects, has been shaped by a whole range of expectations about not only who can know what, but why and how. The range of important topics which have been opened up and explored as a direct consequence of taking gender seriously in educational research has contributed a wealth of significant and now almost taken-for-granted knowledge about school and classroom processes and sex stereotyping (May and Ruddock 1983). The importance of sex role socialization in the early years of schooling has been investigated by Delamont (1980); Browne (1985); France (1986); Davies (1979); Joffe (1971) and Rhode (1990). A social psychological focus upon the development of gender identity is taken up by Archer (1989). Clarricoates (1978) explores the hidden curriculum. The signifance of gender and the socio-cultural construction of the curriculum was the focus of an influential collection of early studies edited by Deem (1980), whereas Dyehouse (1977) focused her attention upon the relationship between the ideological assumptions about wives and motherhood and the development of a curriculum for schoolgirls between 1890 and 1920. Sharma and Meighan (1980) were amongst the first researchers to open up the question of girls and mathematical science subjects. Steedman (1987) produced a highly influential study which moved the research focus forward. *The Tidy House* (Steedman, 1987) is an unusual study, which focuses on the writing of a long story by three 8-year-old working-class girls in a primary classroom. Steedman, who was their teacher at the time, analyses this writing, and the taped conversations that accompanied it, to show that through creating a story about love, sex, marriage, birth and motherhood, the girls are exploring and questioning the ideas and beliefs by which they themselves are being brought up. Steedman related this study of her own pupils' writing to theories about language development, historical uses of children's writing, gender issues and what she calls 'the lost history of working class childhood'. It is a highly readable account, which illustrated the complexity of children's learning, and the importance of cultural context in any study of their writing.

Choice of data-collection techniques

A heightened discussion of methodology has arisen as a consequence of a concern with gender and gender relations. At the heart of the matter is the question of how best to go about developing adequate, non-sexist research strategies which will reveal the gender dynamics of any given situation. In much the same ways that qualitative researchers were critical of methods and techniques which failed to context human behaviour in the lived experience and interpretations of actors, so too, feminist researchers were sceptical, and downright critical of conventional quantitative objective research which failed in their opinion to portray adequately the lives of women. Qualitative approaches and feminism both share, for strikingly similar

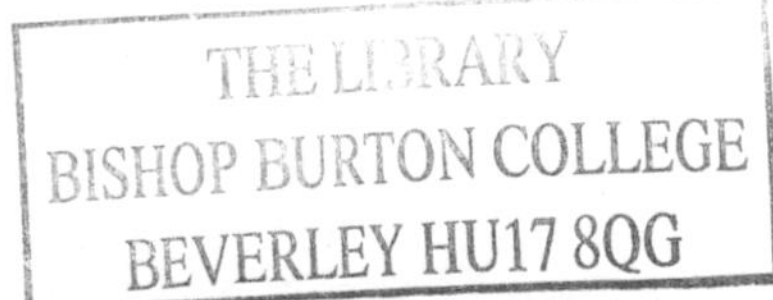

reasons, a rejection of positivism and positivistic research techniques. Both accept and recognize the potential of introspective and biographical approaches to the study of society and educational processes. Under the influence of postmodernism both qualitative research traditions and feminism share scepticism about the notion that there are shared versions of truth. The partiality of knowledge is stressed and a focus upon 'narrative' ensues. Ethnography, life history research, documentary sources and biographical materials are all being used as 'ways in' to understanding gender issues in general and in education more particularly. Quantitative strategies which employ prior, pre-coded closed categories tear experience from its natural (gendered) social context, masquerading the results as objective. Some writers have argued, for example, that interviewing women is a contradiction in terms (Oakley 1981) and that the only way to 'survey' women is through stories (Graham 1983).

All the most popular means of collecting data in qualitative research, namely through fieldwork interviewing, observing and collecting documents, must be explored in terms of the influence of gender. However, it is the case that in qualitative work generally the researcher herself plays such a crucial role as filter of the data that the most obvious affects of gender will be seen here (Warren 1988).

The key thrust of much feminist critique of conventional research methodology is that it is neither sensitive enough nor equipped for revealing the subtle aspects of gender relations in our society. In particular, many conventional methods do not seem able to capture the nature of women's and girls' experiences. This has led many researchers in the direction of relatively unstructured, participatory, introspective, qualitative research techniques, including the life history (Geiger 1986) and others to suggest that a distinct feminist methodology must be explored (Smith 1974; Smith 1979; Roberts 1981; Harding 1988). On the other hand, some researchers have challenged the notion of a distinct feminist methodology. However, perhaps some of the most important research on gender in education has come from recent work employing ethnographic techniques. With its concentration upon the nature of experience and the cultural context ethnographers have been exploring the dimensions of teachers' and pupils' experience of gender and discrimination, with the cultural processes which mediate and sustain these activities. The accounts contained in Part One of *Gender and Ethnicity in Schools: Ethnographic Accounts* (Woods and Hammersley 1993) are admirable testimony to the ways in which a broad ethnographic focus can illustrate these complex issues by use of techniques such as participant observation, field work and conversational analysis.

Choice of data collection techniques will be related to the kinds of problem being explored and research questions asked. Sensitivity towards the gender dimension will need to be built into the research at an early stage and is likely to shape the choice of data-collection techniques. In this sense, gender is no more or less significant than, say, race, ethnicity, age, class or able-bodied/disabled variables. It seems logical, however, that feminist research concentrates on subjective experience, interpretration of the interpersonal dimension, and does this by use of the broad range of qualitative approaches detailed in this book. Reinharz (1992) has provided a useful overview of the use of qualitative methods to look at gender.

The practice of research and subject–researcher relationships

We now realize that research as an activity in the social world of schools, hospitals or wherever, is itself a gendered activity. That is, it is conducted by and upon people of different gender. This has prompted some people to consider the nature and extent of sexism in social and educational research. Eichler (1987), for example, provides a useful account of the nature and extent of sex-bias in social research and offers ways of avoiding it. What we might describe as the 'sexual politics' of subject–researcher relationships are all too often clear to see. Some examples will help to make the point. The intervention of women science teachers to act as positive role models in the Girls into Science and Technology (GIST) Project is a case in point here. School-based qualitative research carried out by a man may be very different in kind from school-based research carried out by a woman. Alternatively, Fuller's (1980) classic account of the sub-culture of a small group of black girls of West Indian parentage and the double discrimination they face owes much to her gender sensitivity. A collection of researchers' own accounts of investigating gender issues contained in Roberts (1981) marked something of a landmark in our appreciation of the ways in which gender influences both the practice of research and the nature of subject–researcher relations. However, one of the major consequences of feminist thinking in this area has been the move towards breaking down the subject–researcher dualism and the substitution of more open, democractic and collaborative forms of relationship between researchers and the people they work with. We saw that this was also a clearly stated principle of action research methods.

In the same way that a focus upon race and ethnicity in education occur as a result of campaigns for multi-cultural, anti-racist education, a focus upon gender arose in part from concerns about the under-achievement of girls, and campaigns for anti-sexist education. Certainly, these became central aspects of the mission statements of schools and colleges in terms of equal opportunities from the late 1970s onwards. As such, it is more than likely that research on gender will have implications for the nature of the researcher–subject relationship and is even more likely than some other kinds of research to have a central concern with the value and significance of the research itself to the subjects themselves. This is likely to be quite acute in school-based practitioner research, and an integral aspect of any action research project such as, for example, GIST. The researcher needs to be alert to the implications involved here.

A DISTINCT FEMINIST RESEARCH METHODOLOGY?

From what has been said so far it is clear to see that the question of a unique feminist research methodology raises a number of central questions. A significant literature now exists which promotes a distinct feminist method, based upon the ideas outlined above. This position seems to entail three main themes: the overarching influence of gender; the primacy of women's subjective personal experience, and the rejection of subject/research dualisms and hierarchies in research. Although we will summarize the arguments for and against each of these themes, researchers will need to reach individual conclusions about the extent to which the case for a distinct feminist methodology is convincing.

The overarching influence of gender

As we noted earlier, gender is seen as a crucial variable both in social life and social research. The debate surrounds the extent to which gender is the crucial variable over and above class, race/ethnicity, age or disability. Advocates of a distinct feminist method argue for the primacy of gender since conventional research for feminists is mainly an expression of male interests and experience. The search for non-sexist research methods and an exclusive focus upon women's experience by women researchers was a characteristic of much educational research work. The problem surrounds the extent to which gender exclusively is the key variable. Researchers have pointed to the significance of other variables in social life and, indeed, to the interaction of these variables in complex industrial societies. Many black women have taken exception to such an exclusive focus. Not all women's experience is the same. Not all women experience oppression in the same way or to the same degree. The gender–class, gender–race axes raise some doubts here. Ramazanoglu (1989) has subsequently spoken about feminism and the contradictions of oppression. (See also Arnst 1986.)

The primacy of women's personal subjective experience

Emphasis upon women's experience as being the only true source of knowledge about women seems to be a central element in the advocacy of a distinct feminist method. Feminist studies are committed to exploring and revealing women's personal experience. The supposed 'double consciousness' of women, their ability to experience and be part of their own culture and that prescribed by men at the same time is seen as putting them in a unique position. Women researchers are therefore best placed to research women. The problem here surrounds the apparent validity of one group's experience as opposed to and/or in conjunction with any other groups. Can we say that one group's insights and perspectives are more valid than another? What complications for this position follow from the suggestion that all experience is socially constructed?

The rejection of subject–researcher dualism and hierarchies in sociological research

Feminists have argued that conventional research models exhibit an unwelcome dualism between subject and researcher. Claims to objectivity, it is argued, are mere disguises for male subjectivity. Feminism puts the subject – women – at the centre of a research orientation which stresses a cooperative, shared, reciprocal rather than a hierarchical relationship, stressing the equal status of participants. Thus, objects of research are transformed into equal participating subjects. The researcher is encouraged to operate in the same 'critical plane' as the subject. As a result, and of necessity, feminist method therefore is entailed in a process of consciousness and awareness raising on the part of both 'subject' and 'researcher'. Research as 'lived experience' in Cook's (1991) words.

Discussion of the role of researcher and subject is not unique or special to feminism. The concern of interactionist sociology with ethnography and participant observation has raised similar points, whereas phenomenologists have highlighted the centrality of the researcher's experience in producing research accounts. Postmodernists take this one stage further by asking questions about the very construction of the researcher's text. This is a topic we unravel in more detail in Chapter 14. What implications for control of research follow from this position? Will only women study women? What is the nature of the researcher's authority, intellectual or otherwise in such feminist research? A number of very important questions emerge which we can only flag here.

We have tried to identify the background themes and issues which have generated claims for a distinct feminist method in this section. We then outlined some of the key arguments on which claims for a feminist method are based. It is important to remember that there are significant differences in feminist thinking here though we have focused upon what appear to be some fairly central ideas. The researcher has to make some personal judgements on the issues raised. We will conclude this chapter by considering an example of research in the area of gender and education.

RESEARCH ON GENDER AND EDUCATION: THE GIRLS INTO SCIENCE AND TECHNOLOGY PROJECT

One of the most influential and interesting examples of research into gender and education was the 1980 Girls into Science and Technology project (GIST), based at Manchester Polytechnic and headed by Barbara Smail and Judith Whyte. The project resulted from concern about the well-documented and continuing under-achievement of girls in science and technology and the general low take-up of science and technology-related subjects by girls compared to boys. The significance of this is considerable since jobs and careers in science and technology often command high status and high salaries. As such, a project designed to explore these issues was important for a number of reasons and posed a series of research questions, for example:

- The need to unravel some of the complex cultural and structural influences which lead to boys and girls receiving differential educational experiences.
- The nature of school and classroom interactions.
- Issues of equality of opportunity.
- The changing nature of work.
- The changing demographic picture.

Clearly, such a project was likely to have many broader consequences and implications, for example:

- Strategic planning, mission statements, aims and objectives.
- School/institutional management.
- Classroom management.
- Subject choice.
- Careers guidance.

We noted in Chapter 3 that the funding and support of any research is a critical issue. It is important therefore to note that the GIST project was jointly funded by the Equal Opportunities Commission and the Social Science Research Council; grants were also obtained from the Department of Industry and Shell UK.

Research design and the GIST project

Research design is crucial and, as we pointed out, takes many forms. For our purposes it is important to see how the design of the project and eventual methodology employed was shaped by the nature of the topic to be explored and the overwhelming influence of gender and sexuality as fundamental organizing principles in the lives of girls and boys and women and men. As such, the project had to come to terms with the fact that gender is an issue that girls and women have to deal with on a regular basis, whereas for boys and men gender is often rendered unproblematic and unrecognized. The design employed was that of an innovative action research oriented project involving teachers and pupils directly. The project was clear in its aims to encourage girls to opt more frequently for science and technology-related subjects and to consider scientific and technological careers. As such, revealing teacher and pupil attitudes was crucial. Eventually, procedures and 'intervention strategies' would emerge which it was hoped would facilitate these changes. Indeed, implicit (and often explicit) in the action research model is the assumption that in principle behaviour is open to change. See for example, Hustler, Cassidy and Cuff 1986; Lomax 1989; Nias and Groundwater Smith 1988; Nixon 1981 and Pollard 1985b.

What the research involved

Working with teachers; teachers' expectations

The project involved a series of school-based workshop activities in order to identify some of the factors which contributed to girls' under-achievement. A number of exercises, some experiential, were used in order to explore personal attitudes and inbuilt sex-typed expectations and unravel the extent of this.

Pupils' attitudes

Clearly, pupils' attitudes were of fundamental significance. The project workers focused upon a target group of children who had completed questionnaires during their first term of secondary school. They found that girls' attitudes were not as fixed as they had thought, but discovered that there was not much experience of 'tinkering activities' on the part of girls. One feature of the direct intervention was the development of clubs for girls designed to provide them with 'hands on' experience of science, technology and related areas.

VISTA Intervention Strategy (1980–1981)

This follows on from the action research model (action research spirals, etc) i.e. that at some point direct intervention in a teaching/learning situations is needed. VISTA was a structured programme of visits to the school by women scientists, technologists, engineers and craftswomen. The idea for this came from the wealth of research which suggests the importance of positive role models for children, in this case positive feminine role models highlighting the fact that women can become successful in science and technology. VISTA also showed the value of a teaching approach which stressed the application of science to the social world, surely a point of equal importance to both boys and girls.

Classroom observation

There is a long tradition of research which highlights the gender imbalances in much classroom interaction, and teachers are often found to distribute their attention in an uneven manner, the turntaking system, as French and French (1984) point out, is often dominated by small groups of boys. The GIST team used a simple, modified classroom observation schedule to generate feedback and found that with guidance, teachers were able to alter the balance of pupil feedback. They also focused upon items such as the shared use of resources. Again, the results confirm other research findings in this area.

Further activities in school

These included the following:

- Parents' evening had slots for GIST.
- Non-traditional careers days.
- A focus upon extended discussion of option-choice.
- Greater emphasis upon social and industrial applications of science.

Certainly, the GIST project provides a good example of the way in which an action research model can be applied to the area of gender and schooling. This was a pioneering and innovative study. However, it is worth pausing, by way of conclusion, to raise a series of questions. Many of these might feature in a wide range of school-based teacher research into this area:

- To what extent was the GIST project explicit about gender issues?
- What realistic expectations of change can we have from action research projects?
- What are the implications of the National Curriculum for issues raised by the project?
- To what extent might it be possible to duplicate aspects of the GIST project at school, college or local authority levels?

Some further issues for school-based research inspired by the GIST project might include:

- The involvement of outside parties in the research.
- The description, monitoring and evaluation of girls' experience of science and technology.
- The implications of family, neighbourhood and peer group responses to non-traditional subject/career choices.
- The nature and organization of industry school/college links.

CONCLUSION

What we have provided in this chapter is an introduction to the issues involved in both understanding and developing an approach to gender issues in education research. Even if your own research is not directly concerned with gender as such, no area of education practice can be studied without taking this dimension into consideration. Teacher–researchers can apply the theoretical and empirical perspectives provided in this chapter to a whole range of research skills ranging from evaluating equal opportunities policies to curriculum development and classroom practices. Career prospects and promotion for women in our educational system are also areas that call out for more research by practising teachers. In asking such questions we hope further work into this vital area of educational experiences and practice will be stimulated.

SUGGESTED FURTHER READING

There now exists a considerable literature on gender issues in social and educational research. The impact of feminist scholarship is great. *Breaking Out: Femininst Consciousness and Feminist Research* (Stanley and Wise 1983) locates the discussion in a broad, philosophical and sociological context and is particularly useful on exploring the nature of the relationship between the subject and researcher. *Non-Sexist Research Methods* (Eichler 1987) offers a good account of the nature and extent of sex bias in social research and ways of avoiding it. Researchers' own accounts of investigating gender issues are contained in *Doing Feminist Research* (Roberts 1981). The particularities of qualitative research methodology in general are discussed in 'Feminist research and qualitative methods' (Webb 1985) in *Issues in Educational Research: Qualitative Methods* (Burgess) and 'Sex and gender in field research' (Warren and Rasmussen 1977). These provide important accounts of the impact of gender upon field-based, qualitative methodologies. 'Feminisms and models of qualitative research' (Olesen 1994), Chapter 9 in *Handbook of Qualitative Research* (Denzin and Lincoln) provides an overview of three different feminist approaches to research, highlighting the problems and possibilities of attempting to hear women's voices.

The focus upon ethnography is taken up in *Doing Qualitative Research: Circles within Circles* (Ely 1990). Very interesting accounts of feminist approaches to ethnography in a self-conscious fashion are presented in this collection.

Three studies which focus upon particular issues in relation to gender and schooling are provided by *A Gender Agenda: A Sociological Study of Teachers, Parents and Pupils in their Primary Schools* (Evans 1988); and *Gender Identities and Education: The Impact of Starting School* (Lloyd and Duveen 1992) and 'Gender imbalances in the primary classroom: an interactional account' (French and French 1984). The research conducted by French and French is the subject of a critical appraisal, 'An evaluation of two studies of gender imbalance in primary classrooms' (Hammersley 1990). Two contrasting studies on aspects of gender and schooling from a broadly ethnographic perspective can be found in 'Qualitative methods and cultural analysis: young women and the transition from school to un/employment' (Griffin 1988) in *Field Methods in the Study of Education* (Burgess 1984b) and *Gender and Schooling: A Study of Sexual Division in the Classroom* (Stanworth 1981). *Gender and the Politics of Schooling* (Arnot and Weiner 1987) contains articles covering a range of perspectives from which to explore the relationship between gender and education. The questions are related to areas such as equality of opportunity, class, race, training and policy.

The interaction of both race and gender as key variables in the educational process are explored in two interesting studies. The first: 'Black girls in a London comprehensive school' (Fuller 1980) in *Schooling for Women's*

Work (Deem) is an important classic qualitative account of the subculture of a small group of black girls of West Indian parentage. It offers a sensitive alternative reading of the girls' viewpoints. The second study is 'To mix or not mix: Pakistani girls in British schools' (Kelly and Shaikh 1989). A brave attempt to explore in greater depth than has often been the case of what children themselves think of teachers' attitudes towards them and the nature of gender bias by use of lengthy interviews has recently been conducted by Cullingford (1993) in 'Children's views of gender issues in school'. Examples of the application of qualitative approaches to the study of gender in schools which highlight both methodological and substantive issues are provided by 'We're back with Gobbo: the re-establishment of gender relations following a school merger' (Draper 1992); 'Gender implications of children's playground culture' (Grugeon 1992) and 'Sex and the quiet schoolgirl' (Stanley 1992) all in *Gender and Ethnicity in Schools: Ethnographic Accounts* (Woods and Hammersley 1993). Finally, *Gender Issues in Field Research* (Warren 1988) offers a short account of the gender dimension in fieldwork. Warren moves the debate on by exploring objectively, feminist theory and the ways in which gender is presented in methodology texts.

5 Designing, planning and evaluating research

INTRODUCTION

This chapter provides a practical guide to the conduct of small-scale research, project or even dissertation work conducted by practising teachers. We are concerned to provide both a 'hands on' guide through the research process and an understanding of the ways in which both the process and products of research may be evaluated. We are not concerned here with a detailed discussion of either data collection techniques or data analysis, that is the subject of Parts II and III, respectively. We are concerned to provide a guide to carrying out research for the purposes of a project, dissertation, exploratory study, some evaluation and other forms of curriculum enquiry. We are also concerned to try and provide the fullest advice and support possible. Even so, this can only be a guide since the particular circumstances of any teacher's research will vary and be subject to different practical and analytical constraints. We wish in this book to explore qualitative research traditions, and provide insights into the application of these techniques to teacher–researchers. However, there are some fundamental questions and issues which all researchers need to attend to, this chapter aims to open up the design, planning and evaluation of research.

One of the ways of approaching this problem is to regard the research process as involving a series of steps and stages which will take the researcher from initial choice of topic and research questions through a particular kind of research design, to data collection, analysis, and writing up and presentation of the study. These stages will incorporate the whole of a research project and will help us to see the complex questions carrying out research raises. Figure 5.1 presents the research process and the kinds of stages to be worked through in a fairly systematic fashion. As such, we hope to provide something of a pathway through the research process which will make things less daunting.

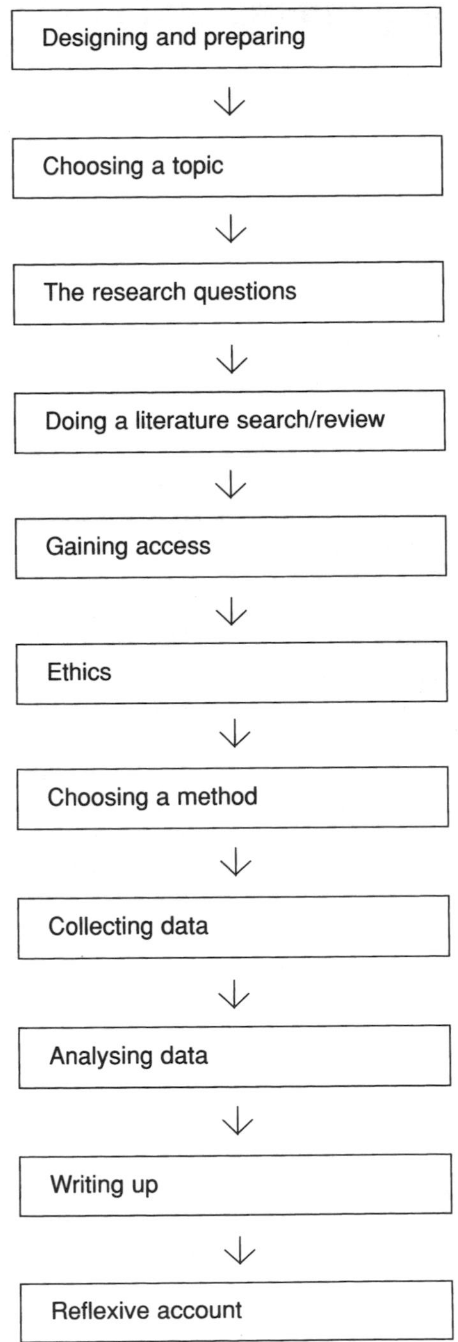

Figure 5.1 Pathways through research

DESIGNING AND PREPARING

All research begins somewhere. All research is underpinned by some basic assumptions. There are a variety of different approaches to research as we have seen; each of these has a different research design, and different blueprint for the conduct of research. A research design will offer the researcher a framework, some key concepts and ideas. The major forms of research design we have identified are shown in Figure 5.2.

RESEARCH DESIGN → DATA COLLECTION → DATA ANALYSIS

↓

Experimental

Survey

Evaluation

Case Study

Action Research

Qualitative/Ethnographic/Case Study

Feminist

Figure 5.2 Types of research design

Obviously the general research design which the researcher selects is going to affect the overall character of the research. Most dramatically, as we have seen, feminist researchers have rejected standard conventional research designs on the grounds that they are frequently male-biased. The research design is often so persuasive that it will start to determine what to look at, how to collect data and how to analyse it. We are concerned with those interpretative qualitative approaches and traditions which tend towards a more open end of the continuum. We have already looked at action research and evaluation designs, in Parts II and III we explore ethnographic research design and the case study.

The design and preparation phases of any research also involve ordinary and mundane sets of tasks and questions. Questions concerning the delineation of a topic or problem to investigate, the location of data sources, and choice of data collection techniques all require attention early on. Walker (1985) has reminded us that research into educational practice is not always straightforward since the problems and questions do not present themselves in a readymade fashion, ready for research. Instead, they will need reshaping in a form that is amenable to research. Research will make practical demands of time, energy and human/physical/financial resources. It is important to spend time early on exploring these questions in the design and preparation phase. A further set of questions will emerge if the researcher is collaborating with other co-researchers. In this case it is essential to be clear about the respective responsibilities of the parties involved and how these will be determined.

CHOOSING A TOPIC

Flushed with the excitement of beginning research many students, academics and teacher–researchers fall into the trap of going for the big '*Aha*'. The topics, problems, issues and approaches are often far too ambitious and grandiose. The design and preparation phases of the research should have clearly identified limitations and constraints which will influence the scale of the study. Very often, training programmes will have word limits, time scales and deadlines. They are less likely to have explicit guidelines and support systems to see the student through the process. Discussion with supervisors and peers may help to clarify the practical realities of a research proposal without dampening the ambition and excitement. After all, the good ideas and motivation amount to nothing if the research is not feasible. Three questions will help to clarify purposes and sharpen focus on choice of topic:

1 Why is the research being undertaken?
2 How will the research further understanding of a problem or issue?
3 Can the topic be realistically explored in the way proposed?

The choice of topic for research purposes will come from the teacher's own professional context. As such, the range of possible topics is massive. However, this is not as daunting as it may first appear. There are likely to be two main sources for generating research ideas which can then be formulated into a series of research questions. The first is the immediate professional context which has identified a contemporary problem or issue, which could be anything from an overview of the implementation of some piece of curriculum change to observing the nature and types of student/pupil interaction and communication with teachers. The second source of ideas for research topics will come from the broader research community and education establishment. Well-researched themes or contemporary educational issues might fruitfully be explored via small-scale or case-study inquiry. Once a broad focus has been identified and a realistic choice of area to explore has been formulated the researcher will have to sharpen this considerably by identifying a series of research questions which can, if needs be, be reworked into a statement of aims and objectives. Certainly, many research projects for formal qualifications have to be presented in a form which includes such a statement.

The following are some examples of possible qualitative school-based research topics:

- Inside 'inside': an exploration of teacher and inmate perceptions of penal education.
- Life histories of adults with learning difficulties: towards life and learning plans.
- An ethnographic account of peer tutoring in the primary school.
- The role of interaction in the development and education of children with hearing impairment.
- The management of change: a micro political study of a secondary school science department.
- A study of gender and texts in Key Stage 2 National Curriculum History.
- Parental involvement in the nursery school.
- Dimensions of teachers' views of pupils.
- Children's friendship groups and the transition process.

These are just a few of the kinds of topics which have been explored by teachers by use of a qualitative framework. They give some kind of idea of the scope available. The key issue, of course, is how these topics are translated into a series of research questions and explored via the collection and analysis of relevant data.

THE RESEARCH QUESTIONS

The identification of a clear research question or set of questions is fundamental. Obviously, there will be degrees of firmness in qualitative research. Many questions might well be formed in a more 'exploratory' fashion. The ability to construct a solid theoretical and methodological framework for a study will depend to a large extent on the way in which the research questions are posed. The way to approach this is through a continuous process of questioning and answering, whereby the researcher develops an internal dialogue, and perhaps an external dialogue with peers or supervisor. In this way a broad focus can be narrowed down, vague ideas clarified and a fairly definite (even though they may well be 'open' and exploratory) set of research questions can be arrived at. This can be achieved by following the steps identified below:

- **Step 1** Outline the general pedagogical educational context of your topic.
- **Step 2** Highlight key theories, concepts and ideas current in this area.
- **Step 3** What appear to be some of the underlying assumptions of your chosen topic?
- **Step 4** Why are these issues/topics identified important?
- **Step 5** Begin to identify the sorts of literature relevant to the research topic.
- **Step 6** Attempt to locate the proposed research in (i) the broader

educational scene; (ii) contemporary debates, and (iii) an underlying body of theoretical ideas.

After doing this the researcher ought to be able to begin to formulate a series of research questions which will guide decisions about methodology in deciding what to collect data on and how to collect those data.

The hardest aspect of this process is moving from the generalities of a research topic to particular research questions. Chapter 2 of Light, Singer and Willet (1990) provides some detailed advice. As they put it, the researcher needs to be able to do three important things here. *First*, express clearly a research question which will subsequently form the basis for design. *Second*, it is fundamental to understand the link between research questions and methodology. *Third*, it is important to learn from the work of others in order to build on, refine and amend the researcher's own ideas. This, of course, is the aim of the literature review which we will now discuss. It should be clear by now how each of the stages in the research process helps the researcher towards greater understanding as each new piece of the jigsaw puzzle is added.

DOING A LITERATURE SEARCH/REVIEW

A literature search will help to focus research more directly and sharpen and refine the research questions. From a search and review of the literature it will be possible to identify major trends in research, any gaps, and key concepts which have been used. Furthermore, a good literature search and review will help the researcher to locate the proposed research in a broader conceptual and theoretical framework. After a literature search and review the focus of the research may change or be slanted somewhat differently. The researcher will then be able to identify common themes in the literature and relate these back to the research questions.

Here we will concentrate mainly upon published materials, including books, articles in journals and theses. A prerequisite of most research is the presentation of a written report, often in the form of a thesis or dissertation; in-service courses and evaluation projects also entail some form of oral or written report. It will, of course, be necessary to find, collate, and evaluate this material. Three questions will therefore appear at the start of a piece of school-based research:

- How and where can you find the relevant publications?
- How can you avoid getting lost in the material?
- How can you record information about the material in a clear and systematic way, which can be used days, weeks, months, or even years after with success?

We will try to answer some of these questions. The starting-point is the library.

Access to libraries

In Great Britain, the teacher will have access to both public and academic libraries, including university, polytechnic, and college libraries. These vary considerably in the range of books and journals stored and services provided. In Great Britain, all public and academic libraries can draw upon the services of the British Library Document Supply Centre, which can arrange for inter-library loans of books and journals not immediately available from their own shelves. You may need to ask for special permission to use the services of academic libraries, especially if you wish to borrow books, but outside the city central libraries they will provide the best source for bibliographies, abstracts and collections of key journals. A visit to the libraries concerned and a talk to the library staff about the range of services and facilities provided is a good first step. A useful guide here is *Study and Library Facilities for Teachers: Universities, Institutes and Schools of Education*, published annually by Hull University Institute of Education.

Planning a library search

A review of the relevant literature, as well as often a course requirement, is an important element of a researcher's work. This will mean initial and subsequent library searches. At the start it is important to bear in mind the following points:

- Define precisely the topic to be studied. The initial library search will more than likely open up new avenues making a subsequent visit necessary.
- Be clear about the parameters of the search and avoid becoming side-tracked. The discussion on 'locating a field' in Chapter 6 will be valuable here since it will help the researcher to clarify the scope and boundaries of a search.
- Further questions will arise. Is the research going to be limited to British publications? Is it going to be limited to recent publications on a given topic, for example, over the past ten years? (It is, of course, important to be flexible on these issues as the research develops.) Authors, bibliographies and reviews of literature are often useful introductions to the key works in any field, since they put the researcher in touch with general findings, ideas and current thinking on particular issues, thereby providing an important background framework.
- The most usual cataloguing system used in British libraries is the Dewey Decimal System, though libraries often modify the basic layout to suit their own requirements.
- British libraries use either a card index or microfiche index (or both) as a means of cataloguing their stock. It will be organized under both subject classification and author's name so that leads can be followed up from two angles. Both will indicate where in the library the books and materials are

shelved by the use of a classification number. When beginning a library search on a new topic with only minimal knowledge, the subject classification provides the best way to locate a book or article. For example, if the teacher was beginning research on 'Appraisal and Target Setting', the obvious starting-point would be the subject classification index under 'Education', and then the subheading 'Education Management'. However, one may find that another related subheading, 'Teachers' or 'Teacher Performance' may be of use. It is important to be prepared to widen the search within the subclassification if necessary and even move into a new classification area. In the example given above this could be 'Management'.

One of the most daunting and, indeed, frustrating aspects of research is finding relevant literature. Hours can be spent searching through dusty book shelves in dark basements to turn up only one or two texts of any use and these might turn out to have only one or two relevant sections. Obviously, this is an element of the research and writing process but it can become very time-consuming and is often not cost-effective. What is needed is a systematic approach. The research community and libraries have recognized this and produced bibliographies, abstracts, and guides to finding materials. However, these are daunting publications; we have therefore listed below some of the key guides and publications it would be useful for the teacher–researcher to consult.

Bibliographies

- Walford, A. J. (Ed.) (1982) *Guide to Reference Material* (4th edition).
- *British National Bibliography* (BNB) (since 1950). This is a cumulative series of volumes so it is important to consult the index. The Dewey decimal number is also recorded in the BNB and because classification numbers sometimes change it is necessary to check these for each year.
- United States Library of Congress, Books (quarterly), Periodicals.
- *British Education Index* (quarterly). Since 1976 the more general format of this has been replaced by one which makes it essential to use the detailed subject index.
- *British Humanities Index* (now available on CD-ROM).
- *Ulrich's International Periodicals Directory*.

Abstracts

The main difference between an abstract and an index is that abstracts provide useful summaries of the work listed. The researcher could initially consult Ulrich and Walford cited above and then discuss what abstracts are available for the particular subjects to be investigated. We have listed below some of the main abstracts:

- *Child Development Abstracts and Bibliography*, University of Chicago Press (since 1972).
- *Current Index to Journals in Education.*
- *Language Teaching and Linguistics Abstracts*, Cambridge University Press (since 1975).
- *Psychological Abstracts*, American Psychological Association (since 1927).
- *Research into Higher Education Abstracts* (since 1982).
- *Sociology of Education Abstracts* (since 1965).

Theses

A lot of research conducted by teachers appears in theses and dissertations for degrees. The following works are therefore worth consulting in order to see what research has been done in a particular area:

- *Current Research in Britain*, British Library Board.
- *Dissertation Abstracts.*
- *Index of Theses* (submitted) 'ASUB', annually with supplements since 1950.

Computerized literature searches

We have, so far, dealt with what might be described as manual searches. Most college and university libraries have now moved to a search system which enables the user (in most cases free of charge) to gain access to information including a range of materials, references, etc. from compact discs (CD-ROM) on a computer. These discs store vast quantities of information on a huge range of topics and can be invaluable for those engaged in literature searches. This facility enables the researcher to access information and to obtain a printout of abstracts, short articles and reference lists covering the particular areas of concern.

CD-ROM stands for 'Compact Disc, Read Only Memory' and is a system which enables the user, via a personal computer, to select from computerized files. Libraries will have a list of available CD-ROM databases from which the user selects those appropriate to his needs. The disc is loaded into the computer and the search begins. The references selected can be printed out or, alternatively, 'down-loaded' on to another disc. Although not every topic is covered on CD-ROM databases, they are an invaluable and time-saving tool for researchers. These databases are simply an alternative way of storing information and should be used in conjunction with other literature searches. Most libraries offer tutorials and guidance for first-time users of CD-ROM databases, so it is always worth asking for help. We have listed and described below some of the available CD-ROM databases which will be useful for those conducting research in the field of education:

- ERIC (Educational Resources Information Center) is a bibliographic database covering education. It includes details of journal articles, research reports, dissertations, conference papers and some books and about 750 journals. Coverage is from 1982. ERIC is an agency of the United States Department of Education, and is a national information service providing ready access to the literature of education. ERIC produces two indexes in printed form: (1) Current Index to Journals in Education (CIJE), covering periodical literature, and (2) Resources in Education (RIE), which includes research reviews, project and technical reports, conference papers, annotated bibliographies, dissertations and some books. ERIC on CD-ROM combines both CIJE and RIE. Much of the material has an American bias, although a fair amount of British material is included. Not all the journals covered by ERIC will be in your library so use of the inter-library loan system will be needed.

- ASSIA PLUS is a CD-ROM database providing information on the social sciences from 1987 onwards. It covers social services, economics, politics, employment, race relations, health, education and penal services.
- BOOKBANK ON CD-ROM is a full bibliographic database (produced by Whitaker publishers) of over 600,000 British books currently in print.
- BRITISH HUMANITIES INDEX (BHI) is a bibliographic database of journal articles in the humanities, social sciences, economics and politics from 1985 onwards.
- BRITISH NATIONAL BIBLIOGRAPHY (BNB) is a database produced by the British Library providing bibliographic details on books published in the UK. Coverage from 1950 onwards.
- CHANGING TIMES contains nearly 15,000 original reports and over 1000 pictures from *The Times* and *Sunday Times* between 1785 and 1985, and grouped into history topics.
- INDEPENDENT ON CD-ROM is a full text database of *The Independent* and *The Independent on Sunday* newspapers.
- INTERNATIONAL ERIC is a bibliographic database covering education. It combines the Australian, British and Canadian education indexes and includes journal articles, theses and research reports.
- SOCIOFILE. The Sociofile database contains information from approximately 1500 journals in thirty different languages, mainly covering sociology and related disciplines but including bibliography citations and abstracts from other sources.
- SOCIAL SCIENCES INDEX (SSI) provides subject access to 300 major English-language periodicals published in the United States and abroad in areas of the social sciences, including anthropology, black studies, economics, environmental sciences, geography, international relations, law and criminology, planning and public administration, political science, psychology, public health, sociology, urban studies and women's studies. This is a very valuable and important database for those working in education.

In addition to the computerized service offered by CD-ROM, there are other services available. These fall into two categories: free-on-line services, which can include access to other libraries; and commercial-on-line services, which require a payment or fee. An example of a commercial on-line database is DIALOG. Many large university libraries now have computerized catalogue and search systems. Here, searches under subject/title areas and authors' names can be undertaken. The information displayed will then show what is available in the library stock under a particular author or on a particular topic. Other computerized services include BIDS which is one of the best databases around and is available in the UK at most university libraries. It covers the Social Sciences Citation Index and other similar publications. This is a subscription service so may not be free.

Advantages and disadvantages of computerized literature searches Obviously, computerized literature searches offer the researcher an amazing opportunity, particularly when the time-saving factor is considered. However, there are disadvantages as well as advantages to computerized search techniques. Certainly, such strategies overcome the rather old-fashioned and cumbersome 'card index and file' approach to searches. The speed, sophistication and scope of CD-ROM databases means that the researcher can get through a lot more material, a lot quicker. The use of CD-ROM will enable up to date searches and facilitate cross-referencing of topics across a wide range of literature. Cross-referencing and specialized detailed literature searches can be completed much more easily via these databases than by use of traditional library search. All in all, there are considerable advantages to using these databases for research.

There are, however, some problems and difficulties it is wise to be aware of. Many students and researchers complain about the North American bias of some of these databases, in particular ERIC. Linked with the fact that journal articles have a tendency to be cited more often than books, the researcher can have problems. There is also the so-called 'shelf-life' problem, whereby other books may not be cited or referenced. CD-ROM discs tend to contain only recent (some since 1980) references, thus making a manual search necessary for other items. The researcher will need to be familiar with the areas being searched beforehand so time is not wasted. The search processes themselves will not necessarily be the same across different discs.

Finally, it is important to note that there are bad computer searches and reviews, just as there can be bad traditional library searches. A lot depends upon the skills of the individual. In this section, we have tried to unravel some of the complexities involved in literature searches. It is almost inevitable that teacher–researchers will have to engage in computerized searches of one form or another.

Keeping records

An essential aspect of any research activity is the systematic organization of the information and materials which have been collected. This is especially important where literature and references are concerned. References and notes written down on bits of paper stand the risk of getting lost or destroyed. A simple card index system is the easiest solution. We discussed the issues surrounding the organization of field notes in Chapter 3 and many of the points we made there apply here. The researcher needs also to develop an organized and systematic approach to ordering information collected outside the field so that it can be retrieved easily at a later point. The best size of card for this purpose is eight by five inches. Additional sheets can always be stapled to the cards later. The cards should list all the biographical details, provide accurate copies of any quotations, and list contents of books or articles. It is important to provide all the details of the book or article, including the author's surname, forename, date of publication, title of the book or article, publisher or title of the journal, place of publication, page numbers, and volume and part numbers. To secure a book through the inter-library loans system, the ISBN number is useful. Hence, reference to a book would look like this.

> Milman, D. (1986) *Educational Conflict and the Law*, Croom Helm, Beckenham, ISBN 0-7099-3521-8

and reference to an article in a journal would look like this:

> Barrow, R. (1986) 'Empirical research into teaching: the conceptual factors', *Educational Research*, **28**, 3, November, 270–277.

If the teacher–researcher keeps these records properly and consistently, as the reading and research goes on it will make the process of referencing the final report much easier. It is useful to draw a distinction between references and a bibliography.

References have to be made in the text to any source which is cited in the report, whereas a Bibliography is placed at the end of the report and lists in alphabetical order all the sources which have been referred to and consulted during the course of the research and referenced in the report. However, reports come in a number of forms. They can list all known current material on a given topic, the sources consulted in a piece of research whether used in the text or not, or they can list works of a particular author. When preparing a report of research the kind of bibliography the teacher–researcher includes will depend upon the nature of the research.

Referencing often causes difficulties. The main reason for this is that there are a number of different methods of referencing. The teacher–researcher will, in the course of reading, discover a variety of referencing systems. What is important is that the method of referencing adopted is adhered to. One of the most straightforward methods, and one which is common in scientific and social scientific writing, is the 'Harvard system'. By use of this system the complete reference to an article or a book appears at the end of the article or book. The author's surname and date of a piece of work is given in the text and would read, for example, as 'Stenhouse (1975) has argued . . .'. If that author published more than once in a given year, letters are added as in 1975a, 1975b, etc. The main advantage of this system is that it does not hinder the flow of the argument. The full list of references should be given at the end of the chapter, article or book (in alphabetical order) and page numbers may be added in the text in the case of a substantial quotation or a passage that draws heavily upon the work of one author.

Referencing: a brief guide

Titles in the text Titles of books, plays, periodicals and major works should be underlined and the titles of articles placed within quotation marks.

Verse If less than one line, incorporate it in the text; if more than one line, indent and single-space it.

Prose Similar principles to the above should operate but up to two lines can be incorporated without indenting.

Figures and diagrams These should be clearly numbered and noted in the contents page.

Pagination Each page should be clearly numbered at the top centre.

References in the text It is very important to reference appropriately. This should be in the following form:

- Refer to the author(s) in the text by name and date of publication: 'Jones and Brown (1978) found that . . .' or 'It was found (Jones and Brown, 1978) that . . .'.
- Where there are more than three authors, use '*et al.*': Smith *et al.* (1979) found that . . .'.
- Where the author(s) has more than one publication in the same year, use a, b, c: 'Smith *et al.* (1979a) found that . . .'.
- Give page numbers in the text wherever it seems appropriate: 'Jones and Brown (1978, pp 12–145) found that . . .'.

Bibliography Books should be cited in the following way:

Archer, J. and Lloyd, B. (1985) *Sex and Gender*, Cambridge: Cambridge University Press.

and articles as:

> Witkin, H. A. (1967) 'A cognitive-style approach to cross-cultural research', *International Journal of Psychology* **2**, 233–250.

Although this is common for reports and articles and in scientific work it may be inappropriate for dissertations and theses and it is important to consider the regulations involved before beginning the research. A particular institution may wish you to follow the numbered note or British system where each bibliographical reference is numbered (1), (2), (3) etc. according to its appearance in the text. A full complete entry should be given either at the bottom of the page (normal in theses and dissertations) or at the end of the chapter, article, or book. This would include the author's name and title, though specific references can be appropriately abbreviated, using short titles. The question of the appropriate use of quotations, correct forms of footnoting, and the use of bibliographies is clearly discussed in Turabin (1980). Particular attention needs to be paid to the use of quotations in a text. The problem is most marked with secondary sources which are useful for supportive illustrations and information. It is best to avoid the use of long quotations since these take up much valuable space that could otherwise be used for the teacher's own ideas. The point to bear in mind is that a string of quotations, however well edited, is no substitution for the teacher's own empirical work and ideas. Even when conducting a literature review, attempts to paraphrase the works being reviewed and to develop a synthesis of the materials and ideas around some key points is much better from both the teacher's and the reader's point of view.

As far as footnotes are concerned the form most appropriate to the particular piece of research needs to be worked out. Once this has been decided it is important to be consistent and not to let the footnotes become a bugbear. Generally, reports and articles need no or few footnotes and these are usefully placed at the end of the piece. Longer studies need more extensive footnoting either at the end of a chapter or, as is normal in the case of a thesis, at the bottom of each page. In the latter case the writer will need to find out from the institution involved what the particular 'house style' is. The same applies to articles submitted to journals for publication.

THE LITERATURE REVIEW

Whilst locating a body of literature presents its own problems, reviewing and evaluating literature, in turn, creates fresh problems. The literature review plays a vital role in any research endeavour. Since the literature review is so important, it is useful to begin by exploring the value and functions of literature reviews:

- A literature review broadens and refines existing knowledge.

- A literature review helps to sharpen and clarify research questions.
- A literature review can highlight gaps and under-researched areas.
- A literature review helps clarify theoretical, methodological and analytical issues.
- A literature review will identify current debates and controversies.
- A literature review may have its own intrinsic merits.

Typically, as we have indicated in Figure 5.1, the literature review will occur early on in the research. Although the researcher will need to take care in the writing up stages not to become over-involved with repetition, a good literature review and its products should *inform* and *underpin* the whole of a research project. The selective use of a literature review and care over presenting a standalone, self-contained literature review, suggests that the literature review can take a number of forms. A review of the literature is not simply a selection or list of materials with short paraphrases of their contents. Whereas it will certainly contain this, a review of the literature must be able to identify themes, issues, topics and questions relevant to the particular research. The literature review ought to present a coherent argument, not just a list of facts. In this way, the research engages in a reflexive dialogue with the relevant materials collected via the literature search. Whilst the literature search is more practical in raising issues about the organization, storage and recording of information, literature reviews are more conceptual and theoretical.

Clearly then, producing a literature review is not a discreet, independent phase in the research process. Rather, it should be ongoing. However, constraints of time, resources and the prescriptions which often surround the requirements for presenting a study mean that there will have to be some cut-off points. A literature review, as we said, must inform the overall research process. A good literature review will be useful at various points in a study and be incorporated at various points in the final written product. One of the ways this may become clearer is to consider different types of literature reviews and the purposes which they can achieve. We identify five major categories of literature review and briefly describe each of these below.

Substantive reviews

These literature reviews focus upon substantive concerns and issues relevant to the general theme, focus or topic of the research. For example, a study of the organization of 'reading' in a primary school will first need to survey the current debates and previous debates on the teaching of reading. Reading is the substantive concern, how children learn to read and ideas about this will have to be reviewed. In this case, there is a considerable theoretical, mainly psychological literature, a vast pedagogical literature, and a growing exploratory literature on the substantive theme of reading in the primary school.

The researcher will need to locate herself in this literature and relate it to the aims and focus of her particular research.

Theoretical reviews

Clearly, reviewing a substantive area will quickly highlight the fact that research into educational processes is underpinned by a simply huge array of different theoretical viewpoints. A theoretical literature review will help to identify what these are, how they have influenced thinking and what the key debates surrounding the substantive concern entail. A theoretical review might, therefore, attend to the following:

- Philosophical debates surrounding the substantive area.
- Philosophical debates and controversies surrounding research approaches.
- Different viewpoints on the nature of evidence.
- Debates surrounding the appropriateness of research strategies.

Methodological reviews

As substantive literature reviews can quickly become theoretical reviews, a theoretical review will quickly become a methodological review. A crucial aspect of the literature review is to locate the author's chosen research methodology in the debates about research methodology. Although this will, of course, differ from study to study, it is essential that the researcher uses the literature review to develop a rationale and argument for her own particular choice of methods. Where qualitative research methods are concerned, these debates are very important indeed.

Furthermore, a methodological literature review will help to identify strengths, weaknesses and practical issues surrounding the chosen techniques. For example, there now exists an extensive literature on interviewing childhren or minors. If the research intends to make extensive use of interview data from children then this literature must be attended to. Methodological reviews are perhaps likely to be the most complex and difficult to organize while being central to a study as a whole. A methodological review in this sense is therefore essential. Not only will it locate and context the researcher's own choice of method, it may go some way towards helping the researcher to establish a rationale for that particular choice of research methodology.

Key authors/key studies reviews

In the course of enquiry, it is impossible to ignore the contribution of key figures. A key author review can be of tremendous value in charting both the contribution a particular individual has made to an area of research in education, and to the ways in which that person's research has changed and developed over time. This could be the subject of a key author review. Alternatively, it is often possible to identify seminal pieces of research in an area and, subsequently, to undertake an in-depth review of a small number of such studies. These types of review have the advantage of being highly focused and tuned in very often to the idiosyncratic needs and concerns of particular research.

Identifying different kinds of literature review will help to clarify a number of points for the researcher. Ideally, the notion of an 'integrative research review', where all these forms of literature review are brought together and made use of, both throughout the research process and in the finished written study, is the goal of the reviewer. Reviewing the literature is a crucial aspect of the research process and essential for the development of scholarly professional work. The busy teacher may be forgiven for feeling insecure about this.

Some valuable resources for literature reviews

What we have said so far might seem to suggest that the literature review is, in fact, a very daunting exercise. It can be. We have spent some time discussing this because of its major significance in the research process occupying as it does a key place in the pathway through research. There are a number of resources which can help the prospective researcher here and we list these below. These sources may lighten the burden somewhat.

Book reviews

Most journals now have lengthy sections devoted to reviews of new books. The more selective and perceptive the journal is, the more focused and narrow the basis of the books reviewed is likely to be. On the other hand, the more general educational research journals will contain book reviews on a whole range of topics. Looking at these is a useful way of covering a lot of ground and identifying relevant sources and materials.

The review article

The review article can be found in many journals. The usual pattern surrounds an invited acknowledged expert in the field reviewing a cluster of anything from two to six studies on a related theme or topic. The difference between a book review and the review article is one of space and complexity. The review article is given much more space and the author develops a range of ideas, questions and issues. As such, the review article can be very helpful in both theoretical and methodological reviews.

Source books and handbooks

We have no desire for our readers to constantly attempt to reinvent the wheel. The substantive focus of this book is the application of qualitative methodologies to teaching, learning and education. We are more than fortunate in that there is a massive literature which is of a very high quality surrounding our concerns. The emergence of source books, handbooks and the like can be used as their authors have intended them to be used. We believe that they have a special value for the literature search and review aspects of the research process. Their use can save considerable time and energy. Two good examples of particular value for students undertaking qualitative research are:

- N. K. Denzin and Y. S. Lincoln (1994) *Handbook of Qualitative Research*. Thousand Oaks, California: Sage Publications, is clearly the most comprehensive overview of qualitative research in the human sciences to date.
- A. Pollard and S. Tann (1993) *Reflective Teaching in the Primary School: A Handbook for the Classroom*, Second Edition, London: Cassell, is a very important handbook designed to promote school-based professional development via reflection and examination of research. This is an invaluable source book of which the researcher can make a variety of uses.

An essential aspect of reviewing literature will be the evaluation of particular research studies. We will briefly now say something about this.

How to evaluate a research paper

A useful skill to acquire whilst doing research and, indeed, a skill that has more widespread significance for the teacher is the ability to critique a research paper, examine the nature of evidence and assess claims made in the light of evidence presented. Bassey (1990) has provided some useful guidelines here which have significance for teachers and teachers as researchers. It is quite clear that the development of a critical, reflective, professional stance is an essential ingredient in the development of research skills. The ability to unpack a curriculum initiative, identify its philosophy, explore its deeper meaning and significance is not unlike the kind of skill required to evaluate and assess a piece of social or educational research. In both cases it will be necessary to get beneath the surface. Doing this with a piece of published research can be daunting and we will consider criteria for evaluating research more generally later on in this chapter. For the time being in the context of literature-reviewing, Bassey's (1990) guidelines are useful:

Frame-work for a critique of a research paper

1 What *contribution to educational knowledge* is claimed? What advancement to knowledge is the author claiming to have made?

2 What *conceptual background* does the author indicate was the starting point for this research? Was it theory-in-the-literature, or commonsense theory, or both?
3 What *methodology* underpinned the enquiry? Was it taken, or adapted from, a method recorded in the literature, or did the author develop it from commonsense theory?
4 Was the *collection of data*, as reported, appropriate, sufficient, ethical?
5 Was the *analysis and interpretation of data*, as reported, appropriate, sufficient, ethical?
6 Does the evidence of the paper, as examined in answer to questions (2) to (5), *substantiate the claim to knowledge* made in answer to (1)?
7 Is the *presentation* of the paper such as to enable the above questions to be answered?

(after Bassey 1990: 41)

GAINING ACCESS AND ETHICAL ISSUES

We have discussed at length the nature of access and ethics in research in general and qualitative teacher research in particular in Chapter 3. By this point in the journey through the research process, access and ethical issues will no doubt have arisen. As such, it is instructive to read the relevant sections in Chapter 4 once more in the light of the discussion so far.

GETTING DOWN TO RESEARCH

Choosing a method

It may appear that it has taken a long time to get to the point at which we can talk about the methodology of a particular piece of research. Designing and preparing, deciding on a topic and posing some research questions, reviewing the literature and thinking about access and ethical issues are all very important tasks. They are likely to influence the choice of method to a great extent. Choice of method is determined by the chosen topic and the kind of data to be collected. The real issue here is the idea of 'fitness for purpose'. Will the method chosen provide the kinds of data needed? In Part II we provide an overview of the major kinds of qualitative research methods available. The researcher will need to have a good working knowledge of the key elements of the method or methods chosen. This can be achieved by reviewing the methodological literature on the particular technique, and by reviewing some of the substantive research which has made use of the technique by way of example and illustration.

A focus upon method, however, may be misplaced. It may be more appropriate to speak about methods since much research combines a variety of data sources and uses more than one method. King (1987) has argued that there is no 'best method', and that we should suit our methods more closely to the topics being explored. Part II therefore extensively considers the main methods available to qualitative researchers.

Collecting data

Choice of method, collecting data and analysing data are all linked. This is a fundamental aspect of qualitative research. The type and amount of data collected needs to be related to the kinds of analysis that are going to be made. Another important point concerns ways in which the data is to be recorded and organized. Many students and researchers have tried to identify problems in advance by engaging in a pilot study or 'dry-run' in order to ascertain the nature and extent of any likely problems before the 'real thing'. All of these questions will ultimately be influenced by the kind of technique being used and the people being studied. For example, as we will highlight when we look at interviewing, the decision as to whether to use a tape recorder is quite an important one. A fundamental consideration for qualitative researchers concerns their involvement in the data collection itself. Again, these questions are explored more fully when we unravel the major techniques of data-collection.

The teacher–researcher following an interpretative, ethnographic research design and using a range of qualitative techniques will find that 'data collection' will involve three basic processes which constitute the main ingredients of any qualitative research technique. These are *observation*, *interrogation*, and *documentary and oral data collection*. The first process involves listening to and looking at what the people in the research setting itself are doing. The second involves talking to these subjects about the meanings they attach to their actions, and the third involves the interpretation of meanings from written or oral data. The outcome of all three processes is collected data which will then need to be sifted, analysed, or evaluated. What the researcher is doing here is creating what we can call either first-order accounts or primary sources and then, by means of analysis, second-order accounts or secondary sources. The processes of data-collection and data-analysis in qualitative research are in a real sense simultaneous. It is perhaps misleading to see them as separate activities.

Analysing data

Obviously, the kinds of analysis which may be made will depend upon the focus of the research and the kinds of data obtained, but what do we mean by analysis? Analysis involves a move from the description of what appears to be the case to an explanation of why what appears to be the case is the case. Qualitative data analysis is a complex affair and has received much less detailed treatment in the literature than quantitative analyses and measurement. An account of qualitative data analysis is given when we look at each technique and an extended discussion is provided in Part III. Put simply qualitative analysis involves breaking down the data and relating particular items of data to one or other categories which the researcher has identified.

Analysis is what the researcher does with data in order to develop explanations of events so that theories and generalizations about the causes, reasons and processes of any piece of social behaviour can be developed. Analysis therefore looks for the major properties of any event or set of events. There are very many different kinds of analyses which ultimately depend upon the nature of the particular research design employed and underlying assumptions held. Researchers have used statistical analysis using mathematical techniques, thematic analysis, class analysis, content analysis, conversational analysis, qualitative analysis. The chapters in Part II unravel some of the important tasks the teacher–researcher will need to engage in when analysing material.

Although analysis is important the purpose of teacher school-based research means that the enterprise does not finish with analysis. What the researcher does with the research findings is often inextricably linked with the underlying design of the research which we outlined in Figure 5.2. Teacher research comes from and inevitably returns to professional practice. This means that evaluation and an examination of the practical and policy implications should feature in the analysis stage of any school-based teacher research. Evaluation might therefore be defined as that process which subjects data and the theories developed to some kind of assessment in terms of specific criteria. The aim is to unravel the effectiveness or otherwise, the success or otherwise of particularly arranged activities to achieve certain ends or goals and, ultimately, to improve the quality of the particularly arranged activities to achieve certain ends or goals and improve the quality of the particular sets of actions involved. The processes of analysis and evaluation take on a special importance in teacher research. This is explored in more detail in Part III.

Within the qualitative tradition there is a certain disagreement as to whether one should develop theories alongside data collection or to collect the data first and then look for a fit between the data and theories. Those who argue for the latter suggest that by doing the analysis last one avoids as far as possible contamination of the data by the researcher. We have found from experience that there is a positive advantage in developing data collection and analysis side by side as it enables one to try out different explanations of the fit between data, theory and ideas as the project proceeds. The key question for the qualitative researcher is how it is possible to obtain as authentic an account of school or classroom life as possible without forcing the data into a theory or avoiding the temptation of 'hammering reality into shape'. These issues are explored more fully when we unravel each technique in detail in the chapters in Part II. The relationship between data, method and theory in qualitative research traditions is distinct from that relationship in quantitative or positivistic research; we tried to identify the major axes of these differences in Chapter 2.

WRITING UP

Writing is all about communicating. The nature of the communication will vary with the audience the researcher is targeting. But whatever the audience, clarity and style will be important. In this section we want to start to look at some of the questions surrounding writing up. We return to this theme in more detail in Chapter 14. What does the researcher do with all the material, ideas and analyses that have been collected and formed during the research? For most people writing is hard. It is also personal. Researchers develop their own ways of writing and working. However, it is important to begin the writing process as early as possible. Drafts and rough chapters can always be changed and edited at some later point. A distinction needs to be drawn between the framework of a study and the ways in which the study is written, that is a distinction between *structure* and *style*. We will look at some of the models available for the presentation of a research project since most readers will be involved in this. Writing for publication in a journal or book involves another set of conventions.

A matter of style

The characteristics of qualitative research with its emphasis upon the involvement of the researcher, first-hand experience, use of subjective materials, and heavy descriptive content means that the researcher is an integral part of a qualitative study and, by definition, a part of the writing of that study. A concern with capturing the rich description of events puts the researcher at the centre of the observations. Positivistic research has been criticized for decontextualizing events, ripping behaviour from social context. The characteristic ways in which 'scientific', positivistic research is written mirrors this. The usual convention is that research must be reported in the third person. The assumption here is that this will be a reflection of the researcher's assumed objectivity. However, fieldworkers, participant observers and ethnographers are likely to find themselves in the role of narrator, use of the first person is therefore justified and some might say essential for capturing the reality being explored. Furthermore, it is important to acknowledge the role of the researcher in qualitative research and identify this in the reporting of the research. The writing up of qualitative research may therefore be rather different from the writing up of quantitative research. Recently, there has been considerable experimentation and creativity on the part of ethnographers in the ways they present their studies and the styles which they have adopted. We consider Van Maanen's (1988) discussion of three typical narrative conventions for writing up qualitative research, realist, confessional and impressionist, in Chapter 14.

The writing process

Mastering an understanding of research design and techniques of data collection is only one side of the research equation. The other involves the teacher–researcher in communicating findings, ideas and suggestions to an audience. This is just as important as the actual research itself. The teacher–researcher will therefore have to consider seriously the way in which her findings are to be written up and presented. This, after all, is part of the process of reflection upon professional practice. The first question to consider is the nature of the written report itself, and second, the nature of the audience for whom the report is intended. In this sense the teacher–researcher will be subject to some of the same rules that apply to the presentation of academic work. Part of the problem lies in the nature of the research and kinds of data collected. Becker and Geer highlight the differences involved in presenting different types of data:

> When fieldwork ends, the observer will already have done a great deal of analysis. He must now put his material into such a form that a reader will understand the basis on which he has arrived at his conclusions. While statistical data can be summarized in tables and descriptive measures can often be reported in the space required to print a formula, qualitative data and their analytical procedures are often difficult to present. The former methods have been systematised so that they can be referred to in this shorthand fashion and the data have been collected for a fixed, usually small, number of categories. The presentation need be nothing more than a report of the number of cases to be found in each category.
>
> (Becker and Geer 1982: 24)

The major dilemma facing the teacher–researcher making use of qualitative materials is, therefore, how best to avoid an exclusive reliance upon illustrative and anecdotal examples. Ethnography has at its heart description, but this description is theoretically informed. Description must always therefore be balanced with analysis. Description without analysis is only half a story. This is undoubtedly a skill that is learned. We stressed that the teacher–researcher will often be involved in the processes of data analysis while collecting the data. The final text then will not only display these elements of the research but the teacher's ability to communicate effectively in written form. The model which the teacher–researcher eventually adopts for the written presentation of the research will depend upon the data obtained, the problems being studied, and the audience who will read the report. There are a number of ways in which the teacher–researcher can present her findings and we will now consider some of these. We would encourage researchers to consider the fact that whereas the structure for presenting the research may be fairly fixed, the style of writing presents an opportunity to be creative and to reflect the true spirit of qualitative enquiry.

The research report

The writing of a research report is perhaps the least problematic though not necessarily the easiest form of research discourse. It is possible to provide a plan of research reports which highlights the key aspects and ingredients of such reports. A classic model for the presentation of a research report is given below:

1 An outline of the research project.
2 A review of previous work in the field in order to place the new research in context.
3 A precise statement of the range and scope of the research outlined.
4 A description of the methods employed in the research.
5 Clear presentation of the data and a discussion of implications.
6 Summary and conclusions.
7 List of references.

(after Nisbet and Entwhistle, 1984: 253)

Obviously, the form that a research report takes depends very much on the nature of the research and the data involved. It may be that an appendix is used to place material which would otherwise clutter the main text, so that it can be conveniently referred to by the reader. The framework provided by Nisbet and Entwhistle (1984) is a useful one. By their very nature, research reports are concise illustrations of the whole of the research and the researcher needs to convey this in as clear and readable a fashion as possible. If the teacher–researcher is dealing with a more practical or applied concern then the relationship of the research to school or classroom practice will become a key element of the report. Also, uppermost in the mind of the teacher–researcher will be the audience being addressed. This may therefore involve the researcher in clearly defining any technical or specialist terms, and providing as far as possible a jargon-free text.

Theses, dissertations, long essays and school-based projects

In a number of situations the teacher–researcher may well be working with a supervisor or another professional. In this situation a working relationship develops and an action plan for writing up for a degree or professional qualification might take the following form:

- A preliminary 'brain-storming' session with sheets of paper, writing down key ideas and concepts. Out of this should emerge a basic plan of the shape of the written text, including main and supportive theoretical constructs and concepts. However, as we observed in Chapter 3 when discussing the analysis of qualitative materials, a thorough knowledge of and acquaintance with the materials is crucial. This will mean reading them through many times.

- A more detailed plan can then be attempted which should include a chapter on themes, each broken down into main and subheadings (even if in the actual project the researcher may not wish to use these). It is also possible at this stage to detail paragraph content in note form.
- A review of the research data and comparison with the plan, looking for omissions and inconsistencies in argument. Care must be taken to ensure a flow between narrative, data presentation and analysis so that as few loose ends as possible are left, or when they are left, that account is taken of them.
- A final working plan will now appear which should be carefully looked at again not only for omissions which may still occur and for weakly supported and over- or under-theorized descriptions but also for examples of over-use of quotations, for ideas that may be a favourite 'hobby horse' but are not relevant to the current research (the prejudice syndrome) and, above all, for ensuring that what you mean to say is in fact conveyed adequately by the text in front of you.

One way of approaching the dissertation is to try and see stages and phases in research and work towards these. Clearly, research in educational settings will be structured to a certain extent around term times and the institution's calendar, making any phasing more important.

A typical dissertation process

Initial dissertation proposal

This form should be completed in such a way as to enable the identification of an area/problem to be studied, a literature to be explored and some indication of how the research will be conducted.

Enlarged proposal

This will involve a revised and extended version of the initial proposal and involve approximately 1500–2000 words and should include the following:

- Provisional title.
- Dissertation objectives.
- Rationale of dissertation.
- Proposed methodology.
- Brief literature review.
- Identification of problems.

Initial report

This initial report will need to contain a statement of your progress to date and include a draft discussion of the framework you will be employing.

Furthermore it will need to contain reference to the practicability of the research. You should consider the following in about 2000 words:

- Restatement of objectives.
- Progress.
- Problems.
- Identification of timescale and timetable.

Draft chapters

You should be submitting draft chapters from May–June onwards so that your supervisor has seen a complete first draft of the dissertation in advance of receiving the submitted manuscript. Such a phased/staged approach might result in the following kind of structure:

- Title page.
- Contents page.
- Abstract/summary (250 words).
- Acknowledgements.
- Chapters
  1 Introduction.
  2 Theoretical basis, research problems and research design.
  3 Literature review.
  4 Justification of research methodology and data collection techniques.
  5 Presentation, discussion and analysis of findings.
  6 Conclusions, recommendations, implementation.
  7 Reflexive account.
- Appendices.
- References.

Applied research

In applied research the question of presentation and organization of research material is a crucial issue as the intention of such research is to improve practice by directly involving those within the educational process in reflecting upon, evaluating, and perhaps changing their practice. In such research a useful organizing principle is often to be found within the issues explored themselves. The balance advocated between description and analysis, action and structure might be difficult to achieve with more applied research (Walker 1985). Stake, for example, has argued that in an evaluation study 'what the evaluator has to say cannot be both a sharp analysis of high priority achievement and a broad and accurate reflection of the programme's complex transactions. One message crowds out the other' (Stake as quoted in Walker (1985: 163). In endorsing this Walker adds perceptively that:

> The same point is generally true in research studies: the kind of investment of time and other resources necessary to complete a survey or testing programme, or to carry out a detailed ethnography, rarely leaves room for a full portrayal of the whole context within which the study was made, a choice has to be made between breadth and depth.
>
> (Walker 1985: 164)

Finally, an important aspect of the writing process is to ensure that the language used neither explicitly or implicitly gives the impression of belittling, patronizing or stereotyping people. Obviously, the research report should not be written in sexist or racist language, there are, however, other more subtle examples of the ways in which wrong impressions and discriminatory language can creep into the writing process. This question is part of the broader issue of equal opportunities. A simple start would be to ensure that the descriptions used by groups themselves form the basis for the language used in a report. This is not simply a matter of being politically correct. 'Queer' suggests something different to 'gay', and writing about handicapped or disabled people is very different from writing about people with disabilities. These issues are now regarded as being so important that guides to the use of language have appeared. The best of these are those produced by The National Association of Teachers in Further and Higher Education (NATFHE, 1993) and the Open University (1993). Both of these documents convey straightforward ways in which problems can be avoided.

The reflexive account

We have stressed the importance of reflection in teachers' professional development regarding the process as an essential professional development criterion. The notion of the reflective practitioner needs to be extended to the research process itself. In this sense it is helpful and instructive to include a reflexive account at the end of any research report. By this we mean an honest, open and critical account of the course of the research and its major strengths and weaknesses. This account should contain comments on problems encountered and solutions found. It is also helpful to think about how the research might be conducted if the study was to be done again. It would be useful to consult the research diary if one was kept during the research. This is likely to be the source of some particularly reflective comments which could be incorporated into the reflexive account. The reflexive account extends and develops the dialogue so crucial to the development of understanding.

In the previous pages we have been charting a course through the research process, providing a pathway with key points of reference *en route*. This pathway was broken down into research designs, data collection and analysis. Part I of this book has been concerned to unravel designs and approaches.

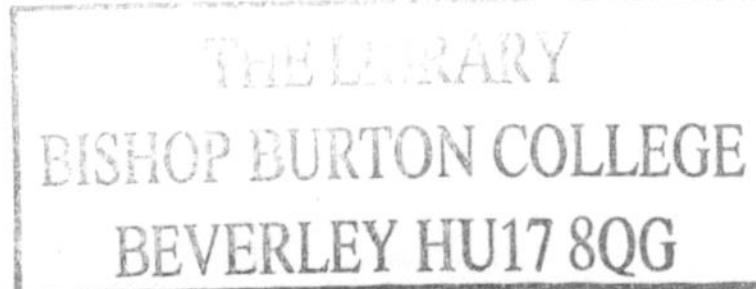

Part II is concerned, in particular, with qualitative data collection techniques, and Part III with the case study, qualitative data analysis and writing. We conclude Part I by providing a framework for the evaluation and assessment of research in terms of the practice and products of research, that is, a look at the nature of evidence, claims made in research and the overall quality of the research and its findings.

ASSESSING RESEARCH: SOME INITIAL CRITERIA

Whilst we have stressed the diversity of research approaches, highlighting the qualitative research tradition which underpins our orientation, it would be easy to assume that there could never be any common ground when it comes to evaluating and assessing a piece of research. A major aim of ours has been to encourage the development of a range of critical skills needed to assess and evaluate the nature of evidence and claims made in the light of evidence in educational research. In order to do this we need to provide some kind of 'across the board criteria' against which we can place our own and others' research. The problem surrounds the identification of 'across the board' criteria which will have some kind of universal currency over a range of research approaches. Given that we have identified very major philosophical differences here we have something of a problem. The suggestion might be that what constitutes a good, acceptable piece of quantitative research may not be the same sort of qualities as those which constitute a good, acceptable piece of qualitative research. Issues such as the scope, range and purpose of a piece of research will feature in such discussions.

Generally speaking, the scientific research community has identified three kinds of criteria by which a piece of research can be evaluated and around which researchers ought to develop their studies. These criteria are *validity*, *reliability* and *representativeness*. It is important to remember that these terms apply equally to the research methodology, the data collection strategies employed and to the kinds of analysis made and explanations offered. Also, it must be remembered that there is considerable divergence of opinion as to what exactly and precisely these three terms mean (Hammersley 1992). As Hammersley (1992) points out the use of these terms derives from a concern with measurement in science and, of course, the experimental method is the obvious way of checking for the truth and accuracy of an explanation since the significance of variables may be ascertained through the element of control which an experimental situation allows. However, for the most part qualitative research is not about measurement *per se* (Pollard 1984) though quantification can and often is necessary in some qualitative, ethnographic research. Qualitative research is about meanings and interpretations. This has led some people to argue that qualitative researchers' search for meaning, their reliance upon themselves as data gatherers and filterers, and the characteristic focus upon small groups, micro-situations and particular cases has rendered the criteria of validity, reliability and representativeness as wholly inappropriate as ways of assessing and evaluating such research. Perhaps this is 'What's Wrong with Ethnography?' (Hammersley 1992). Qualitative research is not beyond assessment in these terms, but what is important is clarification of what is meant by the terms and an appreciation of the nature of the research being conducted. It seems strange to judge interpretative research by a set of positivistic style criteria (LeCompte and Goetz 1982). Furthermore, the kinds of research undertaken by teachers is likely to be of a different order and scope to so-called pure research. Our position is clear. It is always important to scrutinize research, to ask how convincing the evidence is. To consider whether the claims made are justified by the evidence presented. To consider the nature and quality of the descriptions provided. To ask whether the research is convincing. At the same time we must caution against over-sceptical tendencies and negativity. All research, and especially teacher research, operates under a variety of constraints. Very often pragmatism results. There will always be the need to strike some kind of balance. The conclusion of reflective or critical self-commentary at the end of a piece of research is one of the ways in which another look at these criteria can be developed. Despite these problems we believe it is both necessary and possible to develop some fairly uncontentious 'across the board' criteria for the assessment and evaluation of research and pointers for the researcher to attend to whilst undertaking research. It is fair to say that many pieces of research do not make explicit how the research was conducted.

Validity

Validity has to do with a number of things. Generally speaking, validity has to do with instruments/techniques, data, findings and explanations. Validity is concerned with the extent to which descriptions of events accurately capture these events, for example, the extent to which the material collected by the researcher presents a true and accurate picture of what it is claimed is being described. This will relate to the descriptions of events the researcher offers. Hence the notion of *descriptive validity* refers to the extent to which the researcher describes what, in fact, the study set out to do and describe and whether this description was accurate and authentic. Most research, of course, remains at the level of description but makes explanatory claims, develops theories and uses concepts. In moving from describing what *is* the case to analysing and explaining *why* what is the case the researcher offers reasons and explanations. *Explanatory validity* therefore surrounds the extent to which any explanations offered are justified in the evidence presented. Are the explanations internally consistent and logical given the materials available? Are there any alternative explanations or rival factors which could have been considered? Another way of looking at validity is in terms of *instrument/technique validity*. Is the choice of data collection techniques or instruments suited to the type of data required and research questions formulated? – the notion of 'fitness for purpose'. Yet another way of looking at validity is to consider the findings of a study and compare them with another accepted (valid) observation or explanation of the same thing. This is known as *criterion validity*. These are all ways of assessing the accuracy and the quality of a particular study's methodology, evidence and claims. There are, of course, many differences between quantitative and qualitative research but quality is a relevant issue for both types of research. The survey researcher dealing with large quantities of data will be equally concerned with the quality of those data. On the other hand, ethnographers and fieldworkers often work with an unstated and implicit notion of ethnographic adequacy. Ethnographic adequacy refers to the extent to which subjects or members recognize themselves in the descriptions of them and their activities reported by ethnographers in their attempt to 'get it right' and 'tell it like it is', from the 'inside'. Here, the notion of faithfulness to the actors' perspective ought to ensure high degrees of descriptive validity, very often people will judge such work in terms of the apparently soft notion of face validity. Do the descriptions ring true? Do they feel right? The researcher engaged in ethnographic fieldwork or participant observation, for example, will anyway be simultaneously engaged in a validating process as she collects data, moving backwards and forwards between description and explanation, data collection and tentative fairly inductive analysis. Guba (1981) has developed some criteria for assessing the trustworthiness of natualistic studies which is of help here.

The notion of *validity checks* suggests that there are things which the researcher can do to increase validity. The most common way in which validity can be strengthened is by some form of triangulation or diversity of method. The use of more than one method to collect data will result in different sorts of data. This will expand the picture which the researcher has to look at but will also show how an initial idea or hypothesis may be confronted from different angles. Typically, qualitative researchers engaged in case studies will as a matter of course use a diversity of methods and data sources. Another strategy available to the researcher is to compare data obtained within the field to data from outside the immediate field. Yet another option is for the researcher to look more closely at and scrutinize the deviant case—the example which goes against the grain—in order to see what light that will cast upon the rest of the researcher's data. Finally, the researcher can take the field notes or other observations back to the subject in order to check that she has got it right. This is known as *respondent validation.*

It remains to be asked whether validity can ever be satisfactorily and completely demonstrated in qualitative research. In any case there will always be a background research community with its current values and ideologies against which research will be judged. These 'scientific communities' as Kuhn (1970) describes them, determine the judgements of what constitutes appropriate science at a particular point in time. Kuhn's view holds that science is not a carefully constructed and organized set of theories founded upon the meticulous accumulation of facts but rather a set of social constrictions based upon practices and activities in use at the time. Judgements of what is 'right' and 'fact', etc. are based upon world views or paradigms. These paradigms will hold together coherent traditions of scientific research. However, even when research seems superficially to be in general agreement with the current views of the scientific research community there may still be grounds for questioning it. This can be seen in the rather acrimonious debate between Cecile Wright and Peter Foster, see Wright (1986; 1990) and Foster (1990; 1991). Foster's point is that it is important to subject empirical studies to scrutiny rather than simply accepting without question even when, as in the case of Wright's study, findings seem to support the current academic view of black pupils' experience of racism in schools. Foster (1990; 1991) has argued that the kind of evidence presented by Wright was insufficient and inadequate to make the claims she makes and that other plausible explanations are available. This puts in serious doubt the validity of Wright's study.

Reliability

Reliability refers to the extent to which any particular method of data collection is replicable, that is if the research was to be repeated by someone else using a different technique, would the same findings result? Simply put, reliability concerns the extent to which a particular technique will produce the same kinds of results, however, whenever and by whoever it is carried out. It will also involve asking questions about the extent to which different observers of an event will produce the same kinds of observations of that event. For example, coders using the ORACLE manual, must all be coding teachers' questions in the same way for the research instrument to have acceptable levels of reliability. Hence, the ORACLE researchers went on a mini training course. Ethnographic and qualitative research traditions compound the problem of reliability by virtue of their conventions. In particular, the all-encompassing role of the researcher who both collects and analyses the data means that it is that researcher's experience which predominates. Much will simply have to be taken on trust and we will have to rely on the researcher having done what was claimed to have been done. The question of reliability therefore raises the issues of the influence of the researcher, research technique, setting and so on.

Questions of bias and sources of error are very important when evaluating research. We need to ask about the significance and nature of the research technique itself, and the influence of the researcher. This latter point has typically been treated in terms of the influence of key variables, such as gender, class, ethnicity, age and status. Indeed, we regard 'gender' as such a significant variable in the research process that we have devoted considerable space to unravelling the gender–research–education equation.

We need to ask about the ways in which these variables can shape and influence the research process and its products. Is their significance such that they can become sources of error, or generate bias? The problem of reactivity centres on the ways in which the researcher changes, shapes or influences the situation to the extent that it is no longer 'natural'. As we have pointed out, qualitative research techniques tend, in fact, to be highly reactive. Fieldwork, participant observation, unstructured interviewing, taking life histories all directly involve the researcher in intense and often prolonged sensitive interactions with people. Indeed, this closeness, intimacy and the understandings achieved are regarded as positive hallmarks of the qualitative/ethnographic tradition. The suggestion that this kind of research is easily replicable gets us nowhere. The assumption here is that the same situation ought to be able to be researched in the same way, producing roughly the same sorts of findings by different researchers. The fundamental misunderstanding here is that the situation will be the same. Situations never remain the same, they change, are redefined and two individuals will view the 'same' event in rather different ways. We feel that it is much more profitable to critically consider the significance of a range of key personal variables of both researchers and subjects as well as considering the nature of the technique employed itself. The professional and practical context of school-based research will add a range of 'validity issues' which will need to be addressed by the researcher. The emergence over the years of accounts which highlight the essentially socially constructed nature of ethnographic work have gone a long way towards opening up the area of reliability. It is now customary to provide more detailed accounts of the researcher experiences in the field and how this shaped and influenced the study.

Representativeness, typicality and the question of sampling

We now come to the final criterion which might be employed in evaluating research. Representativeness surrounds the extent to which the situation, individuals, or groups investigated are typical or representative of the situations, individuals, or group as a whole. Representativeness therefore raises questions about the choice of situations, subjects and groups.

What is important here is the extent to which the researcher has been able to obtain a good overall view of a setting or situation. Ethnographers who have used the community study/case study approach for looking at schools and classrooms have attempted to place school and classroom processes in a broad socio-cultural context. Although this is done in order to ascertain both the nature of the interaction between, say, home and school, it is also done in order to see the relative significance and importance of certain factors. The researcher must therefore endeavour to obtain data which are typical and representative of the groups, individuals and situations in question. Whilst the scope and range of a study, and the material sources, will certainly place restrictions upon what can be done, some form of sampling will need to take place. Whereas sampling poses special problems for small-scale qualitative research, it is an important aspect of social survey research and the identification of a target group is essential in questionnaire design. It is worth briefly considering the ways in which sampling is undertaken in survey research in order to contrast this with the issues of typicality and representativeness in qualitative research.

Standard procedures for selecting samples or sampling strategies have emerged:

- Random samples are drawn by selecting from a list referred to as the 'Sampling Frame'. For example, if the researcher was concerned with subject or option choice in terms of gender issues then an appropriate sampling frame might be all Year Three pupils who were making their choice of GCSE options. The random sample of pupils from this group may be drawn by use of random number tables to select a group for study. However, this would not necessarily provide a balance between girls and boys so this element would then need to have been put into the sampling frame.
- Stratified sampling provides a means of ensuring greater sophistication in obtaining representativeness. In this approach some form of separation of the group is done by stratifying the group according to characteristics such as age, gender or ethnicity or, indeed, a consideration of these. Obviously, this can become a quite complex process but it significantly increases the degree of representativeness of the sample. Sampling can be as simple or as complicated as the researcher cares to make it. The nature of the target population and its internal dimensions will provide the researcher with an understanding of typicality and representativeness and thereby criteria for selecting samples.

All researchers need to give attention to the selection of respondents or informants. Survey and questionnaire design enables typically larger target populations to be identified, leading to a greater choice of increasing typicality and representativeness. However, qualitative field-based researchers usually have smaller numbers of respondents or informants, but research them in greater depth than is usually achieved in surveys or questionnaires. All the same, qualitative researchers need to pay attention to typicality and attempt some form of sampling. The emphasis needs to be placed upon obtaining as natural and representative a picture of a situation as possible. Some form of sampling then will help the qualitative researcher to at least attempt acceptable levels of representativeness and will anyway identify problems and gaps. The main problem with qualitative research here is that qualitative researchers usually work with a small number of cases. However, a single case will have subsets (cases within cases) and it is important for the researcher to 'sample' across time, space, locale and person. The major difference here is that whereas in quantitative research sampling tends to be random, in qualitative research it will be what we might describe as 'purposive'. Miles and Huberman talk about two interrelated processes in sampling in qualitative research:

> First, you need to set *boundaries:* to define aspects of your case(s) that you can study within the limits of your time and means, that connect directly with your research questions, and that probably will include examples of what you want to study. Second, at the same time, you need to create a *frame* to help you uncover, confirm, or qualify the basic processes or constructs that undergrid your study.
>
> (Miles and Huberman 1994: 27)

Miles and Huberman (1994) provide an excellent account of the options available for sampling in qualitative work. In particular, they highlight within-case sampling, theoretical sampling, and multiple-case sampling, (Miles and Huberman 1994: 29). Their book contains an extensive account of sampling in qualitative research. Let us explore some of the ways in which researchers have gone about handling this problem. The work of Brice-Heath (1982; 1983; 1994) will serve as an example of the ways in which ethnographers try to ensure that they achieve reasonable levels of representativeness.

Brice-Heath (1982; 1983) attempted to develop an in-depth understanding of teaching and learning in one corner of the south-eastern United States via a blend of cultural–linguistic analysis which attempts to intervene positively in the activities of that world. Her work has been prompted by the need to understand low academic achievement and the alienation of some groups of children and, in particular, the need to understand the nature of communication between black and white teachers, children and parents. For Brice-Heath to develop such an understanding in the context of the two communities of Roadville and Trackton in the Piedmont Carolinas she undertook a long in-depth community-based ethnographic study in order to gain insights into both the macro- and micro-community, school and family locations. Her work included participant observations in a variety of settings, talking to a range of teachers and pupils, spending time in the homes of children, looking at the curriculum, the organization of work and labour and so on. The different ways of asking questions at home and at school, the different ways in which children communicated in Roadville and Trackton is placed in a context which has been understood and interpreted as a result of observing a wide range of situations, groups and individuals. In order to develop this thinking the research needed to cover a wide range of contexts, checking for typicality and representativeness. Whilst we would argue that the studies of Brice-Heath (1982; 1983; 1994) do achieve high levels of validity they also seem to be dealing with typical and representative situations to the extent which is perhaps not common in small-scale qualitative studies.

What then might the researcher do to ensure a fair degree of representativeness? First, it is important to understand the nature of the link between evidence and claims made, and the extent to which generalizations, if any, are being made on the basis of this. The kinds of strategies which are likely to result in greater representativeness are varied. Usually, length of study and degree of involvement are seen as being fairly important. But of course the kind and quality of involvement in a setting is what counts. The researcher should aim to study a range of activities and make sure that any informants are selected as far as possible on the grounds that they are representatives of different groups, of different status, different outlook and background, age and gender. In the literature on field research the notion of a 'well informed informant' (Back 1955) has emerged. This is someone who knows the culture well, someone who understands the culture. However, many ethnographies highlight the ways in which a single informant has helped the researcher. Notwithstanding the very many advantages this brings, the well informed informant may not be typical.

One unusual way of approaching representativeness is for the researcher to focus upon the unusual, atypical or deviant case on the assumption that this might cast important light on the ordinary, the mundane, routine or typical.

We have tried to identify a range of criteria by which the process of research and its products may be evaluated. In the following sections the issues surrounding validity, reliability and representativeness in qualitative teacher research will surface again and again in a number of different contexts. However, we may simply be adding to the continuing debate over the nature of these criteria and their application to qualitative research.

In this chapter we have attempted to take the reader on a pathway through researching. In an attempt to make this journey more agreeable we have provided a series of signposts pointing in directions which we hope will help the prospective researcher.

SUGGESTED FURTHER READING

There a number of valuable texts now available which focus upon designing, planning and writing research. A simple introduction is provided by *Doing Your Research Project: A Guide for First-time Researchers in Education and Social Sciences* (Bell 1987). This is somewhat limited as far as qualitative research goes though. An excellent guide, albeit North American, is given by *Surviving Your Dissertation* (Rudestam and Newton 1992) and *Integrating Research: A Guide for Literature Reviews* (Cooper 1989). This is by far the best overall account and is very user friendly. There are particularly good sections on methods and presenting results, with sound advice on literature reviews. Another very good account of the research process which takes a more theoretical approach is *By Design: Planning Research on Higher Education* (Light, Singer and Willett 1990). Literature searches and literature reviews are extensively considered by Cooper in a series of works: 'Scientific guidelines for conducting integrative research reviews' (Cooper 1982) and

The Integrative Research Review: A Systematic Approach (Cooper 1984). Chapter 4 of *The Management of a Student Research Project* (Howard and Sharp 1983) contains sound advice on conducting a literature search.

As we have indicated, the writing process is complex, and presenting qualitative research poses special problems. *A Manual for Writers of Research Papers, Theses and Dissertations* (Turabin 1980) is a good overall guide and *Writing for Social Scientists: How to Start and Finish Your Thesis, Book or Article* (Becker 1986) is written by one of the foremost qualitative researchers with a wealth of experience. The writing process and qualitative research is extensively covered in *Writing Up Qualitative Research* (Wolcott 1990). The article by Woods (1985a) concerning qualitative educational research offers further insights. 'New songs played skilfully: creativity and technique in writing up qualitative research' in *Issues in Educational Research: Qualitative Methods* (Ed. Burgess 1986) and 'On the nature of research in education' (Bassey 1990) provide an excellent overview of a range of important themes in the debate over research methodology.

An interesting account of the concepts of validity and reliability in qualitative research can be found in *Reliability and Validity in Qualitative Research* (Kirk and Miller 1986). The specific questions about ethnography are explored in an important article by LeCompte and Goetze (1982), 'Problems of reliability and validity in ethnographic research'. The complex ethical issues surrounding validity and the kinds of limits which may be reached in qualitative educational inquiry are discussed in a frank article 'On seeking – and rejecting – validity in qualitative research' (Wolcott 1990b) in *Qualitative Inquiry in Education: The Continuing Debate* (Eisner and Peshkin 1990).

Part II

Qualitative research techniques

Introduction to Part II

Part II of this book concentrates upon a range of qualitative research techniques and their organization in small-scale research. We aim to provide a clear rationale for the use of a range of qualitative techniques, with a practical understanding of how these techniques may be employed in qualitative research in education. Whilst Chapter 12 focuses directly on the analysis of qualitative data, we deal in general terms with the kinds of analyses that can be made of data generated by ethnographic observation, interviewing, the observation of classroom interaction and a focus upon spatial arrangements. We also open up the complex issues surrounding the analysis of life history materials and documentary sources. We have tried to look at both the strengths and weaknesses of these techniques but, above all, our intention has been to communicate the range and vitality of qualitative research techniques and explore the potential they offer teacher–researchers and others concerned to explore their own professional practice.

Ethnography and fieldwork provide the framework within which some of the techniques we explore can be placed. Not every qualitative researcher will be engaged in full-blown ethnography or lengthy periods of field research, but they will all be engaged in fairly close involvement with the data and usually the context which produced those data. Central to ethnography is, of course, observation. This model of research offers teachers unique opportunities to trade on their own knowledge and involvement in their own settings to investigate the processes of teaching and learning.

Our choice of individual research techniques has been decided by a variety of factors, including our experience of what has been found to be most useful, the flexibility of the techniques themselves and, finally, the contemporary diversity of qualitative research techniques. However, ethnography, fieldwork, interviewing, biographical life history research, documentary research and classroom observation research are so central to both qualitative research designs and educational research that they were self-selecting. This part of the book is concluded with an in-depth focus upon the ways in which the spatial dimensions of teaching and learning may be investigated in order to highlight the value of qualitative research techniques.

Throughout the chapters in Part II we have made reference to numerous studies and a range of research findings, not so much for their substantive content, but for the techniques and methodology employed. Those interested can follow these references up at a later point. The suggestions for further reading at the end of each chapter cover standard works in the area and highlight more recent studies. Although the focus of these chapters is primarily methodological, dealing with particular research techniques, we explore also a range of substantive areas and themes, some of which might provide readers with triggers for their own research investigations, or substantive concerns which may be followed up at a later date.

From a consideration of contemporary work, and a look at what qualitative researchers do, some of the main characteristics of qualitative research may be identified. These include the following:

- There is considerable diversity apparent in qualitative research, terms, such as 'fieldwork', 'ethnography', 'participant observation', 'case study' and 'life history interview', have all been used to describe qualitative enquiry.
- Qualitative research is practised in a variety of settings and is conducted by researchers from widely differing disciplinary backgrounds, including both pure and applied research.
- Qualitative researchers focus upon natural, ordinary, routine everyday situations, collecting unstructured data which is not heavily structured by the researcher.
- Qualitative data is collected in a number of different ways and in a variety of settings.
- Qualitative researchers are concerned to make sense of, understand and interpret the data rather than to count and measure them.
- More often than not qualitative research deals with a small number of cases.
- Qualitative researchers analyse their data in an inductive way focusing upon peoples' perceptions, interpretations and meanings since they are concerned more with social processes than social structures.
- Qualitative research is not concerned with the 'testing' of preformulated hypotheses, but with developing theories which are 'grounded' in the data. Concepts are used by qualitative researchers to sensitize them to the situation being analysed.
- Qualitative research as currently practised is emergent, creative and open-ended.

We will explore these various characteristics of qualitative research as we examine the ways in which the teacher–researcher can use the techniques we describe in Part II. Whilst there is considerable diversity, it is these characteristics which seem to hold qualitative research traditions together. We begin by looking at ethnography, the approach most commonly associated with qualitative research. In this and the subsequent chapters in Part II we hope to convey some of the excitement of carrying out qualitative research and to show the ways in which the quiet 'qualitative revolution' (Denzin and Lincoln 1994: IX) has overtaken other approaches in the study of education, teaching and learning.

6 Ethnography, fieldwork and the teacher

INTRODUCTION

A young graduate student in his late twenties makes his way through the rain and industrial grime of a northern city, *en route* to begin research in an inner city open plan primary school. On arrival the school resembles the inside of an aircraft hangar. The researcher feels a tap on his leg, 'Hi, I'm Geoffrey, they think I'm thick me but I'm not'. Geoffrey's introduction is as quick as his departure for on turning, the researcher finds Geoffrey running off and a middle-aged short man approaching him. 'Did you get lost?' he enquires. It transpired that the researcher had mistakenly entered the building via the playground doors and not through the 'official' entry point, which led into the foyer with the head and his secretary's offices adjoining it (Hitchcock 1980).

Somewhere in Brixton, London, an American researcher sits in a coffee bar speaking to a group of young Afro-Caribbeans about their experience of school. He says little, nods sympathetically now and again, answers the questions they ask of him, occasionally scribbling down some notes. Later he writes up these notes and files them under various headings and ponders on some questions he might want to ask his friends tomorrow (Cottle 1978).

Elsewhere in a Midlands town a sociologist is getting to know the culture, language, ideas, attitudes and expectations of a group of 'lads' who constitute a school counter-culture. He discovers that the lads are 'learning to labour' (Willis 1977). Meanwhile another researcher is charting the day of a school principal (Wolcott 1973) and yet another researcher is observing children and teachers in an infant school (King 1978). All these people have one thing in common: they are all engaged in *ethnographic fieldwork*.

The terms 'fieldwork' and 'ethnography' are often used interchangeably in social research. However, fieldwork usually refers to the means by which the product, the ethnographic description of a group, organization, culture, or set of practices, comes into being. Such a bewildering array of activities have been conducted under the heading of ethnography that it makes it a little difficult to say exactly what ethnography is. Whereas it may be difficult to describe in anything other than general terms what comprises fieldwork and ethnography, it can safely be said that the use of these approaches was, in part, a response to dissatisfaction with positivistic, quantitative approaches and, in part, a result of modern anthropology's encounters with and attempts to understand others very different from ourselves. In general terms, fieldwork is the primary means by which most anthropological information has been obtained. It involves the prolonged, intensive and direct involvement of the researcher in the lives and activities of the group in question. Observation and participant observation became the key means by which this was achieved. As Malinowski, one of the first social scientists to use the technique of ethnography, has put it, the goal of ethnography 'is to grasp the native point of view, his relation to life, to realise his vision of his world' (Malinowski 1922: 25).

One of the difficulties in talking about 'ethnography' is that it is often used in conjunction with other terms, such as participant observation, qualitative methodology, case study and, to a certain extent, action research. As such it is difficult to define precisely, it is better instead to focus upon the kinds of features which are characteristics of ethnography. Perhaps one of the most striking features about ethnographic research is its utilization of a wide range of sources of data. From observation and interviewing to the use of documents and photographs, ethnographers are concerned as much with the ordinary, routine, mundane aspects of the life of a group or organization as they are with the extraordinary. It is therefore the aim of this chapter to provide teachers with the basic and general principles of fieldwork and ethnographic research in particular as these pertain to the teaching and learning context.

A working definition of ethnography may now therefore be attempted, though in broad terms only. It is possible to distil a summary of the characteristics of ethnography. Ethnography involves:

- The production of descriptive cultural knowledge of a group.
- The description of activities in relation to a particular cultural context from the point of view of the members of the group themselves.
- The production of a list of features constitutive of membership of a group or culture.
- The description and analysis of patterns of social interaction.
- The provision, as far as possible, of 'insider accounts'.
- The development of theory which is grounded in the data and the use of concepts in a sensitizing manner.

Ethnography is typically concerned with a single or a small number of cases or ranges of situations. Data are usually collected from quite a wide range of sources through participation, observation and documentation. As such, ethnography rests on two key assumptions. First, the principle of *naturalism* argues that human behaviour is best understood by exploring behaviour in natural, ordinary routine situations. It is this principle which distinguishes ethnography from experimental research design. Second, ethnography is about *understanding*, the researcher is therefore required to develop rapport, trust and empathy with the subjects of the research.

Thus, an ethnography in fact becomes the realisation of the fieldwork experiences and encounters, formalizing as it does the overt or covert involvement of the researcher in a particular setting and the information obtained, resulting in a written report or document, the 'ethnography'. Fieldwork and ethnography therefore are certainly fairly basic modes of research. Ethnography is about portraying people and we use the term here to refer jointly to a particular style of social research, accepting that there are important variations in this and to the products of that research. Originally ethnography and fieldwork were the key tools of the anthropologist studying a non-Western society, though these anthropological approaches were quickly seen to be of value in studying the ethnically diverse, complex industrial societies of Great Britain and North America. When anthropologists turned their attention towards educational experiences of ethnic minority groupings it was only natural that the tool of fieldwork, ethnography, the use of informants and cultural description were to become important in developing a distinct anthropology of education in North America. Yet the foundations for doing this were laid down some considerable time ago when Malinowski, complete with his tent, pioneered the fieldwork method in his study of the Trobriand islanders in the Pacific.

Clearly, ethnography as a broad qualitative research orientation has much to offer the teacher–researcher. Ethnography makes us pay attention to culture, to neighbourhood, to the backgrounds of children and staff, to class, status, ethnicity, and gender, to the minutiae of everyday interaction and to the particular contextual meanings and significance of events and activities of the school and classroom to members themselves. As such, educational ethnography incorporates a broadly humanistic approach to investigating the social world of the school. But what is it that ethnographers do?

WHAT DO ETHNOGRAPHERS DO WHEN THEY DO ETHNOGRAPHY?

Ethnographers look, listen, ask questions, take part, learn the language, learn and record any specialized use of language or argot, make inferences from what people say, locate informants, develop relationships, become friends and experience different ways of life. Typically, ethnographers will observe ceremonies, collect and trace family trees (genealogies), observe meetings, record daily events, watch children and adults play, keep diaries and write letters home and countless other things besides. In order to put this picture into sharper focus let us briefly consider Wolcott's (1973) description of his work in Ed Bell's school.

In developing his study of an American school administrator or principal

Wolcott developed a range of methods to facilitate his understanding of Ed Bell's work and which enabled data to be gathered on a number of aspects of the school. He outlined six sources of information which supplemented his direct observations. He collected routine distributions of notices, copies of school records, reports and correspondence. He took notes at 60-second intervals for blocks of two hours relating to the interactions and activities of the principal, he obtained impressions of school life from fifth- and sixth-grade pupils, used a tape recorder, and designed, distributed and analysed a staff questionnaire at the end of the school year (Wolcott 1973: 8–18). It is interesting to note that Chapter 2 of Wolcott's ethnography is entitled 'A day in the life' and provides a rich and detailed account of what a typical day in the life of a school principal is actually like. Clearly here, as in school-based research more generally, the researcher will act as the key instrument or funnel through which data are obtained in the research.

Ethnographers become involved in a range of activities and it is not always possible to specify in any detail beforehand what to consider. What the ethnographer does in the field is for the most part dictated by the nature of the composition of the group being studied. The above description conveys the process whereby the researcher attempts to immerse herself in the flow of happenings in the setting. An initial feeling experienced by the novice ethnographer is the desire always to be where the 'action' is. Once the 'action' ceases to be new, but instead becomes routine, ordinary and taken for granted, it has ceased to strange and the ethnographer is truly immersed in the culture and it is time to leave. As Whyte (1955) observed in his classic participant observation study of an American Boston Italian slum neighbourhood, he began as a participant observer and ended up as a non-observing participator (Whyte 1955).

Here we arrive at that special and unique point the teacher–researcher is placed in. Teachers, unless they look at other schools and classrooms, are usually already participants in the worlds they wish to describe and uncover by means of fieldwork and ethnography. Even when they do research in other schools they are considerably tuned in to the world of schools and classrooms. We will examine the implications of this observation shortly. Enough has been said, however, to give an initial flavour of what fieldwork and ethnography is all about in general terms. Let us now consider a breakdown of what might be involved in carrying out ethnography in educational settings.

STEPS, STAGES AND TASKS IN DOING FIELDWORK AND ETHNOGRAPHY IN EDUCATIONAL SETTINGS

It is important for the teacher–researcher to develop an appreciation of the skills, steps, stages and tasks involved in the conduct of ethnographic inquiry. Certain skills need to be spelled out and, from experience, certain things seem to be best done before others. It is helpful therefore to see the fieldwork and ethnographic process broken down into seven elements although there are often overlaps between these stages: see Figure 6.1.

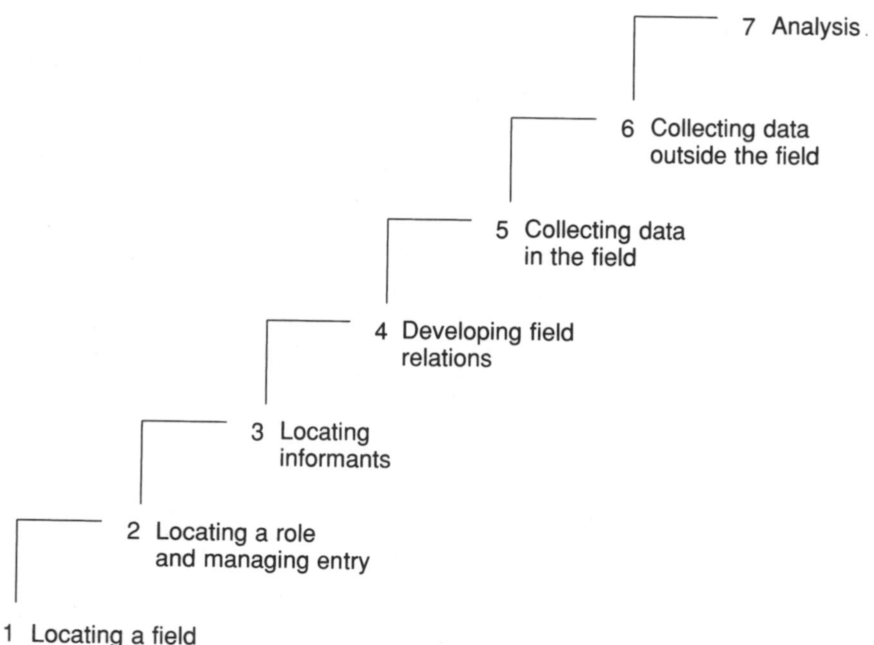

Figure 6.1 Steps and stages in doing fieldwork and ethnography in educational settings

Whilst Figure 6.1 suggests a series of stair-like steps in this process, it is important to realize the research can move backwards and forwards. Analysis, for example, is not one discrete stage in qualitative research, but can occur at a variety of stages in the research process.

Preliminaries

There are incredible strains in conducting any kind of fieldwork. For the most part these stem from the fact that the researcher is the main vehicle of the research. What the researcher sees, hears and becomes involved in constitutes much of the data in ethnographic research. It is clear to see, therefore, how the personal dimension of the fieldwork experience is of considerable significance. A number of writers have provided both sobering and amusing accounts of the fieldwork experience; some of the best of these are contained in Powdermaker (1966), Frielich (1970) and Wax and Wax

(1971). Fieldwork and ethnography, perhaps more than any other research techniques, involve the researcher in a direct and often fairly intense relationship with people and events. No matter how modified these approaches become in the hands of the teacher this personal dimension of the fieldwork equation needs some attention as an important preliminary issue. Emotions, values, attitudes and expectations will all play a part in any fieldwork situation. When the researcher is a familiar participant in the setting, as it is often likely to be the case with teachers, all of these issues can become compounded.

None of these problems or difficulties are insurmountable. For most situations the teacher is engaged in researching, what is required is the development of an attitude or a frame of mind for this kind of research. All in all, the personal skills which are conducive to successful completion of field research, as we shall see, turn out to be similar to those required for the achievement of normal successful social interaction, for example, appearing interested and friendly, sympathetic and willing to listen to others, refraining from appearing dogmatic and overbearing. However, this does not mean that teachers conducting research must hide their intentions or beliefs. The point is quite simple. The more the researcher's views, attitudes and opinions enter into the research situation, the less of the actors' perspectives and ideas will be revealed. These are all undoubtedly matters of degree, and resolution of these problems will depend upon the nature of the research and the setting in question. Locating a field becomes the first problem.

Locating a field

When researchers speak about the 'field' they are referring to the immediate physical and social boundaries surrounding their chosen research area. Obviously, a field in this sense can be quite extensive. It is important for the researcher to locate and delineate the boundaries of the particular field in question. The field for the teacher might be all those situations directly connected with teaching and learning in a particular school. The field will involve a range of activities and typical categories of persons and individuals. It is unlikely that the teacher–researcher is ever going to be able to cover all of the field she sees as being central to her project. It is important therefore to be able to see the field as a whole and to establish its boundaries and decide on what can and cannot be looked at in the project. Furthermore, by doing this the teacher can develop a fair idea of what data and information outside the immediate field might need to be collected. Although the field can be extended or narrowed as the research progresses so that new information can be incorporated, or fresh lines of thought developed, the location of a field in a general way will help the researcher to clarify reasonably well the nature of the issues to be covered and areas and people involved. A useful way of approaching this task is to try and represent the field by means of a diagram. This is the point at which important practical decisions about both the size and composition of the field itself will be made. Such an exercise should help the teacher to appreciate more clearly what the focus of the research is and, indeed, could become. This process will involve the teacher in identifying key persons, key topics and key sources of data. Once such an exercise has been completed the teacher will have a more realistic appreciation of what areas to concentrate on, how to do this and how this meets the initial aims of the project in question. The boundaries for the research will have at least been partially defined.

Locating a role and managing entry

In Part I we emphasized the importance of dealing in an honest fashion with questions of access and ethics. All social research is governed by questions of access to people, information and settings. Once access is obtained, actually entering the field and establishing a role for the researcher are two further central elements of ethnographic work. Whereas there are many differences between educational ethnographic research and ethnography in other settings there are many similarities.

The researcher cannot enter a scene unannounced and begin to conduct interviews. All researchers have to plan and prepare their work carefully; part of this preparation involves securing access and permission to enter the scene being investigated, if this is required, and once in the scene (1) establishing a reason for being there and (2) developing a role, a persona, so that people know who the researcher is, what the researcher is doing there and if necessary why! It follows that a fixed set of guidelines on these matters cannot easily be laid down since situations and circumstances will vary. Furthermore, the character of the researcher will vary also. The teacher embarking on fieldwork and ethnographic inquiry is subject to many of the same sorts of access, entry and role problems other fieldworkers face. But, as far as the teacher–researcher is concerned the differences depend to a great extent upon whether the researcher is doing fieldwork in her own classroom or her own school, or whether she is researching in another school or classrooms unknown or less familiar to her.

Although some of the difficulties fade away when the teacher is conducting fieldwork in her own setting, others are thereby created. Familiarity is simultaneously an advantage and a disadvantage. The teacher knows the school, the staff and children; she has a reputation and an ‘official’ role as, for example, a music teacher, top infants teacher, head of science, deputy head, or head. She has worked in the school perhaps for a number of years; she is established as someone with particular characteristics. The researcher already has an abundant store of important information about the school, its organization and the children inside her head. The problem, of course, is that the all-too-familiar setting is very often largely taken for granted. Hence the teacher engaged in ethnographic research in familiar settings has the problem of rendering the familiar strange in order to avoid missing or taking for granted crucial aspects of the situation or topic being explored. Whilst much ethnographic work is *overt*, that is visible, known about, and recognized as such by the subjects, for example when interviewing or clearly observing them, in contrast, some ethnographic work is done and data gathered by *covert* means, that is when the researcher is engaged or participating in the setting yet unknown to the other people involved in that setting, is observing, watching, listening to them and making a mental record of the actions and conversations that ensue. All of these matters will involve role adjustments and will involve a consideration of the ethics of covert participant observation operations. The teacher might have to step out of her role as a teacher in order to facilitate observation. Her involvement might have to increase or decrease in certain activities. All in all though there are considerable advantages where access, entry and the establishment of a role are concerned if the teacher is doing fieldwork in her own school. None the less it is always important to establish what it is the researcher is doing with the appropriate member of the school management and, where necessary, gain permission and more importantly, support, Walker's (1980) advice is worth considering:

> To gain access to the school, you need first to approach the Local Education Authority; to gain access to the staff, you need to approach the head; to gain access to the pupils, you need to approach the staff. Each fieldwork contact is thus sponsored by someone in authority over those you wish to study and relationships between 'sponsors' and researchers can not be broken if the research is to continue.
>
> (Walker 1980: 49)

The extent to which each of these things is necessary can be ascertained only by the teacher and common sense should prevail. What is certainly a lot more delicate is the actual process of entry and the development of a role with a group of teachers and pupils who are relatively unknown to the researcher. This situation is becoming increasingly common with school interchanges of staff, short courses involving teachers visiting other schools, and so on. A 'softly, softly' approach is usually the best line to take. Often, entry and the development of a role can be facilitated by the help of a key member of the school. Many ethnographers and participant observers have gained entry into a setting with the help of a key informant. The most famous example here is 'Doc' who was responsible for initiating W. F. Whyte into street-corner society so that Whyte could produce his classic account of an Italian–American slum neighbourhood (Whyte 1955). Hitchcock's (1980, 1983b) entry into the world of Cedars Junior, an urban open-plan primary school, was facilitated by Liz, a long-standing college friend who taught in the school and developed a role that was not unlike that of a student teacher on teaching practice. Another problem facing the teacher who is

not familiar with a particular school is the negotiation of gatekeepers. All organizations and institutions have gatekeepers whose function it is to vet personnel entering the buildings, making sure they see only what they are supposed to see.

We must not, however, forget that the issues surrounding access, entry and roles themselves cast important light on to the social organization of the setting itself and may in turn be regarded as an important source of data on the setting in question, as Burgess's (1984a) account of gaining access to Bishop McGregor School and its Newson department demonstrates (Burgess 1984a: 40–5).

Locating informants

The production of adequate ethnographic accounts has focused on the extent to which the ethnographer can offer a description of the features constitutive of membership in the group, culture, or institution being studied, with a description and analysis of what happens in that setting, the knowledge, abilities and ways of interacting characteristic of the group. This has been achieved by anthropologists and sociologists and, more recently, educational researchers, by the use of 'informants': people who were knowledgeable about their society, culture, or the activity in question. Hence, for a long time the idea that not just anybody will do as an informant was an accepted notion. Researchers were encouraged in the methods and techniques of handbooks to search and make use of what Back described many years ago as 'the well-informed informant' (Back 1955: 30–3), someone who knew the setting under investigation well and would be able to provide the ethnographers with the correct information needed. In many cases ethnographers have relied upon a few or even single 'key informants' in constructing their accounts. The ambiguous nature of what might constitute a culturally competent individual, and thereby someone who might be regarded as good key informant material, was initially not questioned. Eliciting accounts, narratives and other information from key informants is a hallmark of ethnographic research. One of the key issues here, identified more recently, is the extent to which the ethnographer or ethnography represents or reconstructs reality. How does the teacher–researcher identify which accounts are more important than others? The question of the location and selection of informants by teacher–researchers is best seen in terms, first, of the practical aspects, and finally, in terms of the distinction between adults and children as informants.

Researchers often speak about the two connected themes of informant reliability and response validity; these, in turn, surround the issues of the truth and accuracy of informants' accounts and the extent to which the accounts are not natural but derive from the nature of the research encounter itself and are thereby influenced by it. A distinction is sometimes further drawn between 'internal validity', that is the extent to which the researcher's presence and choice of informant affects the kinds of data and materials obtained by the fieldworker and the analyses developed can be applied to other school and classroom situations. However, ethnographers tend to be much less concerned with the generalizability of their findings than other researchers.

These technical issues often seem to suggest that there are solutions to the problems of informant selection provided one simply follows technical procedures. The practical and everyday reality of schools and classrooms poses special problems surrounding the selection and location of informants for teachers carrying out fieldwork and ethnography. For example, not everyone in the school will be seen by all members of the school to be valid, reliable and competent commentators and sources of information on the school itself. Political and status issues are likely to emerge here. For example, is 'competence' in these terms equitable with status, length of stay in school, seniority and the like? Teachers need to be wary of developing a too mechanistic view of the selection of informants. Whilst we are not suggesting that everybody's voice has equal influence or power, we are saying that it is important to recognize the existence of as many voices as possible. An important principle emerges here. Fieldworkers quickly discover, in contrast to the advice of technical manuals, that the field itself dictates and demonstrates the relative 'worth', 'significance', 'validity' and 'competence' of its various component voices. Teachers need to attend to this feature as a serious and crucial aspect of their research. Perhaps there is nothing to be done about the fact that the nature of the field and its organization dictates in a large measure whom the researcher can take as an informant. It is, none the less, an important comment on the nature of the setting itself which, in turn, may be treated as important data on that setting. Furthermore, the age, sex, status and possibly subject specialism of the teacher carrying out the research is clearly likely to influence her choice of and encounters with informants.

In much social research, especially sociology, subjects for the research are usually chosen by means of some form of 'random sampling' in order to ensure their representativeness and typicality. This is not the case in ethnography. The selection of informants in ethnography, unlike the subjects for a postal questionnaire, who for example, are chosen more by luck, is dictated by the nature of the field itself and many ethnographers of schools and classrooms like those working in other settings have relied upon key informants. Key informants are those people whom the researcher focuses upon as a key source of data on that setting. They are spoken to by the researcher more often than others in the setting. In more cases than not, the key informants used by the teacher–researcher in educational settings are often neither typical nor representative, but are people whom the researcher feels are integral to the scenes and situations being investigated. The teacher will frequently use informants who by their position, role, status, or gender are not representative of the scene as a whole. This does not mean that they are of no use as a source of data. The question of the selection and use of key informants is not so much one of their typicality and representativeness, but rather with placing what any informant says into the wider picture, which necessarily includes other perspectives, contextual description and the researcher's own observations. Furthermore, teachers in the course of conducting a particular piece of research will collect data and obtain information from a variety of sources, not simply key informants. Again, what is important is for the teacher to be clear on what informant selection strategies were employed and why. In other words, what was the basis upon which certain informants were chosen?

There are, however, a series of practical issues that the teacher needs to attend to concerning informants. These might be regarded as a checklist for the research design stages, as well as during the fieldwork itself:

- Has a range of viewpoints been covered by the informants used?
- Are different positions, roles, levels and status groupings being represented by the informants used?
- Has the informants' behaviour and talk been monitored by the researcher across a range of situations so that the importance of context can be established?
- Do the informants used have specialized subject or general subject/area knowledge, occupy central or marginal positions?
- Has the influence of the researcher's own age, sex, class, ethnicity and status been considered in (a) the informant selection procedure and (b) researcher–teacher, informant–teacher relationships?
- Since schools, like many other institutions, are frequently very hierarchical, has the selection of informants given due weight to the existence of unequal voices?

Teachers will need to recognize the essentially practical and *ad hoc* nature of the use of informants, with the broader analytic and technical consequences of whom they gain much of their information from. Can informants be friends? Can you ask ethnographic questions of those whom you teach? The use of the term 'informant' itself is perhaps too simplistic and mechanical to convey the real nature of the involvement between a teacher and a fellow colleague known for some time. After all the technical and scientific talk in the world it is still easier to get on with some people than others. On the other hand, some informants may not give the fieldworker information for fear of boring them with the commonplace. These are all eminently practical matters: their resolution hinges to a large extent upon the fieldworker's own interpersonal relationships and the question of informants then blurs considerably with issues of field relations more generally which we consider next. However, the question of children or pupils constituting key informants raises important questions that we might briefly discuss first.

Children as informants

We consider some of the questions surrounding pupils' accounts in Chapter 10 when we examine the classroom as a social environment and focus upon classroom talk and interaction. The idea of children as informants raises methodological issues as well as moral and ethical ones. On the surface there is really no problem in using children as informants provided all the usual reasonable precautions one would take with other informants are taken. The whole issue would seem to surround taking children seriously. In many ways the use of pupils as key informants is simply a further extension of portraying the actor's perspective and, as such, any study which did not pay reference to children's views and interactions of pupils' perspectives could found to be lacking.

A number of researchers are now focusing upon pupils' viewpoints or 'pupil strategies' (Woods 1980b). Pollard (1987: 95–118), for example, discusses some of the processes involved in trying to collect information on middle-school childrens' perspectives, whereas Benyon (1984: 121–44) shows how a focus upon pupils as 'data gatherers' enabled Benyon to see how, when starting secondary school, boys' endeavours in 'sussing out' the teacher were a crucial aspect of their school experience. These strategies allowed the children to 'locate' the teacher, develop expectations and maintain their own peer-group organization.

Using children and pupils as informants raises a number of problems. Despite the obvious differences in status, sensitive ethnographers have been able to develop good ethnographic descriptions of child culture and life in school. The prospective researcher might consider the ways in which the following researchers have resolved some of these problems and the kinds of data and analyses they have been able to produce: Ball (1985); Corsaro (1981: 117–46); Davies (1982); Schostak (1982: 175–85); and Waksler (1986: 71–82).

Developing field relations

Once the fieldworker has located the field, managed entry and located key informants the process of developing field relationships becomes crucial to the successful completion of the study. The development of good field relations becomes all the more important if doing fieldwork in someone else's classroom or school, or with a group previously unknown to the researcher. She must build up some degree of confidence, trust and rapport with the subjects. Indeed, one classic textbook on the topic describes participant observation and ethnographic techniques as consisting of 'lore on establishing and maintaining good relationships in the field' (McCall and Simmons 1968: 28).

It is always worth remembering that people do not have to accept you, co-operate with you, or help you. Discretion, sensitivity and common sense are therefore paramount here. Schools, like most other organizations, thrive on gossip, hearsay, innuendo and so on. The researcher will need to cut a path through this, recognizing its importance and being sensitive towards the implications and consequences. Writing down what someone says in an notebook in front of them might on some occasions be perceived as an invasion of privacy, or overly formal, whereas on others it may not be seen as out of place. We will discuss writing field notes later but it is important to bear in mind that how the researcher conducts herself in the field, including how and where she writes field notes, will certainly influence researcher–staff relations and consequently the nature of the data collected. Some ethnographers have, as an attempt to get around this problem, moved to a secluded or private place, such as a cloakroom, simply to jot down broad headings and verbatim comments, to be 'written up' later after leaving the field.

Perhaps the most difficult area for the teacher–researcher to deal with when conducting fieldwork and doing ethnography is her own feelings, emotions and attitudes. Teachers often hold strong views; the researcher herself is likely to have very definite ones. Some of these views have generated the desire to conduct the research in the first place. However, the teacher–researcher must never lose sight of the ultimate goal of her endeavours: the description, elaboration and analysis of the actor's perspective. Undoubtedly, the teacher will be confronted with perspectives and opinions that are diametrically opposed to her own and if certain people are not going to be alienated from the research a way of handling those interactions will have to be developed.

Many of these problems are considerably reduced when the teacher is conducting fieldwork in familiar settings. First and perhaps most importantly, the teacher has a good commonsense knowledge of the interpersonal relationships of the staff in the school; allegiances, friendships and major lines of disagreement are known to the teacher as researcher by virtue of her own practical involvement in the setting. Here, the teacher–researcher must trade on this 'insider knowledge'. In this sense teaching and ethnography have much in common, for teachers themselves have continually to make sense of, interpret and describe the settings in which they find themselves. They are themselves also participating and observing in the course of their routine work. All of this gives the teacher–researcher conducting fieldwork in familiar settings many advantages. However, the problem of the familiar is that it can all too often become taken for granted. Even in familiar settings the fieldworker has continually to be open to everything going on around her. This is how one fieldworker summarized the character and development of field relations in the course of carrying out fieldwork in an urban open-plan primary school in northern England:

The characteristic features of the fieldworker's relationships with staff in Cedars Junior may be summarized in the following manner:

1 The relationships tended to emerge over a period of time.
2 The relationships were to a large extent the product of contextual or situational features.
3 The relationships began by being reasonably fluid and became more stable.
4 Relationships *can* and *do* change.

(Hitchcock 1980: 100)

The development of good field relations is an integral feature of the processes of fieldwork and ethnography. The ways in which the teacher will deal with these issues depends on the field itself, the nature of the research and the characteristics of the researcher.

COLLECTING DATA IN THE FIELD

Researchers often combine various ways of collecting data in ethnography. Fieldwork in educational contexts provides the opportunity for the teacher to collect data in quite a variety of ways. In the remaining chapters in Part II of the book we try to unravel in more detail some of these techniques. The teacher can become involved in collecting different kinds of data in different ways. Combinations of data sources and techniques of collecting data are a feature of many educational ethnographies. Amongst the major sources of data and means of collecting data in ethnography we find participant observation and non-participant observation, making field notes and keeping a field journal or diary, unstructured interviewing and conversations, documentary sources and collecting life histories, collecting evidence of specialized language use or argot, making inventories, drawing maps, plans and diagrams, the use of still photography and video cameras. In the remaining chapters of this part of the book we will concentrate upon interviewing, collecting and using documentary materials and focus upon classroom interaction as important aspects of school-based teacher research. In this section we will confine our comments on data collection in the field to the process of making and using field notes, keeping a field journal or diary, collecting argot, making inventories and still photography.

Field notes

Field notes may be regarded as the basic raw data from which the researcher fashions or moulds the ethnography. In many cases the ethnographer's journal, diary or field notes hardly ever see the light of day in their original state in the finished report. Selections of verbatim transcripts or conversation, anecdotes recounted in the field, or sections from diaries by way of illustration are the usual ways in which these 'raw' materials find their way into the 'polished' finished report.

The teacher making notes is engaged in an important exercise for she is not simply recording events and producing data, but is also engaged in the first stages of preliminary analysis from which ideas and lines of inquiry can develop. Whereas note-taking is a very basic activity, it is none the less an important one. It is vital that the teacher–researcher develops a careful and systematic approach to note-taking. Note-taking, writing up and organizing field notes are quite exciting if painstaking and time-consuming activities.

Notes should be taken by the teacher from the very beginning of the research project. It must be remembered that the notes and records of observations have been lifted from a particular context and are only a partial record. In order to try and get round this the teacher can endeavour to provide some background information on the context of the sequences described in the field notes. More often than not these field notes will be supplemented by other data collected by the teacher. Given the importance of field notes it is preferable that the teacher endeavours to set a particular time aside after a day in the school or classroom in order to write up the field notes. Whilst there are certainly different types of field notes we describe a typical pattern the teacher–researcher might follow.

First, in the school or classroom itself, shorthand, quickly scribbled temporary notes, or jottings concerning the events and activities observed are written down by the teacher in the field at a suitable time and place. Abbreviations or personalized systems of referring to individual staff, pupils, or activities are likely to be generated. Key words or key phrases are frequently jotted down; short quotes are remembered and noted as accurately as possible. In a busy school or classroom situation these are likely to be very rough and probably intelligible only to the researcher.

Second, the rough and often indecipherable initial notes taken by the teacher in the field will have to be translated into something more easily readable and much more permanent since these records are going to be read and re-read at a later date. These temporary notes can act as memory jerkers for the creation of longer, more permanent notes. In the production of this set of more detailed elaborate and permanent field notes certain basic procedures need to be followed:

- Write on one side of the page only, normally of A4-size paper.
- Number each page of the permanent notes consecutively.
- Start a new page for each new day of the research.
- The notes must be prefaced by the date, location, or context of the observations and brief biographical information on the main informants referred to (these need only be written once).
- It is usually preferable to write any verbatim quotations in a different colour pen if in long hand, or underlined so as they stand out from the main body of the notes if typed.

- Finally, it is absolutely *essential* that at least one copy of the original permanent notes is made in order both to guard against loss or damage and to make the process of analysis and writing up easier. The length and detail of these permanent notes will be dependent upon the nature and context of the research. However, the most typical experience is for the researcher to write long and detailed notes at the start of the research while everything is fresh and new, and for these notes slowly to shrink towards the end of the fieldwork or period of observation.

Third, in ethnographic fieldwork the process of initial analysis, classification and organization of the data very often takes place while the researcher is still involved in the field. When writing up and organizing the permanent field notes the teacher will quickly develop her own observations and ideas or hunches. This marks the beginning of the process of analysis. The teacher can use a margin to add any comments, questions or ideas, or if these are likely to be much longer than a couple of sentences, the reverse side of the paper to which these comments refer may be used. Once well into the fieldwork or periods of observation this is the point at which themes, patterns or recurring features may be noted. This is also the point at which the teacher can assess the amount of material collected on a particular topic and whether some activities are described in more detail than others, or, indeed, if there are any gaps of major significance.

Fourth, as a result of the first three processes it is possible for the teacher to consider whether any specialized field notes on particular themes, topics, or substantive areas will need to be made in addition to the general field notes contained in the permanent record. Here, the teacher may wish to construct a checklist or an *aide-mémoire* on the particular topic or area to be looked at in detail in order to focus attention more sharply.

Finally, sorting, categorizing and coding of data are essential aspects of the analytical processes involved in qualitative ethnographic research. Once the fieldwork or observation period is completed the teacher may begin these central and crucial tasks. We discuss this process in detail in Part III.

These are the major stages of field note collection and preparation. It is important that the teacher takes these issues seriously since for most purposes the field notes will form the major basis for many school-based research projects. The teacher needs therefore to be systematic and methodical in all aspects of producing field notes.

The completed field notes of a particular piece of educational research will provide the teacher with a general chronological story, narrative, or picture of the events being considered. The important time dimension provided by the chronological character of the record allows the researcher to appreciate the order in which materials were collected and observations made. This can, of course, be very important if, for example, the teacher is observing and monitoring a child's educational career through a period of time. The researcher also needs to spend some time thinking and responding to the actual circumstances of note-taking itself. The overt or covert nature of making the initial temporary notes is a matter for the discretion of the teacher and the nature of the circumstances encountered. It is usually possible to make brief scribbled notes in a fairly unobtrusive fashion. But the teacher needs to take care and let common sense prevail on this issue.

In general the teacher has to provide descriptions of ordinary as well as extraordinary events. Informants' words should be recorded as accurately as possible with no emendation or alteration by the researcher. The teacher can focus upon a particular unit of observation, for example a staff meeting, a lesson, or other activity and produce fairly detailed notes on this or detailed portraits of individual staff or children can be constructed from the field notes involving those individuals. The possibilities of making field notes and the uses to which they can be put are great.

The field journal or diary

If the teacher has the time it is well worth considering keeping a separate field journal or diary, especially if the research is going to be carried out over a number of months. The natures of these journals or diaries vary greatly and many famous social scientists have kept their own private intimate diaries; some researchers have even written letters from the field. The personal and private nature of these field journals or diaries needs to be distinguished from the professional nature of the field notes. The value of keeping a journal or diary is as much emotional as it is technical or analytical. Indeed, the diary has been the basis for many of the recent more confessional tales of fieldwork experience. The journal or diary allows the researcher to let off steam, to complain, or to moan. They enable some of the pressures which are inevitably placed upon the researcher in such work to be taken off. But the significance of keeping a journal or diary is not only the emotional security it may afford but also for the researcher to reflect on the research, to step back and look again at the scenes in order to generate new ideas and theoretical directions. The fieldwork journal or diary is the place where the researcher, in conversation with herself, can record hopes, fears, confusion and enlightenment. It is the place where the personal side of the fieldwork equation can be recorded. These kinds of journals or diaries need to be distinguished from other kinds of field notes.

Inventories

When anthropologists first encounter an alien group whom they intend to live with and observe, one of the standard tasks they carry out is the production of cultural inventories, that is a listing of the various aspects or domains of culture, and the categories of person, activity and artefacts found within that culture. These kinds of inventories add depth to cultural descriptions and may be used by the teacher–researcher in the course of an ethnographic study. If, for example, the classroom is the main unit of analysis the layout, objects, furniture, as well as the group of children can be listed and noted. The photographing of schools and classrooms can also be used to help construct an inventory and aid description of a particular school or classroom. The role of visual images is discussed later.

Layouts, maps, plans, diagrams

A further way of both collecting and presenting data is for the teacher to make use of any official plans of the school building that she has access to, or to construct her own. Since school layout and the arrangement of furniture and seating are indeed important interactional features of teaching and learning, the teacher can construct classroom plans, or maps and diagrams of particular areas. When the teacher–researcher is concerned to discover aspects of the spatial organization of schools or classrooms these plans can offer an important visual representation of the themes the teacher is exploring. Indeed, a number of researchers have made extensive use of these sorts of maps or plans in educational research. We discuss this area in more detail in Chapter 11 when exploring the spatial dimensions of schools and classrooms.

Argot

Social scientists often note that in most organizations and institutions a distinction exists between the formal or official rules and goals of the organizations and the informal and unofficial rules of the organization. As well as the official language of an organization there will exist an informal specialized language, a slang, shorthand vocabulary, or argot used by the members themselves. Schools and classrooms are no exception here. The existence and importance of the use of a specialized language has been demonstrated by many ethnographers and sociologists carrying out research in workplaces, including factories, schools and hospitals, and amongst numerous deviant and criminal groups. It is essential to develop a working knowledge of the language and specialized terms employed by members in the field. An initial task for the teacher here would be to sift the field notes or even produce from the field notes a glossary of the specialized terms or argot employed by either teachers or pupils. However, this is just a first stage. Learning the argot is not the same as knowing and being able to use it in socially and interactionally approved and defined ways in the setting under investigation. The specialized argot is best seen in terms of the staff's perceived likely outcomes of involvement with the children concerned.

In many ways the talk of teachers and pupils and their utilization of specialized language conveys the ethos and climate of the culture of the school. This is therefore a rich source of imagery on all sorts of aspects of school and classroom life. Many researchers have paid attention to the specialized language or argot used and developed by the pupils themselves in a focus upon 'pupil culture'. For example, Willis (1977) tried to capture the attitudes of the lads in his study of a school counter-culture by using as far as possible their own words, whereas Measor and Woods (1983: 57–76) and Woods (1980b) both pay special attention to pupils' own views as expressed in their talk and specialized terms. In attempting to understand the meanings and interpretations of teachers and pupils, the researcher has a number of techniques at her disposal and a focus upon and analysis of argot in schools and classrooms offers a rich potential.

Still photography

Anthropologists and sociologists have made use of photographs and photography in their research for a long time. Photographs provide an extra source of data and new and fresh angles on the settings being researched. Photography may be seen as a perfectly natural extension of qualitative research since photographs can provide a rich source of descriptive data on a setting providing a sense of the location and the environment. However, those who have made use of photographs do this within the broader context of supporting ethnographically derived data. Photography as a tool in educational research does present an exciting potential and we look at the use and analysis of these materials in more detail in Chapter 12. Photographs fall into two categories: those photographs already in existence and those that are specifically taken by the teacher.

First, the teacher–researcher might come across old photographs of the school and school-related activities that might be of value to the research. If, for example, the research has a documentary or historical focus photographs will almost certainly be of significance. School-solicited photographs – photographs of the school released to the press and local groups – often present the image of the school which its members might seek to promote. Other photographs might be found in libraries, newspapers or magazines. Photographs of major school events and class portraits can be used to identify people and changes. Photographs can in this sense be used as documentary evidence. However, the teacher must always ask who took the photograph, for what purpose and what audience was it intended for? These are the kinds of questions that must be asked of any documentary source as we pointed out in Chapter 5 when we discussed documentary sources in detail. Used with caution and supplemented by other sources of data the teacher can, depending upon the focus of the research, make creative use of these kinds of photographs.

The use of photographs collected by the researcher, as with any other document, raises the question of ownership. Copyright law is extremely complex and contentious. However, there are two main ways in which the researcher can approach this. Humphries (1984: 39–40) distinguishes between 'formal agreements' and 'informal agreements'. A formal agreement will contain a written statement concerning the rights and responsibilities of both parties regarding the materials involved. Informal agreements on the other hand, are based upon the understandings which have been negotiated between the researcher and subjects. We discussed the ethical issues and confidentiality in Part I. Here we have pointed to some practical implications of using photographs and other documents.

Second, the teacher can take her own photographs of the school, classroom, playground, or related activities. These photographs will be taken for particular purposes; for example, they may be used in the consideration of the use of space, classroom organization patterns, or the influence of school design. The presence of a camera, like a tape recorder, may influence people's reactions and it is best to try and avoid 'staged' photographs, aiming instead for as much of a natural pose as possible. One of the ways around the problem of many people's reluctance to be photographed is to get them to take the photograph. The teacher can ask another teacher to take photographs of, say, classroom activities, or indeed anything that the teacher finds significant; this has the advantage of offsetting any potential researcher bias in taking the photographs.

Film

Photography is a readily available means of recording aspects of social reality. In Chapter 12 we will explore in more detail some of the technical and analytical issues involved in working with photographs in ethnographic research on schools and classrooms. The use of film and video recording techniques present an altogether different proposition. There is, of course, a long tradition of documentary film making, yet the relationship of film and the visual image to disciplines of words is problematic. The discipline most closely associated with the use of film as a source of data and as an alternative way of representing a social reality to the written word is anthropology. It is the concerns of the anthropologist which come closest in many ways to the interests of ethnographers and qualitative researchers. The advances made in technology now mean that very sophisticated ways of documenting social life can be achieved, and certainly offer the researcher wonderful opportunities for recording information on life in school and classroom and related contexts. Yet not all would-be researchers are in a position to take advantage of this approach. There are at least five sets of issues to consider here:

1 *Basic technical issues.* A basic mastery of handling equipment in terms of camera operation, lighting control, sound recording, editing and cutting is necessary. Most qualitative researchers will probably want to work with a system which is halfway between professional and domestic quality.
2 *Methodological issues.* Similar to those we will discuss with regard to the use of photography which need to be confronted. For example, subject topic, camera angles and perception, as well as focus. The camera does not have

a life of its own, it is wielded by someone. What we see is filtered through our background experiences. Filming is a highly reactive process, the researcher needs to bear in mind the impact of this on the possibility of performing for the camera.

3 *Ethical issues*. As elsewhere in the research process, and as we have highlighted in Chapter 3, these will have to be dealt with particularly regarding ownership, consent and editorial control.
4 *Theoretical issues*. Involve, more formally, the researcher's underlying perspective, or frame of reference. Since qualitative research traditions operate within a post-positivistic framework it could be argued that the significance of theoretical issues might be the same for all researchers. But this is not the case. Throughout the book we stress the diversity of qualitative research traditions. The impact of movements such as feminism and post-modernism has meant that there are differing theoretical concerns amongst qualitative researchers. This is likely to be further highlighted in the application of qualitative techniques to applied fields, such as the study of education of institutions and processes. In particular, one issue to be dealt with here would be the relationship of the researcher's ethnographic account of the film itself.
5 *Analytical issues*. Concern what the researcher, and to a certain extent the viewer, will make of the film, i.e. reading what the film is saying. Where as the photograph freezes a piece of action in time, film is a moving record of events. In one sense the ethnographic film portrays the analysis by focusing upon some scenes and not on others, by sharpening one image in the foreground and leaving other images in the background. These are all very complex questions which we can only put on the agenda in a simple fashion.

Undoubtedly, film offers the qualitative researcher some wonderful opportunities. There is great scope and potential for the use of film and video in teacher research, but we must be cautious. For those interested in these techniques it is well worth considering what has been achieved in the field of 'visual anthropology' and the genre described as the 'ethnographic film'. This was highlighted by the excellent Granada Television series 'Disappearing Worlds', a set of remarkable films produced in close collaboration with anthropologists. Since 1970, Granada Television has produced over 60 documentaries in this vein. An emerging literature now exists on this field, Ball and Smith (1992) although concerned primarily with still photography, make some passing comments on ethnographic film, whereas Barnouw (1983) charts the history of what is described as the non-fiction film. Other important sources worth consulting are Crawford and Turton (1992) and Loizos (1993), and some important technical and directional questions are dealt with by Rabinger (1992). The researcher is likely to find guidelines coming from the discipline of anthropology, since to date it has been anthropologists who have taken the lead. It would be encouraging to see more teacher and educational researchers becoming involved with the visual image if for no other reason than our field of study is itself so rich, dynamic and, indeed, fast-moving. Playground culture, play, teacher–pupil interaction, the use of space and place all instantly spring to mind as possible topics.

COLLECTING DATA OUTSIDE THE FIELD

It may seem odd at this point to suggest that the teacher might want to collect even more data. One of the characteristic features of qualitative research and ethnographic fieldwork in particular is that amounts of rich, highly descriptive data can quickly be amassed. Indeed, one of the problems the teacher will have to face is knowing when to stop! A range of data from outside the school or classroom can be collected and referred to in the course of the research project. Instantly, government and particularly DES statistics come to mind, but official reports such as, for example, those of Warnock (1978) or Swann (1985), as well as examination board reports, are all important potential sources of data. Most of these sources are readily available in libraries, but some schools now hold copies of major reports.

On other occasions data from agencies outside the school will have to be consulted by the teacher. These agencies themselves will present the teacher with an important source of data. Certainly, it is difficult to imagine how the teacher engaged in researching aspects of teaching and learning where ethnicity is a crucial variable cannot become involved in outside school activities, especially in neighbourhood, community and family contexts. The teacher may, indeed, find herself with two quite distinct types of field in which she has to become involved in order to uncover aspects of a single problem or issue. Obviously, if the teacher finds it necessary to become involved with members of an ethnic community and the parents of, for example, Afro-Caribbean or Asian children, then locating a role and managing entry, locating informants, developing relationships and collecting data in this new field will become very different from the ways in which these steps and stages have been handled inside the classroom. In some cases when collecting data outside the field the researcher may have only brief formal encounters with people or officials. In these cases the emphasis given to the data derived from these encounters must be set against their fleeting or brief character. It is virtually inevitable that the researcher is likely to go beyond the immediate field at some point or other in search of data. This must be recognized and the issues unravelled.

ANALYSIS

Analysis may be described as an attempt to organize, account for and provide explanations of data so that some kind of sense may be made of them. The researcher moves from a description of what *is* the case to an explanation of *why* that is the case. This is usually perceived to be one of the most daunting aspects of research, but as we have pointed out the teacher has already been engaged in initial forms of analysis while collecting data in the field. For example, the teacher has reviewed her field notes in the process of rewriting the temporary field notes into permanent ones and will have begun to see themes and patterns emerging. This process can also suggest new lines of inquiry for the researcher. Up until this point, however, these activities have been largely informal or piecemeal, and usually conducted on an *ad hoc* basis.

Once the teacher has completed the fieldwork, conducted all the interviews or observations and generally has the data required, the formidable task of sorting and organizing begins. 'Data analysis' and 'writing up' the research therefore refer to the process whereby this mass of data, in whatever shape, is scrutinized, coded, or sorted, so that the teacher's own appreciation and understanding of the problem investigated may be furthered and this type of analysis may be conveyed to other professionals. The point of analysis for researchers using a qualitative approach is not so much with testing a preformulated theory or hypothesis, but rather with generating ideas from the data. All we wish to do at this point is to provide a basic knowledge of the ways in which analysis might be approached by the teacher–researcher, this is elaborated further in Chapter 12.

An important distinction needs to be borne in mind by the teacher when thinking about analysis. There is a difference between analysis that is done in the field and analysis that is done after the fieldwork is completed. This is sometimes referred to as informal and formal analysis. The teacher has already done a lot of analysis in the field itself. Once the fieldwork is completed and all the data have been collected more formal kinds of analyses can begin.

The initial task of analysis in qualitative ethnographic research is the organization, sorting and coding of the data, with the development of some kind of system for the retrieval of information on particular topics from the mass of data. Here, the key words for the researcher are patience and care, for time spent at this point will certainly help to develop analytical skills. The initial operation is not unlike that which the researcher has perhaps already been doing in the field, that is reading through the notes and materials in order to see what features and issues consistently crop up, what topics appear more than others and discovering what the researcher has little data on. The process will reveal certain themes, patterns and categories of events and activities. In order to give an idea of what this process involves we can examine the way in which this kind of analysis developed in the ethnographic study of one school.

In the course of an ethnographic study of an inner city open-plan primary school the researcher has collected over 300 pages of A4-sized field notes (Hitchcock 1980). During the initial stages of the analysis of these materials the researcher was able to isolate a series of key topics and units of meaning which tended to feature regularly in the field notes. These were extracted, sorted and indexed in the following way:

- Richard and Geoffrey.
- Problem children.
- Explanations of failure.
- Dealing with trouble.
- Attitudes to parents.
- Categorizing kids.
- Clubnight.
- School holidays.
- Staff relations.
- Attitudes to open plan.
- Using space.
- Building boundaries.
- Parental involvement.
- Relationship between school and outside agencies.
- Socializing the researcher.

These general headings or categories can be written on to the top of a postcard and should include reference to the page number of the field notes on which reference to these topics appears. From the original general categories, the teacher needs to move towards unravelling families of activities, or a series of codes under which groupings of categories can be placed. Using the same set of field notes as above this procedure would result in the following:

- Teacher's definition of the situation code:
  attitudes to children
  attitudes to parents
  attitude to open plan
  relationship with other staff
- Relationships code:
  staff–researcher interactions
  head–staff interactions
  Mrs Smith and the staff
  relationship between infant and junior staff
  parent–parent relationships
  parent–teacher relationships
  school–outside agency relationships
  the local social worker
  the educational psychologist
- Activity code:
  coffee-time
  staff meeting
  dinner-time
  wet playtimes
  clubnight
  sports day
  the school holidays

- Special event codes:
  selection of the children for the holiday
  dealing with Richard and Geoffrey
  stealing on school trips
  involvement of parents
- Physical context code:
  home-base
  enclosed home-base
  Fletcher maths area
  wet areas
  furniture arrangement
  plan of school
  plan of home-bases
  staffroom
  plan of staffroom
  foyer
  playground layout
- Social and organizational processes code:
  dealing with the researcher
  friends and enemies
  dealing with space
  roles and allegiances
  dealing with trouble.

Although these codes are not exhaustive they cover quite a lot of the materials contained in the field notes. The codes refer to basic aspects of social life in the school. 'Teacher's definition' codes refer to the attitudes, values and expectations held by teachers in Cedar Junior towards the issues and events that confront them. 'Relationships code' refers to the more formal sets of social relationships, lines of communication and interaction patterns in the school and between the school and outside agencies. 'Activity code' focuses upon the kinds of routine, mundane, everyday occurrences in school, whereas the 'special events code' highlights the extraordinary events that promoted discussion and debate. 'Physical context code' encompasses the physical architectural aspect of the school, furniture, objects and artefacts and the way these are used by teachers and pupils. Finally, the 'Social and organizational processes code' brings together many of the more informal aspects of the relationships code. Here, informal patterns of communication, friendship networks, social roles and teachers' and pupils' responses to issues, such as the nature of the school, trouble, disruption and so on, could be included. Some researchers would extract certain topics from these main codes and cut out the relevant sections referring to these areas in their field notes and other materials and place them in individual files.

Given the large amounts of material usually generated by ethnographic fieldwork it would be impracticable and time consuming to have to sift through all the field notes and materials to get at one example. Here, the researcher will need to construct some kind of index of the materials collected and ideas and concepts generated in the course of the research. Indexing can be as simple or as complex as one likes. What needs to be remembered is that the production of an index is not the goal. The index is simply a means to an end, a way of enabling the researcher to retrieve and find data, references, or materials quickly. It is possible to produce more than one index depending upon the nature and size of the materials and the focus of the research. Lofland (1971: 118) has spoken about the use of 'mundane' indexes which simply include, for example, names of people, teachers, pupils, everyday events in school, or locations, referring to the page number which contains mention of them in the notes, and to 'analytical' indexes which are used to group together references on particular topics or issues in the field notes. The advent of computer technology has, of course, made this whole process infinitely more sophisticated (see, for example, *The Ethnograph* (Seidel and Clark 1984: 110–25)). In the end, the aim of analysis is to move from accounts of what people do and say as descriptions of their worlds, to explanations of how and why they do what they do and say what they say.

SOME CURRENT DEBATES AND CONTROVERSIES

Up to this point we have taken a fairly straightforward look at ethnography and fieldwork as fundamental mainstays in qualitative research. We have explored the ways in which ethnographic approaches, in general, can help us to understand the world of teaching and learning. Whereas, on the one hand, it is possible to talk about ethnography in an unproblematic, how to do it 'tools and techniques' fashion, on the other hand, it is clear that ethnography as a research technique has received considerable criticism and its protagonists have responded. Ethnography has come a long way since Malinowski peered out from the door of his tent. The ethnography of schools and classrooms has undergone a number of changes. In this concluding section we wish to briefly explore some current debates and controversies surrounding ethnography which have both general and particular significance for teacher research.

It seems to us that the last ten years have seen the emergence of a number of issues surrounding the nature of qualitative inquiry in the human sciences and the practice, purpose and presentation of ethnographic modes of research. First, and most obviously, ethnographers and the practice of ethnography have become altogether more reflexive, self-conscious and open. Second, with the increasing amount of ethnographic inquiries, particularly in applied contexts, has come a greater questioning of the quality of ethnographic descriptions offered and the analyses made. Third, this has, subsequently, developed into a full-scale reconsideration of the kind of criteria used to judge ethnographic research. Fourth, the critique of ethnography from a postmodernist viewpoint, including feminist and ethnic research models, raises questions of both textuality and representation in ethnography. The increasing use of ethnography in applied settings such as health and education, with practitioner research poses fundamental questions about the positioning of such research in terms of funding agents, research participants and outcomes, highlighting, fifth, ethical issues in ethnographic research.

These are certainly complex matters, yet they relate to the current practices of qualitative social and educational research. It is not possible to talk about or consider social and educational research in a vacuum. Neither is it good to attempt to do so. The kinds of developments leading to the debates and controversies we have highlighted above are certainly not new, yet characteristically are left out of research texts which all too frequently present sanitized unproblematic versions of research. Indeed, the impact of the debate over the significance of postmodernist thinking for the human sciences may have been eclipsed by the fact that we might be in the post, postmodernist period. For some this seems to have occurred without first appreciating the impact of either postmodernism or feminism or both, for carrying out social and educational research. In the short space left we will briefly unravel the nature of these debates and controversies. However, some of these concerns were raised in Chapter 4 when we looked at gender and are also raised in Chapter 14 on writing up.

Ethnography, reflective and reflexive

We have been guilty of painting a picture of ethnography as being rather unproblematic. Our 'steps and stages' view of ethnography, for example, suggests an unproblematic series of stepping stones. Indeed, for some time sociological and anthropological ethnographies were largely formulaic, containing unquestioned representations of standard fieldwork practices. With the advent of more open, confessional accounts of what actually happened in the field, the conventional ethnographic format showed itself to be exactly that, a convention and a constructional device which masked the realities of the fieldwork experience. Reflective ethnography sees fieldwork less as a technical mastery of a range of skills, and more as a practical activity, including the construction and reconstruction of social realities, both jointly and individually in the course of fieldwork. This emphasis upon reflection became a preoccupation of many ethnographers working in the field of education: Burgess (1980), Burgess (1984a,b), Hammersley (1983), Hitchcock (1983a,b) and Lacey (1976). The move from a focus upon reflection on the ethnographic fieldwork process, to a realization of the internal reflexivity of these accounts, in terms of recognizing the effects and impacts of both the research and the research strategy on the findings, came later. Influenced by qualitative sociologists, most notably ethnomethodologists, with feminist and ethnic models, a reflexive appreciation of ethnographic realities takes on board the fundamental role of the researcher in the construction and reconstruction of the professional ethnographic monograph. Reflexive ethnography will pose the question, 'To what extent does ethnography represent or construct a social reality?' There is now much greater understanding of this aspect of research in the practice of ethnography and the consequences of this are increasingly being felt in educational research, most notably in the area of gender and schooling, biographical and life history approaches.

The quality of ethnographic descriptions

It is true to say that the last ten years or so has seen greater methodological sophistication and increased theoretical sensitivity on the part of ethnographers working in education and related areas. In particular, educational research journals show the emergence of critiques, and counter-critiques, replies and responses whereby published work was scrutinized in terms of its general validity, reliability and representativeness. There was an undercurrent of feeling that somehow ethnographers had been 'getting away with it' and that their findings were frequently not supported by the evidence presented, or that there were significant problems surrounding the validity or reliability of a study. In addition, it was not often clear what role theory had played, was playing or could play in ethnographic research. Here it is useful to remind ourselves of the kinds of points we made in Chapter 5 about assessing and evaluating a particular study. For many it seemed the case that some ethnographers were not attending to the normal criteria of scientific adequacy in their work. This of course begs the question about the nature of the criteria being applied to the work. There are certainly problems with applying the same kind of evaluative criteria for both qualitative research and quantitative research. We will unravel the distinction between positivistic and post-positivist criteria below. A good example of a protracted debate over the adequacy of an ethnographic study can be found in the interchanges between Foster (1990), Wright (1990) and Foster (1991). These interchanges are indicative of an increasing tendency to question ethnographic findings and the explanations offered, and in Hammersley's (1992) terms to ask, 'What is wrong with ethnography?'

Criteria for judging ethnographic research

Currently, we appear to be in a situation where the very criteria used to judge the adequacy of ethnographic work are subject to discussion. As far as ethnography goes, and more generally qualitative research, the issues surround the quality of the research and the nature of interpretation and analyses offered. Since we are concerned with practitioner qualitative research, a further set of criteria may emerge relating to the perceived practical, professional relevance of the research. Hammersley (1992: 57) identifies three basic positions concerning what criteria should be employed when assessing and evaluating ethnographic studies. Following and adding to Hammersley, these positions may be summarized in the following manner:

- *Applying the same criteria to qualitative and quantitative research.* This position seems to start from the assumption that there are universal criteria by which any piece of research can be assessed. From this viewpoint ethnography is merely one method amongst many and does not entail any distinct underlying philosophy. Typically, standard criteria of validity, reliability and representativeness are applied in the same way in which they would be applied to any piece of research.
- *Qualitative research operates as a distinct paradigm which is oppositional to the dominant positivistic orthodoxy.* This viewpoint holds that qualitative, ethnographic, naturalistic research views the social world as fundamentally different from the physical world, seeing the character of social inquiry as having more in common with the humanities than science. This viewpoint has left a certain amount of ambiguity surrounding exactly what criteria therefore should be applied to the assessment of ethnographic research.
- *The very character, nature and organization of qualitative ethnographic research implies that there are no criteria available for judging the adequacy of such research.* This position doubts the possibility of ever developing fixed criteria for the assessment of qualitative research, refusing to choose one set over and above any other set of criteria. Here, assessing ethnographic research by use of externally derived criteria is antagonistic towards the philosophical orientation of that research approach itself, and therefore of no value. Qualitative research is in this view essentially emergent, creative and open-ended.

The first position may be characterized as *positivist*, the second as *postpositivist* and the third *postmodernist*. The issues are certainly complex. Again, we need to make the point that our own view changes somewhat throughout the book. This is logical and consistent with our efforts to go beyond the straightforward textbook presentation. As we began this chapter with a somewhat conventional view of ethnography we finish by raising a number of problems and controversies. As we explored pathways through the research process in Chapter 5 we traded on some fairly conventional understandings of criteria such as validity, reliability and representativeness. By the time we reach the end of this chapter and work through those in Part III, the position will change again. We will operate mainly with postpositivist and postmodernist criteria yet hold on to the view that there is something very important about the use of criteria such as validity, reliability and representativeness, though subtly and not so subtly these criteria became transformed into subjectivity, authenticity, credibility, realism and the like. This is not to by-pass the key questions, but instead to signal the emergence of further sets of criteria by which we can judge ethnographic work.

The turn to textuality: the politics and poetics of ethnography

Ethnographic research has not escaped the far-reaching intellectual debates that have rocked the human sciences over the last decade or so. The impact of feminism, ethnic models of social research and postmodernism have resulted in what might be described as a turn to textuality, an overriding concern with the ways in which ethnography is written and the political implications of our understanding of the researcher–subject, writer–reader and audience–text relationship. We do not wish to go into this area in depth here. We will come back to some of these points as far as qualitative research is concerned more explicitly in Chapters 8 and 9 and, of course, in Part III of the book. Increasingly, ethnographers are concerned with the nature of their representations and the styles in which they report their findings. Self-narratives, confessions, the use of symbols, collapsing time, the use of poetic and dramatic devices, the use of visual representations, multi-vocal texts and mixing genres are all appearing on the scene; indeed, they have been around for some time. Those ethnographies often described as 'experimental' look very different from standard conventional ethnographic monographs. 'Educational' research has not escaped the postmodernist impulse. The interchanges between P. Woods (1993) and P. J. Woods (1993) or Louden's (1991) account of Joanna are but two recent examples of this in educational research. A heightened concern with writing is one offshoot of this. Again, our view of the writing process in qualitative research moves and, in Chapter 14, we challenge some of the conventional views of writing up qualitative school-based research that we proposed in Chapter 5. We cannot underestimate the significance of these issues. In many ways these debates have been responsible for generating the current diversity of qualitative research. The critique of ethnography from a postmodernist viewpoint has sharpened our awareness of exactly what it is we are doing and maybe might do in the future. Not everyone would agree with this. We are here simply trying to synthesize existing viewpoints so that the current state of ethnographic research in education and its likely shape may be identified.

Ethics and qualitative practitioner research

We have discussed at length the importance of access, ethics and objectivity in Chapter 3. We simply wish to flag some current concerns as they relate to practitioner, applied qualitative research in the ethnographic mode. Two positions are increasingly being rejected by qualitative applied researchers. First, the assumption that the research, however naturalistic is neutral. Second, that anything is justifiable in ethnographic research. Those researchers influenced by feminist, action research and critical perspectives, have gone to great lengths to spell out the nature of engagement on the part of both researchers and subjects. Rather than pretending that evaluation is not about values, attitudes and moral/political standpoints, these researchers argue that it is crucial to understand the positioning of such research and the advocacy of particular idealogies and viewpoints. The role of the research, the standpoint of the researcher and the relationship between researcher and subject are put into sharp relief in ethnographic practitioner research, and will pose special ethical issues. This has come to the surface most explicitly in feminist qualitative research. Furthermore, the nature of these and other problems has caused some people to question whether teacher research is a proper endeavour. Our view is that these issues can and should be faced and solutions to them found.

The term 'smash and grab' ethnography has been used in a critical way to draw attention to the situation whereby a researcher enters a teaching and learning scene, collects data, retreats and publishes the findings with little or no consideration of the subjects' feelings or interests. Specifically, action research and feminist models criticize such a practice. Democratic evaluation, collaborative enquiry and the like stress the need for ethnographers to take greater responsibility for what they do and share more with the subjects of the research. Ethnographic qualitative research ought to be well placed to respond here. The relationship between applied ethnographic research and the notion of empowerment will need to be worked out.

In this section we have simply tried to open up some of the contemporary debates and controversies surrounding ethnography. These debates are healthy and signs of a strong, not weak, discipline. Ethnographic work will continue to pose problems, will change and develop in response to dialogue, but ultimately ethnographers and qualitative researchers will maintain their commitment to studying and revealing the lives of human beings, adding their voice to our understanding of human experience, from the inside and from members' perspectives themselves, and thereby telling us all more about ourselves.

SUMMARY

In this chapter we have presented an outline of the major features of ethnography and attempted to relate these to school-based teacher research. We outlined the major steps and stages in carrying out ethnography, the kinds of data sources used and analyses made. As such, we hope in this opening chapter of Part II to have provided a context for the remaining chapters in this part of the book. We concluded the chapter by opening up a series of current debates and controversies which surround ethnography. Many teachers have rightly been critical of educational research for ignoring the everyday realities which underpin teaching and learning. Ethnography can, we believe, at least lay claim to taking these realities seriously and in describing and explaining them, uncover some of the deeper layers of meaning and interaction that influence teaching and learning in schools and classrooms.

SUGGESTED FURTHER READING

Recent years have seen an explosion of literature in the area of ethnography and qualitative research. We have therefore broken down some of this literature dealing with it under a series of sub-headings.

Some general texts on ethnography

Ethnography is a general approach which can incorporate a number of data-collection techniques, including observation, documentary research, interviewing and participant observation. *Speaking of Ethnography* (Agar 1986) provides a sensitive introduction.

Introduction to Qualitative Research Methods: A Phenomenological Approach to the Social Sciences (Bogdan and Taylor 1975) is a clear account of the ways in which qualitative research may be carried out. The authors cover a wide range of techniques, including interviewing, observation and life history work, and ground the methodological issues in a clear philosophical framework. They show how qualitative approaches are based upon some specific assumptions about the nature of the social world. *Field Research: A Source Book and Field Manual* (Burgess 1982b) provides one of the most comprehensive and important collections of materials on all aspects of field research, containing extracts from classic articles and works. There are clear editorial introductions and excellent bibliographies. This can be read in conjunction with *In the Field: An Introduction to Field Research* (Burgess 1984a) the best introductory text on major aspects of field research focusing upon the practicalities and processes involved. This book has the advantage of making use of illustrative examples from the author's own field work in the Newsom department of a secondary school. The book is wide-ranging and covers areas such as access to the research setting, choosing appropriate research strategies and the political and ethical problems of field research. Among the methods discussed are participant observation and the use of personal documents. The author also develops his argument of interviews as conversations. *Sociological Methods: A Source Book* (Denzin 1978), despite its age, is a very good introduction to the issues surrounding sociological research in general and qualitative or 'naturalistic' techniques in particular, but assumes some social science knowledge. Part 9 contains important articles on participant observation by Gold and Becker while Part 10 deals with the life history method. Important accounts are given by Blumer (1969) and Glaser and Strauss (1967) on the relationship between theory and data and the idea of 'theoretical sampling'. *The Research Act in Sociology* (Denzin 1970) is an important text but, again, assumes that the reader is familiar with social science research methods. There is a useful chapter on triangulation showing how different sources of data and different research techniques can be combined. *Ethnography: Principles and Practices* (Hammersley and

Atkinson 1983) offers a clear and readable account of ethnography which tries to steer a course between narrow and stereotypical definitions of 'positivism' and 'anti-positivism'. Instead, the authors argue for the importance of the location of ethnography within the social world it attempts to study. The book charts the development of these techniques and raises many critical issues. There is an excellent extended, annotated bibliography of ethnographic texts. *Analyzing Social Settings: A Guide to Qualitative Observations and Research* (Lofland and Lofland 1984) is the latest edition of a classic text on qualitative research located in the interactionist tradition. There is much sound advice and suggestion. W. F. Whyte with the collaboration of K. K. Whyte in *Learning From The Field: A Guide from Experience* (Whyte 1988) provides some interesting insights. Anyone conducting fieldwork in any setting could profit from the insights and revelations of one of the most famous field workers in sociology. In particular, for those engaged in school-based research, Whyte's book is important since it emphasizes the nature of applied research. Whyte (1988) draws upon his own extensive experience of field-based research to discuss issues such as planning a project, the development of field relations, observational methods, interviewing, team research and the use of historical data. A critical literature on ethnography is now emerging. A recent critical evaluation of the scope and role of ethnography in social research is given by *What's Wrong With Ethnography?* (Hammersley 1992).

Ethnography and fieldwork in educational research

This research orientation focuses upon participant observation and records of the routine aspects of life in schools and classrooms. Whilst the classroom is often the unit of analysis, this research frequently extends the focus to the wider aspects of culture and community.

Qualitative Research for Education: An Introduction to Theory and Methods (Bogdan and Bilken 1982) is an excellent American introduction to the whole area of qualitative research in education. There are some very good illustrations of the techniques in practice. *The Research Process in Educational Settings: Ten Case Studies* (Burgess 1984c), *Field Methods in the Study of Education* (Burgess 1984b) and *Issues in Educational Research: Qualitative Methods* (Burgess 1985b) are three collections of articles by researchers, talking about their research experiences, that bring together some of the most important recent work on the application of ethnographic, qualitative, field-based methodologies to the study of education. The introductions by Burgess are all clear and many of the key methodological issues are tackled in the chapters from the point of view of particular research projects. 'The two traditions of educational ethnography: sociology and the anthropology compared' (Delamont and Atkinson 1980) is an important article which charts the differing orientations, issues and problems of the ethnography of schooling from sociological and anthropological traditions. *Ethnographic*

Research: Theory and Application for Modern Schools and Societies (Dobbert 1982) is an important American text on the application of ethnography in general terms to research in educational settings. The text has the advantage of incorporating examples from studies to illustrate techniques and problems. 'Qualitative methods for research on teaching' (Erickson 1987) in *Handbook of Research on Teaching* (Wittrock) provides a review of qualitative or interpretative approaches to research on teaching and learning. Erickson focuses upon the kinds of research questions which become the main concern of this work, the philosophical background to these approaches and the development of participant observation. Erickson's account is important because it deals with the theoretical and practical concerns of qualitative research on teaching. The section on data collection and data analysis stress the simultaneous nature of these two activities in qualitative research. *Children In and Out of School: Ethnography and Education* (Gilmore and Glatthorn 1982) contains an interesting collection of papers and overviews: see especially the chapters by Brice-Heath and Hymes. The collection shows how many ethnographers broaden their focus to explore the wider cultural and community context of schooling as well as sociolinguistic dimensions. *Ethnography and Language in Educational Settings* (Green and Wallat 1981) is an important collection of papers on social interaction in educational settings. Contributions come from a number of disciplines and focus upon the possibilities and problems of ethnographic method. A focus upon 'communication' in its widest sense is a salient feature of these studies. *Ethnography and Qualitative Design in Educational Research* (Goetze and LeCompte 1984) contains many useful and original papers on the applications of ethnography to educational settings and summaries of the North American literature. 'Qualitative research traditions: a review', (Jacob 1987) focuses upon five main traditions here, namely: ecological psychology; holistic ethnography; cognitive anthropology; the ethnography of communication, and symbolic interactionism. However, whereas American research is cited, there is a total neglect of the contributions of British ethnographic research on schools. For a counterbalance and critique, see 'Qualitative research traditions: a British response to Jacob' (Atkinson, Delamont and Hammersley 1988). The debate on ethnography in educational research is taken further in the interchange between Woods and Hammersley in 'Methodology debate: ethnography' (Hammersley and Woods 1987). *Doing the Ethnography of Schooling* (Spindler 1982) contains an important collection of case studies and reviews of research. The articles by Heath and McDermott are of special interest. 'The use of ethnographic techniques in educational research' (Wilson 1977) is an early paper which maps out the origins and orientations of ethnographic techniques used in educational research outlining the philosophical rationale of participant observation research.

Ethnography and participant observation with children

Studying the world of children from an ethnographic perspective raises special issues. The best introduction to this area is given by *Knowing Children: Participant Observation with Minors* (Fine and Sandstrom 1988). This book has the advantage of taking a developmental approach looking at participant observation with pre-schoolers, pre-adolescents and adolescents. See also 'Participant observation with children: promise and problems' (Fine and Glasner 1979). 'Studying children's perspectives: a collaborative approach' (Pollard 1987) in *Doing Sociology of Education* (Walford) looks at the problems of obtaining data from young children, and 'Entering the child's world: research strategies for field entry and data collection in a pre-school setting' (Corsaro 1981) deals with a range of important aspects relating to early years of education and its investigation. Another study by Corsaro worth considering is '"We're friends right": children's use of access rituals in a nursery school' (Corsaro 1979). The classic sociological study of infants classrooms in the country is given by *All Things Bright and Beautiful: A Sociological Study of Infant Classrooms* (King 1978). Approaches to the study of child culture have taken a number of directions. However, it is important for the researcher to have an understanding of background theoretical and conceptual ideas relating to child development and socio-cultural context. *Children's Friendships* (Rubin 1980) is perhaps one of the best accounts of the role of friends and friendship in children's social worlds. The more recent emphasis upon context in child development research indicates the coming together of psychology, sociology and cross-cultural analysis in understanding children. This view is well represented in *Growing Up in a Changing Society* (Woodhead, Light and Carr 1991). Interesting studies of play and playground culture include *Playtime in the Primary School: Problems and Improvements* (Blatchford 1989); *Life in the Classroom and Playground* (Davies 1982) and *Growing Up in the Playground* (Slukin 1981).

7 Interviewing, asking questions and conversations

INTRODUCTION

In this chapter we provide an introduction to one of the major tools of social research, the interview. Central to the interview is the issue of asking questions and this is often achieved in qualitative research through conversational encounters. We will outline the different kinds of interviews available and show how the teacher–researcher might make use of interviews and conversations as a source of data in school-based research.

Interviews have been used extensively across all the disciplines of the social sciences and in educational research as a key technique of data collection. This has lead to considerable diversity in the form and style of interviewing as well as the products of such an approach. Researchers have approached the interview in so many different ways that broad types of interview can be identified. The differences refer to matters such as the nature of the questions asked, the degree of control over the interview exercised by the interviewer, the numbers of people involved, and the overall position of the interview in the research design itself. Roughly defined, interviews might be said to be 'talk to some purpose'. However, as we shall see, this definition does not get us too far. We can point to a range of different interview types which can be divided under two headings:

- Standardized interview:
  Structured interview or survey interview.
  Semi-structured interview.
  Group interview (structured or semi-structured).
- Non-standardized interview:
  Group interview (non-structured).
  Ethnographic interview (unstructured).
  Oral history and life history interview.
  Informal interview.
  Conversations and eavesdropping.

It is important to add to this diversity the fact that in social and educational research, interviews have been directly conducted by the researcher or by a team of trained researchers. Interview materials have been analysed by those directly involved in the research and by those who have only a minimal involvement in the research. Interviews have been conducted with both small and large groups. We are concerned to develop an appreciation of the basic principles and initial modes of analysis when using interviews and conversations in small-scale school-based research. As such, we will concentrate upon the type of the interview described as 'unstructured', 'semi-structured' or 'informal'.

The chapter contrasts structured interviewing with unstructured interviewing and also considers conversations and the diary interview. The interview as a research technique may be examined in terms of three key aspects which we will focus on in turn: the interview situation; methods of recording interviews; and the analysis of interview and conversational materials. Most of the key issues facing the teacher–researcher using the interview in school-based research will be examined, however, there are four basic questions, which affect all types of interviewing, and need to be addressed by the teacher at the outset of the research:

1 Why interview?
2 Where do I interview?
3 Whom do I interview?
4 When do I interview?

The teacher–researcher needs to work through these questions, briefly providing answers to them before embarking on the interviews proper. These answers will give the teacher a good idea of what type of interview to use and what specific issues might arise in the course of a school-based project which makes use of interviewing. We will now look at the main differences between so-called 'structured' and 'unstructured' interviewing strategies.

STANDARDIZED INTERVIEWS

The structured interview

The structured interview lies close to the questionnaire in both form and the assumptions underlying its use. Its main advantage over the postal questionnaire is greater flexibility and ability to extract more detailed information from respondents. This is one of the most widely used types of interview, largely because of its versatility both inside and outside the social sciences. For example, structured interviews are used in market research, public opinion research, studies of voting behaviour, attitude research and in a host of other contexts (see, for example, *Interviewing in Market and Social Research* (MacFarlane Smith 1972)). In social and educational research the structured interview is used when a high degree of control over the interview situation is required or seen to be necessary. Researchers who make use of structured interviews usually seek results which can form the basis of generalizations, that is statements about a large number of cases. For this reason structured interviews are very often carried out with quite large samples of individuals. It is possible to isolate the key features of structured interviews so that they can be compared with other types.

Structured interviews display a number of features in common. However, these characteristics take on a greater or lesser significance depending upon the particular research project. Typically, they are arranged around a schedule of questions which are usually both short, direct, and capable of immediate (frequently 'yes' or 'no') responses. Often the researcher will have tried out the questions and their order before the major research by means of conducting trial or pilot interviews beforehand. Since one of the main aims of researchers using structured interviews is often to produce generalized statements, fairly large numbers of people are needed. However, constraints of time, energy and cost often prohibit the use of large numbers. At this point, the researcher will make use of a 'sample'.

Sampling is a procedure which allows the researcher to select people from a large group to question. We briefly considered sampling strategies in Chapter 5, and compared the role of sampling in quantitative research with the place of sampling in qualitative research traditions. All researchers need to target a group of people for their study. This large group is referred to as the 'population' which could be secondary school teachers, middle-school children, or whoever. Since the researcher cannot interview the whole of this 'population' a representative sample has to be obtained. In order to do this the researcher must find a suitable 'sampling frame', that is a list of all the people in a particular group or category from which the researcher will draw off a sample. There are two main ways in which the researcher can do this. These methods are referred to as quota sampling and random sampling. When quota sampling is used, a specified percentage or quota from the categories of people identified in a population is interviewed. Here, attention is paid to keeping equal numbers of men and women, comparable ages, social backgrounds and so on of the people forming the sample. In contrast, random sampling, which is based upon probability theory, refers to the procedure whereby the sample of people to be interviewed is chosen purely randomly from the identified population. The assumption is that the random sampling will thereby reduce any possibility of bias since each individual within the population identified has an equal chance of being chosen to be interviewed. This is, of course, not as straightforward as it appears. For example, how truly random is a sample of individuals drawn by choosing every fourth entry in the telephone directory? Only as 'random' as those people who have telephones and are in the directory!

Another key feature often associated with the structured interview is that the interview schedule itself is capable of being administered by a person or persons who did not design the questions; frequently, trained interviewers are used. Structured interviews have the advantage of being able to cover wide areas and large numbers of people. Furthermore, they are cheap to administer. As we noted earlier, the response categories in structured interviews are fairly straightforward, often only involving categories such as 'yes' or 'no'. This makes the response easy to analyse. Most of the advice on the operation of the structured interview draws upon the experience of large-scale social surveys. It would, obviously be difficult to duplicate the circumstances of such surveys in small-scale school-based research. It is interesting to note the kinds of problems these researchers face, however. In a handbook, MacCrossan (1984) offers some general guidelines and advice for interviewers which might be of interest to the teacher–researcher.

MacCrossan offers some comments on the sample, the interview and the findings. She stresses the need for the sample to be as representative as possible and of obtaining complete interviews with as many members of the sample as possible. The interviewer needs to be able to persuade the interviewees of the importance of the survey, in the hope of ensuring their co-operation. Once the responses have been collected the task of classification and coding responses begins. This highlights the need for interviewers to record answers to questions accurately and as instructed and of 'probing' for full and precise information (MacCrossan 1984: 6). However, although MacCrossan's comments are informative she is referring to situations where the resources for carrying out the research will be far greater than those of the teacher–researcher. All the same, teachers can make use of structured interviews and to this end these observations are of value.

We will briefly consider some of the issues the teacher–researcher will face in setting up a structured interview. Although we are primarily concerned with qualitative research techniques, it is worth considering the elements of structured interviewing procedures since there may be times when even qualitative researchers need to work with a structured interview schedule!

Setting up a structured interview

It is possible to construct a set of tasks we would need to undertake when setting up a structured interview. These tasks are sequential and it is best to approach them in this fashion:

1 Note the areas on which information is required.
2 Translate the broad areas into a series of general questions.
3 Construct clear, direct, and unambiguous questions in line with (1) and (2). Initially, try to develop questions which are capable of being answered in straightforward 'yes' and 'no' fashion. Terms such as 'always', 'sometimes' or 'never' can be introduced to grade and extend the responses.
4 Construct a clear and simple layout and presentation of the questions which will enable the interviewer to tick or circle answers easily so as to avoid confusion when collating and analysing responses.

It is important to note that in the context of school-based research the teacher is likely to be doing all this kind of interviewing herself; she will not have the advantage of a large team to help her. On the other hand, hard structured interviews can provide the teacher–researcher with a fairly large amount of data in a relatively short period of time. Quite large numbers of teachers or pupils could be interviewed in this way, providing important basic data. However, what the structured interview is unlikely to reveal are the complex and emergent factors which shape the social world of schools and classrooms, because fairly rigid, prearranged questions form the basis of this technique. All the same, even the most highly structured interview is usually a good deal more flexible than the questionnaire since it is still a face-to-face situation and the researcher can usually leave room on the interview schedule for residual categories, such as 'anything else', or expansion. Typically, a structured interview is of most value to the teacher–researcher when basic straightforward data is needed quickly for purposes of evaluation. This has led researchers to make use of less structured versions of the structured interview. One advantage is that it allows the interviewer to take into account the level of comprehension and articulacy of the respondent.

The semi-structured interview

The semi-structured interview is a much more flexible version of the structured interview. It is the one which tends to be most favoured by educational researchers since it allows depth to be achieved by providing the opportunity on the part of the interviewer to probe and expand the respondent's responses. This is because the interviewer asks certain major questions of all respondents, but each time they can alter the sequences in order to probe more deeply and overcome a common tendency for respondents to anticipate questions. This can be done by including spaces on the interview schedule for the interviewer to add comments or make notes. In this way some kind of balance between the interviewer and the interviewee can develop which can provide room for negotiation, discussion, and expansion of the interviewee's responses.

In a small school-based research project the teacher can make use of the semi-structured interview, but care does need to be taken in both the construction of the sample, the questions, and the conclusions which may be drawn from the responses. The semi-structured interview is itself quite valuable as a pilot study, that is a short, preliminary, investigative study designed to reveal issues which can be explored in more depth later by means of a variety of techniques. For many researchers operating within the ethnographic framework there are considerable limitations to both structured and semi-structured interviews as a means of data collection in social and educational research. The prospective teacher–researcher needs to appreciate what these reservations are.

The advantages of structured interviews, it can be argued, lie in their approach to data collection which can help to reduce interviewer bias and lead to easier analysis of data. This view rests on a major assumption – that structured interviews are 'context independent' and free from the influence of the interviewer so that a more objective view of the social world of the respondents emerges. But, one can question this view of structured interviews.

One of the most famous criticisms of structured interviews and conventional methods of social research design more generally has come from the American sociologist Aaron Cicourel. In Chapter 3 of his book *Method and Measurement in Sociology* Cicourel (1964) Cicourel makes some revealing comments about the overall nature of the 'interview complex', that is the relationship and interaction between questions, interviewer, interviewee responses, and response interpretation. For Cicourel the main problem seems to surround the relationship between what the interview is intended to achieve and what is in fact interactionally done in achieving this. In other words, in the effort to sustain an objective approach to data collection that will reveal valid and reliable data, the structured and, indeed, semi-structured interview needs to ignore, by-pass, or pay lip service to the socially organized practices which need to be managed in order to actually complete the interview. The interview has to be dealt with as it happens and for many researchers this observation carries with it the consequence that interviews must be flexible, unstructured and sensitive to the context of the interaction. Cicourel has put the matter thus:

> The interviewer cannot check out his own responses in detail and follow the testing of a hypotheses during an interview; he is forced to make snap judgements, extended inferences, reveal his views, overlook material and the like and may be able to show how they were made or even why they were made only after the fact. The interviewer cannot escape from the difficulties of everyday life interpretations and actions. The common-sense 'rules' comprise literal hypotheses testing, but they are necessary conditions for eliciting the desired information.
>
> (Cicourel 1964: 100)

Cicourel's comments point to an important series of issues. It cannot be assumed that the interviewer–interviewee relationship or the nature of the interview discourse is unproblematic. Certainly, the structured interview is highly appropriate for many research situations. An example drawn from outside the arena of educational research may be used to illustrate some of the problems with formalized structured interviewing and survey interviews which reinforces Cicourel's viewpoint.

In underdeveloped and developing countries it is important for a variety of reasons to establish existing and projected fertility patterns. It is important from the health, welfare, social planning, and educational aspects to be able to describe and predict the size, nature, or composition of a country's population. In underdeveloped and developing countries this is quite vital. Cicourel, a longstanding critic of conventional, positivistic orientations to social research, has questioned the claims to validity upon which many traditional fertility studies and, more widely, interview surveys depend. In his study of Argentine fertility, Cicourel (1973) argues that there is essentially a betrayal of meaning in such approaches as he demonstrates that standard elicitation and coding procedures of interview materials routinely distort what 'family size', 'birth control' and so on actually mean to the families involved. In other words, the 'ethnographic context' of the people's lives does not form the background to either the development and generation of appropriate questions or the culture-specific location of the meaning and interpretation of subsequent answers. Cicourel suggests that there will as a result be inevitable distortion. Hence the picture of 'social reality', 'social structure', 'fertility', or 'education' claimed to be revealed by such interviewing techniques will, in fact, have a dubious relationship to the worlds which they are supposed to be researching. Furthermore, the neat, packaged, coded tables that result from such work will not show the interpretative and judgemental work the interviewer/researcher puts into the situation in the first place in order to obtain her empirical materials.

Those researchers adopting what might loosely be described as 'unstructured' interviewing techniques share a rather different set of assumptions about the nature of the social world and the subsequent form of social research which broadly encompasses the ethnographic, qualitative, interpretative model of research design we outlined in Chapter 2. These researchers claim that survey and structured interviewing procedures are not commensurate with the nature of the social world. Such approaches, it is argued, are not sensitive enough to the social contexts of the interview itself, the characteristics of the interviewer or interviewee, and the topic under investigation. Neither are they sufficiently flexible enough towards questions of design and working or sensitive to the problems of recording.

Qualitative researchers point towards the importance of the establishment of rapport, empathy, and understanding between interviewer and interviewee. They point out that it is not always possible to specify in advance what questions are appropriate or even important to any given social grouping before involvement with that group. They offer the observation that people do not always say what they mean in so many words, suggesting that social meanings are complex and not unequivocally revealed by a dictionary-like translation of 'responses' to prearranged 'questions' which can then be mechanically 'coded' to reveal patterns for subsequent analysis and generation of theory. Underlying these criticisms are the personal qualities and interactional skills of both the interviewer and respondent. As Lofland has pointed out in an often-quoted passage:

> I would say that successful interviewing is not unlike carrying on unthreatening, self-controlled, supportive, polite and cordial interaction in everyday life. If one can do that, one already has the main interpersonal skills necessary to interviewing.
>
> It is my personal impression, however, that interactants who practice

> these skills (even if they possess them) are not overly numerous in our society.
>
> (Lofland 1971: 90)

We are not claiming that once teachers possess these skills, automatic success at interviewing is guaranteed. For Lofland the situation seems mysteriously one-sided. The characteristics, composition, and interpersonal skills of the respondent in interaction with the interviewer come together to create a particular social situation. This brings us to a second example.

The unstructured or informal interview depends heavily for its success on the relationship that is developed between the interviewer and respondent. Lofland (1971) stresses the features needed for successful interviewing as a series of interpersonal skills. It is also crucial for the interviewer to develop a familiarity with the biographical and contextual features of the respondent's life history, outlook, customs, and life-style in order to be able to relate more fully and in a more appreciative way with those being interviewed. This will be especially noticeable when interviewing pupils where, for example, Measor (1985) found issues of her own appearance and status as being important factors that were attended to by the pupils she interviewed. These issues and the interpersonal skills Lofland (1971) refers to become crucial when attempting to build a relationship and establish rapport with respondents when one is exploring sensitive or delicate areas. In a study of the sexual behaviour of young people, for example, Schofield (1968) found that due to the characteristics of the young people themselves, the nature of the topic being explored and commonsense attitudes, specially trained interviewers were needed to work with the young people involved. Such a task is not easy but there are a number of examples in educational research that testify to the ability of sensitive researchers to develop these skills when engaged in unstructured interviews with pupils. Two good examples are the study by Measor and Woods (1984) of school transition and Willis's (1977) ethnographic account of a school counter-culture. In situations like these where there is likely to be no shared membership and where interviewer and respondent are clearly in an unequal relationship, the question of personal skills and, of course, ethics looms large. Those relying heavily upon structured interviewing techniques have been criticized for not giving due weight to the fact that the interviews are 'situated activities' and the materials produced 'situated accounts'. Futhermore, it is widely recognized that the social organization of the research process is something which all researchers must attend to. Whilst this message has been coming loud and clear from feminist researchers, interpretivists have been making this point for some considerable time.

NON-STANDARDIZED INTERVIEWS

Group interviews

Interviews of groups have been used more frequently in recent years and can be either standardized or non-standardized in form, though here we will concentrate on the qualitative non-standardized group interview. The strength of group interviews lies in the insights that they can provide into the dynamic effects of interaction between people and the way that this can affect how views are formed and changed. Researchers interested in consensus formation, interactional processes and group dynamics may find the group discussion useful for it allows one way into understanding how people interact in considering a topic and how they react to disagreement. They can be helpful in uncovering and identifying attitudes and behaviour which can be considered anti-social or unlawful, for example racist attitudes and drug-taking.

Lewis (1992) has argued that there are four set research-based reasons for resorting to group interview techniques. These are: to test a specific research question about consensus beliefs; to obtain greater depth and breadth in responses than occurs in individual interviews; to verify research plans or findings; and, more speculatively, to enhance the reliability of interviewee responses.

Group interviews with children

It has been argued that:

> group interviews may . . . be more practicable than individual interviews for a teacher–researcher to carry out. However, the teacher–researcher needs to consider carefully whether or not the children's inter-relationships as well as his or her relationship with the children will distort responses and so render data invalid.
>
> (Lewis 1992: 417)

When organizing group interviews the composition of the group is as important as the size. Small friendship groupings of, say, up to six appear to be the most productive. Another issue concerns the physical arrangements with a circle of chairs recommended and the need to keep eye contact with the group as a whole. The parallel here is with a teacher trying to note how other children are responding, in a class, when addressing a particular pupil (Lewis 1992: 414).

Group interviews with children, especially, need very careful chairing and if interviewers have a focus that they want exploring they may need to bring a group back to the point occasionally. However, the great merit of the group interview is that it allows what Lewis (1992) calls 'soap box stances' to emerge, but the flexibility can be lost with an over-directed approach by the interviewer(s). Furthermore, interviews with children also need recording carefully as the conversation can become animated and the researcher will need good recording facilities to ensure an accurate transcription. Lewis (1992) observes that some researchers have used more than one microphone to capture different respondents' contributions though they have produced only one transcript at the end. Other alternatives include the use of more than one interviewer or videotaping the session though both of these can be intrusive and may affect the responses. A compromise if only one interviewer is present may be to audiotape the interview and make supplementary notes immediately afterwards. The key question here is the purpose of the group interview, if this is to obtain data on consensus views then the need to disentangle individual voices may not be a problem.

Similarly, coding is inappropriate not only for technical reasons but also because one is looking for insights from transcripts and not numerical codings. As Lewis points out:

> Numerical summaries of individuals' comments are inappropriate as the relatively quiet or slow children may not score on some categories of response because these children are timid, need longer thinking time, or were deterred from speaking by preceding speakers' comments.
>
> (Lewis 1992: 420)

If you want to make a distinction between solicited and unsolicited issues then the researcher can ascertain strengths of support for rival or contradictory views by determining levels of support for views within and across the group. A final point made by Lewis is that the process of interpreting group interview transcripts will reflect the research questions (Lewis 1992: 420).

The unstructured interview

In a sense this title is a misnomer for as Whyte has reminded us 'a genuinely non-directive interviewing approach is simply not appropriate for research' (Whyte 1982: 111). There must still be structure then in an unstructured interview. The key difference between the different interviewing techniques we have been discussing so far might be said to be the degree of negotiation between the interviewer and interviewee. In the unstructured interview there is scope for the interviewer to introduce new material into the discussion which had not been thought of beforehand but arose only during the course of the interview. In other words, the unstructured interview allows the interviewer greater scope in asking questions out of sequence and the interviewees of answering questions in their own way. The aim of the unstructured interview is to provide for a greater and freer flow of information between the researcher and the subject. Even so, the researcher using unstructured interviews does not totally abandon any pre-interview work. It is just as important when using the unstructured interview as it is when using the structured interview to consider beforehand the nature of the encounter and the kinds of general areas the researcher wishes to explore. The researcher might work to a rough checklist of ideas or areas she wants to explore in the interview but will be prepared to let the interviewees 'travel' wherever they like.

As a result of the nature of the technique itself and the assumptions underlying its use those researchers employing unstructured interviews as a means of data collection are particularly aware of sources of bias and the range of factors which influence and shape encounters between researcher and respondent. These researchers highlight the need to develop rapport and empathy with those being interviewed. Once this is achieved the belief is that deeper, more meaningful information will be obtained. This will enable the interviewer to move backwards and forwards in the interview itself providing the opportunity to clarify points, go over earlier points, and raise fresh questions. It is fair to say that there is an inherently more equal relationship between researcher and subject in the unstructured interview than there tends to be in the structured interview. The overall aim of unstructured interviewing is to create an atmosphere where the individual feels able to relate subjective and often highly personal materials to the researcher. To allow for this some researchers have even gone so far as to encourage the interviewee to take greater responsibility for the interview, both in terms of planning the interview and organizing the questions.

The unstructured interview is now used widely in educational research generally and in teacher research more particularly. It has distinct advantages for the teacher–researcher working within a known culture with fellow professionals. For example, it can be used in curriculum evaluation, management, and appraisal exercises. Here its value is extensive since it can help throw light on to a number of aspects of both staff and pupils' experience of the school and curriculum change. When comparing structured and unstructured interviews it is clear to see how unstructured interviews offer the teacher–researcher much greater flexibility. Indeed, the teacher–researcher using unstructured interviews will quickly see how these often merge into a conversation. Conversations are, of course, a major element in any kind of ethnographic field research. Conversations not only constitute an important source of data but might also be regarded as a method of research in their own right. Once this happens it is transparent that elements of everyday social interaction will be incorporated into the unstructured interview. It is in this sense that Burgess (1982: 107–9) talks about the unstructured interview as a conversation. Burgess quotes Palmer here who suggests that the unstructured interview:

> assumes the appearance of a natural interesting conversation. But to the proficient interviewer it is always a controlled conversation which he guides and bends to the service of his research interest.
>
> (Palmer 1928: 171, cited by Burgess 1982)

We have explored the differences between standardized and non-standardized interviews. By approaching interviewing as a source of data for school-based research a number of matters will have to be considered by the

teacher–researcher. These might usefully be examined under three broad headings: the interview situation, methods of recording, and the analysis of interview and conversation materials. There will necessarily be overlap between these three aspects but we will consider each in turn.

The interview situation

The interview is a complete piece of social interaction. It is important for the researcher to be aware of what might be described as the dynamics of the interview situation. The following six areas could again act as checklist for the teacher–researcher to consider both before actually conducting the interviews and later when organizing and analysing them:

1 Researcher effects.
2 Characteristics of the researcher/interviewer.
3 Characteristics of the respondent/interviewee.
4 Nature of the researcher–respondent relationship.
5 The interview as a speech event.
6 Interviews have an ethnographic context.

Researcher effects

One of the advantages of the structured interview might be said to be the greatly reduced possibility of researcher effect or bias by constructing the technique and questions before the actual interview takes place. But as we saw in the example provided by Cicourel (1964), this kind of interviewing may be unwittingly involved in destroying the very meaning of items it is concerned to discover. In an important sense, whatever kind of interview is used the fact that an individual, the researcher or interviewer, is directly involved with another individual means, inevitably, that the presence of the researcher will have some kind of influence on the finds or data. Many have argued that the more involved the interviewer becomes with the situation the greater will be the potential for researcher effect. The major problem here surrounds the extent to which the interviewer 'leads on' or influences the respondents' responses. Clearly, there is little scope for this in a highly structured interview with a prearranged set of questions which must be answered in order.

Alternatively, there is much scope for this in the unstructured interview format. If, for example, the teacher and the interviewees are known to each other there may be a degree of reciprocity taking place, that is the respondent may feel that they have to give the researcher the kinds of answers and responses it is assumed the researcher wants. This is especially problematic when conducting interviews with peers as Platt (1981c: 75–91) has pointed out.

When researcher influence and effect are discussed reference is usually made to the personal and biographical characteristics of the researcher. These factors will take on special significance when the teacher is engaged in interviewing in educational contexts. For example, some teachers being interviewed may feel that evaluation or criticism is implied. The teacher–researcher will need to consider the context of each interview and examine the nature of any of her own values or prejudices which might influence the course of the interview. teacher–researchers as well as the subjects of their research have values, attitudes, political affiliations, and often firmly held opinions on what constitutes 'good teaching'. The teacher–researcher can never get rid of these features. The important point, however, is that she attempts to understand the significance and impact of them.

Characteristics of the researcher/interviewer

The main sources of bias and influence upon interviews is generally regarded as being the personal characteristics of the interviewer. Here, the key variables of age, gender, class, and ethnicity will all play a crucial role. Whereas we consider the influence of the characteristics of the interviewee shortly it must be remembered that the total situation must be seen in terms of the interaction of the two sets of characteristics. The age of the teacher–researcher will have an influence on the nature of the interactions she has with her subjects. This, of course, applies to all social research. In specifically age-stratified societies individuals are often excluded from many aspects of the social activities of a group on the grounds of their age. 'Seniority' and 'youth' are factors that do seem to have a particular significance in schools. Teachers' attitudes towards each other are often based upon the age of the respective parties concerned. Age is certainly a dimension the prospective interviewer would need to pay attention to. Lynda Measor (1985) for example, describes how in her research she paid special attention to her dress and appearance. She felt that she had to dress rather conservatively when interviewing other staff. Consider the implications for the interviewer of the following extracts from Measor's interviews:

Mr King: Young art teachers, clueless wonders some of them drab girls, who came looking as though they were selling off jewellery and wiggly hair and long woollen things and skirts that come down to their ankles and toenails that could have been cleaned.

Mr Tucks: I've never worn teacher uniform, I teach in what I'm wearing now [cord trousers, casual shirt, no tie, desert boots] . . . often criticized by colleagues.

(Measor 1985: 58–9)

Clearly, if one happened to be a young art teacher who remotely approximated Mr King's caricature above the implications for getting interview materials that were not grossly affected by the interviewer's age and appearance are quite remote. Conversely, Mr King might have a problem interviewing Mr Tucks. However, as Measor (1985) suggests, appearance can to a certain degree be manipulated, age cannot. There are obviously other occasions, as Hitchcock (1980) notes, where being young, new and a novice can have considerable advantages when interviewing older, more 'senior' teachers provided the right style and demeanour is adopted. But even when the 'old hands' come clean and decide to tell it 'like it is' to a younger member of staff, fieldworker/interviewer, the problem remains as to whether the data and materials obtained from such encounters are not wholly products of those encounters? They may not be a 'real' indication of what the respondent feels is appropriate given the relative ages of themselves and the interviewer.

We have concentrated on age as a crucial aspect of the researcher's identity which can influence the course of an interview, as it can field research in general. Certainly, the gender dimension of an interview is equally crucial. In many cases the teacher–researcher might find it easier to interview people of the same sex, though in other cases different researchers might find it easier to interview people of the opposite sex.

Traditionally, interviewing has been condescending towards women because little account has been taken of gender differences. The gender of the interviewer does matter and when the respondent is a woman added problems can occur especially as questions can ignore exploration of the more affective side of human interaction, i.e. personal feelings and emotions, which have traditionally been more highly developed in women in most cultures. This was certainly the view of Oakley (1981) who argued that to date interviewing had been a masculine research paradigm. Warren (1988) argued that the entry problems associated with the orthodox ethnographic interview are compounded, especially in highly sex-segregated groups or societies where women have low status or limited roles. In our highly diverse and heterogeneous societies, Warren's views need careful consideration before you undertake field interviews. Are there some circumstances where a man cannot interview women effectively or when a woman cannot interview men.

Researchers need, therefore, from the start to take into account the power relationships that not only exist in society and which will affect their respondents but also to be aware that these relations can bring into question the very notion of men interviewing women, no matter how much male interviewers try to take this into consideration when conducting the interview. The same is true of ethnicity. The difference here, of course, lies in the possibility that the interviewer or interviewee may hold stereotypical views of ethnic minority group members which those members either reject or find degrading. The question of the perceived status of the parties involved will create the foundation on which the teacher–researcher must consider the influence of the characteristics of the interviewer.

Characteristics of the respondent/interviewee

All the factors discussed above apply equally to the respondent. These variables will affect how the subject interprets the topics being discussed and responds to the interviewer. Ultimately it is the way in which these characteristics are worked out in the relationship between interviewer and interviewee. Although it is certainly difficult to disentangle these influences the teacher–researcher must at least be aware of them.

Nature of the researcher–respondent relationship

There are a vast number of possible relationships that the teacher–researcher might develop with the people being interviewed which are in the main shaped by the knowledge each has of the other, the relative status and standing of the interviewer and subject, and the outlook of each and the degree of friendship between the two. In many cases the teacher will be interviewing people she knows; in some situations the teacher will only have a passing knowledge of the person being interviewed. What is important here is the identity of both interviewer and interviewee. Obviously, if the teacher is engaged in unstructured interviews or conversations with pupils then a whole range of special factors has to be taken into account. For the most part teachers are going to be interviewing other teachers, but parents and members of outside agencies and bodies having dealings with the school may also be interviewed in some pieces of research. The teacher–researcher will often be researching and conducting interviews with her peers. As Platt has argued, this does present some peculiar ethical, technical, and analytical issues (Platt 1981c: 75–91). The teacher–researcher interviewing teachers is simultaneously teacher and a researcher. This dichotomy is often very difficult to manage since it requires the teacher to be both an interested party but not so interested as to take matters for granted. Furthermore, the teacher–researcher returns to her field after the research is complete. This dichotomy in the researcher–respondent relationship in school-based research has both ethical and practical consequences and can influence the nature of any interviewing which takes place. The researcher, like her subjects, has an identity, a past, a history, a certain reputation. How much of this can be divulged in the interview on the assumption of a reciprocal return of information by the subject? This is further exacerbated when the researcher and subject are of unequal status or standing in the school. How much are both parties prepared to give to each other? This is practical but also ethical in so far as it involves both parties' definition of what the situation is about and how the researcher will use what has been revealed to her.

When interviewing fellow teachers the designations of 'researcher' and 'respondent' and, indeed, 'interview' are too highly formalized and the unstructured interview format is an attempt to take this into consideration. For example, we have heard teachers talk about the way in which all manner of information was revealed to them once the interview was seen to be over. The openness and informality of the unstructured interview carries with it the possibility for the redefinition of what may be discussed in the interview by the respondent. However, what are the possibilities of this developing if the respondent is of 'lower' status or standing in the school hierarchy than the researcher? The basic problem surrounds the teacher's role as both researcher and an individual with a self and an identity in the setting under investigation. This suggests that the view of the interview as some kind of unambiguous research instrument is, in fact, false. The considerations we have been raising here may make such idealized views impossible to realize in practice, that is in the real situations of everyday life.

Probably one of the most well-known examples of the fundamental importance of the effects of interviewer and respondent characteristics on the outcome and results of interviews is provided by the sociolinguist Labov (1969: 1–31). Considered against the background of so-called cultural, linguistic, and deficit models of school failure, Labov has shown that when interviewed in different ways by different interviewers adopting differing roles, the language of black children can be shown to be highly variable. Labov describes the kind of interview situation which produces 'defensive' and 'monosyllabic' behaviour in the child:

> The boy enters a room where there is a large, friendly, white interviewer, who puts on a table in front of him a toy and says:
> 'Tell me everything you can about this'.
>
> (Labov 1969: 26)

He goes on to compare this with a very different kind of interview situation which resulted not in 'monosyllabic' children but children who were capable of using the English language well and who portrayed the extended ability to use the complex and rich ingredients of non-standard black English:

> In the next interview with Leon we made the following changes in the social situation.
> 1 Clarence [the interviewer] brought along a supply of chipped potatoes, changing the interview into something more in the nature of a party.
> 2 He brought along Leon's best friend, eight-year-old Gregory.
> 3 We reduced the height imbalance by having Clarence get down on the floor of Leon's room, he dropped from six feet, two inches to three feet, six inches.
> 4 Clarence introduced taboo words and taboo topics and proved, to Leon's surprise, that one can say anything into our microphone without any fear of retaliation.
>
> The result of these changes is a striking difference in the volume and style of speech.
>
> (Labov 1969: 30)

Whereas Labov is talking about the context of adult–child conversation and interviewing, where certain special factors play an important role, the general points have much wider applicability highlighting the need for careful appraisal of the influence of researcher–respondent characteristics and the nature of the ensuing relationship.

The interview as a speech event

By describing the interview as a 'speech event' we are drawing attention to the communicational and sociolinguistic aspects of its organization and the production of data contained within the interview and conversational materials in terms of what it is that the parties are doing with the words, phrases and idioms that they are using. These issues become most apparent when the interviewer and respondent use different linguistic styles or dialects within the interview or conversational encounter. Many studies on the multi-cultural context of learning and the education of ethnic minority groupings point to the potential for misunderstanding, miscommunication, and resulting educational problems when teachers and pupils from vastly differing cultural backgrounds having different languages and speech styles meet in the classroom. These difficulties may well spill over into the interview and research situation in general and are not confined to the inter-ethnic or multi-cultural context. The language of the researcher and respondent is closely aligned to their definition of themselves, the encounter and the front, image, or presentation of self they wish to convey. However, there is a major difference between the two personae here. As we have already discussed, field research, ethnography, and qualitative research require a range of social or personal skills on the part of the researcher. The nature of the language of the respondents will vary, so the sociolinguistic context of the interview will change. The nature of the presentation of self by respondents will vary also, rendering very different contexts within which the interview takes place. The effect of these differing definitions of the situation and linguistic codes means that the researcher has to take into account the sociolinguistic context of the interview and the allied definitions of the situation and presentation of selves that follow from this. The teacher–researcher needs to consider the implication of these observations not just for the interview situation but in the subsequent analysis of the materials.

Interviews have an ethnographic context

All the points we have been making so far about the interview situation highlight the need to recognize the influence of a variety of social, cultural, institutional and linguistic factors. Interviewers and respondents have identities. They have perceptions of themselves and of each other. This knowledge, of course, varies and changes as people become more familiar with each other. There is a past to the encounters and situations the researcher observes. There is therefore always a context to be taken into account. We might describe this as the 'ethnographic context' of the interview, unstructured interview, or conversation. It points also to the need for consideration of the fact that the informal interview, however unstructured, is still an unusual situation for most people to be in.

RECORDING INTERVIEWS

One of the most important aspects of interviewing is the question of how to record interviews. One major exception is Whyte's (1982) excellent article on interviewing in field research generally. Basically the considerations relate to the type of interview involved and the decision to use one or other method of recording. First of all it is clear to see that some of the problems regarding the recording of interview materials diminish if the interview is heavily structured since the use of pre-coded categories allows the researcher to record answers quickly and easily. Conversely, the flexibility and freedom entailed in the unstructured interview present problems as far as recording goes since the answers or responses and questions are likely to be lengthy, complex, and even 'rambling'.

The researcher has to make an early decision on how to record the interview materials though it is possible for the teacher to change the ways in which the materials are recorded as a relationship develops and as barriers are broken down. The teacher really has three possibilities to consider. She can (1) tape record the whole of the researcher–respondent exchanges, (2) take notes verbatim as the interview is happening, or (3) write up the main features and exchanges of the interview at some point after the interview is completed. Furthermore, recording unstructured interviews is somewhat different from recording structured, formal interviews since the interviewer in unstructured interviewing takes a much more active role in the encounter. This means that it is important not simply to record the respondent's responses but the interviewer's contributions also.

The tape recording of the interview session will produce the most complete record of what was said. However, the researcher must recognize certain consequences of using a tape recorder. The interviewer will have to manage the inevitable formality and structure that the introduction of a tape recorder will bring to the situation. The effects of this will vary depending upon whether the teacher has a long-established relationship with the respondent or, in contrast, if the relationship is new or fairly superficial. The researcher must never play down the possible effects which the presence of a mechanical recorder can have upon what people say and the way that they say it. Much will depend on the teacher's handling of the situation and the rapport that she has established with the subjects. The teacher–researcher will in any case have to obtain the permission of individuals to tape record the interviews and conversations. If this looks as if it might be difficult then the best course of action to follow would be simply to resort to note-taking. A series of practical issues, such as placement of the microphone, the problems of interference, and locating the tape recorder in as unobtrusive a fashion as possible, all need to be attended to by the interviewer before the interview (see also Chapter 9 on the oral history interview).

Taking notes during the course of the interview is another option open to the teacher, but this also has its disadvantages. Note-taking can introduce as much formality into the interview as can the presence of a tape recorder. The act of note-taking in the course of an interview means that the interviewer may not be able to give sufficient attention to what is being said because she is so busy trying to record it. If a teacher has not been interviewed before she or he may clearly feel self-conscious, something which may be heightened if the interviewer is writing down everything that is said. The teacher–researcher will have to 'read' this aspect of the research very carefully. In any case it will be important to record not just the subject's responses but the interviewer's questions also. It is simply not possible to write as fast as someone is talking unless one is using shorthand. One of the ways in which the teacher–researcher can take notes in the interview is by making use of a checklist or an *aide-mémoire* as a relatively informal way of organizing the interview which might make the recording process easier. This could involve the researcher writing up the notes on the interviewee's responses next to an appropriate section which the researcher has put down on a sheet of paper before the interview. However, some might argue that this procedure would introduce an unacceptable level of formality into the interview.

Finally, it is possible for the teacher–researcher to 'write up' the interview and reconstruct the reality of the encounter from memory at a later point. Some teachers we have worked with find this the only appropriate way to handle interviewing their colleagues since interference, anxiety and self-consciousness can be reduced to acceptable levels only by minimal intrusion of recording techniques. The main problem with writing up the interview after the event is that the whole of this process is retrospective and there will always be the potential of recording features in the written record which were not present in the original encounter. There is the risk therefore of introducing distortions and making errors. MacDonald and Sanger (1982), for example, have argued that note-taking and recording are not simply different ways of recording data but actually constitute different ways of going about research. Walker's comments make the difference clear:

> Note taking draws the researcher into the interpretation early in the study and in one sense makes the researcher more of a person in the eyes of the subject. Tape recording lends itself to a recessive process by burying it in the editing and selection of extracts from transcripts.
>
> (Walker 1985: 109)

This brings us swiftly on to the complicated and difficult question of the analysis of interview materials.

ANALYSING INTERVIEW AND CONVERSATIONAL DATA

Once the teacher has undergone the daunting and frustrating task of transcribing tape-recorded informal interviews, or has sorted out a mass of field-notes, or transcribed a series of verbatim conversations, then the next question is what to do with these materials. The analysis and explanation data is in many ways the culmination of the research project. At this point the teacher will begin to think about explaining, evaluating, and possibly suggesting ways of changing. However, the teacher will have been forming ideas, developing notions and thinking about the data as they were being collected. The more formal process of 'analysing interview and conversational materials' can occur at any point in the research once the materials become available. It is therefore important to locate these materials in the overall context and aims of the research. Very often the teacher will have not only the products of more than one interview to consider but also possibly transcripts of group interviews. All these features need to be kept in mind in order to place the interview materials in a meaningful context so that any analysis of their content is justified.

Preliminary issues in the analysis of interview and conversational materials

Many of the issues surrounding the analysis of materials collected by the teacher apply across the board to social research more generally. It is useful to reconsider at this point the questions that were raised about the analysis of ethnographic materials towards the end of Chapter 3. The question of the analysis of qualitative data is taken up more fully in Chapter 12. Although many teachers will use interviews of the structured or semi-structured variety using precoded questions, others will be using informal, unstructured interviews and conversations. As such, we will concentrate upon unravelling some guidelines for the qualitative analysis of interview and conversational data. However, even if the teacher–researcher is involved in the coding and quantification of fixed responses to structured interview items many of the points we will make below are still relevant.

One initial observation may be made at this stage. After all the time spent collecting data and conducting interviews the teacher–researcher is likely to be anxious to get on with 'doing something' with the materials. The danger here is that the teacher–researcher might begin to impute things to the data which are not perhaps borne out by more detailed careful analysis. There is no quick easy route to effective analysis. We feel that it is important for the researcher to get a 'feel' of the interview or interviews, conversation or conversations as a whole to begin with. Once this is done specific categories and meanings can be generated later avoiding the tendency of the researcher to impose categories on to the materials at an early stage. It is possible to unravel some general guidelines the teacher–researcher might follow when approaching the analysis of interviews and conversations.

Guidelines for the qualitative analysis of interview and conversational materials

It is fair to say that the organization and conduct of interviewing has received much greater attention than the analysis of interviews. However, there are certainly some examples in the literature which focus upon the analysis of interview materials and the prospective researcher could profitably consider Spradley (1979), Wragg (1984), Hycner (1985) and Powney and Watts (1987) here. We would point to nine related areas in considering the qualitative analysis of interview and conversational materials:

1 Familiarity with the transcript.
2 Appreciation of time-limits.
3 Description and analysis.
4 Isolating general units of meaning.
5 Relating general units of meaning to the research focus.
6 Patterns and themes extracted.
7 Nature of typifications and perceptions.
8 Self-revelation and researcher reflection.
9 Validity checks, triangulation, re-interviewing, and re-analysis.

Familiarity with the transcript

It is important for the teacher–researcher to have a thorough familiarity with the interview or conversational materials before attempting to develop any kind of systematic analysis. The process of reading and re-reading the materials will engender a sense of their coherence as a whole. Where possible, if a tape recording of the interview or conversation is available this should be done with both the written transcript and tape recording since this is the best way of gaining an appreciation of the subtle features of tone, pitch, intonation, and other crucial aspects such as pauses, silences, emphasis. Some researchers would want to add descriptions of the paralinguistic and non-verbal dimension to the interview encounter. This process of familiarization then is a fundamental prerequisite to the successful analysis of these kinds of material.

Appreciation of time-limits

What has been suggested above implies that a fair amount of time will be spent on reading and re-reading interview and conversational materials. This presents the teacher with an important practical matter to resolve. Given the restraints facing teacher–researchers it is much better to analyse a few interviews well than a large number badly.

Description and analysis

As we have stated elsewhere description and analysis are integrated in qualitative ethnographic research styles. The researcher moves backwards and forwards between description and explanation. In effect this means developing what the American sociologists Glaser and Strauss (1967) describe as 'grounded theory'. By grounded theory is meant the production of analysis and explanation which is grounded in the data the researcher collects, since it requires the researcher to move consciously backwards and forwards between the data and the emerging explanations, analyses and, eventually, theory. The researcher continually moves around amidst the raw data contained in the field notes, transcripts or accounts and then back to analyse, synthesize and formulate what has been found. The researcher can then return once more to the data and descriptions for further evidence, examples or clarification.

Isolating general units of meaning

The researcher by this point will be in a position to consider the very general units of meaning, that is the broad themes and issues which recur frequently in the interview or conversation. It is important at this stage to have a number of copies of the interview transcripts or conversations because the researcher will need to make notes and comments in the margins against particular utterances or responses. The general units of meaning refer to the range of issues the respondent refers to and these in turn are related to the overall focus of the research by the researcher. An example will serve to illustrate this process here. If a teacher provides comments or perceptions on a particular curriculum development project or an examination scheme then general units of meaning may be identified in the transcript which refer to issues such as teachers' perceptions of teaching, attitudes towards the underlying philosophy of the syllabus or project, views on the children involved. The researcher needs to identify, extract, and comment on these general units of meaning.

Relating general units of meaning to the research focus

Once the teacher has isolated the general units of meaning from the interview or conversation this is the point at which she can hold them up against the research focus, topics and concerns in order to see whether and to what extent they throw light upon them. It is important to note that the materials themselves are placed against the research focus and not the other way around which might lead to forcing the materials into the researcher's prearranged ideas and hypotheses. This would run counter to the general ethos of 'grounded theory'. It may turn out that the materials relate only tangentially to the research focus or are ambiguous. The researcher will then have to re-think the general focus of the research. Since, by definition, unstructured and informal interviews and conversations are fluid, the scope for straying from the relevant issues to other 'relevant' issues is quite large. Whatever the case the teacher is likely to find that there is much in the so diligently collected and transcribed materials which bears very little relation to the task at hand. This ought to be so since everyday life is such that all manner of varied topics are likely to emerge in the course of an interview or conversation.

The extracting of general units of meaning which relate directly to the focus of the research will necessarily involve leaving much out. What does the teacher–researcher do with the sections of the interview or conversation she is not using? This is in many ways a presentational matter. Depending upon the research and the audience complete transcripts of the whole of the interviews or conversations used *may* be included by the teacher–researcher in the final report. This relates to one of the advantages of ethnographic work on schools and classrooms. By including as many of the data as possible in the report itself the researcher enables the reader to provide alternative readings and analyses of the data and to consider the way in which the teacher–researcher arrives at her analysis.

Patterns and themes extracted

This is the point at which the teacher–researcher can explore in greater depth the major themes which emerge for the data and the ways in which these relate to the focus of the research in particular. The question of the research focus itself has already been established. There is almost a limitless number of topics the teacher–researcher might explore. The constraints will surround the time the teacher has to explore these topics and the ways in which she intends to do so. Most of the issues the teacher–researcher chooses to focus upon will come from the immediate classroom, school or neighbourhood context. Hence the patterns and themes extracted from the interviews and conversations might be seen in relation to these. Those teachers whose research is part of a course of study may well have been exposed to elements of psychology, sociology or anthropology as well as educational studies. These disciplines have generated their own analytical categories and the teacher–researcher might extract patterns or themes in relation to some of these categories.

The patterns and themes extracted may indeed turn out to be very particular and local. It is important, however, to remember that there is both a particular individual school context of teachers and pupils as well as a cultural, neighbourhood, community and societal context of those schools and classrooms to consider. Learning is inextricably linked with both of these contexts. Hopefully the patterns and themes extracted and the kinds of analyses made of the interview or conversational materials will throw some light upon the local and particular as well as the wider situations in which we teach and in which our children learn.

Nature of typifications and perceptions

One of the most influential approaches within the human sciences over the last few years has been that which has been associated with phenomenology. The philosopher Edmund Husserl (1965) is usually associated with 'phenomenology', a philosophical position concerned to describe the phenomena of consciousness, that is the foundations of our commonsense taken-for-granted assumptions about the social world. In order to achieve this Husserl, in his famous phrase, argued that we had to go 'back to the things' themselves. The way to achieve this for Husserl was to adapt the method of 'epoche', or bracketing the phenomena, that is to free ourselves from all presuppositions about the phenomena in order to see what they are made up of. This method of phenomenological reduction refers to suspending our belief in the world and thereby in Garfinkel's phrase, making activities 'anthropologically strange' (Garfinkel 1967). The aim of this approach therefore becomes the abandonment of all our prejudgements and preconceptions of phenomena so that nothing may be taken as given; this would therefore reveal, in Husserl's terms, the essence of the elements of consciousness and thinking themselves.

Whilst all of this may sound typically philosophical, phenomenology, as a philosophical position, and the sociological approaches it has shaped, ethnomethodology and interpretative approaches in the human sciences, have been responsible for mounting major criticisms of conventional, positivistic social science. Furthermore, these approaches have generated fresh ways in which qualitative materials like those derived from ethnography, unstructured interviewing, conversations and participant observation, may be analysed.

A number of key concepts feature in the work of those social scientists who have been influenced by phenomenology. Consciousness they argue is always consciousness of something, people intend actions, that is they play a crucial role in making things happen themselves. We experience the life-world of our 'intuitive environments' as a world we share in common with our fellow human beings. This world then is an inter-subjective world where the other people with whom I come into contact are assumed to make the same kinds of assumptions as I do and that, furthermore, if indeed we were to change places with others, they too would see the world as we do in exactly the same way. This confirms the principle of the interchangeability of standpoints. For phenomenologists these features constitute the natural attitude, the ordinary commonsense mundane practical reasoning of everyday life. Human beings, they argue, share an unshakeable faith in the 'facility' or realness of their everyday world.

Alfred Schutz (1899-1959) is usually regarded as being the key figure in unravelling the sociological implications of phenomenology but it was with the publication of Garfinkel's book, *Studies in Ethnomethodology*, in 1967 that the direct practical research implications of phenomenology for sociological investigation were worked out. Schutz was concerned to unravel the nature of commonsense thinking, that is the ways in which we routinely and ordinarily make sense of events and activities in the world around us. For Schutz our commonsense understanding of the world is facilitated by our use of language. Language provides us with a store of labels or types which provides for the mutual recognition of objects and events in our world by different people in the same or similar ways. Schutz describes these processes as constituting 'stocks of knowledge' which are in turn dependent upon the process of 'typification'. We understand the actions of others by employing constructs, models or idealizations of typical courses of action, typical people and typical motives, objects, events or activities. We obtain these 'ideal types' from our continual experience of the everyday social world. As Schutz puts it, we have a 'cookbook recipe for actions' which relates to our typifications of real-life situations so that typical people can be associated with typical events which are likely to bring about typical consequences. When we go to the bus stop we expect a bus with a particular number on it to arrive, not the *Starship Enterprise*! This enables us to apply rules of thumb to situations in order to make sense of them and we have 'recipe knowledge' from which we can extract explanations and provide solutions to problematic situations in everyday life so that if someone did arrive at the bus stop expecting the *Starship Enterprise* to arrive we can describe them as typically 'deluded', 'nuts', 'a weirdo', or the like.

The notion of typification might therefore be useful in analysing interviews and conversational materials. Most obviously teachers have typifications of their children and students based upon their everyday experience of them, with their biographical situations. These typifications also embrace expectations and assumptions about how the types of child or student so identified will behave in certain typical situations. Of course, typifications are not confined to individual actors, but groups of actors, classes, subjects, even teaching styles. One of the ways of approaching the analysis of interview materials therefore is through elaborating, unravelling and explaining these processes of typification.

Consider the following typifications of children, parents and families contained in materials collected during conversations and unstructured interviews in the course of an ethnographic study of an urban open-plan primary school:

Bill: You know these kids, I mean for all that's wrong with them they're game for anything you know, they're really keen at sports, full of enthusiasm they give it their all.

Mrs Smith: What I find with these kids is that they need more than the average security, it's their backgrounds, these high rise flats and things, a big planning mistake you know. You know what I mean.

Anne: Some of these kids you know get so frustrated and pent up inside if people keep on telling them off the way some people talk to them. They're human beings after all.

Anne: I don't know, some of these parents don't seem to care about their kids at all, they send 'em out any old way, you wonder why some of these lot ever bother having families at all.

Elaine: I don't know, they're crazy, you just can't do anything with these kids in a situation like this, at least I can't it's really getting me down.

Liz: I mean there's really two kinds of kids in our school it's quite clear really you can tell. There's my yellow group kind these kind of kids are the really, really bad ones, you know the dirty smelly ones, can't do anything, the ones with sore feet, 'Miss I've got sore feet' [laughs]. Birks, and oh Geoff.

G.H.: What do you mean 'sore feet'?

Liz: You know sore feet, they put their shoes on the wrong feet.

G.H.: Really?

Liz: Yea, but then there's the other kind my red group, they're really good workers, Teresa, Joanna, Martin.

Mr Brown: The trouble with these kids is if you give 'em a bit of freedom you find they go everywhere and get all of the things out all over the place.

Mr Brown: You can tell these kinds of kids, the dim ones their trays are always in a mess, look at that [pulls out Linda's tray] you can tell the brighter ones, they don't need much tidying up.

Mr Brown: You see the kinds of parents we tend to get here often tend to get things wrong and start taking things the wrong way . . . you see we've got three types of parents really, the sort of right-wing type, who look in their English books checking the spellings, mind you some of their spellings are nothing to write home about judging by the letters I've seen but that's beside the point, then there's the overprotective ones who can't leave their little ones without saying good-bye, and then there's those who just come to gossip and meet other parents in the morning.

(Hitchcock 1980: 334–6)

Numerous studies have pointed to this important process of typification in the educational world and these studies might be consulted for the ways in which they have focused upon typifications in their analyses of school and classroom processes. One thinks particularly of Rist's early classic study of American kindergarten teachers' expectations of their pupils based upon social class factors (Rist 1970: 411–51), Sharpe and Green's (1975) study of teachers' ideologies in Mapeldene infant school, a so-called progressive school, Hargreaves, Hestor and Mellor's (1975) study of deviance in secondary schools, and more recently Pollard's (1985a) account of a primary school. These studies point to the potential of focusing upon typifications as a way of analysing the materials contained in interviews and conversations.

Self-revelation and researcher reflection

The occasion of research often puts individuals into situations that they would not normally find themselves in. Unstructured interviews, no matter how loosely or informally organized, ask individuals to sit down, take stock and reflect, albeit in as natural and unprovoked a manner as possible, on particular topics. One hopes that there will certainly be moments in the unstructured interview when the degree of rapport and empathy between the teacher–researcher and subject or interviewee is such that the respondent may reveal themselves in more detail than ever before. When respondents do become involved in this process of self-revelation, of 'baring all' to the researcher so to speak, then the researcher needs to be prepared to reflect on the themes exposed. The nature of teaching itself is such that individuals do tend to develop highly organized conceptualizations of who they are and what they are able to achieve. The unstructured interview offers teachers and pupils the opportunity to verbalize and attempt to articulate some of these aspects of their lives. It is important for the researcher to attempt to pick up on these aspects of the interview and, in the light of any other data that have been collected, reflect upon these points.

Teachers' perspectives are by definition complex. They are often revealed only partially and in different ways to different audiences. The teacher will have to be sensitive towards the possible fluctuations in the way in which teachers themselves may try to present or reveal aspects of themselves in the interview. It is important to remember that the subject may be very concerned to present a positive self-image thereby influencing the content and nature of the replies and accounts as we indicated earlier.

Teaching is full of situations which place the individual in difficult and contradictory circumstances. Students of organizations often speak about the differences between the formal organization of an institution such as, for example, a school or factory, and its informal organization. This refers to the distinction between what is supposed to happen in an organization, its rules and official reasons for operating on the one hand, which is often described as formal organization, and the unofficial, unwritten, taken-for-granted and informal organization on the other hand. In teaching, these kinds of differences often find expression in what we describe as the dichotomy between professional themes, such as a 'whole school approach', 'integrated day', and so on, and the practical arrangements of ordinary teachers and ordinary pupils routinely trying to make a 'whole school approach' or an 'integrated day' happen. The two often turn out to be somewhat different.

A focus upon these self-revelatory aspects of the interview may help the researcher to see how some of these problems are resolved by the teacher.

For example, they may help to see how contradictory attitudes to examinations are resolved, or how teachers handle curriculum or syllabus objectives they perceive to be unrealizable. A close examination of the interview or conversational materials may throw light on these and other complex questions.

Validity checks, triangulation, re-interviewing and re-analysis

It is possible and important to develop checks on the data in qualitative research and we will briefly examine how the teacher might do this with interview materials in this section.

First of all, as we stressed earlier in this chapter, familiarity with the actual materials themselves is a vital first step for the teacher. From the wealth of data the teacher has on the setting itself, she will have inside her head a considerable amount of intuitive knowledge which she can bring to bear on the materials in such a way as to identify lack of consistency, potential errors and comments that are simply untrue. Basically, two approaches have been used to validate interview and conversational data. The processes of triangulation and of re-interviewing and re-analysis are the two main options open to the teacher–researcher. These procedures apply to other data collection techniques to check on validity and authenticity but they are especially useful for the teacher making use of unstructured interviews in small-scale research.

'Triangulation' refers to the use of more than one method of data collection within a single study. However, a number of other terms have been used to describe this process, for example, mixed method, multi-method, or multiple strategies (Burgess 1982: 163–7). As we have seen, almost by definition, field research will be directly involved in some form of triangulation since the field researcher will obtain data from a variety of sources and in a number of different ways. Triangulation encourages this flexibility and can, as in the case of the analysis of interview and conversational materials, add some depth to the analysis and potentially increase the validity of the data and consequently the analyses made of them. Whilst there are clearly advantages of a multi-method approach to data collection for the teacher–researcher, not least because she is likely to have at hand a variety of different sources of data, there are also disadvantages and problems. The researcher has always to be careful that the data elicited by means of the different techniques are actually comparable. In other words, there are many different kinds of data and one data source cannot be used unproblematically to validate another source of data. Documentary sources of data are very different from observational sources or accounts. Alternatively the researcher can engage in different types of triangulation.

Denzin, a long-time supporter of triangulation, has argued that it is a basic principle of social research. Denzin (1970) distinguishes between 'within methods' triangulation and 'between methods' triangulation. Within methods triangulation refers to the replication of a study by use of the same techniques as a way of checking on the reliability of the study and the nature of the theories generated. Between methods triangulation refers to the use of more than one method of data collection within the same study. Given the circumstances the teacher–researcher is likely to be faced with, methodological triangulation is likely to be the most readily available method for checking the data.

Once the teacher has organized and read through the unstructured interview materials she can compare these with other sources of data she may have on the situation which may be derived from participant observation or other sources. One of the best examples of the use of this kind of triangulation in educational research can be found in the study of Cicourel *et al.* (1974) of social interaction in both classroom and testing situations in first-grade and kindergarten classrooms in two districts of southern California. This study was designed to show how the 'facts' of a child's competence and abilities were actually subjectively and socially accomplished in the routine ongoing activities of the classroom and testing situations. The authors produced audio and video tape recording from which the analyses were made. The term widely used in these articles is 'indefinite triangulation' and it refers to the ways in which different sources of data were brought to bear upon the same event. What the authors did was to compare the participants' performances in test and classroom situations with data which were gathered through interviews where the teachers were shown the video tape or test answers and asked to explain their actions and reasons. As such a further level of meaning and interpretation is added to the analytical equation. How far this triangulation process can go is, of course, an interesting question.

Another way in which triangulation can take place with a view to warranting the subsequent analyses of the materials may be found in the 'diary–diary–interview' method as described by Zimmerman and Wieder (1977: 479–500). The diary can be used for a variety of purposes. We have worked with many teachers who, while engaged on research into their own classroom, have kept diaries of events and activities. The teacher could therefore ask the people within her research if they would keep a diary; this diary could be used as a basis for subsequent unstructured interviews. Hence the diary may be used as a question-generating device and as a validity check also.

Zimmerman and Wieder's (1977: 479–99) study of the 'counter-culture' in California is a good example of the ways in which methods and sources of data may be combined in a research project where all the activities engaged in could not be observed by the researchers. As a result the people involved in their study were paid $10 for keeping a diary for seven complete days and were given a Who? What? When? Where? and How? formula to record events in chronological order. The triangulation takes place when subsequently the subjects are interviewed about the accounts and activities recorded in the diary of the seven days of the individual's life. As Zimmerman and Wieder put it:

> the diarists' statement is used as a way of generating questions for the subsequent diary interview. The diary interview converts the diary – a source of data in its own right – into a question-generating and, hence, data-gathering device.
>
> (Zimmerman and Weider 1977: 489)

Clearly, the diary–diary–interview method is one that could be of considerable use in school-based research.

The second major way in which the teacher–researcher might attempt to check or validate the interview materials is to go back to the respondent with the complete transcript or a summary of the main themes and emerging categories. Alternatively, it may be possible to re-interview the individuals concerned and become engaged in subsequent re-analysis. Both of these courses of action offer the subject the opportunity of adding further information and the researcher the opportunity of checking on what data have been collected. A second interview could be used to focus upon themes and issues which emerged, or those on which the researcher was not clear.

These are some of the ways the teacher–researcher might attempt to check and validate the data. One cannot, however, rule out the possibility of intentional error. As we have noted elsewhere, the first task in establishing the accuracy of accounts in the field is to place them in their ethnographic context and consider whether or not they hold up under scrutiny. The procedures we pointed to in Chapter 3 regarding informants' accounts could easily be applied to the subject matter of interviews and conversational materials. In an important sense, of course, even lies can be regarded as an important source of data.

SUGGESTED FURTHER READING

Interviewing is one of the most widely used research techniques. A number of useful texts and articles will need to be consulted by those making use of interviewing. The following will provide important information and advice: *The Research Interview: Uses and Approaches*, (Brenner, Brown and Canter 1985); *Interviewing* (Breakwell, 1990); *Learning How to Ask: A Sociolinguistic Appraisal of the Role of the Interview in Social Research* (Briggs 1986); 'The unstructured interview as conversation' (Burgess 1982a); in *Field Research: A Source Book and Field Manual* (Burgess); 'Interviewing: the art of science' (Fontana and Frey 1994), in *Handbook of Qualitative Research* (Denzin and Lincoln 1994); *The Long Interview* (McCracken 1988); *Research Interviewing: Context and Narrative* (Mishler 1986) offers a reflective account of the interview process; *The Ethnographic Interview* (Spradley 1979). The most comprehensive account to date of interviewing in educational research is found in *Interviewing in Educational Research* (Powney and

Watts 1987). The articles 'Conversation piece: the practice of interviewing in case study research' (Simons 1981) in *Uttering, Muttering, Collecting, Using and Reporting Talk for Social and Educational Research* (Adelman 1981); 'Interviewing: a strategy in qualitative research' (Measor 1985) in *Issues in Educational Research: Qualitative Methods* (Burgess 1985b) and 'Group child interviews as a research tool' (Lewis 1992) all offer valuable insights into the processes and practicalities of interviewing in educational contexts. The gender dimension to interviewing is explored by '"It's great to have someone to talk to": the ethics and politics of interviewing women' (Finch 1984) and 'Surveying through stories' (Graham 1984) in *Social Researching Politics, Problems and Possibilities* (Bell and Roberts). 'Interviewing – an "unnatural situation"?' (Ribbens 1989) provides an interesting critique of interviewing from a feminist perspective focusing explicitly upon the power dynamics in an interviewing situation, stressing the socially structured nature of interviewing and interview data. Oakley, of course, sees interviewing as a contradiction, see 'Interviewing women: a contradiction in terms' (Oakley 1981) in *Doing Feminist Research* (Robert 1981).

Interviewing and observing children presents special problems. The following works all deal with the issues involved here: 'Entering the child's world: research strategies for field entry and data collection in a pre-school setting' (Corsaro 1981), in *Ethnography and Language in Educational Settings* (Green and Wallett), 'Children's perceptions of social interaction in school' (Davies 1979); and *Life in Classroom and Playground: The Accounts of Primary School Children* (Davies 1982).

Although the practice of interviewing is reasonably well covered in the literature the analysis of interview materials, especially the products of unstructured interviews, is much less well covered. Whilst the comments we made earlier about the analysis of qualitative data in general apply here also, in addition to considering earlier suggestions for further reading the following articles provide some specific indication of the ways in which it is possible to forward the analytic process: 'The phenomenological research interview: a phenomenological and hermeneutic mode of understanding' (Kvale 1983), and 'Some guidelines for the phenomenological analysis of interview data' (Hycner 1985). These articles need to be read in conjuction with the discussion of analysis in Chapter 12.

8 Biographies: the life history interview

INTRODUCTION

We have spent considerable time exploring the nature of interviewing in social and educational research. The range of interview types was discussed, focusing in particular on unstructured, informal approaches. The growth in the use of personal documentary sources in educational research, including autobiography, biography, letters, diaries and personal narratives in general warrants consideration since the teacher–researcher may well find these sources of considerable value. One such source of information is the life history produced via the life history interview. We will try to provide a context for understanding the emergence of personal documentary research in general and life history approaches in particular. This will be followed by a detailed overview of life history research and its use by teachers in school-based research.

PERSONAL DOCUMENTARY SOURCES

All sorts of people from philosophers to social scientists have concerned themselves with first-hand oral or written accounts. This tradition is a long one and ranges from early Greek attempts to collect first-hand accounts of warfare, the diaries and reminiscences of white Christian missionaries, to the social commentary of people such as Mayhew and Webb. Within the social sciences themselves a concern with life stories has preoccupied social psychologists in the form of psychobiography (Erikson 1959; Runyan 1982), whereas Gordon Allport was writing as long ago as 1942 about the value of personal documents for psychology in general (Allport 1942). The development of Chicago Sociology and, subsequently, symbolic interactionism (Rock 1979; Hammersley 1989) was based upon a respect for individual actors' accounts and a desire to portray as accurately as possible, an individual's interpretations of social events. In social history and recent historiography the emergence of so-called 'people's history', the study of mentalities and 'history from the bottom up', places individual accounts in the form of 'documents' from the 'past' in a pre-eminent position and allocates these materials an important role in the development of both descriptions and subsequent analysis. However, one of the fullest and most prolific expressions of a deep concern with recording individuals' life stories and experience is to be found in the development of oral history in the USA. One of the most famous oral historians is, however, a non-academic and unattached Chicagoan, Studs Terkel. In particular, his *Hard Times: An Oral History of the Great Depression in America* (1970) and *Working: People Talk About What They Do All Day and How They Feel About What They Do* (1974) are wonderful examples of the depth, richness and feeling which Terkel is able to entice from his interviewees. Oral history also played in a major role in the study of delinquency (Bennett 1981). The practice of oral history is considered in Grele (1975) and Gittens (1979).

Personal documentary sources constitute a largely neglected source of data on the social world of schools and classrooms, especially when compared to the extensive use of the survey technique, structured interviewing, or systematic observation. We suggest that used with care and in conjunction with other kinds of data, personal documentary sources offer the teacher–researcher a number of possibilities. As we have seen, ethnographic accounts of school and classroom processes tend to pinpoint the immediate 'here and now', contemporary quality of the situation, thus possibly lacking historical depth. One of the values of personal documentary sources, especially the life history, could be said to be its ability to represent subjectively meaningful experience through time. Whereas ethnography and the case study are concerned with what might loosely be described as situational analysis, that is interactions in schools, classrooms, staffrooms, curriculum planning meetings and so on, personal documentary research is concerned with biography, that is individual experiences, memories, reflections and interpretations. The situational and the biographical are, therefore, two sides of the same coin since the situational will be influenced by the biographical and vice versa. A focus upon the biographical can therefore help teacher–researchers to appreciate more fully the situational.

THE LIFE HISTORY

Recently, the life history technique has been enjoying something of a revival, and educational research is in part responsible for this. Since the subject occupies such a central place in this research it may be argued that a certain democratization of the research process itself takes place. Added to this, the life history approach draws the subject and researcher into a much closer interaction than conventional research where the researcher is encouraged to remain aloof, objective and eventually apart from the subject and data obtained. Furthermore, the life history approach offers a clear potential in terms of considering the ways in which culture is both represented and reproduced, and of how culture is moulded, changed and created by individuals through time.

For those working in the field of education and similar areas, the life story approach facilitates a deeper appreciation of an individual's experience of the past, living with the present, and a means of facing and challenging the future. The life history technique is one of the most extended and developed aspects of the life story approach in the human sciences. The approach uses qualitative techniques, in particular the unstructured or semi-structured interview, which are designed to provide individuals with the opportunity of telling their own stories in their own ways. This facilitates the reconstruction and interpretation of subjectively meaningful features and critical episodes in an individual's life. The basic concern of the life history approach is the presentation of experience from the perspective of the subject or subjects themselves. As one of the advocates of this approach has put it, the life history technique is in many ways superior to other methods since it enables the researcher to build up a mosaic-like picture of the individual and the events and people surrounding them so that relations, influences and patterns can be observed (Becker 1966). The retrospective quality of this kind of research enables one to explore social processes over time and adds historical depth to subsequent analysis.

LIFE HISTORIES AND QUALITATIVE APPROACHES

Qualitative research can be defined as a particular orientation within the human and social sciences that 'fundamentally depends on watching people in their own territory and interacting with them in their own language, on their own terms (Kirk and Miller 1986: 9). As such, it is committed to research 'in the field', i.e. observing in a school classroom or interviewing a colleague, and its methods of collecting data and analysing data reflect this. In the use of qualitative methods in this century and especially their employment in educational research over the past twenty years or so it has been participant observation rather than the use of life histories which have predominated. The reasons for this are complex but, as will be shown below, from the late 1930s onwards the method was neglected by the majority of mainstream social scientists in both the USA and in Britain.

This neglect was largely the result of the apparent institutionalized need for the social sciences in this period to develop abstract theories and adopt a form of research design which was closely allied to laboratory experimentation. A problem with life histories was the difficulty in such research designs of achieving both representiveness and generalizations. They seemed a poor base from which to develop or test abstract, universal theories. Even in the 'Chicago school' the life history fell out of favour giving way to other ethnographic devices, notably participant observation. This was partly the result of the decline of Chicago University as a dominant centre of research in sociology and to the research orientations of two sociologists, Blumer and Hughes. Both of them emphasized group rather than individual experience (Goodson 1980: 76). In contrast, the life history approach is essentially retrospective in orientation though how far back the researcher and subject will go varies considerably and depends on the topic, nature of the subject and other factors.

It is important to remember also that whereas there are many examples of research which only utilizes life history data, life history data is more and more being incorporated into research as another source and level of data. The ethnographic framework itself by definition involves the researcher collecting data from a number of sources and in a variety of different ways. As such, life history work sits easily with qualitative and ethnographically oriented research in general, constituting a distinct 'life-story' approach in sociology (Bertaux and Kohli 1984).

WHAT ARE LIFE HISTORIES?

Put very simply, life histories are stories or narratives recalling events in an individual's life. As such their origins are very old. For centuries men and women have been writing their autobiographies or, as biographers, recounting other people's lives. Life histories are a particular narrative form whose origins lie in the anthropologists' desire to understand contemporary cultures and the oral historians' desire to understand past ones. Within psychology and psychoanalysis the individual case history has always had an important place (Runyan 1982). As a consequence, the forms life histories have taken have varied considerably.

Some of the earliest life histories were collected by anthropologists studying the culture of North American Indians at the start of this century. The technique was taken up and developed by sociologists during the 1920s and 1930s, especially associated with work undertaken by the so-called 'Chicago School'. A key book of this period was that of Thomas and Znaniecki, *The Polish Peasant in Europe and America* (1958, originally published in 1918–1920) focusing upon Polish immigrants in the USA and based principally on autobiographical accounts, diaries and letters and other documentary sources (see also Bulmer 1983). The authors saw these personal documentary sources as constituting one of the most important sources of data the sociologist could get hold of. So much so, that they were led to comment in a famous passage:

> In analyzing the experience and attitudes of an individual, we always reach data and elementary facts which are exclusively limited to the individual's personality, but can be treated as mere incidences of more or less general classes of data or facts, and can thus be used for the determination of laws of social becoming. Whether we draw our material for sociological analysis from detailed life records of concrete individuals or from the observation of mass phenomena, the problems of sociological analysis are the same, but even when we are searching for abstract laws, life histories as complete as possible constitute the perfect type of

> sociological material, and if social science has to use other materials at all, it is only because of the practical difficulty of obtaining at the moment a sufficient number of such records to cover the totality of sociological problems, and of the enormous amount of work demanded for an adequate analysis of all the personal materials necessary to characterize the life of a social group. If we are forced to use mass phenomena as materials; or any kind of happenings taken without regard to the life histories of the individuals who participated, it is a defect not an advantage, of our present sociological method.
>
> (Thomas and Znaniecki 1958: 1831–33)

The life history technique involves the collection of individual subjective experiences of a life either written down by the individual themselves or related orally to the researcher who then writes up and presents the life history account. The technique therefore reconstructs, interprets and presents some of the main aspects of selected areas of a single individual's life. Empathy between researcher and subject is therefore an essential ingredient in this research as a result of the highly collaborative nature of the activity itself. This points to the suggestion that life histories are seen as the joint production of researcher *and* subject. By concentrating upon internal subjective experiences in either a contemporary or a retrospective fashion the research aims to develop a clearer appreciation of the complex processes of social life, identity and change. An important feature of conducting life histories therefore is the development of a dialogue between the subject and the researcher as well as the subjects with themselves. The resulting data are characteristically rich, evocative, highly localized and subjective. Researchers have differed in the degree to which they have edited, ordered and reassembled the narrative materials. Whereas many of the early users of the technique tended very much to impose categories on to the data and edit the materials heavily, later researchers, especially those influenced by phenomenological and feminist critiques, have sought to reverse this by stressing the need for the subject's voice to come through, intact as it were, in the final writing. These issues have all been explored by, amongst others, Frank (1981; 1984 and 1985), Hoskins (1985), Myerhoff (1978) and Shostak (1981).

Few researchers pay attention to the impact of their research upon the subjects themselves. With its focus upon key episodes in a life, turning points or reminiscences, the subject is given the opportunity to look back on a life or career. Woods (1987: 122–5) has gone so far as to argue that life histories, because of their special qualities in revealing the self, have an important role to play in 'the construction of a meaningful, relevant and living teacher knowledge', Woods (1987: 136). A clear case for the use of life history approaches in a variety of contexts has now been well made.

Clearly, there is likely to be tension between retaining the rich descriptive character of these accounts and allowing time and space for their analysis, a tension that is evident and to a certain extent unavoidable. Distinctions between *types* of life history may be noted here. It is possible to distinguish between 'retrospective' life histories based upon the reconstruction of a life or aspects of a life from memory, dealing with individuals' feelings and interpretations about past events now, and 'contemporaneous' life histories focusing upon the description of aspects of an individuals' daily life in progress (Langness and Frank 1981; Frank and Vanderburgh 1986: 188). Contemporaneous life histories are possibly likely to draw the research more into the discussion and interpretation of materials. Whilst there are different kinds of life history with varying emphases there are also clearly different modes of presenting a life history. On the one hand, there are 'naturalistic' first person life histories where most of the actual published life story is in the words of the individual subject, perhaps with a brief introduction by the researcher, providing background detail and context and possibly a conclusion. Second, there are thematically edited first person life histories where the words of the subject are retained intact, but where the researcher has presented them in terms of a series of themes, topics or headings, usually in a chapter by chapter form. Third, there are what might be described as interpreted and edited life stories where the influence of the researcher is most marked since the researcher sifts, distils, edits and interprets the words of the subject and, although retaining the feel and authenticity of the subject's words, presents a written version of the life story, sometimes making use of extensive first person accounts to tie the researcher's text together.

Certainly there are considerable advantages to use of the life history technique in school-based research. The retrospective quality of life histories can provide historical depth. They will also be able to reveal the differing ways in which an individual perceives educational situations, issues and changes. A number of substantive research concerns themselves seem amenable to investigation by means of the life history technique, for example, teachers' careers, teachers' and pupils' values and attitudes, and the ways in which the variables of class, gender and ethnicity can influence the learning process. We could add to this list some of the themes explored in the studies reported here, for example, the local management of schools, the ethnic experience in further education and special needs. As a result of the flexibility and adaptability of the life history technique it can be used in a variety of situations. This perhaps is the reason why versions of this approach have been used in such diverse fields as education, welfare, medicine, psychology, sociology and anthropology and gerontology. The use of these kinds of personal documentary sources in the study of education by teachers themselves has special and distinct advantages.

PERSONAL DOCUMENTARY SOURCES AND EDUCATION

Teachers and others have complained that the contextual particulars of the routine day-to-day activities of schools have often been ignored by researchers. Much of this research, it was claimed, did not pay attention to either teachers' pedagogical or practical problems. The use of autobiographical narratives or life histories of particular teachers and pupils when considered alongside certain themes as, for example, occupational histories, subject histories, or 'deviant' histories can help the researcher to see the ways in which individual experience relates to wider school and societal processes. One of the characteristic features of these personal documents is their ability to convey an individual's experience of the past. The teacher–researcher who takes the time to collect, interpret and analyse a life history, for example, has the opportunity not only of seeing events in a different way but also of discovering how apparently unconnected events seem to come together and shape future experience and behaviour. First-hand accounts of children's and pupils' experiences collected by the teacher can throw light on a whole range of issues and demonstrate the value of this kind of research focus. Two examples can be used here to highlight the value of collecting pupils' life stories, accounts and experiences.

As a result of a series of in-service workshops for ILEA teachers on the investigation of gender issues in the secondary school (Adams and Arnot 1986) one of the areas examined was the impact of parental aspirations and family culture on pupils' lives and values. The teachers were encouraged to focus upon collecting a pupil's first-hand account. The following account, provided by a white girl from a traditional working-class area, shows how mothers can influence their daughters' feelings of discontent, fantasy, domestic responsibilities, and the pressures to conform to traditional roles and expectations: all factors likely to influence girls' attitudes to school and learning:

> Me in ten years' time, that's a joke. I'll probably be chained to the cooker with three kids yapping around my ankles. I hope not. I hope I'll be living in the Caribbean with a millionaire husband with servants to wait on me hand and foot. I'd have a Porsche car and perhaps an old Rolls Royce to pop up the shops in. I'd have a new suit every day and my hair in a different style every week.
>
> I'll tell you the truth now as you can gather [that] was only a fantasy. In ten years' time, I should think I'll be married, I might have some children. I hope to have a nice car, doesn't have to be brand new but at least it will be decent. My husband will have a good job and we'll regularly go out to the pub or somewhere special. My house will be clean and I shall have nice furniture. My husband will have a car too, so when he goes out I'll still have a car in case I want to go out. I shall also have a job, it doesn't have to be full-time but at least it will be bringing more money into our

> home. My job will probably just be a part-time shop assistant or work mornings in a factory or warehouse.
>
> If I see myself like that in ten years' time, what's the point of me being here working like mad, getting as many exam passes as I can. It doesn't really seem worth coming to school but you only get in trouble if you don't.
>
> My mum and most of the women I know have lives like this. I think that I will be like them because to me a married woman with kids has a life like that, as they should enjoy the time with their families.
>
> This is what will happen to me if I don't do anything about it, not that I'm complaining, it's a decent life for someone like me.
>
> (Adams and Arnot 1986: 89–90)

Another example is provided by the work of Tom Cottle. In an extensive series of studies Cottle demonstrates the value of what he describes as the 'life study' in describing the lives of urban Black Americans and British West Indians (Cottle 1973: 344–60; 1978). An example of this approach can be found in his short account of a young female American prostitute, Matilda Rutherford (Cottle 1972: 519–63), and in his description of the lives of West Indians in London (Cottle 1978). Cottle's work is reminiscent of the Chicago urban ethnographers yet has a journalistic feel to it. His work develops out of long-term friendships and interviews as a form of conversation with the subject. These conversations can take place any time, anywhere. Cottle does not use a tape recorder. He believes that it intrudes too much on the naturalness of the situation. Instead he listens, makes notes and writes up the conversations later There must be, in his terms 'mutual recognition' that is a trusting and informal relationship between researcher and researched. Most of Cottle's work has been done in the USA; however, his work on poor West Indian families in London (Cottle 1978) does deal quite extensively with British West Indians' experience of the education system. These 'life stories' reveal the reality behind the Swann Report but no doubt also the alienation of many West Indian children in our schools. The following extracts from Polly Davies' story show considerable insight:

> Every day I walk by this brick wall. You have to go through this little passageway to get to school. There's usually a cat there climbing around. When I see him I tell him, bring me good luck. He usually runs away, which I tell myself is a good sign. Then I tell myself, no matter what anybody tells you, don't be upset, don't be afraid. Sometimes it works, but most of the time it doesn't especially if Jessie isn't with me. It's better when she's with me. I'd rather have someone yell out, 'There goes two nigger girls' than have me be there all by myself. You don't know what they're going to do next when they do it, and it's always happening. You don't know what's the best thing to do either. Like they's say, 'Hey, you short nigger, what are you – some kind of a pygmy?' That's my own special name because I'm short. Aren't they clever! I never know what to

do. Some people say you shout back at them so they won't do it again. But I couldn't get myself to do that. What am I supposed to do when it happens, like, when we're on the playground or on the stairs? Or in the class too? It happens in class too. 'Hey, pygmy, you read the lesson for today?' What am I supposed to do? Jessie says I should keep my mouth shut and tell one of the boys, like, the biggest person I see and tell him that kid over there called me a pygmy. That's what she says to do because she says if we don't start fighting back they'll never stop doing it to us. Maybe she's right, but I can't see myself going up to some guy and telling him what someone said to me.

(Cottle 1978: 57)

THE IMPORTANCE AND CENTRALITY OF THE INTERVIEW

At the heart of the life history approach is what has come to be described as the 'life history interview' which is different from other forms of interviewing in very many respects. Interviewing is, of course, one of the most popular and widely used techniques of data collection in the social sciences. Interview types can be identified in terms of the kinds of relationship between researcher and subject which characterize the interview situation, the nature of the questions asked, the kinds of information and discoveries sought, and the corresponding views of science which underpin these matters. In asking about the centrality and importance of the interview process in life history work we are raising some more general questions about the whole methodological basis of life history work. This is at once problematic.

The life history approach has occupied a highly marginal position in social and educational research compared to the use of systematic forms of observation, experiment, hypothesis testing and surveys. Furthermore, although there are many texts dealing with the mechanics of interviewing there is a corresponding absence of any highly developed theoretical and epistemological framework for life history research. What is distinct and unique about the life history technique itself provides the basis and framework from which such research may begin. In this sense the concern of life history work with revealing the subjective, phenomenal consciousness of an individual, as experienced by that individual, demands certain prerequisites of the overall methodological framework or strategy itself. Certain basic features of life history work may be outlined before considering the ways in which data are obtained in this approach. These themes relate more generally to the underlying concerns of qualitative research traditions.

Introspection is a central element of this approach with its concern to encourage subjects to reflect on the past and to look again at their own life and experiences in an introspective and subjective fashion. It follows that for the purposes of research, introspection cannot be recorded, presented or analysed without the involvement of another party. Hence life history work presupposes direct involvement of the researcher with the subject. Doing a life history then becomes a highly interactive and collaborative exercise based upon mutual understanding, empathy, trust and rapport, and some shared perceptions.

The life history is a document, a record or a text. Like all other documents, records or texts it has to be interpreted and presented. In Chapter 9 we explore in more depth the classificatory and analytic issues surounding documentary sources in general. Some people have argued that the life history speaks for itself and have left the text to stand by itself as a rich 'thick description' of a setting, situation, culture or organization. Can life histories be treated as if they are the direct interpersonal subjective experiences of an individual? Or, alternatively, is the role of researcher, as interpreter and the joint collaboration of researcher with subject, such that interpretation and selection is inevitable? Furthermore, what processes are involved when the reader 'reads' the text? In this sense interpretation, collaboration and introspection seem to be key ingredients of life history work, it is in this sense that life history research is different to many other research styles.

These features of life history work suggest that the role of the interview, or more appropriately conversation, becomes very different to that of interviewing in other kinds of research. The kind of interviewing strategies employed may be loosely characterized as being unstructured. However, this term is something of a misnomer since it conveys the impression that neither the subject nor researcher bring any preconceived ideas or structure to the interview, which is clearly not the case.

The concern with biography and the production of life history accounts means that considerable freedom can be given to the subjects to respond and talk in ways they wanted to about the issues they wanted to, prompted by the researcher's general concerns. In the light of the major characteristics of life history work we highlighted above it would be more true to say that we are talking about interviews, or more appropriately conversations, which enable the interviewee to introduce subjects, materials or themes as they see fit, which will to a large extent determine the nature of the interview itself. In this sense there is a diminishing role for the interviewer as social science researcher and an extension of the role of sympathetic listener, friend, colleague and fellow human being. William Foote Whyte has said much the same thing whcn he comments that:

> The good research interview is structured in terms of the research problem. The interview structure is not fixed by predetermined questions, as in the questionnaire, but is designed to provide the informant with the freedom to introduce materials that were not anticipated by the interviewer.
>
> (Whyte 1982: 27)

The kind of interviewing we will be dealing with has been called 'unstructured' but as we pointed out earlier this is a misnomer for no interaction between two people in which one is seeking information can be completely unstructured. Teachers in their everyday job are constantly asking and answering questions and to this degree have a fund of experience on which to draw. The difference lies in the fact that interviewing, as we have defined it, becomes a conscious activity, conducted according to rules and with a clear aim in view. Conversations and interviews are no longer random and largely unrecorded but become a principal source of data which we can use to develop an understanding of the world of teaching and schools.

As such, this book reflects both the increasing tendency for teachers to engage in small-scale research into areas of professional concern and the renewed interest in so-called 'qualitative methods' as means of collecting and analysing data in educational research. Indeed, as Brenner, Brown and Canter (1985) have argued, one can widen this tendency further and say that across the spectrum of the social–human sciences discipline divide, the use of interviews as a means of data collection has grown rapidly in recent years and has led to the emergence of new forms of interview. Life history research presents one such expression of this. We are concerned to show how such approaches can be developed within the context of school-based research.

ORGANIZATIONS AND THE LIFE HISTORY APPROACH

The life history offers some important possibilities when it comes to unravelling the complex interconnected sets of meanings, interpretations and expectations which go to make up schools as complex organizations. The fundamental way in which these meanings take on a rational, understandable and workable form is through the use of language and the development of an organization's vocabulary or grammar, its rhetoric, and its argot or a specialized language, through which the reality of teaching is constituted. Teachers' accounts of their experiences and their viewpoints will frequently be couched in this vocabulary and grammar. It is through these accounts, stories, reminiscences and popular myths (all of which the life history may focus upon) that the collective reality of the organization is transmitted, accepted or contested. At times of change these vocabularies and grammars themselves must change and adapt as is currently happening in the UK. In this way life history research is not just useful for exploring teachers' careers but is a very important research orientation for curriculum research in general. In examining individual careers and histories, the relationship between individual and group processes, professional themes and practical arrangements, relationships between groups and institutions and, more importantly, the way these change over time, life history research has much to offer. It is these features which underly the 'reality' of schools as organizations. Jones (1983) has put the case for life history research and a focus upon personal documentary sources in such settings in the following way:

In using the life history methodology to approach such issues the re-

> searcher's aims to uncover the grammar of an organization's language, to expose the ways in which the typifications offered by a particular organizational language condition the experience and action of organization members, and to understand how members themselves account for the premises contained in the organizational language. The methodology can be used to generate and analyse life history accounts of organizational members in a variety of ways.
>
> For example, suppose that the researcher is interested in the study of organizational socialization or career development and the ways in which dominant organizational members seek to impose their definitions of the situation on others. One form of account immediately available is that contained in the autobiographies, diaries, and correspondence of prominent entrepreneurs, philanthropists, and politicians.
>
> (Jones 1983: 155)

However, such studies do not simply take us to the individual, cultural milieu, mapping individual changes and responses through the life cycle, they are also better equipped to reveal the relationship between the individual and wider structural arrangements; the interaction of biography and history. All the same, the life history technique is not appropriate for every research project the teacher–researcher will become engaged in. A number of factors will come into play including individual circumstances, the nature of the project and practical constraints of time and energy. Once the decision has been taken to use the life history technique the researcher will need to attend to some preliminary issues, the process of data collection, and making sense of and analysing life history materials. We will explore each of these phases in turn.

PRELIMINARY ISSUES

This phase of any research is crucial. The observations we make here are really best considered when the research is being planned and thought about, that is at the stage of research design. Practical as well as technical matters are involved. Since the life history technique relies so heavily on the goodwill of the subject or subjects, it is essential to make adequate and effective prior arrangements. For similar reasons it is important that the teacher–researcher has a reasonably clear idea of the kinds of question she wants eventually to ask and the general areas on which information and ideas are sought. Choosing a person to work with will be dependent upon the availability of the individuals with whom the researcher wishes to work and their position *vis-à-vis* the topic or theme of the research. Here it is important to bear in mind the points made in Chapter 6 and about the ways field researchers select informants. The researcher using the life history technique, perhaps more than any other researcher, must be able to develop a close, sympathetic and understanding relationship with the subject.

Obviously, teachers will have to consider status differences between themselves and any teachers they work with, as well as any problems arising from working with children or older pupils.

DATA COLLECTION PHASE

The prospective teacher–researcher might profitably gain from re-reading the sections on data collection in Chapter 5. The initial problem for the researcher concerned to produce a life history is how to record the conversations and narratives. No hard and fast rules can be laid down. It is preferable for a number of reasons to use a tape recorder to collect the life history materials. It is the best way of quickly and accurately recording data. Alternatively, the researcher can write down the subject's comments and replies to questions or ask the subject to write down their own commentaries and life stories. Life history researchers have made use of all these methods of recording the materials. Whereas the use of a tape recorder offers the easiest form of recording the data the presence of a tape recorder often makes people ill at ease. Furthermore, school and classroom contexts do not always present the easiest places to record in. Often the researcher might take notes during the early periods of involvement with the subject and once a friendly atmosphere has developed introduce the tape recorder. The major problem with taking notes as the subject is talking concerns the fact that the speaker usually talks more quickly than the researcher can write. Finally, some researchers have quite successfully asked their subjects to write their own accounts.

The problem of recording rests upon the nature of the research and the general stance of the researcher. Certainly not all researchers have found that the tape recorder is the solution to all problems. For example, Cottle (1978) found the tape recorder an unnecessary burden and his comments are worth considering:

> Futhermore, I used no pre-arranged interview schedule. Nor did I concentrate on designing a scientifically determined sample. I made a number of friends, most of whom I met in informal ways, if not purely by accident. I visited schools, housing and employment programmes, clinics and hospitals, social service agencies, churches and of course people's homes. As I grew familiar with particular neighbourhoods, meeting people became no problem at all.
>
> As a methodological note, my conversations were not tape-recorded. Like others I found the tape-recorder to be a cumbersome intrusion in friendship.
>
> (Cottle 1978: 57)

Thus, Cottle's informal approach to recording extends to the whole tenor of his research. Some, however, would regard this as being unsystematic or too informal. Perhaps the only way to assess the success of this approach is to consider the quality of the materials Cottle is able to assemble by the use of such an approach.

Once the question of how the materials are to be recorded is decided the teacher–researcher must begin to think about the general questions to be asked, areas to be covered, and how this is to be achieved. For the most part the teacher–researcher is likely to rely upon the kind of extended informal conversation used by researchers such as Cottle (1978) and elaborated in more detail by Woods (1985b: 13–26). Here, the teacher–researcher cultivates the art of listening, imposing herself as little as possible into the situation since the more the researcher is to the fore, the less the subject's voice will come through. Any researcher interjections or criticisms must be conducted with care. Empathy, understanding and the ability to lend a sympathetic ear are all ingredients in the successful production of life histories. One might think that these are qualities teachers would already possess.

The actual conduct of the interview or conversational exchanges themselves will depend upon the extent to which the researcher wants the subject to wander freely from one topic to another or to focus upon particular themes or topics. The number of meetings or conversations involved will vary from project to project and the time available. There will usually be a combination of the subject talking generally and particularly interspaced with the researcher asking general and focused questions. In this way the life history gets built up. Once the involvement with the subject comes to an end many researchers have one final meeting where some of the emergent themes that the researcher is beginning to isolate can be raised and the subject's views recorded. Again, as we noted in Chapter 6, whilst engaged in collecting qualitative materials the researcher is also conducting a preliminary analysis of these materials. Many of the themes the researcher might follow up later will appear spontaneously as the data are being collected.

ANALYSIS, EXPLANATION AND PRESENTATION

Once the teacher has collected the life history materials and organized them the task of analysis can begin. However, the analysis of life history materials has been conducted in a variety of ways. Some researchers feel that it is simply best to leave the life history materials to stand on their own, whereas others have edited and analysed the materials in more detail. This points up one of the central tensions in life history research, namely the desire to retain the rich detailed descriptions on the one hand yet to develop some analysis and explanation of the materials on the other. Undoubtedly, the many published life histories available and those produced by teachers that we have seen all have their own intrinsic merits. They are all a good read. But the teacher–researcher is concerned to try and develop more systematic knowledge and understanding of the factors which influence professional practice and school learning. As such, the teacher–researcher will want more from the materials and will consequently have to develop some analysis of them.

Part of the process of analysis will involve the researcher establishing the extent to which the materials are valid, reliable, and representative of the concerns of the project. These issues tend to take on a rather different character for the researcher relying so heavily upon first-person accounts. The researcher needs to establish the truthfulness and accuracy of the accounts so far as she is able. How does the teacher know that people are not telling the researcher lies? How is it possible to establish whether the researcher and the subject are engaged in the elaborate creation of a congruent fiction? These are important issues in any research but the use of first-hand subjective accounts brings them to the fore. A major concern of school-based research must be that it goes beyond the 'merely' anecdotal and moves towards analytical as well as authentic accounts of school and classroom processes. Researchers working within the ethnographic tradition have developed ways in which it is possible to check on the validity and accuracy of the qualitative materials. The teacher–researcher using the life history technique might consider the following as a short checklist against which they could place the narratives which they have collected:

- Note the circumstances surrounding the recording and collection of the data.
- Consider the relationship between researcher and subject.
- Are there any 'facts' in the accounts which are easily checked on?
- Compare statements in one section of a life history with statements in another section of the same life history.
- Compare the statements in one life history with those in other life histories from different people within the same setting.
- Compare the statements in the life history with data from other sources within the same setting.
- Compare the statements in the life history with other statements in published life histories of teachers and pupils.
- If possible, get a second opinion on the materials by showing them to colleagues.

Although none of these procedures guarantees the absolute accuracy of the materials retained, together they do go some way towards establishing validity. Furthermore, this procedure will help the teacher–researcher to consider the typicality of comments and the relationship of the materials to the setting as a whole. This process is an important one because reasons are going to be attributed to the accounts and subsequent explanations of them will be offered. This is no easy task, as the case of Vincent Van Gogh's left ear demonstrates. Whereas there is no doubt that Van Gogh cut off a portion of his left ear, what is debatable is why he did it. Runyan (1982: 38–41) elaborates thirteen different sets of explanations!

Perhaps the best way to think about the analysis of life history materials drawn from school contexts is to approach them in terms of themes. This kind of approach to analysis is therefore described as thematic analysis and involves the researcher examining the kinds of themes that emerge from the materials regularly, and how they relate to the concerns of the project. The researcher could therefore concentrate upon, for example, a teacher's occupational history, a particular child's deviant 'career' or the involvement of staff with a subject area or curriculum development project. Some guidelines do exist in the literature and the reader should consult some of the suggested further reading at the end of this chapter. By way of illustration we will briefly consider one way in which life histories may be analysed.

An anthropologist, Mandelbaum (1973), has developed a way of looking at life history materials which may be of use to the teacher–researcher. Mandelbaum's solution to the vast and often highly jumbled flood of raw data the life history produces is for the researcher first to organize the materials into some kind of chronological ordering but then to focus upon three aspects: dimensions, turnings and adaptations. Dimensions of life, including the individual's general, social, cultural and psychological experiences, and the subject's subjective world; in other words, how an individual grows up, for example, and the attitudes and values surrounding individuals. Turnings refer to those turning-points or transitions or changes of status an individual goes through. These turnings occur when the individual takes on new roles or a new status and as a result takes on a new social identity; it is appropriate therefore to look and ask for key turning-points in a life. Turnings are, of course, extremely varied, from religious conversion to promotion to a senior teaching post through to marriage or divorce. Finally, adaptations refer to the ways in which individuals at some point or other in their lives must slightly amend, alter, or change their values, attitudes and behaviour patterns to accommodate and handle new situations. Mandelbaum's scheme seems to be quite illuminating and it is one which we suggest is particularly appropriate to the educational context. Mandelbaum's scheme was employed in his famous life history of Ghandi.

The methodology of life history research applied to schools and as it may be used by teachers is relatively underdeveloped, though of course elsewhere in the social sciences this is not the case. However, pioneering work in this field by Goodson (1983) and Sikes, Measor and Woods (1985) raises important methodological issues and shows what kind of analyses may be made. Watson (1976: 95–131) has provided a framework, based upon the ideas of hermeneutics and phenomenology, for understanding the life history. He makes a number of points which are worth considering here that provide the basis of a framework for understanding teachers' life histories.

'The sociocultural context'

Following the ideas of intepretive sociology and phenomenology social events can only be fully understood if placed within a particular context.

This is part of a more widespread current interest in the realm of the cultural in understanding social life and, in particular, the ways in which cultural factors shape and mediate individual subjectivity. As far as the life histories of teachers presented here are concerned the teacher–researchers have drawn upon their own extensive knowledge of the wider cultural and historical context of teachers' careers and professional development in not only conducting the interviews but in making sense of the materials also. This sociocultural context will include all the salient features which surround the individual, topic or theme being explored. As Watson puts it:

> The details of economics, family structure, politics, religion and educational transmission, for example, must all be known to comprehend fully the contextual meaning of events and experiences described in the life history.
>
> (Watson 1976: 102)

'The individual life in context'

It will be important to try and place the life history materials within the context of ideas about pedagogy the individual teacher holds. This is, of course, quite difficult since individual's viewpoints do not always present themselves clearly or unambiguously. However, this must be attempted if crude stereotypes are to be avoided. As well as the age, gender and social class background of the teacher, factors such as religious persuasion and outlook are all likely to influence the ways in which an individual sees the social world. Furthermore, it is important to set the life history materials against the individual changes as a direct result of the life cycle. Young teachers may experience school and their training in very different ways than otherwise similar older teachers. Female teachers experience the world in different ways to male teachers. All these features will go towards shaping the general sociocultural context of any individual teacher's life.

Watson suggests that as well as appreciating the general cultural and social context within which an individual operates, it is also important to focus upon the relationship of the individual concerned with this general context. Here, teachers' experiences are mediated by individual variations as a result of many factors.

'The immediate context of life history data gathering'

Watson draws our attention to the all important practical aspects of the way in which the life history comes into being, and the way in which it is recorded and interpreted. The way in which the life history is elicited will shape the kinds of expectations and understanding of both parties. In the particular context of teachers' professional lives it is crucial that the teacher–researcher explains fully to the teacher the basis of the research. What kind of bargain has been struck between researcher and subject? What is the basis of this relationship? How do teachers perceive the exercise? How are the individual teachers who are the subjects of the life histories *and* the teacher–researchers themselves, defining their roles and their identities within the interactions? The teacher who is the focus of the research may bring a number of assumptions to the research situation that are or are not shared by the researcher. The teacher–researchers themselves will undoubtedly have their own views of the situation. These factors may not only influence what the individual recalls from memory but also the way in which this information is presented. The teacher–researcher subsequently filters these materials through her own perceptions and experiences. Appreciation of the way this done is important. This brings us to another issue raised by Watson.

'Preunderstandings'

Using the ideas of phenomenological philosophy, Watson (1976) suggests that it is crucial to be aware of our own perceptions of the events and activities we wish to research and investigate. In this sense it is important for teacher–researchers to explore the nature of their own *preunderstandings*. Since the aim of life history research is to locate and record individual subjective experience as it changes during the life cycle, researchers have to avoid the temptation of understanding these materials only in terms of what the researchers themselves want to understand. In other words, life history research is not about what we, (the researcher) understand, but is rather about attempting to understand what the subject understands. Teacher–researchers need to try and avoid prejudice and make every effort to explore their own preunderstandings.

These are just some of the kinds of features it is important to consider when making sense of life histories. Clearly, many more emerge in the course of particular pieces of research. These questions are all part and parcel of the problems and possibilities of life history research.

SOME IMPORTANT QUESTIONS ABOUT PERSONAL DOCUMENTARY SOURCES

The teacher–researcher needs to think in advance of the possible strengths and weaknesses of the use of any research technique or source of data. She also needs to bear in mind the way in which the findings of the research can be presented to others and some of the implications for professional practice contained in them. The following might be regarded as a preliminary checklist for the teacher–researcher to attend to when using personal documentary sources as a substantial part of a piece of school-based research:

- What is the nature of the document or documents in question? Are they largely solicited or unsolicited? What consequences follow?
- Who is the subject and what grounds for subject choice can be given?

- How are the issues of validity, reliability and representativeness to be dealt with?
- What is the nature of researcher involvement in the project?
- How is the material to be organized, edited and analysed?
- How are the research findings to be communicated to other professionals?

These questions by no means exhaust all the issues associated with the use of personal documentary sources in school-based research. They provide the teacher–researcher with only a general guide to some of the issues which will have to be dealt with. The 'answers' to these six questions will, however, form a substantial part of any research involving personal documentary sources. The reader might like to consider the ways in which other researchers, notably Goodson (1983) and Woods (1985b: 13–26), deal with some of these issues at this point. The issues suronding presentational aspects of qualitative research in general are dealt with in Chapter 14.

LIFE OF PUPILS AND TEACHERS

A clear case may be made for the teacher–researcher focusing upon the biographies, experiences and interpretations of pupils and teachers. All educational practices and systems have a history. A focus upon teachers' and pupils' life histories can help to relate individual experience to the wider school, community or societal context. Individuals' perceptions of the learning environment shape and influence their experience of and involvement in these environments. The teacher–researcher is concerned to step back and take a systematic look at her own and others' professional practice. To this end we suggest that some of the following themes may be explored by use of the life history technique.

Suggested themes for exploration in pupils' life histories:

- Pupils' experience of previous schools.
- Pupils' views of subjects.
- Pupils' attitudes to gender issues.
- 'Disaffected' pupils.
- Pupils with 'special needs'.
- Pupils' experience of ethnicity .

Suggested themes for exploration in teachers' life histories:

- Teachers' professional training and perception of pupils and subjects.
- Teachers' career patterns and experience of previous schools.
- Teachers' involvement in curriculum innovation or development.
- Teachers' experience of roles and authority.
- Teachers' attitudes to pupils.
- Teachers' attitudes to gender issues.
- Teachers' attitudes to children with learning difficulties.

A focus upon pupils' viewpoints is a relatively recent phenomenon. But, Blishen (1969), Hammersley and Woods (1976), Woods (1980b) and Measor and Woods (1983: 55–76) have all considered ways of investigating pupils' worlds, which face different circumstances. The teacher will have a position in the school, a 'reputation' amongst both staff and pupils. These factors can play quite a determining role in the research process and the teacher–researcher will have to consider the ways in which these factors influence matters. Of note here would be factors such as the age of the pupils, their familiarity with the researcher, differences in language usage between pupils and the researcher, and the topics being explored. Perhaps most obvious is the question of the truthfulness of pupils' accounts. But, as Measor and Woods (1983: 55–76) point out, even pupil myths have a serious and important reality to them. Indeed, these matters are crucial aspects of school culture which perform important functions in peer socialization, the formation of groups and so on. For the most part when working closely with pupils in the construction of life histories the teacher will need to adopt a sympathetic and understanding stance, refrain from imposing her authority and 'definition of the situation'.

Whereas the production of pupils' life histories is not without its difficulties, neither is the production of teachers' life histories. The nature of the relative position and status of researcher is crucial. Again, a realization on the part of the teacher–researcher that schools are social situations like anywhere else, made up of people who get on and don't get on, gossip, hearsay and rumour will serve to sharpen her awareness of the context of the research. The recent teachers' dispute, for example, created serious rifts in many staffrooms. These are all realities behind teacher research in general.

In an important article Goodson (1983: 129–54) has attempted to demonstrate the importance of collecting and using teachers' life histories. By focusing upon the work of the American educational ethnographer, Louis Smith, in particular *The Complexities of an Urban Classroom* (Smith and Geoffrey 1968) and Smith's later research on the same school, Kensington School, *Anatomy of an Educational Innovation*, (Smith and Keith 1971), Goodson demonstrates the importance of trying to link the life histories of individuals with the histories of schools as a whole and patterns of educational innovation. Smith's follow-up study was concerned to see what had happened to the original staff and what effect the Kensington experience had had on them. By adopting such an approach and collecting life histories of the heads of the school through retrospective interviews an important picture of the changes the school underwent began to emerge. Smith's problem was to develop a methodology that could deliver descriptions of the major changes and innovations the school experienced. His solution was to widen the focus from life histories of the individual heads and their periods of office to the testimonies of other teachers and the wider history of the school district.

Goodson has also gone on to discuss the sorts of materials that can be collected in producing life histories of teachers, in particular their involvement in subjects and curriculum change in *School Subjects and Curriculum Change* (Goodson 1982). The aim of this project was to try to establish the background to the introduction of a new school subject, Environmental Studies. Goodson began by collecting the life histories of the key figures in the promotion of the subject, arguing that, in fact, the life histories of these teachers became the life history of the subject. It is therefore possible to develop insights into the teachers' changing perception of work set against the background of school organization. Goodson's work demonstrates the importance and value of focusing upon teachers' careers, work experience and location in a particular socio-cultural milieu through the life history.

Peter Woods has recently discussed the conversational aspects of the life history method (1985b: 13–26). Woods reports on research with a sample of fifty secondary school teachers grouped according to age and subject, the aim of which was initially to concentrate upon the ways in which teachers adapted to crises and critical incidents in the course of their careers. The life history was seen as the most appropriate method there, but as a result of the circumstances Woods and those working with him felt it had to be adapted. The point is strongly made that one of the major values of the life history and its reliance upon conversations between teachers and researchers is that it contrasts strongly with the more traditional 'researcher–researched' model, where the latter provides the data and the former the interpretation; and yet avoids the limitations of some 'teacher–researcher' approaches, as Woods argues, 'life history approaches offer real prospects for bridging the divide between education research and the practice of teaching, and the empirical supports of sociological theory'.

A good example of the way in which 'biography' can be used as the basis of a research strategy is promised by Louden (1991) and reviewed by Hitchcock (1992). Louden develops the 'story' of Johanna, a Canadian Community School teacher (a public alternative school for children in Grades 7 and 8, aged 12 and 13 years). It is also the 'story' of William Louden's attempt to capture and make sense of the traditions which underlie the teaching of one able and interesting person. This book represents an innovative and sensitive account of teachers' knowledge focusing upon central themes of continuity, the settled practice and sets of routine which frame the everyday experience of teachers which shape any responses to change. This is what Louden tries to do.

Louden's study is not easy to read, but then why should it be? For many years the study of curriculum and schooling has been undertaken simplistically and with faint regard to the autobiographical, situational and interpretive aspects of teachers' lives and work. It is only with the development of notions such as the 'extended professional' and 'reflective practitioner' that a full appreciation of the importance of biography is beginning to emerge. This has been aided by the renaissance of life history approaches across the human sciences that we discussed earlier, on the one hand, and the influence of both hermeneutic interpretive traditions and critical theory, on the other. Louden's theoretical underpinning comes from people such as Schon, Habermas and Godamer. Louden's methodology will be familiar to field-based ethnographic research. However, the focus upon one single informant and the corresponding high degrees of respondent validity achieved, with the researcher's changing role, significantly push this methodology forward. Louden thereby might overcome or at best balance some of the weaknesses of life history research. The result is a richly descriptive and superbly sensitive account of what it is like for this person to be a teacher, how this teacher gives meaning to and makes sense of the syllabus and the activities which surround it. Louden's book then is in the genre of intensive case-studies providing an autobiographically sensitive classroom perspective on the knowledge this teacher has and uses.

The study retains the feel and sense of person and place characteristic of good ethnography. The story unfolds around an initial account of Johanna's life, her dreams, hopes and loves. Chapter 2 provides an account of what Louden describes as Johanna's repertoire 'those lessons which have been rehearsed and refined over the years and which form the experiential basis for the new lessons she invents each day' (Louden 1991: 24). This takes the form of six stories of Johanna's teaching during Autumn 1988. In the course of the stories Louden raises some important issues about narrative voice and layers of interpretation, issues we have already touched upon. The next two chapters focus, respectively, on a series of writing and science lessons. In Chapter 6 the concentration is upon reflecting on the kinds of dimensions and categories which may be useful in conceptualizing the ways in which Johanna's understanding of these changes in her teaching were achieved, and throws some light on the problems and possibilities concerning the analysis of such materials. Again, Louden is at pains to point out the collaborative nature of the process. The book concludes with an interesting chapter on the whole process of continuity and change in Johanna's teaching practice.

Louden has, with the help of an amazingly articulate teacher, written a remarkable book. The message is clear: change in teachers' work is a change in teachers' lives. Any attempts at reform, school improvement or innovation which do not take account of this fact will inevitably fail. Biography and life history research has a clear function to play here.

PROBLEMS AND POSSIBILITIES

For a long time life history research occupied a marginal position in social research, in part due to the declining use of the approach in Chicago and later interactionist sociology. Many critics pointed to the highly subjective nature of the approach, and in their view, the limiting reliance upon single informants. A number of issues may be raised here and, indeed, some are discussed in the following chapters. The general worry of most of these criticisms is the potential flight into individualism which the methodology offers. Indeed, it is important to guard against seeing teachers in isolation from the wider context.

Other worries include things such as practical concerns, including the time-consuming nature of this kind of work, the development of rapport, interpersonal skills and skills in interviewing; ethical issues; representativeness, reliability and validity; and, finally, the question of analysis, interpretation and theory.

Life history research in particular is extremely time-consuming, it places responsibilities on both subject and researcher and involves the subject and researcher in extended periods of one or two hours or longer together. Of course the work does not end here and transcribing and developing analyses are further time-consuming activities that have to be accounted for before writing up the finished project. From what has been said so far it is clear to see that the development of rapport and empathy between subject and researcher are crucial elements in interactive techniques such as the life history interview. Indeed, qualitative, ethnographic field work by its very nature puts the researcher in a high profile position and demands involvement and participation with members of the field or setting. Not everyone has the interpersonal skills necessary to conduct such work. This is even more the case when it comes to highly interactive and collaborative techniques such as the life history with its emphasis upon the discovery of subjective meaning.

The role of interviewer in this kind of research, as it is in all other qualitatively orientated social and educational research, is very different to the predominant structured and objective survey type interview. This is in part due to the fact that the very purpose of the interview in life history and qualitative research is different to that of other research approaches and is based upon different goals, aims and assumptions. Elliot Mishler (1986) has cogently argued the case that most conventional approaches to interviewing in social research present severe limitations at best and at worst are restrictive practices which eradicate much of the context, and hence meaning, of what it is interviewees and interviewers are saying. In contrast he argues:

> An interview is a joint production of what interviewees and interviewers talk about together and how they talk with each other. The record of an interview that we researchers make and then use in our work of analysis and interpretation is a representation of that talk.
>
> (Mishler 1986: vii)

However, this is not the way in which the interview is typically viewed. So often 'questions' and 'answers' are seen as stimuli and response and not forms of speech or speech events. This is further evident in the use of extended and elaborate coding and statistical analyses characteristic of much interview data and analysis. The neglect of the respondent's and interviewer's personal and social contexts and, conversely, a concern with getting around 'researcher bias' are matters which become translated in life history interviewing into what Mishler (1986) has described as the problems of 'meaning expressing' and 'meaning understanding'. The studies in the remaining chapters have all had to confront these problems but begin from some fundamentally different assumptions about what an interview is, to that of the conventional wisdom surrounding the research interview.

The teacher–researcher, like all other researchers is a moral agent and will have views, opinions, values and attitudes. Clearly, ethical issues will have to be faced. These may be broken down into two aspects. First, there are the general issues of trust, confidentiality, anonymity and the ownership of the knowledge produced by the research. Second, it is fair to say that particular research strategies pose special ethical problems, for example, there are differences between conducting overt participant observation and covert participant observation (Bulmer 1982). In some respects the teacher–researcher role solves many ethical problems but simultaneously generates new ones. In much conventional research the researcher raids the school for knowledge and escapes with it in order to write it up for professional research. The point is that this is often one way, is sometimes covert, and frequently puts little if anything back into the professional and pedogogical context. School-based teacher research, because it is done by teachers, albeit often in conjunction with so-called 'academics', can avoid this kind of hijacking. The resulting knowledge belongs to teachers themselves though, of course, it will stand as important contributions to our general understanding of schools and classrooms. Crucial issues regarding the ownership of knowledge, privacy and individual rights are raised. The life stories presented here are produced by teachers in interaction and cooperation with other teachers. The knowledge is shared, the aim being an enhanced appreciation of professional practice, an important democratization of the research process ensues.

We now come to an area that has concerned many people, that is the status of life history accounts and the life history technique as a rigorous, scientific instrument. The so-called problems with life history work on these grounds in part explain the limited role it has played in social research when compared to other strategies. To the fore are questions surrounding the use of single informants and individual cases, the involvement of the researcher and the highly personalized and subjective nature of the data. The representativeness, reliability and validity of life history materials have all been questioned. Whilst not wanting to dismiss these concerns, they clearly are *conventional* questions which routinely get asked about conventional social research. LeCompte and Goetz (1982: 31–61) make the important point that as ethnographic research is very different in kind to experimental research, consequently, the issues of reliability and validity need not be defined, or even applied, in the same ways by these two differing approaches. It is debatable whether teacher–researchers' work will ever satisfy criteria of representativeness since they will be unable to 'sample' large numbers of teachers, pupils, schools or classrooms in order to demonstrate typicality for purposes of making generalizations. The 'sample' is in effect one, in life history research.

There are, however, a number of strategies available here. Within the case study, or small-scale school-based project, the representativeness of groups observed or interviewed and the typicality of what they say can be monitored. Similarly, the teacher–researcher can establish the validity of the life history materials, that is whether they are a true and accurate reflection of a situation, from that person's viewpoint, by employing some simple validity checks or 'validation strategies'. For example, life history data can be compared with documentary sources and data obtained from other sources by means of different techniques via some form of triangulation. A negative case may be examined, that is an instance or situation which seems to contradict the general substance of the materials. Alternatively, some form of respondent validation could be approached whereby the data and analysis are taken back to the subjects for comment. Finally, the teacher–researcher could attempt some form of theoretical sampling as outlined by Glaser and Strauss (1967). However, there are other ways to conceive of these issues. Instead of speaking about validity of life history accounts one could ask instead about their authenticity, that is the extent to which they ring true, the ways in which the researcher feels that they are legitimate, authentic accounts. It would seem a nonsense to ask questions about the reliability of life history work, and the extent to which the end products are simply products of the technique employed because they are exactly that. Life history work produces detailed personal subjective accounts because that is what it precisely aims to do. The notion of replication is similarly problematic since the life history interview is so heavily dependent upon the kind of mutual communication and interaction which develops interpersonally between two human beings. Instead of speaking about reliability *per se* one could begin instead to think about the data as being joint productions and exploring the co-production of meaning. Representativeness might therefore also be translated, as referring to narrative authority and control, that is the way to which the narrative account itself is structured. What is included and omitted, and the way in which what is said is *said*. Clearly, we are some way away from a more complete elaboration of the significance of these issues for both social and educational research. All the same, teacher research in general and life history work in particular are likely to bring these questions up. Ultimately, what we are talking about here is teachers trusting their own experience and perhaps discovering that the colleague with whom they work and perhaps thought they knew turns out to be someone else. The life history is concerned with the social construction of reality with which any individual operates. We are in no way denying the significance of validity, reliability and representativeness, but are instead arguing that teacher research requires a little more creativity in the ways in which these criteria are employed and assessed.

This brings us on to one final issue which surrounds the status of the knowledge produced using these approaches and what kinds of analysis and interpretations may be made. What is the theoretical basis of this research and how might it further enhance our study of the curriculum?

The current political context of teaching and research has contributed to a general decline in support for and funding of independent research and inquiry. We have strongly encouraged a teacher–researcher role as being a crucial element of teachers' professional practice. Underlying our view of the teacher–researcher, Schon's (1983) notion of the 'reflective practitioner' and Lawrence Stenhouse's (1975) 'self-reflective teacher' lies a commitment to *empowering* professionals and, in particular, to generating critically effective, emancipatory activities that feed back into professional practice. Perhaps there has never been a more appropriate (or critical) a time for teachers to take greater control over research into their own professional practice than the present, they should own this knowledge and do something with it! It can in part provide some of the basis for sound professional judgements. But research is not curriculum development, neither is it evaluation. Research is something else. But what, in turn, is the knowledge base of this research? On what is it based and where does it come from? In our opinion the social sciences must form the baseline from which teacher research develops, utilizing its frameworks and techniques and becoming involved in the same controversies and debates. As such, we are clearly not promoting the de-skilling of teachers, but, on the contrary, this process is concerned with empowering them, enabling teachers to become more critical, reflective practitioners, responsible for their own professional development and aware of the complex variables which influence both teaching and learning thereby putting them in a better position to evaluate evidence. It follows that the questions of analysis, interpretation and theory in teacher research will follow similar lines to the ways in which these matters are approached in the social sciences more generally. However, the end point of any teacher research is rather different and in one sense more overtly applied, since this knowledge, analysis and findings and the various skills employed goes back to the context of professional practice where something is done with it. For example, the skills required to conduct the projects described here might be argued to be precisely those which will be needed for the practice of teacher appraisal interviewing or in staff development work.

CONCLUSION

This chapter has focused upon biography and the ways in which life history research can provide a way into understanding the significant influence of personal biography on teaching and learning. We have looked at the nature of life histories, the product of such research and the life history interview, the process which produces the product. Increasingly, life history research is featuring in the work of health professionals, as in the case of research, into the life of a congenital amputee (Frank 1981; 1984; 1988), and in the area of social gerontology, the study of ageing (Myerhoff and Tufte 1974); Myerhoff (1978); Fry and Keith (1986); (Frank and Vanderburgh 1986). The relationship between this research and policy formation and implementation is interesting and teacher–researchers using life history and autobiographical techniques would do well to explore this field.

We have attempted to explore life history research and highlight the value and, indeed, potential of this approach for teacher–researchers. Life history and autobiographical research takes us back to the intersection of an individual life with the social structure, or cultural and organizational processes with large side structural and institutional arrangements. Whilst early work using these techniques regarded the autobiography or life history as largely unproblematically self-referential, recent work has focused more explicitly upon the social production, interpretation and writing of the life history. Life history research has not escaped the debates which currently beset the intellectual cultures of the social and educational (human) sciences. The impact of postmodernist philosophy, feminism and literary turns in ethnography (Clifford and Marcus 1986) are increasingly being embraced by those concerned with biography. Self-consciously, researchers are concerned with the 'art' of their work as much as, or more than, the science of their endeavours. Such developments in life history research raise important questions about the nature and form of cultural representations in general, and representations of the lives of teachers and pupils in particular. Do life histories represent or construct social realities? Life history texts are indeed social productions which make use of a variety of genre conventions. How is the validity of life history research established? The overall effect of these and other questions is a heightened awareness of the analytical and methodological boundaries of life history research. There is clear evidence that educational research and teacher research is likely to be at the forefront of these developments (Woods 1987; 1993 and P. J. Wood 1993). We would encourage teachers to take up the challenge presented by life history research in order to realize not simply the promise but the undeniable potential such an orientation offers.

SUGGESTED FURTHER READING

There are some excellent introductory/overview texts and articles which may be consulted when considering life history and biographical approaches. These usually come from either an anthropological or a sociological perspective. Amongst the best here are *Biography and Society: The Life History Approach in the Social Sciences* (Bertaux 1981); *Interpretative Biography*, (Denzin 1988); 'Doing life histories' (Faraday and Plummer 1979); 'Finding the common denominator: a phenomenological critique of life history method' (Frank 1979); *Documents of Life: An Introduction to the Problems and Literature of a Humanistic Method* (Plummer 1983); 'Biographical method' (Smith 1994), Chapter 18 in *Handbook of Qualitative Research*

(Denzin and Lincoln 1994); and *Interpreting Life Histories* (Watson and Watson-Franke 1985). Increasingly, life history approaches are featuring in educational research. One of the earliest collections of studies using this approach can be found in *Teachers' Lives and Careers* (Ball and Goodson 1985). In addition, the following studies highlight the promise of such a focus, 'Institutional change and career histories in a comprehensive school' (Benyon 1985) in *Teachers' Lives and Careers* (Ball and Goodson 1985); 'Life histories and the study of schooling' (Goodson 1980) and *Studying Teachers' Lives* (Goodson 1990).

A significant critical literature now exists on the use and value of life history and biographical approaches in both educational research and professional development. See, for example, 'Life histories and teacher knowledge' (Woods 1987) in *Educating Teachers: Changing the Nature of Professional Knowledge* (Smythe 1987); 'The use of teacher biographies in professional self-development' (Woods and Sykes 1987), *Planning Continuing Professional Development* (Todd 1987) and 'Sponsoring the teacher's voice: teachers' lives and teacher development' (Goodson 1991). See also the example in *Insights into Teachers' Thinking on Practice* (Day, Pope and Denicolo (1990)). Ethical issues are explored by 'Ethics and methodology in life history' (Measor and Sykes 1990) in *Studying Teachers' Lives* (Goodson 1990). Finally, the 'interpretative' and 'textual' directions which life history and biographical research seem destined to take in the future are echoed in the absolutely fascinating and insightful trio of articles by Peter Woods, David Thomas and Peter J. Woods. See 'Managing marginality: teacher development through grounded life history' (P. Woods 1993); 'Empirical authors, texts, and model readers: a response to "managing marginality"' (Thomas 1993), and 'Keys to the past – and to the future: the empirical author replies' (P. J. Woods 1993).

Some of the complex questions concerning narrative method are pursued in two articles, 'Stories of experience and narrative inquiry' (Connelly and Clandinin 1990) and 'On narrative method, personal philosophy and narrative unity' (Connelly and Clandinin 1986).

9 Using documents

INTRODUCTION

Following on from our discussion of the life history, in this chapter we provide an introduction to some of the methodological and theoretical questions surrounding the use of documents as a source of data in social and educational research. This discussion draws heavily on the techniques and problems which have emerged over recent years. In particular we highlight the contribution of historians and oral history researchers, the debates over hermeneutics and semiotic approaches, and try to place documentary sources within a qualitative framework. An important place to begin, however, is with the classification of documentary sources.

CLASSIFICATION OF DOCUMENTARY SOURCES

Given the range and nature of documents which may feature in a piece of research it is important to attempt some kind of classification of these sources. Documents are mainly written texts which relate to some aspect of the social world. Such written texts or documents range from official documents to private and personal records, such as diaries, letters and photographs, which may have been intended for the public gaze. Documents may be distinguished in terms of their accessibility. Documents will range from those which are readily accessible, usually public records, to private documents which have little or no formal means of access. As teachers we come into contact with a wide variety of written texts, from official documents relating to education policy issues by both national government and by local education authorities and other agencies concerned with education and training, to documents produced within a school, college or training institution. Researchers themselves can also be producers of documentary data in the form of interviews, life histories, field notes or even photographs collected during the study.

Once a written text has been created, for whatever reason, it becomes a potential source of data. For example, minutes of a school committee meeting, or a school prospectus issued to parents are forms of documentary data. In reality the teacher–researcher is both a user of existing documents and the creator of new ones, and what we are talking about here is the process akin to that whereby the historian seeks out and interprets primary documentary data and then creates a second record, one open to public scrutiny (the thesis, dissertation or report – Hexter 1972).

Although we will be concentrating on written documents it should be stated that a whole range of physical artefacts and printed ephemera, such as photographs, school uniforms and so, on are also potential sources of data. How useful these can be to the researcher will depend on the purposes of their production and use. School uniforms may be important carriers of values and a way into understanding the whole question of schools as agencies of social reproduction. That being said the normal criteria for interpreting documents still apply. These can be valuable sources of what has been termed 'unwitting testimony', that is, they reveal information not always directly intended in the document about things such as values and social attitudes (Scott 1990: 13; Marwick 1977: 67). At this stage it is worthwhile classifying different sources of documentary evidence and drawing a distinction between documentation, and archival records. This is how Yin divides up these sources of data in his review of data sources in case studies:

Documentation

Letters, memoranda and other communiqués.
Agendas, announcements and minutes of meetings, and other written reports of events.
Administrative documents – proposals, progress reports, and other internal documents.
Formal studies or evaluations of the same 'site' under study.
Newsclippings and other articles appearing in the mass media.

(Yin 1984: 85)

Yin provides a good example of the use of these kinds of documents in some research he conducted.

> Sometimes a case study can be about an exemplary 'project '– such as a research effort or a federally funded activity. In this type of case study, much documentation is likely to be relevant.
>
> This type of case study was conducted by Moore and Yin (1983), who examined nine separate R&D projects, most of them in university settings. For each project, the investigators collected such documents as project proposals, interim reports and working papers, completed manuscripts and reprints, correspondence between the research team and its sponsors, and agendas and summaries of advisory committee meetings. Attention was paid even to various drafts of the same document, as subtle changes often reflected key substantive developments in the project.
>
> These documents were used in conjunction with other sources of information, such as interviews of the research team and observations

> of the research project's activities and work. Only when all of the evidence produced a consistent picture was the research team satisfied that a particular event had actually occurred in a certain manner.
>
> (Yin 1984: 86)

In contrast, and by way of comparison, Yin also identifies a range of archival records which may be of value to the case study researcher.

Archival Records

> *Service records*, such as those showing the number of clients served over a given period of time.
> *Organizational records*, such as organizational charts and budgets over a period of time.
> *Maps and charts* of the geographical characteristics of a place.
> *Lists* of names and other relevant commodities.
> *Survey data*, such as census records or data previously collected about a-'site'.
> *Personal records*, such as diaries, calendars, and telephone listings.
>
> (Yin 1984: 87)

Yin again provides an example of the use of archival sources in a piece of research:

> Archival sources can produce both quantitative and qualitative information. Numerical data (quantitative information) are often relevant and available for a case study, as are non-numerical data (qualitative information). *Seventeen Case Studies of Medical Technologies* were commissioned by the US Office of Technology Assessment between 1979 and 1981 and illustrate the integration of quantitative and qualitative information, derived mainly from archival evidence of a unique sort; reports of scientific experiments. Each case covers a specific technology, whose development and implementation are reported in qualitative fashion. Each case also presents quantitative information, from numerous prior experiments, on the apparent costs and benefits of the technologies. In this manner, the case studies arrive at a 'technology assessment', intended to aid decision makers in the health care field.
>
> (Yin 1984: 88)

The classification provided by Yin is instructive. It enables us to consider both the range of documentary sources available to the researcher and the purposes to which they may be put.

Lincoln and Guba (1985: 277), on the other hand, classify documents in terms of whether the text was written with a view to formalizing a transaction. This forms the basis for a distinction between *records*, such as for example, bank statements, driving licences, contracts, marriage certificates, etc, and *documents* prepared for personal rather than official useage, such as letters, diaries, field notes, memos, etc. Clearly, records and documents are very different, they are different in their function, design, location and accessibility. They will engage the researcher in different kinds of interpretation. It is likely that both records and documents will be encountered by the qualitative researcher.

From what we have said so far in an attempt to classify documentation, archival records, records and documents it is clear that qualitative researchers and fieldworkers are likely to pick up a wide range of documents from their research sites. One of the principal tasks of qualitative data analysis is organizing and making sense of data. For purposes of retrieval and subsequent analysis a document will need to be readily available for consideration. Here it is important for the researcher to be able to recognize quickly the significance of a particular document and what it has to say about what. Miles and Huberman (1994: 55) have come to the rescue here. Recognizing the problems likely to be encountered they suggest that it is useful to develop and fill out document summary forms. These have the advantage that they can be collected together and coded and categorized at a later date. The value of the use of these kinds of forms is that they will help to put any particular document into a context. We reproduce an example of a documentary summary form from Miles and Huberman (1994) in Figure 9.1. There is no reason why the researcher could not develop another kind of form more suited to the needs of a particular study.

An example of the range and nature of documentary sources available to the teacher–researcher may be gained by looking at a proposed hypothetical research topic. The impact of new curriculum initiatives often has an effect on the morale and organization of any institution and could well be the focus of a case study investigation. Such a case study might consist of field work undertaken in the school or college and the collection of qualitative data in the form of fieldnotes or observations. Alongside this the researcher could collect a range of documentary sources both external and internal. External documents could include Acts of Parliament, Parliamentary debates and Select Committee minutes, Government Green and White Papers, Department of Education policy and other documents. Documents from official and quasi official bodies, such as the former National Curriculum Council or Training Agencies and Examination Boards, might also be included as well as local education authority policy statements and guidelines and professional association policy statements, guidelines, policy documents and documents relating to the funding of courses, i.e. Further Education Funding Council. Internal documents could include those relating to school and college committees, staff meetings and their minutes, syllabuses and course outlines, field notes, diaries, interviews and life history narratives.

These examples give us an insight into the scope and range of documentary sources available for carrying out qualitative practitioner research. However, they only hint at the problems likely to be encountered. Documents are produced in context – for some purpose. Their interpretation is not self-evident. Here, historians can help us.

DOCUMENT FORM

Site: Carson

Document: 2

Date received or picked up: Feb 13

Name or description of document:
The Buffalo (weekly sheet)

Event or contact, if any, with which document is associated:
Paul's explanation of the admin team's functioning

Date: Feb 13

Significance or importance of document:
Gives schedule for all events in the district for the week. Enables coordination, knits two schools together.

Brief summary of contents:
Schedule of everything from freshman girls' basketball to 'Secret Pals Week' in the elementary school.

Also includes 'Did you know' items on the IPA program (apparently integrating the IPA News).

And a description of how admin team works (who is on team, what regular meetings deal with, gives working philosophy (e.g. 'we establish personal goals and monitor progress'... 'We coordinate effort, K12, and all programs' ... 'We agree on staff selection'). Concluding comment: 'It is our system of personnel management.'

Also alludes to the 26 OPERATIONAL GUIDELINES (Document 16)
((I'll guess that the admin explanation does not appear every week - need to check this.))

IF DOCUMENT IS CENTRAL OR CRUCIAL TO A PARTICULAR CONTACT
(e.g. a meeting agenda, newspaper clipping discussed is an interview), make a copy and include with write-up. Otherwise, put in document file.

Figure 9.1 Example of a documentary summary form
Source: Miles and Huberman (1994: 53)

USE OF HISTORICAL APPROACHES IN DOCUMENTARY RESEARCH

An essential characteristic of much past qualitative educational research, based on ethnographic approaches, was its exploration of the 'here and how', with little regard to the historical context from which both the actors and the situations studied emerged. Indeed, until fairly recently most books on social science methodology contained little or no advice on the value of the historical context or on the use of documentary sources and oral or life history approaches.

First, what do we mean by 'history' in the context of this chapter? We are less concerned here with history as a distinct discipline, or even with the ways in which historical approaches can both deepen and strengthen qualitative research into certain areas of schooling. When we speak of history we are talking about the time dimension of social affairs which has often been missing from much educational research outside the area of the history of education. It has been argued that field researchers are in danger of misinterpreting the present if historical sources on the past are neglected (Pitt 1972).

Starting from the position that both science and history are given to generalizations about reality, it may be argued that whereas the former aims for generalizations that are predictive and universal, the latter might be described as being more retrospective and concerned to summarize experience within the boundaries of time and space. In this sense the enterprise of the historian has much in common with that of the qualitative social scientist in that both are engaged in uncovering subjective areas which are difficult to quantify. As Stenhouse (1981) pointed out, these subjects are made up of essentially unpredictable elements since human beings are in essence creative and have the capacity to change and be changed over time. One of the main areas of the application of an historical–time dimension in educational research has been in the field of curriculum change and innovation. We will focus upon this area in order to illustrate the value of the time dimension in school-based studies.

Reid (1986) has observed that those who think curriculum work is practical rather than technical and consists of the deliberate solution of problems about what to teach, how and to whom, will value the assistance that history can give (Reid 1986: 159–66). To Reid it is the concreteness of history, its placing of action within a context and its concentration on the particular which makes it so useful. History supplies practical contexts against which such evaluation can take place. Goodson (1985) and others working in the field of curriculum change have done much to show the importance of the historical context. For Goodson there are three clear levels of the contemporary curriculum which are amenable to historical study:

1 The individual level;
2 The group or collective level;
3 The relational level.

The relational level explores the interrelations and permutations that can exist between groups and individuals, and individuals with other individuals. Of course, these levels often overlap. His own study (Goodson 1985) of the development of rural studies from the 1920s, with its mixture of life histories and curriculum history, is a useful starting-point for researchers wishing to understand this approach which owes much to the recent growth of interest in 'oral history' and one which mixes oral sources with written materials. It is important at this point to be clear that researchers such as Goodson reject any notion of the primacy or superiority of written as against oral data in historical or other research. Documentary data, as we described it earlier, includes both written and recorded oral sources. Oral data is one type of historical source among many and has its own strengths and limitations. Clearly, qualitative researchers have much to learn from the work of historians.

WHAT IS A DOCUMENTARY SOURCE?

Once a written source has been created, for whatever reason, it becomes a 'potential' historical fact and therefore documentary data. For example, minutes of a school committee meeting, or guidelines issued by a school to parents are forms of documentary evidence. In reality the researcher is both a user of existing sources and the creator of new ones since she too will be engaged in the process of writing down information gained from participant observation, or making field notes. Everything is potentially a significant 'document' and this prompted Stenhouse to argue for the creation of an archive of raw data of school-based research. The further one goes back into the past the more one has to rely upon existing documentary sources. However, most research done by teachers is likely to draw upon written and oral sources of the more recent past, as was the case with Goodson's work. Using Hexter's formulation, the researcher both seeks out and interprets raw data and then creates a second 'interpreted' record, one which is open to public scrutiny (Hexter 1972).

HOW TO LOCATE AND ESTABLISH THE AUTHENTICITY OF WRITTEN SOURCES

We need to start from the position that the historical record is inevitably bound to be partial in that a complete record of past events, however recent, is impossible. This highlights the importance of being familiar with and having access to as wide a range of written and non-written sources as possible on the topic being investigated. It brings into focus the essentially interpretative role of the researcher in this work since the researcher's collection and choice of materials becomes so crucial. There might be said to be five main traditions which have utilized documentary sources in their work: historical studies; literary studies; quantitative context analyses; ethnographic studies; and personal documentary research (Platt 1981a; 1981b). Although all the above share common problems and solutions the following sections are written from within the historical tradition and will therefore use its terminology.

Historians have usefully divided their sources (data) into two main categories: those that are classed as primary and those that are secondary. A primary source is one which has come into being during the actual period of the past the historian researcher is studying. A secondary source is the interpretation, written (usually much later) by the historian researcher.

The more recent one's period of study, the greater may be the problem of availability and access to documentary sources. This was the case with Saran's action research on the Burnham Committee, the teachers' pay and conditions negotiating machinery since the Second World War (Saran 1985). The particular problem here was access to unpublished material and this necessitated a considerable amount of letter writing to key figures in various organizations to obtain access. These are precisely the kinds of problems that face all users of documentary records and, indeed, all fieldworkers, namely, access, availability and the scope of materials involved. Things that one may have wished to interpret may not have been written down in any form at all. Documents are destroyed, either intentionally or unintentionally, and it is clear that the loss of data is not uniform across the range of sources. Saran found a number of problems:

> By contrast, the management side of Burnham kept no regular minutes of its ordinary meetings during the era of Alexander's secretaryship (1944–1977), though the archives contained occasional typed minutes, as well as a book of easily decipherable shorthand notes of Management Panel meetings covering several years in the 1950s.
>
> (Saran 1985: 219)

Thus, it is clear to see the problems of relying on single documentary sources. The work of Saran provides a good guide to the historian's craft of reconstructing the recent past and in use of the matching evidence for comparative purposes. Saran (1985) made use of journals, newspapers, personal documents and cited one particular example, *Teachers in Turmoil* (Burke, 1971) which provided an account of some of these events written by a 'well-informed observer'. Saran (1985) suggests that matching and comparing a wide range of documents is an essential aspect of the researcher's craft. In some instances 'sampling' of documents will also be a task that the researcher has to engage in (Platt 1981a; 1981b). If the teacher–researcher turns towards the historian she will find plenty of sound and solid advice on problems with documentary sources. However, before going on to consider the problems of the use of documentary sources and the phases which the researcher will pass through, we will pause to consider some aspects of oral history research which offer interesting comparisons with other forms of documentary research.

ORAL HISTORY

Simply stated, oral history might be said to be the study and investigation of the past by means of personal recollections, memories, evocations or life stories, where individuals talk about experiences, life-styles, attitudes and values to a researcher. The data so produced become oral evidence. It is clear that in this sense oral evidence and oral history approaches might be involved in participant observation and ethnographic work generally as well as life history research. These endeavours, however, are not usually characterized as oral history. What characterizes oral history and oral evidence is, indeed, the spoken character of the data. Oral history then deals specifically with what people say about the past as they have experienced and seen it. Various sources of data may be combined with oral evidence in the same study. The use of oral evidence and oral history requires the researcher to take a particular stance concerning the collection and interpretation of data.

We can look at oral data on at least two levels: that of the historically transmitted transcript of oral evidence and that of the oral historical interview. The former is found in, for example, the published or unpublished documents of numerous official or semi-official bodies, including British Parliamentary Royal Commissions, or a case study conference dealing with a pupil in school. The latter is solicited by the researcher, taking the form of a face-to-face encounter with an individual in the here and now. The main problem with oral evidence concerns the need to recognize the orality of its generation. In other words, the researcher has to find some way of expressing the spoken nature of the words in the first place, complete with intonation, pitch, gesture and the like since these features are likely to bear upon the way the testimony was intended and hence will influence what interpretations may be made of it. This may in part be overcome by use of the original tape recording of the written transcript as well as the transcript itself. Every care should be taken not only over the production of the interview transcripts but also in describing the nature of the interaction between the subject and researcher. The problems are further compounded by the fact that the teacher might make use of both 'researcher-solicited' and 'researcher-unsolicited' oral evidence. There will be quite major differences between oral sources produced in a context not under any form of control by the researcher and those circumstances where the researcher does have some control. Especially important are, for example, the power relationships between the subjects involved.

Oral sources are therefore very different in kind from the other documentary sources discussed in this chapter. Since teachers are likely to acquire oral data from interviews the special character of those interviews and the skills needed to conduct them are worth discussing. Whereas the interview technique employed by oral historians has a number of similarities with other interviewing methods used in the social sciences and the issues we discussed in Chapter 7, some special features do need highlighting and we will briefly focus on these here.

THE ORAL HISTORY INTERVIEW

The researcher is fortunate since *The Handbook of Oral History: Recording Life Stories* (Humphries 1984) offers some excellent advice, sound guidelines and important references and materials in connection with oral history methodology. Humphries offers five straightforward simple 'dos' and 'don'ts' for interviewing, that if followed are likely to result in a reasonably successful interview:

> Do make an interview checklist (containing essential biographical and career details).
> Do be friendly and reassuring.
> Do be clear.
> Do show interest.
> Do use questionnaires flexibly and imaginatively.
> Don't talk too much.
> Don't interrupt.
> Don't impose your views.
> Don't contradict or argue.
> Don't rush away as soon as the interview is over.
>
> (after Humphries 1984: 19–22)

These are practical, interactional and technical matters. Interviewing, with its concentration on the past and the personal, throws some of these issues into sharp relief. In addition the teacher–researcher should attempt to find out as much about the interviewee before the interview and be prepared for more than one or two interviewing sessions. Again, the researcher must never attempt to stick rigidly to a prearranged set of questions. The best and most effective oral history interviews are those that allow the interviewee to drift backwards and forwards through time and space allowing the individual's subjective experience to come through to the surface. This, of course, requires the researcher to be sensitive and understand the skills of handling interpersonal communication. Although a well-ordered series of questions may be what the researcher needs, the best interviews are those where the interviewer listens to what the interviewee is saying. It is always possible to pick up points to be followed up at a later interview. In other words, whilst a structured interview conducted from a pre-set questionnaire may be what the researcher feels she needs, it is more likely that an unstructured interview or series of such interviews will produce the best results. In a real sense oral history is incomplete in that no one can exhaust the entire historical memory of a subject. One can fill in other details by the use of documentary sources, as Goodson (1982) did in his work on curriculum change, by putting oral history alongside a documentary history of the period under study. Indeed, this is perhaps the most usual way in which oral history is used. The researcher will look for complementary links between these oral history sources and documentation.

A final point on oral history interviews is worth making. It is likely that the subjects initially may be as apprehensive as the researcher and will probably want to provide information they think the researcher wants. One way of overcoming this is to talk as little as possible and to watch for any gaps, hesitations, or avoidance of certain topics in the conversation. It is also important to remember that in the course of an oral history encounter, documents of a variety of kinds might well be introduced and discussed. This will provide the researcher with an excellent opportunity to evaluate the documents themselves perhaps using Scott's (1990) criteria which we will discuss below.

TRANSCRIBING: FROM ORAL ACCOUNT TO TEXT

The transcription of any piece of qualitative research will put extra demands upon the teacher–researcher. It is in many ways the most exacting part of the process of using oral materials. Transcribing generally, as we will see in Chapter 10 is far from easy. A 30-minute tape may take anything up to two hours to transcribe. Transcribing is time-consuming and demands concentration and this should be planned for at the research design phase. Teachers need to recognize that after all the data have been collected, putting them into a form that is manageable and presentable is just as important an aspect of the research process. Many otherwise good projects have been spoilt by badly presented or transcribed materials. Transcribing the oral history interview is a rather special case. As we have indicated it is important for the researchers to keep all records of the interview.

Once the oral history interview has been conducted and the transcription is complete the researcher will have a 'text', indeed, a document. This will then be subject to analysis and interpretation and scrutinized by the researcher in ways not dissimilar to other documents. Of particular significance here is the historical accuracy and authenticity of the recollections contained in the oral history 'document' or account. From here on the researcher will need to use and develop criteria for interpreting and analysing these oral history texts as well as criteria for evaluating them.

The value of oral evidence and oral history approaches lies in their ability to add crucial historical depth to individual subjective experience. As with the life history an oral history delivers the subjective world of actors for analysis in ways which other research finds difficult to achieve. These sources of data may be combined very effectively with other documentary sources. We now turn to the phases through which documentary research will move.

PHASES IN DOCUMENTARY RESEARCH

It is helpful to break documentary research down into a series of phases. Each of these phases gives the researcher different problems to resolve and questions to answer. If followed systematically the full potential of a document may be revealed.

First phase: location

During the first phase the researcher needs to locate potentially useful sources and will need to:

- Find out the principal primary and secondary sources for the topic being researched.
- Find out where the documents are housed and/or how they can be obtained, what permission if any is needed to gain access to them, and how best to use them.
- Read around the topic area, not only compiling a bibliography for a preliminary review of literature but also becoming familiar with the special terminology and approaches used in sources, both primary and secondary.

Second phase: classification and evaluation

This phase will involve the classification of the documentary data which the researcher has collected. Scott provides a useful classification here which might be added to the systems we discussed earlier (Scott 1990, 13–17).

Scott distinguishes between official/public, non-official/private, visual/aural. As well as attempting some form of classification during this second phase the researcher will need to develop some criteria for the evaluation of the different kinds of documents collected. The concept of willing and unwilling testimony might be useful here, and we have discussed the notions of validity, reliability and representativeness in Chapter 5. Scott (1990) has developed a further set of criteria which overlap with these ideas yet are slightly different. Scott refers to *authenticity*, soundness and authorship, *credibility*, sincerity and accuracy, and *representativeness*, survival and availability (Scott 1990). He also considers the notion of meaning in terms of literal and interpretative understanding. During this second phase the researcher will need to ask whether the document is authentic, credible and representative. We will explore each of these in turn.

Authenticity

We have identified validity or truth and accuracy as criteria for assessing both evidence and research. Qualitative researchers often talk about authenticity. Indeed, as we have noted, the terms validity, reliability and representativeness relate to qualitative research in a different way than they do to quantitative research (LeCompte and Goetze 1982). The times when the researcher will encounter deliberate falsehood in documentary sources are fortunately rare. But it is more common to find that records or factual accounts have been slightly altered to suit the author's original purpose or later by someone else. One therefore needs to be alert to unexpected changes in the text, such as those of paper, handwriting or attempts to erase words or numbers. One needs also to check for consistency and plausibility both internally and externally. Establishing authenticity is a practical, technical undertaking. Looking for consistency and plausibility is an essential part of this process and the following might provide a useful list of questions:

- Does the document make sense or does it contain glaring errors?
- Are there different versions of the original document?
- Is there consistency of literary style, handwriting or typeface?
- Has the document been transcribed by many copyists?
- Has the document been circulated via someone with an interest in altering the text in any way?
- Does the document derive from a reliable source?

Credibility

Credibility in a document refers to whether it is free from errors or distortions and to the questions of sincerity and authorship. Again, a series of questions can be asked of the text:

- How much time has elapsed between the event being described and the written text being produced?
- Is the account a first hand one, i.e. by someone who was actually there or is it second or third hand?
- What interest had the observer–author in the events described in the document?

The issues here revolve around four further interrelated questions. Why was the document brought into existence? When was the document brought into existence? For whom was the document brought into existence? And, finally, perhaps the most important question, in what context was it brought into existence?

Representativeness

The use of documentary sources of data in large-scale quantitative survey style research will involve the researcher in some form of sampling. However, even in qualitative research the sheer amount of documentation may mean that it is necessary to use a sample of the available data (Platt 1981a:

31–52). If not, then one still needs to ask the question how representative is the data of the 'reality' I am investigating in this document? One document may be adequate or it may not. Is any portion of the document missing? If so how much and is this important? This, to some degree, depends on one's own judgement of the research situation. The ethnographer faces the same problem when asking about the typicality of an event or representativeness of the actors involved.

The above considerations are practical ones which are basic to the collection, selection and classification of documentary data. However, the researcher must always remember that the problem of availability and accessibility can still remain. Historians have long acknowledged that their knowledge of past events is affected by what documentary sources *remain*. The twentieth century revolution in communications resulting in the increasing use of the telephone has also tended to affect the availability of data and has led to the need to balance documentary sources with interviews and other sources. Even recent historical work in education can be affected, as we saw in the study by Saran (1985) into the workings of the Burnham Committee showed. Matching and comparing a wide range of documentary sources is an essential aspect of the researcher's craft, as Saran showed.

Third phase: interpretation and meaning

We now turn to the question of interpretation and meaning remembering that documents are socially constructed texts and that the context of their production must always be taken into account.

Documents demand two kinds of analysis in attempting to grasp their meaning and significance. The first is to understand the surface or literal meaning of the document before us. The first two phases of documentary research outlined above have involved the researcher in this process. At this first level of reading one is required to understand the particular definitions and recording practices adopted by the form or genre in question and the stylization employed in writing the text. Genre, here, refers to the varying conventions governing a particular type of document, for example, government report as against a private diary. The researcher will be particularly concerned with definitions and use of concepts and be aware that these can change over time and are subject as well to cultural and gender dimensions. Stylization refers to the use of *literary devices*, such as metaphor, allusion, allegory and irony, in a text.

However, it is important to go beyond the literal reading of a text to become involved in the second kind of reading for *meaning*, though this is more of a continuum than a clean break. This involves the researcher in looking for deeper meanings in a given text. To a great extent social scientists have favoured the spoken word over the written text. It is not difficult to see why given the potential problems of interpretation. A document is a text and it can never be understood apart from the circumstances of its production.

Furthermore, these texts (documents) need also to be understood in terms of the ways in which they are *read*. Clearly, this is ground for the interpetive, qualitative researcher to explore. Over the last century essentially two kinds of approaches have been developed to deal with the problem of the analysis and interpretation of texts. One is essentially quantitative, the other is interpretative. We will contrast each of these.

CONTENT ANALYSIS OF DOCUMENTARY SOURCES

Generally accepted as being the major system for analysing documentary sources, content analysis aims to produce objective, systematic and quantifiable analysis of documentary data. The major figure in this approach is Berelsen and the key source is Berelsen (1952) *Content Analysis in Communication Research*. His aim was to produce objective, systematic and quantifiable analysis of the overt surface content of documents. That is what they were unambiguously about, not what they might be about, or what hidden deep messages they may contain. The content analyst is not concerned with either the motives of the producer of the document or the circumstances of the document's production. This is seen as being one of the major attractions of the approach and a means of ensuring objective and valid analysis. This is ultimately dependent upon the content analyst producing systematic codes and categories which may be applied to the document in question. We have indeed been this way before. Content analysis has very much in common with systematic observation approaches in classroom research. Both approaches start from the same objectivist position. Both are dependent upon the universal application of procedures by any and all the researchers in the same way to ensure validity, reliability and consistency. In the same way that systematic observation researchers are concerned with the *frequency* of particular occurrences in the classroom, for example, categories of teacher questions, the content analysis of documents is concerned with the frequency with which certain pre-established categories surface in the documents in question. The similarities between content analysis and systematic observation are such that we would suggest that the criticisms of systematic observation we make in Chapter 10 apply in equal measure to the content analysis of documents.

Content analysis attempts to provide a quantitative solution to elucidating meaning by rigorous enumeration of the frequency by which textual items (words, phrases, concepts) appear in a text. Put another way, frequency equals significance. The problem which faces the researcher using content analysis is that frequency does not, in fact, necessarily mean significance and that a striking word or phrase may turn out to be more important in determining meaning. This suggests that a more qualitative approach may be better suited to analysing these materials. Furthermore, the researcher is still left to argue why such frequency is significant by using a qualitative synthesis of the meaning and its impact upon a reader.

THE HERMENEUTIC TRADITION

Of the two qualitative approaches that we shall discuss here the oldest established is that of the *hermeneutic* tradition which is the theory and practice of interpretation. This approach developed in the nineteenth century and is particularly associated with the work of Droysen and Dilthey. These ideas formed part of the counter tradition to that developed by Comte and positivism and J. S. Mill who emphasized the continuity of the scientific study of nature and society. Dilthey argued that the subjective, meaningful character of human conduct has no counterpart in nature. Hermeneutics was then to be the basis for a science of the human world distinct from the natural world. The natural sciences will develop causal explanations of 'outer events' which are essentially meaningless phenomena; the human sciences, on the other hand, are concerned with the 'inner' understanding of 'meaningful' conduct, that is with human action as opposed to movement (Outhwaite 1975; Giddens 1978: 276; Hammersley 1990: 9–43). Though it must be added that Dilthey still wished to emphasize the need to make the human sciences as precise and empirical as the natural sciences and this, argues Giddens, led to a tension between the empirical and the idealistic in both his work and that of later sociologists, such as Max Weber (Giddens 1978: 278).

Dilthey's distinction between the outer experience of 'nature' and the lived inner experience of the human world is epistemological. That is, it contrasts two distinct views of knowledge. The natural physical sciences and the social sciences which emulate them (positivistic approaches) look for causal links and connections between events. The human sciences, on the other hand, are for Dilthey, concerned with understanding, that is with '*Verstehen*', or interpretative understanding. Viewed this way lived experience is essentially and inherently *meaningful.*

Dilthey argued that 'cultural phenomena are to be understood . . . by grasping them as "totalities", by discovering the inner connections of the meanings "objectivated" in them' (Scott 1990: 30). Applied to the analysis and interpretation of a document which becomes in this view a text, certain practices follow. Three processes will be involved. First, an interpretative understanding of individual concepts embedded within the text. Second, an appreciation of the social and cultural contexts through which the various concepts are related to a particular discourse and, third, a judgement on the meaning and significance of the text as a whole. A good example of this would be the way in which Max Weber 'read' and 'interpreted' the works of Puritan Divines so as to obtain a picture of the way in which the early English Puritan communities made sense of their lives in his classic work of the early twentieth century, *The Protestant Ethic and the Spirit of Capitalism.*

In undertaking the first of these tasks the researcher is seeking the selective viewpoint from which the text is constructed and in so doing uncovering the standpoint from which the concepts acquire their relevance. This is essentially a form of 're-enactment' or 're-living'. But this is no easy task for what comes in the way of a straightforward reading are the assumptions that form the frame of reference of the researcher. One frame of meaning can only ever be understood from the viewpoint of another. So, one has to enter, as a researcher, into a dialogue with the author, the so-called 'hermeneutic circle'. The point here is that this approach has particular relevance to reader's involvement in the creation of meaning and it implies that a text may have totally different meanings for different readers at different times. Readers bring to a text knowledge, assumptions, cultural difference, experience and insights all of which affect their interpretation. In other words, we are both constructors and re-constructors of meaning.

Writers in the hermeneutic tradition, such as Gadamer, reworked the concept of '*Verstehen*' (understanding) and detached it from this process of re-enactment:

> Thus, for Gadamer 'Verstehen' is to be treated not as a special procedure of investigation appropriate to the study of social conduct, but as the ontological condition of inter subjectivity as such and not as founded upon an empathetic grasp of the experiences of others, but upon the mastery of language as the medium of the meaningful organization of human social life.
>
> Giddens (1978: 279)

This link between *Verstehen* and language as the medium of inter-subjectivity not only reflects post-positivist views in the philosophy of science but also keys it in to the semiotic approach to the study of texts.

SEMIOTICS

Semiotics is the study of signs and sign systems. It developed largely as a result of the way in which a very influential European philosophy, structuralism, in the hands of people such as Barthes, Althusser, Foucault, Lacan and Levi Strauss, reworked the ideas of a famous linguist, Saussure.

The concern was to produce a science of signs which went beneath the surface of the language (parole) to the underlying deep sign systems (Langue) themselves. Obviously there are similarities here with symbolic approaches. As developed by Barthes the message in any given text lies not in the individual words and phrases but in the underlying system of rules that structured the text as a whole. The task of a reader is to unlock these rules and decode the underlying, hidden meaning that the text carries. Clearly, a semiotic approach to the interpretation of documents looks enticing.

The problem with interpretative approaches it can be argued, is that they have failed to provide a firm basis for distinguishing between different readings and so have raised questions about the validity of one reading against another. Furthermore, there is the problem of relativity here. If everything is relative what is the reality? As Giddens (1979) has argued, the debate about this problem has led, in the twentieth century, to a separation of the text from both its author and its audience:

> One of the major emphases that structuralism shares with hermeneutic phenomenology is the insistence that a gulf divides the text, as a particular articulation of language, from whatever intentions an author may have had in writing it.
>
> (Giddens 1979: 40–1)

So it is argued that the 'message' a text may contain for an audience may be different from what an author intended. This position of 'relativity' of meaning may be one that the researcher can adopt towards certain texts which, like literary ones, might encourage a plurality of meanings. We would argue here that in educational research it is not possible to separate the author from the text and its readers. So although we would agree that meaning in a text should not be seen as a fixed form we would still wish to argue that an author is an acting subject. Giddens again:

> To study the production of the text is at the time in a definite sense to study the production of its author. The author is not simply 'subject' and the text 'object', the 'author', helps constitute him or herself through the text, via the very process of production of that text.
>
> (Giddens 1979: 43–4)

This has special implications for the teacher–researcher who as we have stated earlier in this chapter is a producer of documentary texts. The tenor of much recent work in the cognitive sciences (anthropology, linguistics, philosophy, literary theory and psychology) has been to emphasize that meanings are culturally located and hence, shared and public (Bruner 1992). The problem that arises for the researcher using life history narratives and teachers' stories as documents is how to give the reader a full view of the text and a critical awareness of subjective nature of the interpretation. As a recent critique of the use of life history interviews has pointed out:

> If a researcher has developed a warm rapport with a teacher who is prepared to communicate a life history it is difficult, and perhaps indefensible, to go 'public' with an interpretation which is other than celebratory.
>
> Thomas (1993: 473)

The plea here was for research journals to publish a teacher's life history in full, separate from a researcher's comments.

In research which is not intended for publication, maybe a dissertation or thesis, this matter may be less important or can be overcome by the full texts of interviews always being available to a potential reader. One solution is to use Mishler's (1990) criterion for the trustworthiness of an interpretation. This concerns the degree to which we would regard the text as a satisfactory basis for action. For Mishler the key questions are complex:

> What are the warrants for my claims? Could other investigators make a reasonable judgement of their accuracy? Would they be able to determine how my findings and interpretations were 'produced' and, on that basis, decide whether they were trustworthy enough to be relied upon for their own work?
>
> Mishler (1990: 414–41)

To sum up we need to start from the position that texts must be studied as socially situated productions, constructed and reconstructed. As Giddens concludes:

> One of the main tasks of the study of the text, or indeed cultural products of any kind, must be precisely to examine the divergencies which can become instituted between the circumstances of their production, and the meanings sustained by their subsequent escape from the horizon of their creator or creators. These meanings are never 'contained' in the text as such, but are enmeshed in the flux of social life in the same way as its initial production was. Consideration of the 'autonomy' of the text, or the escape of its meaning from what its author originally meant, helps reunite problems of textual interpretation which broaden issues of social theory.
>
> Giddens (1979: 44)

The teacher–researcher needs to be aware that the text in front of her does not provide immediate access to the social world and that in attempting to ascertain its significance you need to take into account the rules of 'speech', grammatical constructions and the fact that language use is often ambiguous to a reader. Authors use conventions, write within particular genres, i.e. autobiography, biography, a report, a dissertation. In addition, a whole range of intermediates come between a text and its audience, censors, literary editors and, in the case of historical documents, the ravages of time. One must equally be aware of the importance of understanding the power relationships within any given discourse that 'language gives the conceptual framework which determines the boundaries of each discourse'.

An example of the need to understand the importance of discourse and power may be found by focusing on documents concerning the National Curriculum over the years since 1988. One would need to place any document within the frame of reference 6of all the participants within that field of discourse, the Government, Departments of State, the National Curriculum bodies, heads and teachers in schools, etc. As a recent study has argued:

> The translation of educational policy into legislation produces a key text (ACTG). This, in turn, becomes a 'working document' for politicians, teachers, the unions and the bodies charged with responsibility for 'implementing' the legislation.
>
> Bowe, Ball and Gold (1992)

Although questions about the status and the nature of particular policy texts remain empirical in understanding the significance of National Curriculum texts, a useful conceptual starting point might be to use the distinction Barthes drew between literature which gave the reader a role, a function, a contribution to make, and that which did not. The first can be called 'writerly' texts and the latter 'readerly' ones. Examples of the latter would be key National Curriculum texts with their technical language of levels, attainment targets, standardized testing and programmes of study where the signifier (author) – signified (policy) is clear and inescapable. An example of the former would be the published secondary texts or non-statutory guidelines which subconsciously invite the audience to join in their interpretation. What this example shows, is that one always needs to see texts as part of a wider social practice and that if a researcher is to make an assessment of the intention and consequences of education policy, one needs to be aware, not only of by whom and with what intention texts are produced, but also to look at how they may be and are interpreted in practice by their intended audience.

The above discussion will have alerted the researcher to the need to take into consideration the importance of language as a means through which the social world is both constructed and perceived. Documentary sources should, therefore, be seen as important carriers of values and ideologies, either intended or not. Documentary data are one of the most available sources to which teacher-researchers have access and will probably form at least part of the material collected. Yet it is also, as we have seen, simultaneously one of the most problematic sources of data to deal with. What the researcher must bear in mind is the need to evaluate all texts critically, and to be aware of both 'witting' and 'unwitting' testimony, with the myriad problems of interpretation.

CONCLUSION

In this chapter we have tried to outline the nature of documentary sources and the methodological issues surrounding their collection and interpretation in qualitative research. These materials represent an important and rich source of data for the researcher to explore. We tried to unravel some of the theoretical issues involved and explore the contributions from historians and oral history researchers, content analysis, hermeneutics and semiotics. There are some extremely complex questions involved here, that complexity in part constitutes the excitement of using documentary resources. A challenge which we hope teacher-researchers will take up.

SUGGESTED FURTHER READING

Documentary research has a long history in the human sciences. The first extended sociological focus upon human documentary sources is generally regarded to be *The Polish Peasant in Europe and America* (Thomas and Znaniecki 1958) (originally, 1918–1920). It is clear that different traditions exist in documentary research, 'Traditions in documentary analysis' (Jupp and Norris 1993), in *Social Research: Philosophy, Politics and Practice* (Hammersley 1993) explores the problems and possibilities of positivistic, interpretive and critical traditions in documentary analysis. This is done by focusing upon personal documents, life history and letters, quantitative content analysis of newspapers and the production of official documents on crime. Of value also here is 'Positivism and its critics' (Giddens 1979) in *A History of Sociological Analysis* (Bottomore and Nisbet) *Introduction to the Study of History* (Langlois and Seignobis 1908) still provides a sound basis from which to begin an understanding of the historian's approach to documentary sources, while *The Pursuit of History* (Tosh 1991) contains a useful section on using documents. This could be read in conjunction with 'Using documents' (Macdonald and Tipton 1993), in *Researching Social Life* (Gilbert 1993). Two articles by Jennifer Platt were amongst the first and most important contributions that sociologists have made to this area: 'Evidence and proof in documentary research: some specific problems of documentary research' (Platt 1981a) and 'Evidence and proof in documentary research: some shared problems of documentary research' (Platt 1981b). However, the best textbook to date on this subject is the very clear and useful book *A Matter of Record* (Scott 1990). 'The interpretation of documents and material culture' (Hodder 1994), in *Handbook of Qualitative Research* (Denzin and Lincoln 1994) takes a broad overview of the relationship between documents and material culture and is good on specifically non-written documents. The starting point for a consideration of content analysis is *Content Analysis in Communication Research* (Berelsen 1952). Overviews of the methodology of content analysis can be found in 'Content analysis' (Carley 1990), in *The Encyclopaedia of Language and Linguistics* (Asher *et al.*), *Methods of Social Research* (Bailey 1982) and *Content Analysis: An Introduction to Its Methodology* (Krippendorf 1980). The extent to which this kind of quantitative content analysis can be integrated into a qualitative research design is problematic. Some attempts at integration have been made. See, for example, 'Integrating positivist and interpretative approaches to organizational research' (Lee 1991), for some ideas.

10 Interaction in schools and classrooms

INTRODUCTION

Schools and classrooms are complex social environments. They consist of different groups of people interacting with each other in various ways. The individuals who make up these groups all have their own identities, perceptions and values. Teaching and learning will naturally be affected by these features. The most obvious situations where the influence of these factors can be observed is in the pupil–teacher and pupil–pupil interaction and communication patterns.

Over the years much research into this area has been carried out. Research has focused upon the verbal interchanges between teachers and pupils including issues such as the influence of styles of teacher talk and learning. Other research has focused upon the ways in which a child's culture and neighbourhood or family background shapes communication and interaction in the classroom. The common denominator in all of this research is that what teachers and pupils actually say and do becomes the major focus for attention. The growing body of classroom research seeks to uncover the 'black box' of the classroom in order to discover the factors which shape and influence pupils' experiences of school and classroom life. In this chapter we will introduce the teacher–researcher to some of the main themes in this research and try to show how the teacher–researcher can develop her own research into classroom interaction.

The expansion of research in classroom studies over the last twenty years has meant that many different topics of research and ways of exploring these topics have emerged. Teachers have often been sceptical of the findings of much of this research. Whereas some of the scepticism is justified, much, we believe, is misguided. It is important for classroom teachers to treat research findings with caution. We therefore try to provide the teacher with a clear overview of the main traditions in classroom research so that she can adequately assess some of the claims being made and consider in a more critical fashion the nature of the research in question. We will stress that many classroom studies are not unambiguous or unequivocal, a point which we made strongly in Chapter 1. Quite a lot of classroom research is tentative and exploratory. Classroom research cannot tell teachers how to teach but what it can do is to alert them to some of the subtle and complex processes of interaction that directly shape and influence learning. What 'research' here can do is to describe the circumstances, background and parties involved in the interactions which routinely take place in schools and classrooms. Furthermore, it can begin to unravel the complexities of communication in the classroom. We therefore aim to do two things in this chapter:

1 Provide a general overview of the main trends, approaches and strategies in classroom research.
2 Provide the teacher–researcher with a basic insight into the mechanics and processes of research into classroom talk and interaction.

The teacher–researcher may quite legitimately use some of the techniques employed by so-called professional researchers. However, in many cases these will have to be modified or adapted to suit individual circumstances. The teacher–researcher can focus upon the same kinds of topics as previous research has done yet may also introduce her own areas of interest. In the following pages we will explore the nature of classroom research and point to some of the implications of this for the prospective teacher–researcher. The chapter concludes with a practical guide to observing, recording and investigating classroom talk and interaction.

INTERACTION ANALYSIS AND SYSTEMATIC OBSERVATION

No one who has observed a classroom lesson will underestimate the complexity of even the most apparently organized lessons. Any attempts to consider the nature of classroom interaction must be aware of both the diversity and complexity of the processes involved. Interaction analysis and systematic observation were two attempts to produce objective and systematic accounts of what happens in classrooms. In the USA the name of Ned Flanders is associated with the development of interaction analysis, whereas Galton, Simon and Croll (1980) are seen as epitomizing the use of systematic observation in their work in Britain.

Interaction analysis as a technique used to investigate classroom interaction grew from a concern with the improvement of classroom teaching. Many different schedules have been devised but all of them tend to involve a trained observer recording certain features of teacher or pupil talk in accordance with a pre-arranged schedule so that numerical counts or 'tallies' could be made of certain features of classroom talk in terms of a set of pre-coded categories. This results in 'ratings' of teaching style, the climate of the classroom and the 'quality' of the teaching. This information should be used to improve teacher education and hence develop more effective teaching. The work of Simon and Boyer (1967; 1970; 1975), *Mirrors for Behavior*, charts the varieties of schemes and schedules used to do this kind of research. The overriding concern seems to be with the quantification, in statistical terms, of elements of classroom verbal interaction and, in turn, the need to sharpen and refine constantly the research instruments themselves. As such, interaction analysis and systematic observation are observer-oriented efforts to quantify classroom interactions. The best-known example of interaction analysis is contained in Ned Flanders' coding scheme, known as the Flanders' Interaction Analysis Categories (FIAC) (Flanders 1970).

Flanders was concerned with improving classroom teaching and his approach and findings were to be incorporated into the training programmes of student teachers in the USA. He was concerned to identify two contrasting modes or styles of teaching which he describes as direct and indirect. His system involves the identification of analysis of talk in the classroom in terms of the coding and categorizing of utterances according to ten pre-arranged categories. This enables the researcher to characterize any kind of communicative event in the classroom. Flanders' categories are divided up into *teacher talk*, which can be either direct or indirect, *pupil talk*, and *silence.* There are seven categories for teacher talk, two for pupil talk, and one for silence. The system is displayed in Figure 10.1.

The system requires a trained observer to place each three-second period of a total observation 'episode' into the category which it best represents. Each classroom behavioural episode can then be represented by a sequence of category numbers which can, in turn, later be used to construct a matrix enabling scores to be calculated of, for example, features such as the type, amount and direction of teacher or pupil talk. Ratios could therefore be calculated from this.

Interaction analysis was one of the first attempts to look systematically at classroom interaction. However, although the approach is one which can be used by the teacher–researcher it has received considerable criticism. The researcher is assumed to be objective and neutral and capable of maintaining a significant degree of detachment from the subjects of the research. An emphasis upon the measurement of classroom verbal interactions in terms of the pre-arranged categories results in quantifiable data. These two features of the FIAC and similar systems has resulted in some strong criticism. All the same there was a clear argument here.

The use of trained observers and an 'uncontaminated' coding scheme ensures, it is argued, a measure of objectivity and neutrality reducing the possibility of any researcher effect or bias. The use of pre-coded categories and counts or tallies lends itself to statistical treatment and analysis. The ability to cover large numbers of situations enables interaction analysis and systematic observation to develop generalizations and, in the long run, to make suggestions about effective teaching. These observations provide the most important sources of criticism and have led to much acrimonious and sometimes unhelpful criticism. People speak of 'Flandering' around, mechanical models and atomizing classrooms. The major criticisms can be found in Hamilton and Delamont (1974: 1–15), Walker and Adelman (1975: 73–6),

Teacher Talk	Response	1 *Accepts feelings.* Accepts and clarifies an attitude or the feeling tone of a pupil in a non-threatening manner. Feelings may be positive or negative. Predicting and recalling feelings are included.
		2 *Praises or encourages.* Praises or encourage pupil action or behaviour. Jokes that release tension, but not at the expense of another individual; nodding head, or saying 'Um hm?' or 'go on' are included.
		3 *Accepts or uses ideas of pupils.* Clarifying, building, or developing ideas suggested by a pupil. Teacher extension of pupil ideas are included but as the teacher brings more of his own ideas into play, shift to category five.
		4 *Asks questions.* Asking a question about content or procedure, based on teacher ideas, with the intent that a pupil will answer.
	Initiation	5 *Lecturing.* Giving facts or opinions about content or procedures; expressing *his own* ideas, giving *his own* explanation, or citing an authority other than a pupil.
		6 *Giving directions.* Directions, commands, or orders to which a pupil is expected to comply.
		7 *Criticizing or justifying authority.* Statements intended to change pupil behaviour from non-acceptable to acceptable pattern; bawling someone out; stating why the teacher is doing what he is doing; extreme self-reference.
Pupil Talk	Response	8 *Pupil-talk — response.* Talk by pupils in response to teacher. Teacher initiates the contact or solicits pupil statement or structures the situation. Freedom to express own ideas is limited.
	Initiation	9 *Pupil-talk — initiation.* Talk by pupils which they initiate. expressing own ideas; initiating a new topic; freedom to develop opinions and a line of thought; like asking thoughtful questions; going beyond the existing structure.
Silence		10 *Silence or confusion.* Pauses, short periods of silence and periods of confusion in which communication cannot be understood by the observer.

Figure 10.1 Flanders' Interaction Analysis Categories (FIAC)
Source: Flanders (1970: 34)
Note: There is no scale implied by these numbers. Each number is classificatory; it designates a particular kind of communication event. To write these numbers down during observation is to enumerate, not to judge a position on a scale.

Delamont (1976), McIntyre and Macleod (1978: 111–29) and McIntyre (1980: 3–30). We will condense some of these criticisms and add a few of our own in order not simply to be negative, but to suggest some basic principles for the investigation of classroom talk and interaction.

Context and meaning

Classrooms are complex social situations. The meanings of events which take place within them are not always clearly and automatically self-evident. Classrooms and lessons have a history. The teachers and pupils make constant reference to the social context of the lesson and the identities of the participants. It is impossible to appreciate fully what is happening without paying attention to this context. By a concentration upon observable behaviour and in effect taking it at 'face value', interaction analysis can become involved in by-passing the viewpoints and intentions of the teachers and pupils themselves.

Walker and Adelman (1975) provide a good example of the importance of context. They describe a lesson where one of the students shouted out 'strawberries, strawberries' after another member of the class had been told off by the class teacher for not doing his homework properly. This promoted much laughter amongst the members of the class. The only problem was that the researcher was unable to understand the joke. It was only some time later that the researcher discovered that the meaning of 'strawberries' was dependent upon the teacher's previous witty comment, 'Your work is like strawberries, good as far as it goes, but it doesn't last nearly long enough!'

Problems associated with the use of pre-coded categories

As we have seen, interaction analysis focuses upon that which can, in effect, be categorized and coded, that is measured. The FIAC can produce large quantities of data on teacher–pupil talk in any individual classroom. A series of issues arise from the use of pre-coded categories. The major question surrounds the identification of a particular category such as, for example, 'lecturing' of 'giving directions' (FIAC). How are these categories decided in the first place and what is their location in the data on classroom processes? The categories developed by interaction analysis researchers are constructed on the basis of the researchers' own pre-judgements. The problem is one of the relationship of these categories to the realities of the classroom.

Quantification and the neglect of the qualitative

It is clear to see that interaction and much systematic observation research is engaged in quantification by the observer as opposed to qualification through the participant. The debate here surrounds the value of non-participant observation alone as a valuable research technique in researching classroom processes.

Problems associated with using the Flanders system in informal classrooms

From what has been said about the actual procedures of interaction analysis and use of schedules such as FIAC it is evident that many settings will not instantly lend themselves to observation in these terms. If teaching and learning are simply seen in terms of the communication of information by the teacher and the reception of this by the pupils, then systems like FIAC will be able to cope reasonably well with what is perceived to be going on. However, if the teaching and learning situation is viewed more in terms of relationships and interpersonal communication or pupil/student-centred learning then rigid pre-coded observation schedules are at the very best going to miss out on capturing the true nature of the interactions, or at worst they will simply distort them. Such an approach will be unable to capture the particular, the idiosyncratic, and the local aspects of life in individual schools and classrooms. Hamilton and Delamont have formulated this problem of interaction analysis succinctly.

> In the interests of 'objectivity', many interaction analysis research studies feel compelled to survey large numbers of classrooms. It is argued (correctly) that small samples may fail to provide statements relevant to the population at large. However, such an approach (even if it can achieve true randomness) may fail to treat local perturbations or unusual effects as significant. Indeed, despite their potential significance for the studied detail, they are treated as 'noise', ironed out as 'blurred averages' and lost to discussion.
>
> (Hamilton and Delamont 1974: 5)

In attempting to maintain objectivity the surface elements of classroom interaction are examined while the deeper 'hidden' or, as Smith and Geoffrey (1968) describe them, the 'silent languages' of the classroom remain virtually unexamined.

In summary these criticisms of interaction analysis suggest that although the approach may offer some insight into the general patterns of communication in the classroom, there are considerable problems. These problems may be summed up in the idea that interaction analysis relies upon the outside observer's frame of reference and interpretations and not the inside frames of reference and interpretations of the teachers and pupils concerned.

SYSTEMATIC OBSERVATION IN THE UNITED KINGDOM: THE ORACLE PROJECT

The *Observational Research and Classroom Learning Evaluation Project* (ORACLE) conducted over a five-year period was concerned to evaluate the nature of primary classroom teaching in the wake of the findings and recommendations of the Plowden Report (1967). Galton, Simon and Croll (1980) *Inside the Primary Classroom*, and Galton and Simon (1980) *Progress and Performance in the Primary School*, deal respectively with the general analysis of pupils' and teachers' activity and different patterns of teacher and pupil behaviour, and with the supposed effects of these patterns on pupil progress.

The ORACLE research team employed a number of different tests, but the main method of observing teachers and pupils in classrooms was through the use of observation schedules which involved the researchers' recording at 25-second intervals what was happening in the classroom in terms of the categories of their pre-arranged observation schedule. The observation systems used were designed for 'live coding' by trained researchers who had primary teaching experience.

A short examination of the main instrument employed by the ORACLE researchers, *The Pupil and Teacher Record: A Technique for Observing the Activities of Junior School Teachers and their Pupils in Informal Lessons* (devised by Deane Boydell and revised by Anne Jasman) highlights both the strengths and weaknesses of systematic classroom observation as a way of making sense of classroom interactions and their consequences for learning.

The Observation Categories of the Teacher Record (see Figure 10.2) is part of the manual mentioned above designed for use by the members of the ORACLE research team. The detail reflects the need for all of the researchers to use the manual and the categories contained within it in the same way. If this is not done of course the validity of the instrument is immediately questioned. If we consider in more detail the observation and coding of teachers' questions we can see how the ORACLE team developed a highly complex scheme for classifying teachers' questions and they went to great lengths in order to establish that the observers were all coding the teachers' questions in the same way.

The manual identifies five different types of question and provides numerous examples and definitions of what constitutes each of these types of question. But as Scarth and Hammersley (1986) have argued, there are simply enormous problems involved in differentiating between the different kinds of question. How is the observer going to distinguish between Q1-type questions 'recalling facts', and Q5-type questions 'referring to routine matters?' Furthermore, how are the fine-grained distinctions between Q2-type questions (closed) and Q3-type questions (open) to be drawn, not after a long period of thought and consideration, but at 25-second intervals? These general problems in fact relate to the pre-specified nature of the coding categories. The real problem surrounds how these categories emerged in the first place. If it is not known what the teachers and pupils meant, how can the observer be absolutely sure that a question or utterance fits one category or another? Barrow (1984b) puts the issue this way:

Questions	Task	Q1 recalling facts Q2 offering ideas, solutions (closed) Q3 offering ideas, solutions (open)
	Task supervision	Q4 referring to task supervision
	Routine	Q5 referring to routine matters
Statement	Task	S1 of facts S2 of ideas, problems
	Task supervision	S3 telling child what to do S4 praising work or effort S5 feedback on work or effort
	Routine	S6 providing information, directions S7 providing feedback S8 of critical control S9 of small talk
Silence *	'Silent' interaction i.e. interaction other than by question or statement	Gesturing Showing Marking Waiting Story Reading
		Not observed Not coded
	No interaction between teacher and any pupil in class	Adult interaction Visiting pupil Not interacting Out of room
	Audience	Class, group of individuals
	Composition	Identification of pupils involved
	Activity	e.g. Creative writing, practical maths, etc.

Figure 10.2 The observation categories of the teacher record
Source: Galton, Simon and Croll (1980: 17)
Note: Although it was recognized that the term 'silence' was in some instances a misnomer, its use for everyday purposes was preferred to the cumbersome term 'silence or interaction other than by question or statement'.

> The point is that judgements of this kind require a thorough overall grasp of the lesson and its place in the wider context of class life, a thorough awareness of the state of mind of the children in question and a thorough conceptualisation of cognitive content, none of which is catered for in the ORACLE approach.
>
> (Barrow 1984b: 185)

Researchers have pointed to the importance of paralinguistic features such as facial expressions, eye movements, glances, expressions and so on in interpersonal communication. The meaning and significance of utterances, questions and answers is in part dependent upon the paralinguistic and contextual clues and features accompanying them. It is highly unlikely that these aspects could be attended to by the ORACLE observers. This suggests that there may indeed be fundamental problems with the validity of the observation categories of the teacher record as a research instrument.

What emerges as the main problem of the teacher record observation schedule is the relationship between the observer's decision to code a teacher's question in a particular category and the teacher's and pupil's perceptions of and orientation towards the utterances in particular ways. The question therefore refers to the validity of the findings based upon the Teacher Record. When we ask about the validity of data and findings, as we pointed out in Chapter 5, we are referring to the extent of which such data and subsequent findings present true and accurate pictures of the events they claim to be describing. Is the observer actually capable of making accurate judgements and correct interpretations of utterances in the space of 25 seconds? This, in turn, leads on to the question of reliability.

We defined reliability in terms of the issue of replicability in Chapter 5. When researchers speak about the reliability of research findings they are referring to the extent to which the agreement between different researchers, or in this case observers, using the same instrument or schedule, do in fact observe or code the events in substantially the same way. In the event of a piece of research being repeated would the same findings result from the work of another researcher using the same methods to research the situation? This is especially important for work like that of the ORACLE project because so many different observers were used, their findings being subsequently amalgamated.

Some implications for the teacher

Systematic observation schedules such as those used by the ORACLE team are highly complicated. Whilst we share many of the criticisms of ORACLE outlined above it is certainly possible for the teacher, bearing these comments in mind, to adapt or make use of systems like these as part of some classroom research. Alternatively, the teacher could use the FIAC system or the ORACLE schedule for coding teacher's questions as one of a number of techniques of data collection employed in a single study. The results could be used as a way of orientating the teacher–researcher to a set of topics for further investigation. The teacher–researcher need not stick with either of these schemes as a number are now available.

It is often difficult to assess the value and applicability of these schemes and so the teacher–researcher might wish to consult the checklist worked out by Boehm and Weinberg (1977: 58–9) which focuses upon the appropriateness of particular observation systems in terms of questions such as observer reliability, sampling, representativeness and the practicality of use of a particular system for certain situations. There is also the possibility of the teacher developing her own systematic observation system or coding schedule to suit her own purposes. We have worked with teachers who have successfully used observation and coding schemes to consider diverse topics such as aggressive talk in the classroom, gender imbalances, sexist or racist talk, evaluating aspects of children's project/topic work and musical skills. Both systematic observation and ethnography begin from the same starting line, *observation*, but the way in which that observation is conducted, what is observed and the findings arrived at, involve these two approaches running in very different races. Other traditions have employed observation in very different ways.

THE ETHNOGRAPHY OF COMMUNICATION AND ANTHROPOLOGICAL APPROACHES

Anthropological approaches to school and classroom life have made use of ethnographic research and participant observation. The research we shall consider in this tradition focuses upon the socio-cultural level of analysis, that is the ways in which neighbourhood, community, family, ethnicity and culture shape and influence the interaction of teachers and pupils as well as pupils with other pupils in school and classroom contexts. Language is here seen in terms of the social, cultural and interactional aspects which underpin its use in all social settings. The ethnography of communication and anthropological approaches more generally, view the classroom as being composed of a series of communicative events which are influenced by the cultural and social processes which surround both the school and classroom. Hence family, community, tradition, class, ethnicity and gender all feature in the research on schools and classrooms in this tradition.

The ethnography of communication aims to 'examine the situations and uses, the patterns and functions of speaking as an activity in its own right' (Frake 1962: 101). Four key figures are associated with the development of this approach in North America: Charles Frake, Dell Hymes, John Gumperz and William Labov. Developments in the ethnography of communication and the inclusion of anthropological perspectives in research into classroom talk and the interaction open up a wide range of possibilities, especially in terms of the relationship between language, culture and classroom behaviour. It is against the background of urban school failure and underachievement of children from particular ethnic backgrounds in the USA that some of the most important studies from an anthropological perspective have been generated. The focus allows for consideration of the way in which factors such as ethnic identity, home and family background, dialect and bilingualism shape and influence a child's learning.

Two studies highlight the interrelationship of language, culture and the classroom, those by Wax and Wax (1971) and Phillips (1972). Both these studies deal with native American children and examine the involvement and participation of the children in the classrooms using anthropological insights.

The anthropologists Murray and Wax were involved with the study of native American Indian families for a long period of time. Their focus upon the educational experiences of native American Indians and reservation education is well documented (see, for example, Dumont and Wax 1969: 217–26 on Cherokee society and the classroom). Their examination of some of the underlying assumptions of the Sioux Indians on the Pine Ridge Reservation held by white educators highlights the need to see educational failure in interactional and intercultural terms as opposed to being simply and mistakenly a matter of the cultural or linguistic deprivation of lower-class or ethnic minority groupings.

Wax and Wax (1971) describe the background to their study of the educational system of an Indian reservation in terms of culture clash and reactions to cultural differences. Their study tried to involve all parties to the educational process, pupils, parents, administrators and teachers. They found that the white teachers were operating a 'vacuum ideology' with regard to the abilities and achievements of the children. The teachers saw the children in many respects lacking or deficient. It was claimed that their parents did not read them stories or take sufficient interest in them. This indicated to the teachers that school failure was located in the child's culture. As Wax and Wax have put it:

> It places upon the Indian home and the parents the responsibility for the lack of scholastic achievement of the child. Since the child is entering the school with an empty head, then surely it is a triumph he is taught anything whatsoever. Moreover, the ideology justifies almost any activity within the school as 'educational' (just as it derogates any communal activity outside the school): *for if the child is presumed deficient in almost every realm of experience, then the task of the educator can properly encompass anything and everything*. Finally, the ideology justifies the educators in their social and cultural isolation from the lives of the parents of their students; if the child actually has a culture including knowledge and values, then the educators ought properly to learn about these and build upon them, but if, on entering school, he is merely a vacuum, then what need to give attention to his home and community?
>
> (Wax and Wax 1971: 129)

A misunderstanding about the relationship between culture and education on the part of the white educators on many of the reservation schools results in the continued low achievement of Indian children. Wax and Wax (1971) therefore raise issues concerning what is in fact being learnt in any of these schools, and the value of incorporating elements of Indian culture into the school curriculum and classroom setting. If the Indian children are described by people as being apathetic, uninterested, or passive, this has as much to do with the socio-economic position these children find themselves in and the teachers' perception of them as it has to do with their culture.

Similar situations have been documented for some ethnic groups in this country as well as for black American children. For example, Brice-Heath (1982) contrasts the kinds of questioning and question situations the children of Tracton, a southern USA urban black neighbourhood, experienced in the home with the kinds of questions they were routinely faced with at school. Again, the low achievement rates of these children are explained in terms of the operation of cultural differences. Using her extensive skills she draws our attention to the differing role that questions have from culture to culture and the educational consequences of this (Brice-Heath 1983). A focus upon the relationship between home life and family patterns and school and classroom organization is the starting-point for those who see the major differences in the two sets of experiences as providing the potential for interference, hostility and barriers to learning. However, Rosen (1985) has argued that whereas Brice-Heath's study is, in many ways exemplary ethnography, she can be criticized for not fully considering the effect of ethnicity, class and racial prejudice on 'school success'.

Phillips (1972) in her comparative study of an all-Indian class and a non-Indian class on the Warm Springs Indian reservation in central Oregon provides another important account. Many of the teachers reported that the children were generally very reluctant to talk and participate in the classroom. In comparing the nature and degree of involvement in classroom lessons of reservation-reared children and non-Indian children, Phillips draws attention to the nature and organization of the classroom lessons themselves. What Phillips discovered was that the Indian children tended to become more involved in the lessons, participating more freely in them, when situations which required the children to present themselves publicly, as it were, as individuals to the rest of the class, were absent. These and similar situations gave the teachers the opportunity to correct children and generally to control and direct their performances which conversely resulted in lower degrees of participation and involvement on the part of the Indian children in the classroom. Phillips relates these apparent preferences on the part of the children to the way in which they experience relationships more generally on the reservation and in the home. In other words, where there is a 'congruence' between the sociolinguistic styles and social relationships of both the school and the reservation then the children tended to perform better and develop greater levels of verbal interactional participation. Conversely, Phillips argues that the generally poor levels of achievement by many Indian children is directly related to the predominance of classroom organization which effectively puts the Indian children in uncomfortable and alien situations; typically those are the situations and circumstances associated with conventional and formal classrooms!

Phillips's (1972) study is a good example of the way in which an anthropological and sociolinguistic approach can provide a deeper appreciation of the nature and explanation of participation and involvement in classroom learning. Her idea of 'participation structures' is a useful one. She uses this concept to describe the broad and complex range of factors such as attitudes, values, mutual rights, and obligations which ultimately influence relationships, perceptions and ways of behaving that spill over into and affect the learning environment. It is an idea that the teacher–researcher, as well as the average class teacher, might profitably consider since many of the studies conducted in the British context support her general findings. The total relationship of home, neighbourhood, school and wider social and cultural contexts undoubtedly plays a crucial role in influencing and affecting learning. Perhaps this is nowhere more evident than in the multicultural context. Many teachers will have to face the ways in which ethnic minority children's participation and performance in school is influenced by family, neighbourhood and cultural factors as well as linguistic factors. The concern will be with a qualitative focus upon cultural factors. This could act as the focus of a piece of school-based research and hence the studies by Wax and Wax (1971), Brice-Heath (1982) and Susan Phillips will be worth considering. It is surprising that by and large these approaches have not been popular in the UK, and it is clear that there seems to have been something of a reluctance to pursue studies like this in the UK context. More recently, Brice-Heath and McCloughlin (1994: 471–90) have provided a rich account of American, inner-city youth by contrasting these young people's experience of youth organizations as places where they can be safe, with the typical school scenario. Heath and McCloughlin highlight the rate at which the young people they studied learn in these youth clubs. Again, the study is the product of detailed observation and fieldwork.

SOCIOLINGUISTIC APPROACHES

Sociolinguists ask the question, 'Who says what to whom, when and where?' Over recent years many sociolinguists have turned their attention to the classroom context. These researchers therefore recognize and try to respond to the fact that language is diversified and that linguistic forms and speech patterns exhibit huge variation. One of the general aims of sociolinguists is therefore to unravel some of the patterns within this diversity and variation. The ways in which social factors influence the development of language patterns, dialects and so on, as well as the factors affecting particular speakers are areas that sociolinguists research. Following Hymes (1962: 15–53) we outline a series of key factors which affect the diversity of language by focusing upon the dimensions of sender, receiver and setting. We also add some further dimensions of our own.

- *Sender* The identity, status or position of a speaker is often seen most clearly in what might be described as social class, dialects or accents. The social stratification system of any society places individuals in different positions, the language used by any speaker will reflect this.
- *Receiver* The social characteristics of the receiver, the person who is being spoken to, will clearly influence the speech style used by the sender. This is most obvious in situations such as adult–baby or adult–child conversation. It is also clearly expressed in various categories of official to inmate talk, for example, prison warders to prisoners. Whenever a social hierarchy or a status hierarchy exists the social characteristics and identity of the receiver is a crucial variable.
- *Setting* The context of the setting in which communication takes place is clearly oriented towards by speakers and participants. This is a crucial determining factor in language use and will influence the style of talk.

In addition to these factors, we would add the following which are likely to be of central importance in the classroom:

- *Age* The age of the children and the age of the teachers provides an important dimension to classroom verbal interaction.
- *Class* An individual's social class is generally regarded as being defined by socio-economic or occupational position. Social class therefore provides people with a frame of reference, an outlook and typical sets of experiences. But social class is a relational concept in that many factors come together to generate the experiences and outlooks usually associated with a particular class position. The relationship between social class, family background and educational achievement is well documented. Bernstein was one of the first researchers to consider the influence of linguistic codes presumed to be associated with social-class background on educational performance. Class variables enter the classroom social linguistic context in both subtle and overt ways. Bernstein, for example, argued that many children from middle-class backgrounds were able to make use of the same linguistic code which is characteristic of the school situation and turn it over to their own advantage.
- *Gender* In the same way that attitudes to the social class of both speaker and hearer influence the nature of verbal communication and interaction, gender adds yet one more dimension. Gender may be said to refer to the socially constructed and structured perceptions and expectations associated with male and female roles and behaviour. Gender will therefore affect communication in a number of ways from rights of access to talk, to changes in tone, style and vocabulary used. These aspects were explored fully in Chapter 4.

These are some of the more obvious factors which affect verbal interaction. The important point, however, is that these factors combine and interact with each other and provide talk and communication with its unique characteristics. Sociolinguists looking at schools and classrooms have concentrated upon the functions that language performs as a way of unravelling this complexity and diversity.

Nowadays sociolinguists tend to concentrate upon three major ideas, namely communicative competence, speech community and the relationship between language and social networks. The notion of social networks, including kinship, friendship and work and peer group relationships, has been discussed by a number of sociolinguists, for example, Milroy (1987) who discusses sociolinguistic method in detail. The notion of communicative competence includes a range of concerns containing the appropriateness or correctness of an individual's speech in particular circumstances and the ability of an individual to manipulate the situation linguistically to his or her own advantage and to change speech styles effectively from situation to situation. Speech community, on the other hand, refers to the larger groupings of individuals who are said to share a linguistic outlook in common: that is they adhere to the same underlying set of linguistic rules, norms and values. The two concepts of 'communicative competence' and 'speech community' are intimately linked since the individual's communicative competence cannot be seen without reference to the various 'speech communities' of which the individual is a part.

SOCIOLINGUISTICS AND EDUCATION

Sociolinguists have had a long involvement with research in educational settings and provided very many important insights into the organization of classroom verbal interaction. This kind of work which sociolinguists have carried out in classrooms has covered a wide range of topics. The importance of an appreciation of the sociolinguistic dimensions of classroom talk should now be clear. There are clearly a number of policy-related areas where sociolinguistic research has made an impact and certainly has much to offer. For example, the question of bilingualism and bilingual schools, mother tongue teaching, teaching standard English to speakers of non-standard English, the organization of classroom talk and, in particular, teacher talk itself, have all been examined using a sociolinguistic perspective.

Talk in the classroom, however, displays some important individual characteristics. Classroom talk is in many ways different from other kinds of talk. Typically, much classroom talk is organized around the completion of tasks or activities. Possibly one of its most distinguishing characteristics is the way in which one category of speaker, the teacher, attempts to control and direct that talk. Sociolinguistic analyses may be developed by the teacher–researcher in any of these areas. The data will constitute audio, and in some cases video, tape recordings of classroom lessons. The teacher–researcher can focus upon the characteristics of teacher talk, pupil talk and the nature of the conversational sequences. In this way, sociolinguistic analyses can focus upon the way in which talk is oriented towards particular parties, that is how are teachers' utterances or questions heard by pupils as demonstrated in the contextual features of the transcripts and, conversely, how do teachers hear and respond to pupils' contributions to the lesson? For example, arrival times, quiet times and group work in infant and junior classrooms all display particular sociolinguistic characteristics which are worthy of exploration. Indeed, much learning is going on in infant schools during 'arrival time'. Similarly discussion work and formal 'chalk and talk' lessons in secondary schools exhibit particular features. Lessons are opened, are started, are developed and are brought to a close.

These are just a few lines of development a sociolinguistic approach to classroom talk and interaction suggests for research. The prospective researcher might begin by considering some of the more well-known studies by Bernstein (1972; 1974), Barnes (1969; 1971) and Sinclair and Coulthard (1975).

Clearly, sociolinguistic approaches have done much to open up the complexity of verbal communication in the classroom. The prospective researcher will find the insights of sociolinguistic studies and the use of close observational techniques of considerable value in considering the relationship between language and learning.

Recently the boundary between traditional linguistic and sociolinguistic approaches, on the one hand, and more general ethnographic approaches, on the other, has become increasingly blurred. There are a number of important points of contact between a lot of sociolinguistic and ethnographic research in educational settings. Both are concerned with what participants are doing in making sense of each others' utterances and both look at patterns and regularities in classroom talk. However, ethnographic approaches tend to widen the focus of interest to include a much broader range of factors that may influence what goes on between the teacher and the pupils in the classroom. Ethnographers tend to suggest that the 'classroom' is not the only unit of analysis. Some of these differences will become clearer as we consider in more detail what has come to be known as the 'ethnography of schooling', a series of qualitative, micro-ethnographic studies of school and classroom life.

THE ETHNOGRAPHY OF SCHOOLING

In this section we will outline some of the ways in which ethnography has been used to examine the social processes in classroom talk, communication and participation. Like sociolinguistic approaches, the ethnography of schooling displays considerable diversity. What ties ethnographic studies of schooling together is their attention to detail. Close detailed descriptions of everyday events provide the starting-point for ethnography. Ethnographers become involved in the setting under investigation and collect data from a variety of sources in a number of different ways. This orientation has meant that ethnographers interested in classroom interaction and social processes in school have made use of techniques such as audio and video tape recordings of classroom lessons, unstructured interviews and participant observation in the setting itself. The ethnographers' concern with a central concept in the human sciences, culture, directs ethnographic researchers towards describing and analysing what it is individuals and groups of individuals share in common, what it is that helps to produce meaning and stability in their lives. It is a focus upon culture which gives the ethnography of schooling its distinctive flavour.

An examination of the kinds of research in schools and classrooms carried on under the general heading of the ethnography of schooling shows the range of topics which have been explored. Figure 10.3 highlights these areas. The teacher–researcher can of course focus upon any of these areas as a basis for some school-based research. These areas have all featured prominently in the literature on the ethnography of schools and classrooms.

In order to consider both the contribution of the ethnography of schooling and the implications for the teacher–researcher we will examine three areas: culture and interaction; teachers' expectations, and micro-ethnography. Indicative studies will be used to illustrate the methods employed and analyses made.

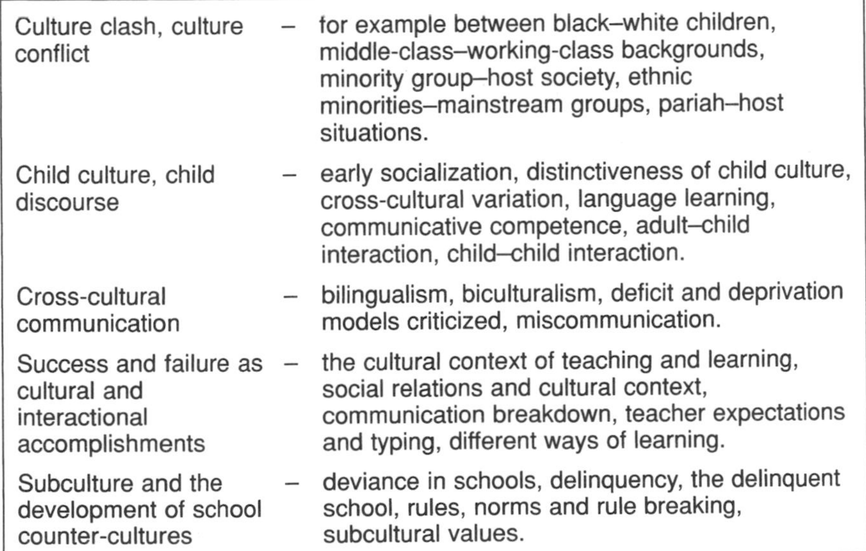

Culture clash, culture conflict	–	for example between black–white children, middle-class–working-class backgrounds, minority group–host society, ethnic minorities–mainstream groups, pariah–host situations.
Child culture, child discourse	–	early socialization, distinctiveness of child culture, cross-cultural variation, language learning, communicative competence, adult–child interaction, child–child interaction.
Cross-cultural communication	–	bilingualism, biculturalism, deficit and deprivation models criticized, miscommunication.
Success and failure as cultural and interactional accomplishments	–	the cultural context of teaching and learning, social relations and cultural context, communication breakdown, teacher expectations and typing, different ways of learning.
Subculture and the development of school counter-cultures	–	deviance in schools, delinquency, the delinquent school, rules, norms and rule breaking, subcultural values.

Figure 10.3 Some characteristic features of topics explored in the ethnography of schooling

Culture and interaction: Louisa Lewis

Louisa Lewis, an American researcher, carried out an ethnographic study of some public schools in Berkeley, California. By making use of extended close observations of these schools she developed an understanding of the relationship between culture and interaction (Lewis 1970). Her main concern was to examine the cultural factors which affect the education of Afro-American children in the Berkeley public school system. This study focuses upon the ways in which the cultural contact of black children and teachers shapes the learning that is taking place and reports on observations of grade 2 and grades 4–6 classrooms. Lewis sets herself the following question 'To what extent does a difference between a child's cultural background and that of his teacher and his scholastic milieux affect his classroom attitude and performance?' (Lewis 1970). Lewis's study was carried out at a time when popular explanations of the failure of minority groups were in terms of the family and cultural backgrounds of these groups themselves. Rather than seeing school failure in both individual and cultural terms, Lewis highlighted the importance of interaction in the classroom itself. The nature of Lewis's study and the findings she came up with can best be seen by considering her observation of two teachers.

Mrs A's interactions with the black pupils in the class displayed a number of recurring features. She displayed a detached and formal air and was reluctant to build upon and develop the children's spontaneous comments which tended to have the effect of discouraging them. She was not prepared to let black children work in pairs as a team, instead giving them turns. From Lewis's observations Mrs A clearly had low expectations of these pupils. The issue here is not one of straightforward good or bad practice, but rather with the fact that on almost every point Mrs A's treatment and organization of the black children in the classroom is the opposite of what they have come to expect from and experience in their families, neighbourhood and culture. As Lewis argues:

> William Labov (1969), in his extensive study of black peer group interaction patterns in New York, found that black children live in a predominantly peer-group oriented social milieu. This peer group orientation arises in part probably from such current socio-economic factors as extended family patterns and working or absentee parents. However, this tendency to frequent one's age-mates rather than one's elders is a well known feature of many traditional African societies where age-grades and sets are the primary units for social interaction, and a great deal of deference to elders and members of higher age-grades is maintained. Thus whereas family relationships in middle-class families would generally tend to be hierarchial or parent–child oriented, lower-class black familial relations would tend to be laterally or peer-group directed. Children who were acculturated in the latter milieu would probably tend to perform more effectively in groups rather than individually or competitively.
>
> (Lewis 1970: 12)

Lewis goes on to describe another Californian public school teacher, Mrs B. Half of Mrs B's class were black. Lewis describes a spelling game where the children were grouped as 'families'. One of the children would be asked to spell a word and the rest of the children from that family would shout encouragement. However, if the child was unable to spell the word correctly, another member of the family was called upon by the teacher to have a go in order, as it were to restore the 'family' name. Lewis makes the following observations:

> In observing Mrs B's classroom, we were struck by some of the following:
>
> 1. Although the students had to perform individually, they were performing in co-operation with, rather than in opposition to, the rest of the members of their 'family'. One could almost feel the supportive influence of the rest of the members of his group. For if none of the 'family' successfully spelled the word, it was passed on to another anxiously awaiting 'family'. There was therefore the supportive influence of the group in addition to the stimulating opposition of the competing groups.
>
>   Such an arrangement approximates more closely the peer-group and group-solidarity-oriented play groups to which many lower class black children have been acculturized.
> 2. There was little direct hierarchical exchange between teacher and child. The child's primary reference group is his 'family', and, by opposition, the other families. Such an arrangement seems to approximate more closely the 'social relations' which, as we have seen earlier, black children have been socialized into.
>
> (Lewis 1970: 16)

Despite the fact that this is only a small exploratory study it displays the value of ethnographic reporting in documenting the subtle and complex relationships between culture, social interaction, and success in the classroom. As such, more light may be thrown on the continuing underachievement of Afro-American children in school.

Teacher expectations, labelling and typing: Hargreaves, Hestor and Mellor, and Rist

It is almost an educational commonplace now to speak about the influence of the teachers' perceptions and expectations of pupils and their subsequent performance. The whole issue of teachers' expectations stems in part from a famous piece of experimental research by Rosenthal and Jacobson (1968) *Pygmalion in the Classroom*. These authors designed an artificial situation in order to test the hypothesis that individual pupils' performances were significantly influenced by their teachers' expectations of them. Whilst telling a group of teachers that the children had been given a test, the results of which would enable the teachers to see those who were likely to progress quickly and those who were not, in reality the researchers had assigned the results of the test to the children on a purely random basis. Returning a year after the test the children were again tested and the results this time showed that those found to be 'bloomers' on the first test score had, in fact, increased their results on average much more than those who were not assigned to this category artificially in the first test. Rosenthal and Jacobson's research led to what we now describe as the notion of the 'self-fulfilling prophecy'; if we believe a child to be a 'D-stream' child, label her so, and expect her to perform badly then the chances are, it is claimed, that she will live up to this expectation, do less well and in effect become a 'D-stream' child.

Of course, this study raises a number of ethical and moral issues about the extent to which research intervention can be allowed to influence the lives, and in this case, the futures, of the subjects of the research. Whilst clearly unravelling an important feature of the educational process, Rosenthal and Jacobson (1968) broke many of the ethical rules and principles we explored in Chapter 3. It is unlikely that this would happen today.

Rosenthal and Jacobson's study attempted to show that there was a direct causal connection between teachers' expectations of their pupils and the actual behaviour and level of attainment of these pupils by creating an artificial set of circumstances. Although this was a pioneering study in many respects, it is not without its critics. What does seem to be missing from Rosenthal and Jacobson's research is the context in which the teachers make inferences about particular children in such a way that certain outcomes tend to occur with a fair degree of frequency. Ethnographers have tried to document the processes involved in the generation and development of teacher expectations of particular children in real-life situations. These researchers have been considerably helped by two concepts, namely the notion of labelling and typifications, generated respectively from interactionism and phenomenology, two major perspectives in the discipline of sociology which focus upon the organization of face-to-face social interaction at the micro-level. We discussed the notion of typification in general in Chapter 4 on the analysis of interview materials. We will concentrate briefly, therefore, on the notion of labelling, before examining in more detail some of the ethnographic studies of teacher expectations.

Symbolic interactionism, as a way of trying to make sense of the social world, begins from the assumption that social groups and the individuals who compose them actually create the order of social life by generating meanings, rules, attitudes and perceptions in common. The aim of social and educational research from this viewpoint is to document the actor's perspective. One of the most extensively investigated areas of social life these social scientists have become involved in was the area of deviance. What became known as the 'societal reaction', transaction, or labelling theory of deviance emerged during the 1960s and was associated in particular with the work of Becker (1963) and Matza (1964). The assumption of these writers is that social groups themselves actually create deviance by making the rules the breaking of which constituents deviance. Hence, deviant behaviour is behaviour that people so label; it is, in other words 'in the eye of the beholder'.

In stressing the relative nature of what constitutes deviance in any one situation at any particular moment in time, these researchers drew the attention of those working in the area of classroom research. This theory, it was anticipated, might throw some light upon features such as school counter-culture, failure and many other features of the school environment. From this viewpoint 'deviants' have to be seen in relation to the group, culture and eventually the wider society of which they are a part. Deviance could therefore be described and understood as involving a series of social processes. These are worth considering since they might provide some key concepts the teacher–researcher might wish to relate to any data which she has collected.

All teachers are aware of the ways in which certain children carry with them particular 'reputations'. This is especially true of the transition of pupils from one school to another. Researchers would want to ask questions about the origin of the reputation and the grounds upon which the child's reputation is said to be founded. For example, are teachers actually reacting to a child's behaviour, or to what they expect of the child and what the reputation seems to suggest? The other side of the coin is accounted for in the use of concepts such as identity, self-image or self-concept. These concepts draw our attention to the subjective experiences and attitudes of those labelled in terms of the pictures of the individual which are offered by any particular label. Many pupils may, in fact, find it easier to live up to what is involved in any label than to behave in alternative ways. Labels often have a stigmatizing effect; they set people apart and create suspicion around the person labelled. At worst, stigma leads to ostracism and separate treatment. Once an individual is labelled in a particular way and if that label carried with it negative connotations, the person may be forced into seeking subcultural support from others in similar situations. It is in these subcultures that the so-called deviant may indeed gain a positive self-image and identity. Labelling in this sense may have the effect of actually developing and further reinforcing the behaviour in question since the stereotyping of individuals necessarily only focuses upon certain aspects of an individual to highlight and not the whole of the individual's characteristics.

These concepts and ideas ought to be seen as having a sensitizing role. They can sensitize the researcher towards looking at situations in fresh ways. Much educational research has made valuable use of these terms and they offer the teacher–researcher an important set of ideas. School failure and classroom deviance might therefore be seen as being learned or, indeed, an actual accomplishment. The educational 'life chances' of pupils are seen as being related to these factors as well as those of individual characteristics, social class background, ethnicity and gender.

Early studies in sociology of education, such as those of Hargreaves (1967) and Lacey (1970), using participant observation techniques both made reference to the importance of teachers' attitudes and expectations. Hargreaves maintained that in the secondary school he observed, a distinction could be drawn between an 'academic' subculture and a 'delinquescent' (anti-school) subculture which was clearly related to the streaming system in operation. There were progressively more pupils in the delinqescent anti-academic subculture as one moved down the streams. Some time later Hargreaves, Hestor and Mellor (1975) went on to focus upon teachers' typification of pupils in terms of conformity or non-conformity to classroom rules. These researchers developed ethnographic interviewing techniques for use with samples of secondary-school teachers in order to try and explicate the commonsense knowledge the teachers used in order to link behaviour of the pupils to rules, and thereby define certain acts as deviant. The most impressive feature of this research is the way in which the researchers are able to develop a model of the stages through which the teacher's typification moved. From their research they argue that:

> Given the apparent absence of conceptual distinctions in members' accounts of rules, it was possible for us to organize the rules in school in terms of the threefold classification which we shall call *institutional, situational* and *personal* rules.
>
> (Hargreaves, Hestor and Mellor 1975: 34)

Institutional rules were typically the 'rules' of the school, situational rules apply to the particular situations, namely the classroom, whereas personal rules were those relating to the idiosyncrasies of particular teachers. This study throws light upon the processes whereby rules are made, interpreted and applied in school settings and within different phases or 'stages' of a lesson.

Hargreaves, Hestor and Mellor (1975) concentrated upon the teachers' expectations and definitions. Another important piece of research was that carried out by Rist (1970: 411–51) again using ethnographic techniques. He followed the progress of a group of kindergarten children in an elementary school of a black neighbourhood in St Louis as they moved into the first and second grades. His main concern was with the ways in which the teacher's differentiation of the children into fast and slow learners and on to specific tables appeared to be the result of a series of non-educational criteria, such as the teacher's social-class-based assessment and typifications of the children.

Rist's (1970) focus upon teachers' expectations of the children and the subsequent organization of classroom interactions demonstrates the power of the so-called self-fulfilling prophecy. He found that the teachers were using roughly constructed 'types' in order to consider the kinds of features it was deemed any particular child needed in order to succeed. He found that the teachers made very quick assessments of the children during initial early encounters with them. Eventually, these assessments became more formalized into specific patterns of interaction between the teacher and pupils taking on the character of a rigid caste-like system. The divisions between the groups of children were further reflected in both the seating arrangements in the classroom and the kind of scores the children were achieving. Thus, by the second grade:

> No matter how well a child in the lower reading groups might have read, he was destined to remain in the same reading group. This is, in a sense, another manifestation of the self-fulfilling prophecy in that a 'slow learner' has no option but to continue to be a slow learner, regardless of performance or potential.
>
> (Rist 1970: 435)

These social as opposed to educational distinctions are given considerable symbolic force since the highest reading group of children in the second grade were given the name 'Tigers', whereas the middle group were described as 'Cardinals', and those assigned a first-grade reading level were known as the 'Clowns'. Many of these issues are taken up in more detail in Rist's book, the subtitle of which is '*A Factory for Failure*' (Rist 1973).

The focus upon teacher expectations, the consequences of developing low self-images in children, and the processes of labelling in schools did much to alert student teachers and those already in the profession to some of the problems involved. This is a good example of the way in which 'research' has direct consequences for classroom practice and to the importance of seeing the classroom as a complex social environment.

Micro-ethnography and the work of McDermott

In this chapter we have been concentrating upon the verbal aspects of classroom communication and interaction. The routine everyday processes of classroom life are also made up of the vastly complex and subtle aspects of non-verbal behaviour or the paralinguistic features which are often taken for granted, yet none the less actually maintain what is being said. Movements, facial expressions, glances, and so on as well as posture and bodily movements all influence the nature of interaction in small groups and certainly may shape and influence teachers' evaluations or perceptions of their pupils and conversely pupils' evaluation and perception of other pupils and their teachers. The general term for the study of these features is 'micro-ethnography'. This approach recognizes that important messages are being conveyed in the non-verbal and minute interactional aspects of classroom life and tries to decipher what these may be and how they affect learning. These micro-ethnographic approaches have made extensive use of audio and video tape recordings.

In a series of studies McDermott (1974; 1977; 1978) has developed and refined this approach to the study of classrooms. McDermott makes use of close observational techniques for examining classroom processes and draws on both anthropological and psychological research findings to interpret the data. He has used this approach to examine the achievement of poor reading skills (McDermott 1974), how the way in which teachers and pupils 'make sense' of each other creates specific social contexts for learning (McDermott 1977), and the social processes involved at getting turns at reading in one American elementary school (McDermott 1978). This research represents some of the most detailed work on classroom interaction and has clear implications for classroom organization.

Micro-ethnographic research using audio and video tape recording techniques demands a fairly high level of technical sophistication. It is likely that this research will take time to set up. Cameras are highly obtrusive and can have a marked effect on people's behaviour. The analysis of video recording itself is not an unproblematic affair. Despite these difficulties and reservations teachers can gain much from a close examination of classroom recordings.

In this section we have explored some of the contributions of the ethnography of schooling to understanding the social, cultural and interactional aspects of schools and classrooms. In doing so we highlighted the kinds of techniques employed by various researchers. The teacher–researcher may pick up some possible topics for research and ways of exploring those areas by reading the studies referred to here and in the further reading section at the end of this chapter.

ETHNOMETHODOLOGY, CONVERSATIONAL ANALYSIS AND DOING TEACHING

These linked approaches offer those involved in educational research fresh and exciting ways of investigating classroom interactional processes. Ethnomethodology and conversational analysis have opened up questions about learning, understanding, effective communication and miscommunication. Ethnomethodology originated in the west coast of the USA, in particular California, during the 1960s and 1970s. A group of sociologists who shared a similar qualitative and interpretative approach to investigating the social world began to do some small-scale studies on the way in which people ordinarily interacted with each other in everyday situations. A focus upon the 'methods' by which individuals make sense of, construct and thereby give meaning to the world emerged as a hallmark of this approach.

Ethnomethodology shares some basic premises with qualitative sociology and ethnographic approaches to social research more generally. Ethnomethodologists stress that the social world is made up of shared meanings and shared viewpoints. So much so that if actors changed places they would quite likely see the world in much the same way. Our knowledge of the world is generated through interpretations. There have been two main trends in ethnomethodological research which the teacher–researcher might consider. First, a number of ethnographic studies of institutions and social processes have been carried out which are based upon the assumption that people's actions can be explained only by making reference to the context within which they take place. As such, these studies were concerned with how individuals acquired the cultural perspectives of their societies and displayed them in the course of their daily lives. Second, 'conversational analysis' (CA) emerged as some of the most elaborated and extended body of research coming out of the ethnomethodological tradition. Conversational analysis focuses upon the organization of talk in everyday social life and conversational analysts, most notably the late Harvey Sacks and a group of researchers, including Gail Jefferson, Jim Schenkein, W.W. Sharrock and R.G. Anderson, attempt to consider how a sense of orderliness and coherence is displayed in conversational exchanges. The most striking feature of this approach is the technical machinery developed to analyse naturally occurring talk. One of the earliest attempts in this direction was Harvey Sack's work on telephone conversations to a suicide crisis agency, where he treated the calls themselves as an object for description and analysis. Conversational analysts use raw data, not refined or invented data. They make a series of assumptions and procedural points on the nature and organization of talk:

- Talk is organized by parties to that talk.
- This orderliness and organization of talk must be displayed in the raw data.
- Talk is sequentially organized and speaker change recurs and occurs.
- Talk displays a turn-taking system and turns are not fixed but vary.
- Describing conversational events must be context specific.
- The insistence that data must be recorded as accurately as possible and collected from naturally occurring settings, usually by means of audio or video tape recordings.
- The emphasis upon the sequential and interactional organization of talk reflects a major departure from much linguistic and conventional sociolinguistic approaches.
- The unit of analyses for conversational analysis becomes not the sentence, but rather the utterance.
- In analysing conversational interaction it is argued that the focus must be on participants' orientations to utterances in terms of previous utterances.
- As a result of the first nine points it is clear to see that the members have a methodological resource for making sense of talk; CA attempts an elaboration of this.

CA is nothing if not a highly technical and extraordinarily detailed approach. It offers the teacher–researcher a novel and valuable way of focusing upon classroom talk. We look at the value of CA as a type of qualitative data analysis in Chapter 12. In an important article Sharrock and Anderson (1982) have outlined an argument and a rationale for a focus upon classroom talk. Talk, they argue, is fundamental to all activities that sociologists claim to be studying and in turn if we are to understand these activities, of which teaching and learning are a part, we need to develop an understanding of talk in the classroom. Furthermore, Sharrock and Anderson (1982) make some specific points about the way in which this can be done in terms of a focus upon how talk is organized in particular lessons in particular ways. This requires researchers to look at the ordinary, the routine and the normal aspects of teaching. If research does not tell us this, they argue, then it cannot deliver much by way of insight into how lessons are organized and, subsequently, how learning takes place.

An impressive body of research now exists in the area of the classroom studies which makes use of ethnomethodology and CA. We will briefly consider some of these studies in order to provide the reader with a flavour of some of this kind of research and what light it can throw upon classroom organization and learning. For purposes of this discussion it is useful to distinguish between studies of the social organization and classroom lessons, and studies of the turn-taking system and conversational organization of classroom lessons.

The social organization of classroom lessons: Mehan, Cicourel

A growing number of American researchers influenced by the ethnomethodological perspective began to investigate the traditional areas of the testing of children and the assessment of children's abilities and performance. Mehan (1973: 309–28) focuses upon what he describes as 'children's language-using abilities', highlighting the ways in which speakers and hearers apply their linguistic, social and interpretive knowledge in routine everyday situations, especially those in classrooms and more particularly testing situations. In a study of some formal testing situations in American kindergarten schools, Mehan (1973) found that the tests failed to capture the child's reasoning abilities and obscured understanding of the extent to which the child had understood the questions and how well the child had done because they were clearly based upon the teacher's subjective interpretations and narrow definitions of measurement. Mehan illustrates this point with an amusing but none the less telling example from one of the testing situations he examined:

> Another question instructs the child to choose the animal that can fly from among a bird, an elephant and a dog. The correct answer (obviously) is the bird. Many first-grade children, though, chose the elephant along with the bird in response to that question. When I later asked them why they chose that answer they replied 'That's Dumbo'. Dumbo (of course) is Walt Disney's flying elephant, well known to children who watch television and read children's books as an animal that flies.
>
> (Mehan 1973: 315)

Thus, a child's response does not always indicate a lack of ability, but rather the use of an alternative scheme of interpretation to that being used by either teacher or tester. Mehan (1973) provides the following observation on this sequence:

> These descriptions demonstrate that the child can exist simultaneously in a number of different 'realities' or worlds . . . that is the factual world of everyday life and the world of fantasy. The child who says that animals can fly and talk is (from the adult point of view) mixing and blending the characteristics of fantasy and everyday worlds. The test, however, assumes that the child is attending to stimulus only from the viewpoint of the everyday world in which dogs do not talk and elephants do not fly. The test assumes further that the child keeps the world of play, fantasy and television out of the testing situation. Yet as these anecdotes demonstrate, the child of age 4–6 does not always keep his realities sequentially arranged. Because the child may be operating simultaneously in multiple realities, valid interrogations must examine why he answers questions as he does and determine what children 'see' in educational materials; testers must not use answers exclusively.
>
> (Mehan 1973: 317)

These issues and many more are taken up in an important and influential collection of papers deriving from some American research. *Language Use and School Performance* by Cicourel *et al.* (1974) reports on the social organization of language used in both the testing and classroom situation in first-grade and kindergarten classrooms in two school districts in southern California, as well as some of the home settings of the children. The studies report on a range of situations and the richness of this work can be appreciated only by actually reading them. For our purposes there are two features which deserve attention. First, the major point of many of the studies contained in this volume suggests that a considerable portion of the teachers and the testers operated with highly limited versions of the child's competence. The authors show through the analysis of verbatim transcripts and video tape recordings how, given the child's stock of knowledge at hand and cultural capacities, the answers to the often ambiguous questions can be demonstrated to be highly ingenious and acceptable. So much so that the 'facts' of the test scores and children's classroom answers are not a direct reflection of the individual child's abilities, but rather a reflection of the social processes and interactions and interpretations of both teachers and pupils. Second, of major interest here is the methodology these researchers employed. They made use of in-depth observations, audio and video tape recordings of testing and classroom settings as well as interviews with the teachers. The authors developed what they describe as a system of 'indefinite triangulation'. This involved recording the classroom or testing situation and playing these materials back to the teacher later and discussing the data with the teacher after the event, as it were.

The whole thrust of this volume is the fact that children's cognitive abilities must be set against teachers' perceptions and childrens' interpretive skills within the testing and classroom context. Children's 'performance' then needs to be seen as an outcome of all these features.

Conversational analysis, turn-taking and classroom talk: French and French

As we noted above, CA has developed a conceptual machinery for unravelling the organization of conversation so that it may be described and analysed. It is easy to see how such a detailed focus upon transcripts of recorded lessons scrutinized in such a way will reveal the properties underlying the order of such lessons. The organization of classroom talk, the nature of turn-taking and the conversational strategies employed by both teachers and pupils can help to throw light on diverse issues such as participation profiles of individual children or pupils, gender imbalances, miscommunication, starting a lesson, dealing with latecomers, the assessment of pupils' reading abilities, the achievement of success or failure in the classroom and so on. All of these areas have been considered by those researchers influenced by ethnomethodology and the programme of work developed by conversational analysts. One example will serve to demonstrate the value of such a focus upon classroom talk.

Jane and Peter French have been working on the organization of classroom talk and its effects on learning in a number of different settings for a considerable period of time. Their research has been based around the analysis of transcriptions of tape-recorded classroom lessons together with their own observations of the settings concerned. The study by French and French (1984) may be considered since it shows how a focus upon the verbal interactional dimensions of the primary classroom might, in fact, be the cause of the gender imbalances reported by many researchers in schools. In mixed-sex schools and classrooms, research has shown that boys tend to receive greater attention than girls. Boys tend to have more direct involvement and interaction with the teacher than girls and certainly do better in science subjects than girls. The study undertaken by French and French (1984) involved the analysis of the verbatim transcription of a fourth-year junior school lesson. The lesson was a teacher–class discussion of 'What I do on Mondays and what I would like to do on Mondays'.

This study like many others showed the same kind of gender imbalances between boys and girls. However, unlike other researchers these authors do not see the situation as simply a result of sexist bias, or even poor classroom management, but instead in *interactional* terms. This they do by means of a concentration upon the distribution of interactional terms between boys and girls. Taking this view, the responsibility, if this is not too strong a word, lies with both the teacher and the pupils who collaboratively produce the activities of the lesson. In the lesson reported, a focus upon the numbers of turns of boys and girls showed that a disproportionately high number of turns were taken by a small sub-set of four boys. Furthermore, the ability to obtain a turn to talk was frequently associated with ability to offer 'newsworthy items' which was a resource that was exploited by some children more than others. It is through interactional manoeuvres such as presenting newsworthy items and taking up unusual positions, that boys were able to secure more of the teacher's attention. The major significance of French and French's (1984) study lies in its suggestion that gender imbalances within the classroom may not be simply or only due to the sexism or psychological predispositions of the teachers, but in part the ability to manipulate the turn-taking machinery.

Implications for the teacher–researcher

In this final section on major approaches to classroom talk and interaction we considered the contributions of ethnomethodology and CA. The kinds of research developed by these investigators are particularly suited for adoption by the teacher–researcher. Quite simply, the teacher need do no more than tape record and transcribe one of her lessons. In other words, both the ways of researching classrooms and the kinds of analyses represented in this section are amenable to ordinary teachers themselves. As Payne and Cuff (1982: 8) have pointed out, the most important elements of the attitude needed by teachers to do this is that they suspend some of their own commonsense assumptions about classrooms and teaching. By making the familiar strange it is possible to get closer to the phenomena themselves and in doing so develop tighter and more detailed descriptions and analyses.

Such approaches will inevitably increase teachers' awareness and understanding of classroom processes. In this final section of this chapter we try to show how the teacher might go about looking at her own or other teachers' classrooms and suggest some possible topics and areas to focus upon. To conclude we outline some of the issues involved in transcribing.

A PRACTICAL GUIDE TO OBSERVING, RECORDING AND INVESTIGATING CLASSROOM TALK AND INTERACTION

We have been focusing upon the classroom as a social environment in this chapter and have paid special attention to the importance of analysing classroom talk and interaction. The teacher–researcher can profitably make use of any of the approaches we have highlighted. Indeed, a focus upon the nature of classroom talk and interaction can be achieved without the teacher even having to move from her own classroom. A focus upon the transcriptions of class lessons can reveal the complexity and subtlety of much classroom communication. Furthermore, these materials can be used in conjunction with other kinds of data which the teacher might have collected in the past or proposes to collect in the future.

Whilst there is much the teacher can do this is not without its difficulties. The major problem here, as elsewhere in school-based research, is the problem of the familiar. The data which the teacher–researcher collects on classroom processes may be all too familiar to her. This familiarity may mean that the teacher neglects or simply passes over as uninteresting important features. It is important to bear in mind therefore that familiarity with the data, although clearly an advantage, is not without its disadvantages.

Some possible topics for research

Throughout this section of the book we have offered suggestions about possible areas and topics the teacher–researcher might wish to follow up. We have not been prescriptive since the teacher herself must consider the particular and immediate context of her own teaching in defining a project area. The ten questions listed below are areas the teacher–researcher might like to consider in the light of the preceding discussion in this chapter. These questions might be regarded as some initial preliminary questions requiring some general observations which can, in turn, become more focused at a later stage. In approaching interaction and communication patterns in any classroom the teacher–researcher might like to consider these ten questions as a checklist of items to make notes on. The following examples of topics is intended only as a guide to possible areas for investigation in greater depth.

1 What types of classroom language are employed?
2 What are the characteristics of teacher talk?
3 What are the characteristics of pupil talk?
4 What form does teacher questioning take?
5 What form does any classroom discussion take?
6 How large are the main working groups or group?
7 How does the teacher direct learning?
8 What is the balance between formal and informal talk?
9 How are turns to talk or rights to talk distributed?
10 How much teacher talk and how much pupil talk is there?

These questions can act as a guide for some general observations. We will now consider a series of more focused topics which it is possible to explore.

Control over classroom communication

Teachers are able to exert a considerable amount of control over classroom communications in terms of what is said (topics), over the way what is said is received (relevance) and how much may or may not be said (amount). Teachers adopt a number of strategies to aid them in this regard. It is important to consider the ways in which these strategies may influence learning.

A possible topic of investigation arising from a focus upon control over classroom talk might be a consideration of the differences in teacher styles and classroom organization upon the degree of 'conversational freedom' children are allowed, and the quality of adult–child interaction in the classroom that might ensue.

The right to speak

In our culture children in a number of situations may clearly be said to have limited rights to speak when co-present with adults in interaction. This superordinate–subordinate adult–child relationship is manifest in one of its clearest forms in the teaching situation. The way in which the turn-taking machinery is exploited by different children, different groups of children, or by boys compared to girls is important in order to discover the nature of learning in any one situation.

What does the teacher want?

Teachers, in the course of their day-to-day activities, are involved in what has technically been described as 'recapitulation', 'getting the children to respond', 'feedback' and so on. Mehan (1973) has discussed in some detail the kinds of 'searching practices' the children he observed were engaged in where the teachers or adults involved provided further information for them to respond to original questions. Such activities and strategies can be analysed for the kinds of conversational mechanisms and the cultural knowledge they exhibit. This is of special interest because such activities are characterized by the co-presence of parties with unequal access to the very conversation they are engaged in.

Sociolinguistic barriers

In one of the best general introductory texts on language schools and classrooms, Stubbs (1983: 76–83) offers some topics for investigation. Notably he suggests that it is possible and important to consider what 'sociolinguistic barriers' may exist between schools and their pupils and specifically teachers' attitudes to children's language. This is especially important in the multicultural context. Teachers' attitudes about 'right' and 'wrong' language can have many consequences and can generate in pupils negative images of their language and consequently their social worth in the classroom. These are certainly whole-school issues as well as areas of concern for individual class teachers. The development of any school language policy could certainly benefit from the investigation of these areas because attitudes to language are, indeed, crucial in determining both the classroom environment and the organization of classroom communication.

These are simply a few suggestions for the possible focus of a research project. Other areas that may be considered might include language use and special needs, gender imbalances, subject or task-oriented classroom talk, the nature of child–child talk and interaction, adolescent talk and many more. Whatever the focus and however the teacher–researcher explores the materials she collects, the experience will be fruitful and the data exceptionally rich. Policy and practical implications will certainly follow. To conclude this chapter we need to explore the technical aspects of putting classroom conversation into a readable and presentable form, that is the job of transcription.

TRANSCRIBING: TRANSCRIPTION SYMBOLS AND SYSTEMS

One of the typical features of qualitative ethnographic research is that it produces vast quantities of seemingly unmanageable data. An important aspect of the research process concerns how the researcher is actually going to present the data. The questions here relate to the overall nature of the research design as well as to the data-collection techniques employed and the kinds of data which result. These questions need to be borne in mind whether the teacher is relying upon field notes, interview materials, or transcriptions of classroom lessons. Questions of degree of detail, accuracy and comprehensiveness will vary according to the situation and the materials involved. Generally speaking, if the research is to be focused upon 'classroom interaction' and 'lessons' a transcript which is sufficiently detailed to enable the kinds of analyses we have been talking about will have to be produced. It follows that the teacher–researcher needs either to make use of an existing system or develop her own system and symbols for transcribing the materials. Sometimes researchers describe the transcription conventions they have used (Payne and Cuff 1982: ix; French and French 1984: 134). We offer below our own system for transcribing lesson tape recordings. This scheme has evolved during our work with teachers over the years; it can, of course, be adapted and modified. The main point, however, is that a reasonably high degree of consistency is achieved and that the same conventions and symbols are used in the same way throughout the transcript.

Some transcription symbols and conventions

T. C. P.	Usually for purposes of anonymity it is best to identify speakers by means of T. for teachers, C. or P. for pupil; individual childrens' or pupils' names can, of course, be used provided they are changed yet keep the gender of the speaker clear.
. . .	A pause; dots signify length roughly in seconds.
(1.5)	Alternative symbol for pause timed roughly in seconds.
[ ]	Indicates overlap of talk at point of overlap.
//	An interruption of one speaker.
( )	Denotes an unidentified speaker or utterance.
(( ))	Indicates that the transcriber does not know or cannot effectively make out what the utterance is.
L-A-W-N-S	A speaker spelling out a word.
YES	A phrase or word spoken loudly with emphasis.

	An alternative symbol for indicating loudness or emphasis.
-- --	Indicates a hesitation or pause.

The difficulties involved in transcribing and the time spent should not be underestimated. Indeed, this should be built into the research design itself and taken into account when planning the research so that sufficient time is in fact left for it to be done properly. There are no tried and tested rules for transcribing. Transcribing is for the most part a slog. However, it does have one major advantage. The length of time the researcher has to spend with the data in order to transcribe them accurately means that she is also developing familiarity with the data.

From our experience the mechanics of transcribing can be seen to involve the following series of stages and tasks:

- Listen to the complete tape at least twice through without attempting to write anything down. This will provide the transcriber with a sense of the materials as a whole, the rhythm, tone and substantive content of the talk together with an 'ear' for who is talking at what point.
- The use of headphones gets the researcher or transcriber closer to the data and eliminates any distracting extraneous background noise.
- Transcribing proper will involve listening to short 'chunks' of talk and noting it down and playing and replaying the tape backwards and forwards in order to get an accurate transcript.
- Once a reasonable transcript has been made from the tape the researcher or transcriber should listen to the tape again as a whole while going through her own transcript of it and making any additions or corrections as she goes along, stopping the tape at the appropriate points in order to facilitate this.
- If possible, it is always useful to get another person to listen to the tape and cross-check the transcript.

Transcribing is time-consuming and is often seen as an unrewarding exercise. All the same, it is a necessary process and demands the same kind of commitment and serious approach that any other aspect of the research itself involves.

SUMMARY

In this chapter we have provided an overview of the main approaches to classroom talk and interaction and have stressed the importance of seeing the classroom as a social environment. In many ways the points we have been making in this chapter relate to the wider aspects of a teacher's professional responsibilities. Research into such areas can only enhance this. The prospect is an exciting one and we hope only that some teachers will be prepared to take up this challenge. We finish this part of the book with a look at space.

SUGGESTED FURTHER READING

A vast amount of research has been carried out into classroom interaction. Many different approaches have been used and a variety of topics explored. *Interaction in the Classroom* (Delamont 1983a) is one of the best introductory texts dealing with the classroom as a social environment and covers many of the perspectives outlined here. One of the best accounts of systematic observation as a research technique applied to classrooms can be found in *Systematic Classroom Observation* (Croll 1986), whereas criticisms and evaluation of both the Flanders FIAC system and systematic observation have been made in 'Classroom research: a cautionary tale' (Hamilton and Delamont 1974); 'Systematic observation of classroom activities' (McIntyre 1980) and 'Interaction analysis in informal classrooms: a critical commentary on the Flanders system' (Walker and Adelman 1975). Debate over the ORACLE project is continued in 'The logic of systematic classroom research: the case of ORACLE' (Barrow 1984b) and 'Questioning ORACLE' (Scarth and Hammersley 1986). The importance and influence of anthropological perspectives in classroom research is examined in two articles: 'The two traditions of educational ethnography: sociology and anthropology compared' (Delamont and Atkinson 1980) and 'Anthropology and educational studies' (Vierra, Boehm and Neely 1982), in *The Social Sciences in Educational Studies: A Selective Guide to the Literature* (Harnett 1982). Studies derived from the ethnography of communication tradition can be found in *Functions of Language in the Classroom* (Cazden, John and Hymes 1972). For those unfamiliar with sociolinguistics, *Sociolinguistics: An Introduction*, (Trudgill 1974) remains one of the best introductions. *An Introduction to Sociolinguistics* (Wardhaugh 1986) though longer and more detailed, covers a lot of different studies and is worth consulting for reference purposes. The most accessible overview of sociolinguistic approaches to the classroom is the short book, *Language, Schools and Classrooms* (Stubbs 1983). *Investigating Classroom Language* (Edwards and Westgate 1986) could be profitably read after Stubbs' work. Edwards has taken up the issue of ethnicity, multicultural issues and education in two important and readable works: *The West Indian Language Issue in British Schools* (Edwards 1979) and *Language in Multi-Cultural Classrooms* (Edwards 1983). The classic and highly influential essay by William Labov is reprinted in this country as 'The logic of non-standard English' (Labov 1973), in *Tinker, Tailor . . . The Myth of Cultural Deprivation* (Keddie). A collection of articles demonstrating the value of ethnomethodology and conversational analysis in the study of classroom activities can be found in *Doing Teaching: The Practical Management of Classrooms* (Payne and Cuff 1982).

Communication and Learning in Small Groups (Barnes and Todd 1984) unfortunately out of print, is a classic study of small group talk in classrooms. The authors describe their own study of 13-year-olds working together in small groups without a teacher. They analyse both the cognitive strategies and the social skills displayed by these pupils. In the light of their findings they suggest detailed practical advice for teachers wanting to research talk and learning in small groups. They also outline an analytic framework involving 'content' and 'interaction' frames, which can be used to look at meaning in conversation. *Investigating Classroom Talk* (Edwards and Westgate 1986) looks at a wide range of approaches to recording and analysing classroom talk, from a sociolinguistic perspective. They review the methods used by various researchers, including different ways of doing transcriptions, in relation to the researchers' theoretical orientations and practical purposes. The book focuses on teacher/pupil dialogue (there is little on pupil–pupil talk) and gives a useful basic overview of research in this area. *Describing Language* (Graddol, Cheshire and Swann 1987) is essentially a reference book which explains the basic conceptual framework and technical vocabulary used by linguists describing and analysing language. It includes explanatory material on, for example, sentence and word structure, meaning, writing systems, face-to-face interaction, discourse and text. There are more specific instructions for the analysis of the data, and a discussion of the methodological issues involved in transcription. *Ways with Words: Language, Life and Work in Communities and Classroom* (Brice-Heath 1983) is a very influential ethnographic study by an anthropologist of language practices in two contrasting local communities in the Piedmont Carolinas. Brice-Heath shows how young pre-school children's learning about how to use language, and about narrative and literacy, is intricately tied up with their becoming a member of a particular community. She contrasts the language practices acquired by these children with those of the nearby townspeople, and with those used in schools and classrooms, one of the most detailed studies to come out of American ethnography of communication tradition. *Observing and Analysing Natural Language: A Critical Account of Sociolinguistic Method* (Milroy 1987) provides a general discussion of sociolinguistic method both in practical terms and in relation to theory. It focuses on work in the Labovian tradition, and looks at issues in data collection, analysis and interpretation. It covers questions to do with sampling, collecting natural speech, individual speaker variables, analysing phonological and syntactic variation, and style shifting and code switching. Although not directly concerned with school and education, this book is useful to anyone who is studying language in naturally occurring social contexts.

Children's Writing and Reading: Analysing Classroom Language (Perera 1984) is aimed at teachers who want to assess and extend their pupils' grammatical abilities, this book focuses on the grammatical structures of children's own writing, and of their textbooks, work cards, and examination questions. The author presents a grammatical framework for the description of English, an outline of children's own grammatical development and a description of the differences between speech and writing. She then applies these to a study of children's writing and their reading materials. A definitive source for anyone involved in analysing the structure of written classroom texts. *The Tidy House* (Steedman 1987) is an unusual study, which focuses on the writing of a long story by three 8-year-old working-class girls in a primary classroom. Steedman, who was their teacher at the time analyses this writing, and the taped conversations that accompany it, to show that through creating a story about love, sex, marriage, birth and motherhood, the girls are exploring and questioning the ideas and beliefs by which they themselves are being brought up. Steedman relates this study of her own pupils' writing to theories about language development, historical uses of children's writing, gender issues and what she calls 'the lost history of working class childhood'. *Discourse Analysis: The Socio-linguistic Analysis Natural Language* (Stubbs 1983) is written from the perspective of a linguist with a particular interest in education. Stubbs discusses the descriptive and theoretical issues which arise in the collection and analysis of naturally occurring spoken or written discourse, with detailed references to examples from conversational data, and classroom dialogue. He considers how far the concepts in linguistic theory are useful in discourse analysis, and also looks at the relevance of Speech Act theory. There is a useful final chapter which provides advice and ideas for students and researchers involved in collecting and analysing natural language. This could well be used in conjunction with other sociolinguistic texts. In Chapter 4 we provided an overview of the relationship between gender and education. A considerable amount of research has focused upon gender dimensions in school and classroom interaction. The following are worth considering in this respect: 'Interaction: the work women do' (Fishman 1983), in *Language, Gender and Society* (Thorne, Kramaroe and Henley 1983); 'Differential treatment of boys and girls during science lessions' (Galton 1981); *The Missing Half* (Kelly 1981); *Logo Mathematics in the Classroom* (Hoyles and Sutherland 1989); 'Gender differences in pupil–teacher interaction in workshops and laboratories' (Randall 1987), in *Gender and the Politics of Schooling* (Weiner and Arnot 1987); *Girls, Boys and Language* (Swann 1992); 'Gender differences in a co-operative computer-based language task' (Underwood, McCaffrey and Underwood 1990); 'Classroom practices and organization' (Windass 1989) and 'The relations between teachers and Afro-Caribbean pupils: observing multi-racial classrooms' (Wright 1987), in *Gender and the Politics of Schooling* (Weiner and Arnot).

11 Space and interaction in schools and classrooms

INTRODUCTION

In this chapter of the book we focus upon the spatial dimensions of schools and classrooms and try to show why space and place might be an important focus of research for the practising teacher. We will consider the importance of space in the learning situation and offer a 'hands-on' appreciation of how the classroom teacher might begin to go about looking at classroom interaction and the main traditions of classroom research we outlined in Chapter 10. By way of conclusion we examine Sally Lubeck's (1985) comparative ethnography of two early education settings in America, *Sandbox Society*, first in order to consider the ways in which both time and space dimensions structure activities in the schools, and second because her study raises many of the issues of research design we tried to unravel in Chapter 5. Her book shows some of the ways in which ethnographic and field research methods can be applied to educational settings and provides a good example of the way researchers move through the research process. Whilst not holding up this study as a definitive model of the research process, it offers many insights into ethnographic research and might act as a useful benchmark for the prospective teacher–researcher. Furthermore, it is an important contribution to understanding the pre-school educational process and early years education often neglected by researchers.

SPACE AND PLACE AS A RESEARCH FOCUS

By referring to space and place, or to spatial arrangements and spatial organization, we are pointing to the complex relationships between the physical, interactional and symbolic factors which shape and influence everybody's lives in countless and complex ways. From how close we sit next to strangers on a train, to the ways in which we organize and arrange the furniture in our classrooms, space is a crucial aspect of human social life. How people use, orientate towards, and make sense of features such as spaces, places, and the physical features of these settings, contributes to the orderliness of social interaction. In other words, spaces and places have 'social properties' and we all have a stock of commonsense knowledge which tells us how to act in particular settings, what to expect in them, and the likely consequences of interaction in such settings.

Spaces and places contain symbolic messages and social information. Researchers can ask a series of questions. What is it that a particular spatial arrangement is actually saying? How do people construct spaces to give off messages and how does this influence the interaction which takes place in them? The answers to these questions move us towards considering some of the most basic social and cultural features of our societies.

As a topic of research interest, space allows us to ask a series of important, but often neglected, questions. For example, how do people attend to and make sense of the features of spaces and places? How do people physically conduct themselves in particular spaces and places? How do they act, stand, queue, walk, etc? How are territories or boundaries developed, maintained and crossed? Answering such questions is no easy matter since for the most part the rules governing our behaviour are simply taken for granted and unstated.

How human beings orientate towards and structure the visible and invisible boundaries we refer to as space, environments, territories, or places and how we interact and react within these features has long been a topic of interest to social scientists. Hall (1969), for example, began his studies by asking why it was that Arabs in the USA felt uncomfortable while co-present with Americans during interaction and, conversely, why it was so many Americans felt uncomfortable with 'strangers' abroad. Others, notably Newman (1973) and those people having an interest in the architectural features of our society and the ways in which these features have affected us, pose questions about the correlation between crime rates, housing styles and the composition of many urban environments. On the other hand, more recently researchers such as Goffman and Scheflen have examined in detail the ways in which people co-ordinate their face-to-face interactions in both public and private places, 'upstage' and 'backstage', manipulating these features to their own advantage. In the world of education, most notably in the Plowden Report (1967), the influence of the spatial arrangement and organization of classroom activities was spelt out. Other social scientists, notably anthropologists and sociologists, were focusing upon what was described as 'territoriality'.

In a series of works, Hall was concerned with unravelling the use of space as a 'specialized elaboration of culture'. As such he was concerned with the dynamic use of space and the ways in which human beings could shape and control communication and interaction through the use of both the fixed features and semi-fixed features of space. Examples of the fixed features of space would be things like buildings, houses, schools, those features that it is not possible to move; semi-fixed features, on the other hand, are environmental factors that have the capacity either to increase or to decrease the amount of social interaction with others or will affect the nature of that interaction: hence actors can develop certain amounts of control over these features. Hall can be credited with developing the suggestion that space is indeed a sociocultural phenomenon. Different settings create different patterns of interaction, different cultures have different codes and rules for the use of spaces and the physical proximity of different kinds of actors.

Hall (1969) follows the distinction drawn by Osmond (1959) in his study of the development of mental hospitals between the notions of *sociofugal* and *sociopetal* space as ways of describing two quite distinct kinds of spatial arrangements. Examples of sociofugal spatial arrangements would be railway station waiting-rooms, or the classical/formal Victorian English classroom; the concern and emphasis in these arrangements is to keep people apart by establishing degrees of distance between participants. Sociopetal space, on the other hand, can be found in the typical French pavement café or indeed the progressive, informal English primary school. Here, the spatial arrangements have the reverse effect of actually encouraging social interaction, developing informality, closeness and co-operation. Joiner (1976), for example, from his study on the spatial arrangement of small offices shows how places, such as reception areas, lobbies and so on, can be used to develop impressions of the setting those on the outside of the organization will receive. In a similar fashion, the sociofugal arrangements of many open-plan schools are designed theoretically to provide a more flexible, less constraining, learning environment. In an important sense the way in which any organization is spatially organized provides important information about the culture and ethos of that organization. These ideas may provide the researcher with something of a theoretical framework to make use of when looking at space and place in the context of school-based research. However, this book is written from a qualitative perspective and there has certainly been much research in qualitative traditions which can help us here, in particular the contributions of interactionist sociologists are noteworthy here. Cultural rules define legitimate and deviant behaviour as we travel from one territory to another. This framework might be usefully applied in a descriptive manner to any school, classroom or learning environment. Another source of ideas here are the ever insightful observations of Goffman (1959; 1971).

It is clear to see how all aspects of our lives are influenced both by the nature of the physical spatial arrangements we find ourselves in and our interpretations of them and orientations towards them. It can be argued that these are crucial variables in the learning process and that as part of a teacher's professional responsibility these aspects of schools and classrooms demand close scrutiny. However, before we consider the ways in which the teacher–researcher might embark on investigation of the spatial dimensions of classrooms, let us broadly consider the grounds for wanting to do so in the first place.

SPATIAL DIMENSIONS OF SCHOOLS AND CLASSROOMS

Schools and classrooms may be conceived as 'arenas of interaction'. School buildings, classrooms, areas and locations are interpreted and identified by different people in different ways. Teachers and pupils routinely cope with and manage the physical arrangements in schools. The ways in which they do this has all manner of consequences. Dealing with these aspects of life is fundamentally an interactional affair; it is in this way that space and learning are linked. The ways in which classrooms are organized and arranged is not arbitrary; indeed, the organization of a classroom often reflects the kind of spirit in which learning can take place and can furthermore be said to reflect conceptions of knowledge. The organization and layout of a school or classroom tells as much about the character of the school and the orientations of participants. The aim of research on school and classroom spatial organization is pragmatic. Such research should aim to unravel the ways in which space and learning interact so as to reveal some of the educational consequences of the spatial and physical organization of the immediate environment. This knowledge will enable the teacher–researcher to reflect back upon practice.

The spatial organization of a school or classroom provides possibilities for learning but at the same time constraints. The school buildings and classrooms themselves express and embody conceptions of teaching and learning. In looking at the spatial organization of any school or classroom, the teacher–researcher will need to bear in mind the overall assumptions which are likely to influence any one situation. For example, conceptions of children, the status of the pupils, interpretations of schooling in formal or informal terms as subject- or child-centred, together with teachers' and pupils' attitudes, will all affect the nature of classroom interaction and the influence of the spatial organization and physical context upon this. The pervasiveness of these features and their perceived importance is illustrated by the way in which this issue has received considerable attention in the educational and professional literature. This is reflected most notably in the primary area and the so-called 'progressive' approach to primary education and, of course, in the debate on open-plan schools. Space has also been a focus of attention in unravelling the reasons why girls do not achieve as boys do in science subjects, particularly mathematics.

The implications of the recommendations of the Plowden Report (1967) were quickly felt. Discovery learning and the rejection of the compartmentalization of knowledge meant that the physical and spatial organization of many primary schools was changing. Increased 'activity work' meant provision within a classroom for often a number of different activities taking place simultaneously. Similarly, the introduction of the 'integrated day' or 'team teaching' were attempts to provide greater flexibility within schools and individual classrooms, as well as encouraging greater pupil autonomy.

Consider for a moment some of the implications of Dearden's (1971) definition of the integrated day:

> Learning takes place in an open or openly interconnected space where the teachers move from individual to individual, or draw aside groups according to an overall and agreed programme. Something like the traditional class and its teachers still residually exists at the beginning and end of the day. This is the homebase from which children and teachers alike move out to wider contacts.
>
> (Dearden 1971: 51)

or of Rintoul and Thorne, on the features of open-plan organization in the primary school:

> 1 The organization of classroom spaces so that children can learn as individuals and in small groups for some time.
> 2 The integration of subjects so that different activities may be going on at the same time.
>
> (Rintoul and Thorne 1975: 13)

However, this is really only one side of the coin, the professional side of the professional themes and practical arrangements issue. This points to the way in which teachers have constantly to translate the educational theory, ideas and professional themes, into what they can do in practice, within the constraints in which they work and in relation to their own interpretation of these themes. As Hamilton puts it with regard to open-plan schooling, though the point has more general applicability:

> Open-plan schooling, like any other kind of schooling, is not simply a cluster of theoretical assumptions, still less a set of individual practices. Its realisation is a combination of both practices and theory.
>
> (Hamilton 1977: 107)

From the professional literature then, spatial organization in school is an important matter. Primary teaching is no longer here seen as being about instruction in places of instruction, but rather about developing and creating environments for learning, where teachers provide direction, stimulation and encouragement. These are professional themes and the extent to which they influence and affect practice is not unproblematic, and anyway these professional themes are now being questioned. As we said above, teachers have to translate this, which they do in various ways, in the light of their definitions of the area, the children, their past experiences, and their jobs. It is in this way that the social organization of space in schools and classrooms reflects the practical routine day-to-day considerations of teachers. It is clear to see how the organization of space in any school or classroom situation often reflects the pedagogical underlying practice. It is one of the tasks of the teacher–researcher to get beneath the surface of this.

Possibly the earliest and best-known research that has been conducted in the area of space and education is the work of Robert Sommer, a social psychologist. In a series of studies Sommer (1967; 1969) was concerned with unravelling the influence of seating arrangements and classroom arrangements and classroom spatial organization on the levels of pupils' participation. In one study of an introductory psychology class, the students directly opposite the instructor were found to participate more than those on the sides (Sommer 1967: 489–503; see also Sommer 1969). In classrooms where desks were arranged in straight rows students in front were found to participate more than those in the rear, and students in the centre of each row participated more than those on the side. It is argued that these and other findings back up what is known as the 'expressive contact hypothesis' which relates direct visual contact to increased interaction. Sommer's concern was primarily practical, being involved mainly with the problem of the ecology of classroom participation; his work rests upon the implicit assumption that increased participation makes for better teaching and he is therefore establishing the kinds of physical arrangements that will best facilitate this.

Sommer's approach was one of the first systematic attempts to consider these issues. However, there are problems surrounding this research. There appears to be little recognition of the fact that different groups and, indeed, individuals within any one group will have their own ideas about spatial arrangements. In many ways Sommer's work relates to standard classrooms, but in reality how many classrooms are 'standard'? As we noted in Chapter 6, one of the persistent criticisms of Flanders' interaction analysis system (FIAC) was its inability to cope with non-standard and informal classrooms (Walker and Adelman 1975: 73–6).

Rivlin and Rothenberg (1976), however, conducted their research in a rather different manner. This study is noteworthy not so much for its conclusions, but rather the methodology it adopted. Rivlin and Rothenberg in their study of space in open classrooms in the USA made use of descriptions of the rooms and the users of the rooms and the location of individuals within the room in relation to other individuals. The researchers made observations of two public elementary schools using open-plan classroom approaches located in large urban areas of the USA. The authors described their methodology in the following way:

> The specific techniques that were used included repeated observations of classrooms, repeated *tracking* (following the complete days of individual children), interviews with teachers, children and parents and use of a model of the classroom in conjunction with an interview with students.
>
> (Rivlin and Rothenberg 1976: 481)

These researchers also made use of a behavioural mapping and time-sampling technique which focuses upon the location of any one individual at specified periodic moments. Their use of triangulation by means of interviewing and discussions after the event is also interesting here.

A different line of research is pursued by the well-known American educational researcher Rist (1972) in his study of inequalities in an American ghetto kindergarten classroom. Rist speaks about the 'social distance' that the teacher in his study was able to maintain between herself and her pupils so that a 'some can do it and some can not' attitude developed. Rist's (1972) study was based upon lengthy periods of observation in the kindergarten classroom of a group of black children; he also conducted interviews with both the class teacher and the principal. Rist argues that the actual spatial arrangement of the classroom echoed the kinds of social distinctions which were developed between the teacher and the pupils. Rist offers some revealing observations on the ways in which spatial arrangements in the classroom can further contribute to inequalities and underachievement:

> The permanent seating of the children in the classroom on the eighth day of school took on additional significance when it is noted that they appear to have been seated based on a number of social-class criteria independent of any measurement of cognitive capacity and ability to perform academic tasks.
>
> (Rist 1972: 274)

Rist's study points to the way in which aspects of the spatial organization of classrooms, in conjunction with other factors, can have a considerable effect on the pupils' learning.

In an ethnographic study of the social organization of space and place in one urban open-plan primary school in northern England, Hitchcock (1982) found that the teachers were involved in the elaborate creation of boundaries in a school where there was a general absence of walls and 'classrooms'. Teachers in this school faced a problem. On the one hand, there was the theory and professional themes of open-plan teaching and, on the other hand, they were faced with the realities of teaching in their school in a 'difficult', 'downtown', inner-city neighbourhood. As a consequence, teachers developed a series of practical responses and adaptions to the open-plan context of the school. In other words, this research showed how the professional themes of what should and ought to be going on in open-plan schools such as this were mediated and translated into what could go on and be made to work in these types of location by the teachers themselves. This researcher found three general processes that teachers became involved with in translating the professional themes of the school into the practical arrangements of day-to-day teaching. First, the teachers might be described as being engaged in a process of 'normalization'. The teachers had collaboratively learnt to recognize and interpret certain events in school as being 'normal for here'. This had the effect of rendering a whole range of activities as being non-problematic while elsewhere they could quite easily have been regarded as being highly problematic. Second, the teachers had also learnt to disregard certain kinds of disorderliness and disciplinary problems as a direct response to the visibility of action within the school. Finally, the researcher observed that the widespread practice of the retreat into the home-base seemed to be a response to try and compensate for the absence of walls by using their home-bases, and the five-feet-high partitions of which they were composed, as barriers and partitions within which particularly sought-after behaviour could be encouraged and developed (Hitchcock 1982: 76–84).

The responses and adaptions made by these teachers have important consequences for the amount and kind of learning that takes place in school. Many published studies point to the importance of space and place in schools and classrooms. Furthermore, this research displays a great amount of variation in the methodology employed and data collected. Rivlin and Rothenberg (1976) and Lubeck (1985) made use of flow charts. Rist (1972) used non-participant observation and Hitchcock (1982) used participant observation. In the following section we will examine some of the ways in which the teacher might go about investigating space in schools and classrooms.

HOW TO RESEARCH SPACE AND PLACE IN SCHOOLS AND CLASSROOMS

Whereas observation is likely to be the major source of data for the teacher–researcher interested in considering the importance of space and place in schools, perhaps more than any other topic, the question of classroom and school spatial arrangements lends itself to the triangulation of sources of data and methods of data collection. Moreover, the spatial organization of classrooms and its relation to learning may crop up as part of another research topic or curriculum evaluation exercise. In this sense focusing upon space may constitute a small part of an overall study, or in contrast, the main issue in a single investigation. We will outline some of the main issues involved in researching space. However, to begin with the teacher–researcher needs to bear two crucial points in mind.

First, it needs to be recognized that patterns of interaction in classrooms do change and develop over time. Any research into the spatial dimensions of schools and classrooms will have to take this into account. Second, it is important to give due consideration to the typicality or representativeness of the group, class, or subject being observed. It is important therefore for the teacher–researcher to consider a range of situations in order to get a fair picture of what is happening.

There are likely to be three main ways in which data can be generated on the spatial arrangements and organization of schools and classrooms. Observation, and in particular participant observation, the use of diaries, and interviewing could all be used here. However, a range of visual materials, as we will point out below, are particularly helpful while examining this area.

The teacher's familiarity with the setting can be both an advantage and a disadvantage; the kinds of observations made will therefore have to consider this. The observations may be quite formalized or, alternatively, they may be more descriptive and extended accounts of a classroom setting or particular area. Observations could also be made of the development of a class lesson or activity, focusing upon descriptions of the physical layout of the classroom and the movements of teachers and pupils. The researcher should aim to produce as detailed descriptions as possible from these observations.

The diary offers the teacher an excellent means of gaining fairly detailed descriptions of the routine features of teacher–pupil interaction and the use of space in classrooms. The teacher records the timing and activities she has engaged in during the course of a school day, paying attention to the relationship between timings, locations and the participants involved. The teacher–researcher can do this in her own classroom or alternatively ask another teacher to keep a diary of these features of classroom life. Of course, if a number of diaries are kept the teacher–researcher can engage in a comparative exercise, when similarities, differences and patterns could be established across the materials.

The unstructured or semi-structured interview can provide the opportunity to reconsider the materials the teacher has collected via observations, a diary, or some other means. Here, the teacher–researcher can seek to clarify, for example a teacher's perceptions of the spatial dimension of a particular classroom. The interview might also be used to develop further lines of inquiry. Here it will be useful to have developed beforehand a checklist or an *aide-mémoire* of the salient features it is intended to explore in the interview. In many cases this interview material will act as supplementary data. Whatever method or combinations of methods are used to explore this area, the general aim ought to be the production of as rich and detailed descriptions as possible. With this in mind let us examine some of the data available for the teacher–researcher to collect, the ways in which they may be collected and the kinds of questions which may be raised. The list below sets out some of these aspects:

- Photography and video tape recording.
- Layouts, maps, plans and diagrams.
- Relationships between locations and activities.
- Boundaries.
- Seating arrangements.
- Tracking teachers and pupils and time-sampling.
- Gender dimensions of classroom activities.
- Subject or classroom tasks and spatial arrangements.
- Workshops with staff and parents.

Photography and video tape recording

As we discussed in Chapter 6, still photography has for a long time been considered to be one of the basic tools of the ethnographic fieldworker. Visual records of all kinds may help the researcher to develop a closer feel and appreciation of the setting. There is certainly scope for the use of photography when investigating classroom spatial arrangements. We explore the role of photography in ethnography in detail in Chapter 12. Photographs can add depth and richness and are useful as descriptive resources from which the teacher may tease out ideas and lines of analysis. The photograph, however, can never hope to capture the dynamic ebb and flow of classroom life, though the photographs contained in Prosser's (1992) study show just what can be achieved. This might mean that photographs are more useful for some kinds of classrooms than others. Static, frozen images of classroom activities must always be placed within the ongoing and constantly moving patterns of classroom interaction. In this sense, the use of audio-visual techniques has very definite advantages. Many schools nowadays have access to a 'back-pack' video camera outfit and certainly a number of schools have video tape recorders and playback provision. If video tape recording a classroom lesson, for whatever purposes, the teacher will have to bear in mind the nature of the lesson, the subject involved, age and orientation of the children, and the teacher's style, with the possible effects the presence of a camera will have upon the interactions themselves. Moreover, the teacher will also need to pay attention to the angle or angles from which the filming is done. This is especially important if the teacher uses a fixed tripod. Questions surrounding the possible exclusion of certain areas in the classroom or groups of children need to be considered alongside the kind of film that will emerge from placing the camera at the back, front or sides of the classroom. Although many of these problems are minimized when the classrooms in question are conventional ones, they are conversely increased in, for example, informal infant or primary schools. We have worked with video tape recordings of classroom lessons where the backs of childrens' heads have been virtually all that one saw of the children. Despite these difficulties the video tape recording of classroom lessons can provide the researcher with an important moving record from which to consider the spatial ecology and social organization of space within the classroom. Those thinking of using film or video will need to reconsider the five sets of issues we identified in Chapter 6 on the use of these techniques as a means of collecting data in social and educational research.

Layouts, maps, plans and diagrams

Many teachers and other researchers find the construction of classroom layouts, maps, plans or diagrams of locations within a school or classroom a particularly valuable exercise (see, for example, Hitchcock 1982). The following examples show the kinds of diagrams and plans it is possible to construct from the school and classroom situation. The degree of detail will depend upon the nature of the topic under investigation. Although not absolutely essential, these layouts and diagrams should be as near to scale as possible. Obviously the degree of detail in these will depend upon what the researcher is looking at.

Figures 11.1, 11.2 and 11.3 show the kinds of features it is useful to indicate on a sketch map, plan or diagram of a particular classroom or part of a school. The teacher–researcher also needs to remember that the semi-fixed features of space recorded on the plans and diagrams can and do change. This might mean that more than one plan will have to be produced for a single classroom. If the school's original architect's drawings are available these, too, can help to develop a sense of scale. It will be necessary to include a key to the items contained on these plans. A few of the things the teacher–researcher might want to include would be seating arrangements, position of furniture and desks, numbers of children in the classroom or group, and the main lines of travel or apparent 'thoroughfares' within the classroom.

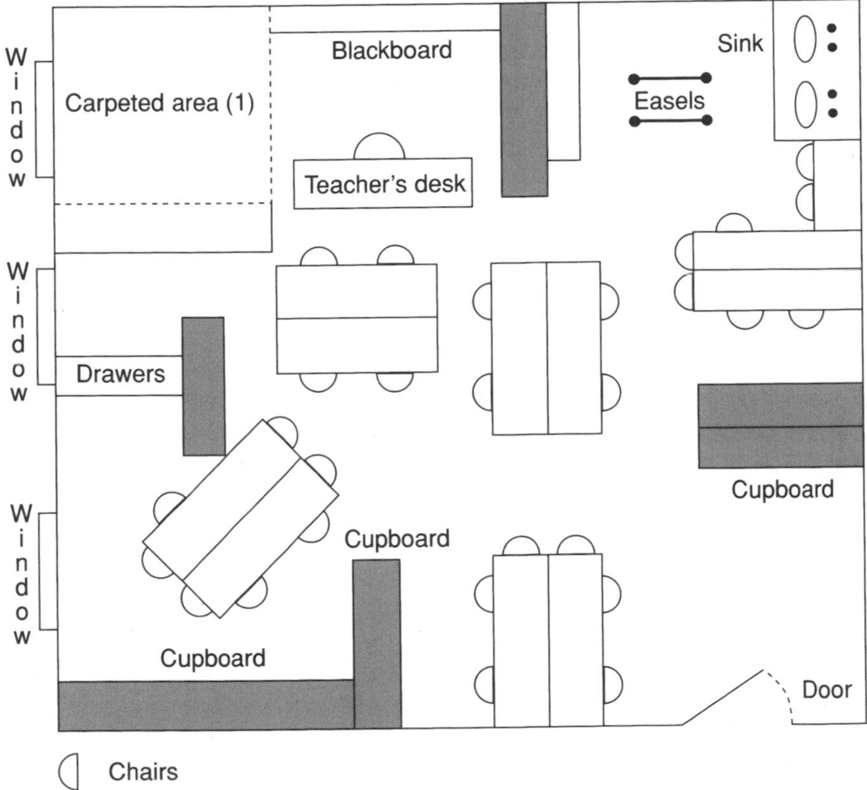

Figure 11.1 An infant school classroom

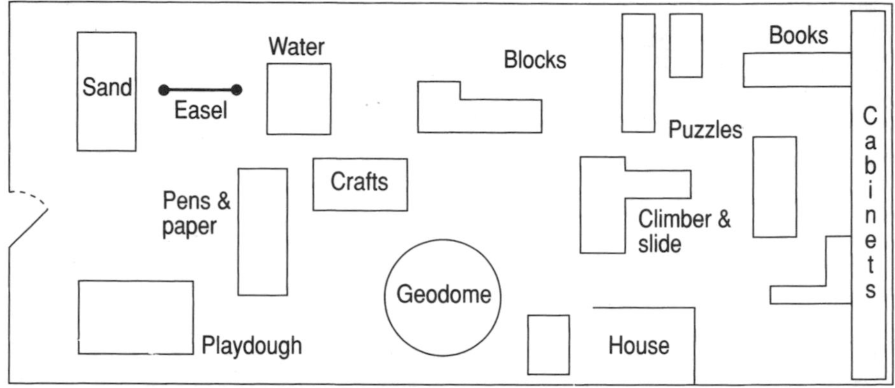

Figure 11.2 Floor plan of Harmony Pre-school
Source: Lubeck (1985: 84)

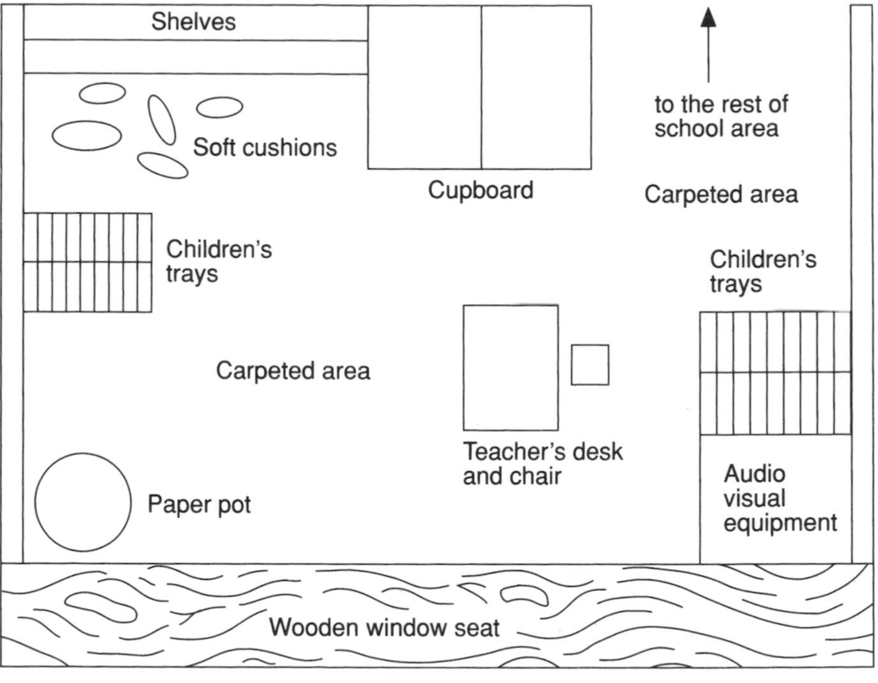

Figure 11.3 Plan of a home-base in an open plan primary school

Relationships between locations and activities

Human beings are indomitable categorizers. We routinely devise categories for people, places and activities. The importance of this lies in the observation that certain categories are seen to 'go together'. Teachers, in the course of their routine work, see certain categories as going together, knowing this categorization system enables the smooth running of organized social activities. Schools in this sense are made up of complex interconnections of locations and activities. Teachers and children come to have specific understandings of the way things get done, where and how. The teacher–researcher concerned to uncover the spatial dimensions of schools and classrooms might focus upon expectations about locations, behaviour and categories of people within the school system. Such a focus will enable us to see any discrepancies between the intended uses of particular locations and the way in which they are used in practice. All the time the teacher is concerned to describe what is actually going on in any school or classroom situation in relation to how the participants themselves orientate towards what they see to be happening. Here, it is interesting to see the ways in which artefacts, furniture, signs, posters and so on play a part in alerting people to the actual nature of a particular location. In other words, participants' understanding of the features of locations in school is constantly affirmed and reaffirmed in the physical and symbolic arrangements found within the schools and classrooms themselves. In many cases, especially with young children, it is important that a working knowledge of this kind of categorization system is developed if classroom activities are going to run smoothly. The teacher–researcher will therefore find these fundamentally important, even if in the event they appear largely to be taken for granted.

Boundaries

One of the interesting features of school and classroom life is the way in which barriers, boundaries and gatekeepers function to shape and influence interaction and eventually learning in schools and classrooms. The school, like any other organization has to let people know where school life starts and finishes. Most schools secure entry into the building so that anyone entering the premises will have to negotiate a series of gatekeepers, school secretaries, receptionists and caretakers. These people are charged with protecting what Goffman (1971) describes as the 'front' the school wishes to present to the outside world. Boundaries are generated across the whole realm of school and classroom life. They generate arenas or stages upon which certain kinds of interactions take place. The development, use and maintenance of boundaries is an important interactional aspect of teachers' work since it enables them to create an order to their worlds.

Seating arrangements

These are obviously an important aspect of class management. The issue here surrounds the ways in which seating arrangements, proximity of pupils to the teacher and the position of the teacher in relation to the class or the group are seen to shape and influence the nature of interaction within the classroom. Sommer's work (1967; 1969) sought to establish a relationship between levels of participation and seating arrangements in the classroom. A number of studies on the gender dimensions of schooling and girls' poor performance in science subjects compared to boys point towards the marginality of girls in many mixed-sex classrooms in terms of being outside the 'action zone' (Turner 1982: 45). Again, the teacher will need to prepare seating plans carefully, asking questions about the degree of choice the pupils are able to exercise, and also the kinds of interaction patterns that might seem to be related to where the pupil sits.

Tracking teachers and pupils and time-sampling

In order to get at the normal use of space in any one classroom and the routine ways in which teachers and pupils make use of this space and interact with each other, a number of teachers in the past have made use of what might be described as tracking. This is an observational technique which involves an observer/researcher monitoring the teacher, pupil, or groups of pupils in the course of a single lesson, or whole school day in order to see the interactions and activities they become engaged in and the consequential use of physical space and places. Although this technique will obviously produce fairly detailed data, the researcher would do well to remember the kinds of criticisms that were made of systematic observation schedules such as those of Flanders and the ORACLE project in Chapter 10. Our point would be that any attempts to track or log the teachers' or pupils' interactions and use of space would need to be combined with other more qualitative data. However, this tracking, mapping and coding can be as flexible or as controlled as the researcher sees fit. Lubeck (1985), for example, shows how this can be done in order to produce 'flow charts' of individual children's movements; uses of spaces and activities in the course of the school day. Often a time-sampling technique can be incorporated into this approach whereby at certain prearranged regular intervals the teacher is logged in terms of her position or location in the classroom, or the tasks that the pupils are engaged in. Rivlin and Rothenberg (1976) in the study mentioned earlier made use of what they described as 'behavioural mapping', a 'naturalistic time-sampling technique for describing patterns of activities and use of physical space'.

Another opportunity open to the teacher–researcher is to focus upon one child's day and to follow the child through an ordinary day noting the interaction patterns, locations and activities the child becomes engaged in. With care and an eye for detail, a fairly comprehensive 'natural history' of the child's day can be painted from which the teacher–researcher can draw inferences about the importance of and orientations towards the spatial organization of school and classroom.

Gender dimensions of classroom activities

There has been considerable research done into the different kinds of educational experience of girls and boys together with research into the reasons for girls' poor achievement in maths and science subjects compared with boys, see, for example, the Equal Opportunities Commission Research Bulletin 6 (EOC 1982). Clarricoates (1980), and Stanworth (1981). Most research has focused upon aspects of the hidden curriculum, teacher and pupil attitudes to subjects, and a general sexist bias in education. An important focus for the teacher–researcher might be upon the gender dimension of school and classroom spatial organization. It may be that seating arrangements and the spatial/physical arrangement of the classroom will influence interaction patterns differently for boys and girls. If teachers are seen to spend more time with boys than girls how much of this might be to do with the spatial organization of the classroom? There is certainly much more research needed in this complex area, some of which may be done by teachers themselves. The point is, however, to consider the influence of gender variables in conjunction with other factors, including the spatial organization of the classroom, as influencing learning and, moreover, attitudes to learning.

Subject or classroom tasks and spatial arrangements

Another important aspect concerns the actual subject of the lesson or, alternatively, the nature of the tasks the pupils are engaged in. The teacher–researcher needs to bear in mind the general ethos surrounding the subject or activities in question and the teachers' and pupils' perceptions of what is involved. Clearly, different kinds of lessons are likely to display different uses of space and spatial arrangements of classrooms when using these materials.

Workshops with staff and parents

Finally, it is worth making the point that the teacher–researcher need never be on her own. Staff meetings with parents are useful points at which to bring up observations and ideas. Alternatively, workshops designed to discuss particular issues may be arranged. Many teachers in the primary section have people helping them in the classroom, and as such they offer an important source of information on the setting as well. The workshop is a useful way of reminding ourselves where our research comes from.

These are just some of the ways in which the teacher might begin research into the spatial organization of schools and classrooms. The data obtained in the ways we have outlined above will probably need to be supplemented by other sources of data, using different techniques. The remaining question surrounds the analysis of these kinds of materials. The visual character of the data and descriptions which the teacher is likely to generate when looking at space and place raises some special issues. The teacher may wish to consult, for example, the highly influential work by Goffman (1971) *The Presentation of Self in Everyday Life* or to consider the guidelines, suggestions and kinds of focus outlined in some of the published studies, for example, King (1978: 201–9) or Hitchcock (1982).

By way of conclusion not only to this chapter on the spatial dimension of schools, classrooms and learning, but also to this part of the book, we consider an American ethnographic study of early childhood education, or what we would describe broadly as nursery education.

CASE STUDY: SALLY LUBECK, *SANDBOX SOCIETY*

A focus upon time and space in ethnographic research

It seems fitting to end our discussion in this part of the book and our examination of space and education in this chapter by focusing upon one study. We have chosen Lubeck's (1985) interesting and well-written book for a number of reasons. First, this book is based upon a doctoral thesis and shows how research for degrees may be turned into a published work. Second, the study makes use of the case study, ethnography format and clearly shows how the researcher in such work can move backwards and forwards between description and explanation analysis, an important theme of qualitative research we have encouraged teachers to develop throughout this part of the book. Third, by focusing upon two schools Lubeck develops comparisons and hence shows how ethnographic research can throw light upon more general processes. Fourth, the overall research design of this work is clearly presented and while displaying certain weaknesses can provide the teacher–researcher with a useful model or benchmark from which to develop her own work, with an insight into the research process itself. From within the context of early education in the USA the book deals in a sensitive way with the complex aspects of time, space, and interaction variables. *Sandbox Society* is an excellent example of the ethnographic approach to educational research.

Lubeck's book is based upon studies of pre-school settings in suburban America. One is a pre-school centre where the children and teachers were white, the other is part of a 'Head Start' programme with black teachers and children. The study was based on a year's fieldwork and her main focus was upon activities, materials and teacher–pupil interaction, together with the use of time and space. She aimed first to try and understand how poor minority black children actually adapted to a 'distinctive social history', how these adaptations were in fact reproduced in the black Head Start programme, and how these were transmitted to the next generation. Second, she aimed to understand, conversely, the processes by which mainstream white middle-class cultural values were adopted and transmitted in a white pre-school not a mile away from the black Head Start school. Lubeck paints a picture of two very different experiences of pre-school education, of two different orientations to pre-school education, and ultimately pre-school education of differing quality. She comments on her book that:

> The story that needs to be told is one that has no obvious beginning and seemingly no end, and so its rendering is but a pinprick in time. It is a story of a single city in the United States, a story of a suburb of that city, a story of two early education programmes in that suburb, a story ultimately of the few people in the act of re-creating the social order by transmitting their values, attitudes and life orientations to the next generation. There, near the sandbox, in this littlest of worlds, children take in cues of who they are and of what the world they will inhabit is like.
>
> (Lubeck 1985: vi)

In order to try and unravel this complex issue Lubeck went for an anthropologically informed ethnographic study based upon the controlled comparison of the two classroom settings we described above. Her perspective sought to 'look at the day-to-day processes by which adults teach children to adapt to the reality which they themselves experience' (Lubeck 1985: 1). Whilst the delineation and analysis of time and space relations, as lenses through which the social organization of a group or culture may be observed, predominates in anthropological literature this is largely missing from research in pre- and early school settings.

The research of 'Sandbox Society'

If the teacher is writing for the purposes of some degree or other course, a literature review is normally regarded as a central aspect of the project or dissertation and we considered the nature and purpose of literature reviews in Chapter 5. It is useful for the teacher to locate her research in current trends, ideas and practices. Lubeck provides such a review of related literature in Chapter 2 of the book. This is important for a number of reasons, but perhaps most important of all is the way in which such a review of relevant related studies can serve as a comparison with the present research findings. This helps to locate a piece of research within the context of a broad research problem. The researcher aims here not at the production of extended, detailed reviews of every single study of the topic that she can find, but rather to set the scene noting the salient themes, topics and findings of the research.

We have mentioned throughout this book the possible use by teachers of a pilot study in conducting small-scale school-based research. Lubeck conducted a four-month-long pilot study which involved close descriptions, many field notes and some intensive in-depth formal interviewing of teachers in the context of a traditional integrated pre-school setting in an inner suburb of a large mid-western city. This was an exploratory study, but Lubeck had a major problem. She wished to investigate and develop, before conducting the case studies proper, a research methodology which would allow her to stop the action sufficiently 'in an environment where the wash of movement, activity and interaction could be overwhelming to the prospective observer' (Lubeck 1985: 51). How can the researcher, especially the qualitative ethnographic researcher whose work depends upon involvement, be protected from being totally swamped and overwhelmed by the density of the data themselves in such settings? Lubeck's pilot study, which involved spending over 100 hours 'in the field' and the development of a series of flow charts of the activities of individual children, enabled her to come to some appreciation of the flux and to explore the possibilities of developing multiple methods for 'stopping the action'.

Lubeck's book is based upon a comparison of two case studies, one of a traditional white middle-class pre-school, the other a black Head Start centre. Lubeck developed the traditional role of participant observer taking field notes and making observations. She would record child–child and teacher–child interactions, analyse the classroom schedules and layouts of the school and, by means of flow charts, plot the children's activities and use of space. Lubeck also became involved in helping out in the routine day-to-day activities of school life.

Noting the issue of validity in ethnographic research, Lubeck attempted to build in some validity checks. One of the important checks Lubeck employed here was to ask the teachers to respond and to agree or disagree. As she became more established in the setting she began to discuss what she was seeing more openly with the staff. Lubeck's study is a good example of the way in which the researcher constantly moves backwards and forwards between description and analysis, between what is the case and why it is the case. Furthermore, the study shows how careful comparison of cases can be used to reveal crucial factors in children's pre-school educational experience which can influence their later educational careers and performance. Lubeck's study is important not only for the way in which the research was designed and carried out, but also for the contribution it makes to our understanding of time and space within an educational world.

The use of time

Lubeck argues that, in effect, differing uses of time reflect different conceptualizations of time. In many ways much conventional educational research seemed to suggest that schools and classrooms were first educational institutions and the participants, especially the pupils, were individuals. The ethnographic approach stresses that schools are socially generated organizations made up of complex layers of meanings which are created by the shared interpretative work of groups of people. Furthermore, a person's history and culture provide them with an orientation to the world and a way of handling that world. Lubeck suggests that time was used and understood in the two classrooms she explored in different ways and, as such, there were differing educational consequences (Lubeck 1985: 69). What is important for Lubeck is that each of the two schools she observed devoted differing amounts of time to differing activities which, in turn, Lubeck is able to link to the individualistic orientations of the white middle-class pre-school and to the emphasis upon kinship and peer group loyalty on the part of teachers in the black Head Start school. Lubeck produces comparisons of the daily routine schedules in the schools and the amounts of time spent on each activity. Timetabling differences show that in effect the Head Start school seemed to be reinforcing group values, whereas the white middle-class pre-school was encouraging individual development. By the use of this approach Lubeck was able to examine the different weightings given to particular activities.

One of the neatest examples here is the way in which the concept of 'free play' is used and interpreted in very different ways in the two school settings. In the white middle-class pre-school it is clear to see how, in fact, much of the children's day is devoted to free play allowing the children the possibility and freedom to direct the nature of the activities they become involved in themselves. This resulted in minimal direct overt control by the adults in this school setting. By way of contrast 'free play' takes on a rather different character in the black Head Start school. Here, free play involved the children playing on their own much of the time, enabling the staff to get on with administrative and other activities. These differences taken together with the amount of time devoted to 'free play' in the two schools point to some quite significant differences. Lubeck comments on this situation thus:

> Whereas the Head Start teachers value and practice reciprocal relations among peers, the pre-school teachers assume that their primary function is to establish relationships with the children and to facilitate their growth. Case histories reveal, however, that this is not merely a matter of educational training or of knowledge of psychological principles, rather it is an orientation that reflects their own socialisation; each teacher had been the product of a nuclear family where the mother had not worked and where she had been the principal child rearer in the home.
>
> (Lubeck 1985: 81)

Again, Lubeck moves backwards and forwards between the situations she observes and the developing analysis of them. She demonstrates the ways in which methods of data collection and different types of data can be brought to bear on the same issue. Here we find a good example of triangulation since participant observation, staff case histories, interviews, conversations and flow chart data are all combined to support and to check out the researcher's ideas, adding depth and density to the study.

The use of space

The problem for the ethnographer and educational researcher interested in space is well put by Howard Becker when he comments that we need to 'stop seeing only the things that are conventionally "there" to be seen' (cited in Wax and Wax 1971: 10): in other words to stop taking for granted what most of us take for granted most of the time. Again, in overcoming this problem, Lubeck made use of a multi-technique approach mixing observations with conversations, to build up data, extract ideas and reflect upon them as the research progressed. This could then be related to earlier work in the area.

Lubeck focuses upon two different yet related aspects. First, descriptions of the physical arrangements of the classroom, that is the planned environment, noting the kinds of changes which take place day to day and week to week. Once more Lubeck makes excellent use of diagrams here to identify the uses of space in the settings. But these descriptions might only be able to give limited accounts of the dynamic uses of space in the actual school day. Alongside these general descriptions went intensive observation of how the spaces were used in practice, a matter of seeing through. For example, she is able to comment upon the white middle-class Harmony Pre-school that:

> The environment is carefully planned and modified slightly from week to week. For example, a balance beam is set up next to the sand table one week; the beam is pushed against the wall to make way for a water table the next . . . The teachers keep material not in use in large cupboards against the back wall. These are unlocked each day, and different activities are set up in different areas . . . Notably teachers and children share the same space. No separate area or desk is sectioned off for the teachers only. The utilization of space appears to be a physical manifestation of the form of social interaction practised in the classroom.
>
> (Lubeck 1985: 84)

Second, the fluidity of the picture needed somehow to be captured. Here, Lubeck makes extended use of flow charts which are constructed to demonstrate the movements of individual children as they went about the classroom, with timings of their use of given spaces. This was conducted over periods of time in order to establish some kind of consistency. Figure 11.4 shows a flow chart for 'Sue' taken from Lubeck's study.

Conversely, it is possible to construct a flow chart of the teacher's movements in the classroom. This will reveal the amounts of time the teacher spends in particular locations and with groups of children or individual children. Flow charts of both children and teachers can then be compared thereby highlighting subtle and often taken-for-granted aspects of classroom organization.

SUMMARY

This chapter has made a case for the importance of space and place in schools and classrooms as issues worthy of attention by the teacher–researcher. We have tried to show some of the ways in which the teacher–

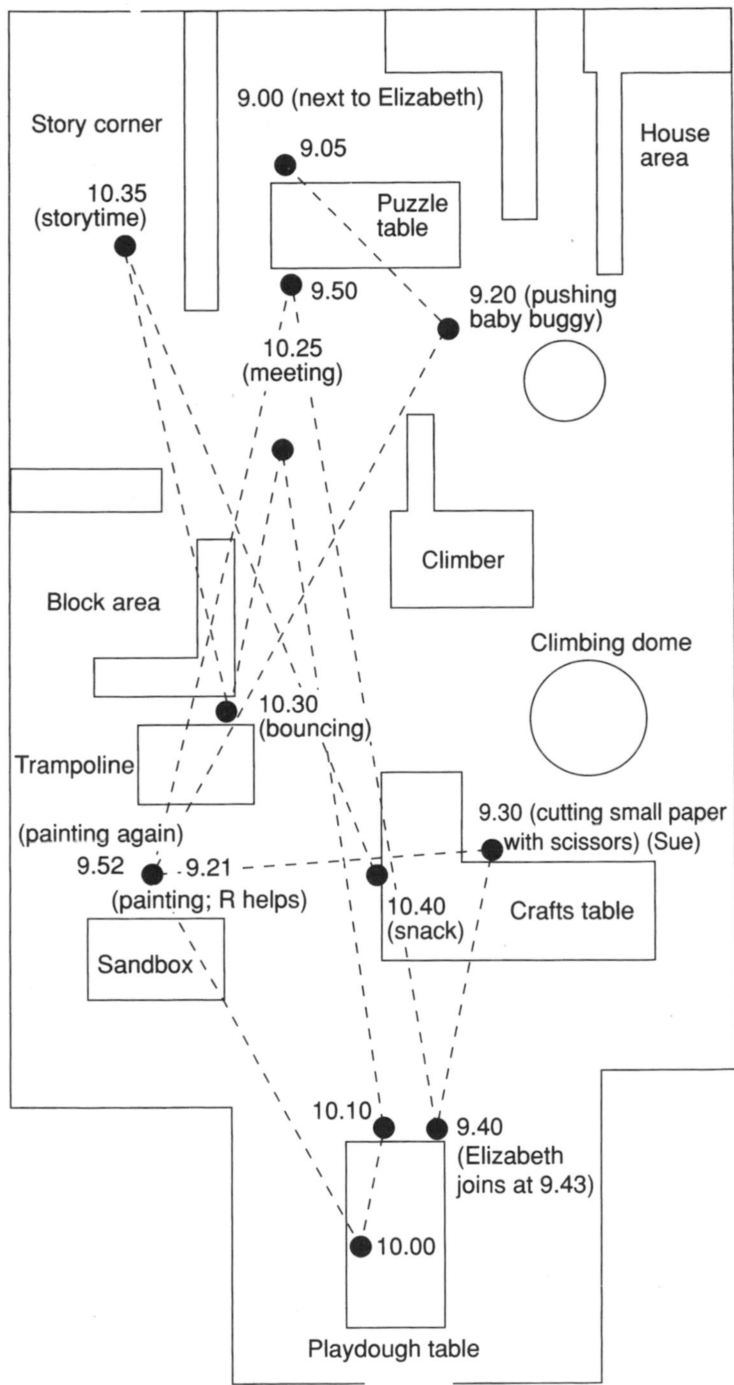

Figure 11.4 Flow chart for 'Sue', Harmony Pre-school
Source: Lubeck (1985: 47)

researcher might profitably go about investigating this area from a qualitative perspective, and concluded the chapter by considering one study undertaken in this area. Since *Sandbox Society* (Lubeck 1985) is an important study it demonstrates what can be achieved by adopting the ethnographic qualitative framework for research in schools and classrooms we have been unravelling and advocating. It also provides a good example of the pathways through research, which we identified in Chapter 5. It is possible to question the validity of Lubeck's findings and to criticize her theoretical perspective, but the study is fundamentally a good example of ethnographic research design in school and classroom locations. We have tried to show in this short review how research works out in practice by focusing upon both the research design of Lubeck's study and some of her substantive findings. It is hoped that the complex yet simultaneously exciting aspects of ethnographic research in education will have been conveyed to the prospective teacher–researcher. There is, of course, one important caveat. Lubeck had all of the advantages, with the disadvantages that accrue from the role of the outside researcher, and it would, of course, be difficult for the practising teacher to emulate such a piece of research. The teacher–researcher will find much of interest the findings of Lubeck's study but also much by way of insight into the ethnographic research process itself. On these grounds it provides a fitting conclusion to our introduction to the main techniques of qualitative research.

We now come to the complex processes of analysing the data and writing up the research. Whilst we have introduced these aspects of the research process at different places in the book, Part III focuses exclusively and in detail on these questions.

SUGGESTED FURTHER READING

There is no text which deals exclusively with research into the spatial organization of schools and classrooms; however it may be useful to begin by considering some of the professional statements made in the Plowden Report (1967), *Children and Their Primary Schools,* and *The English Infant School and Informal Education* (Weber 1971), but both deal with the early years of schooling. Of the observational studies available, 'Teaching and learning in English primary schools' (Berlak *et al.* 1976), in *The Process of Schooling: A Sociological Reader* (Hammersley and Woods 1976); 'The head and his territory' (Evans 1974) and 'The social organization of space and place in an urban open-plan primary school' (Hitchcock 1982), in *Doing Teaching: The Practical Management of Classrooms* (Payne and Cuff 1982), are of interest. General, issues surrounding school architecture and learning are considered in *The English School: Its Architecture and Organization, 1870–1970* (Seabourne and Lowe 1977); and 'The organization of junior school classrooms' (Bealing 1972).

Part III

Qualitative data analysis, case study and writing

Introduction to Part III

In this final part of the book we come to the point where data analyses, presentational forms and writing begin to loom large in the research process. Whilst there are undoubtedly very practical aspects to these processes there are some fundamental conceptual and theoretical issues which need to be dealt with. We have linked analysis, case study and writing because qualitative researchers have strongly argued for the interconnection of these elements of the research process. Qualitative data demands different kinds of analysis to quantitative, numerical data. The nature of qualitative research itself means that both different ways of writing about qualitative research and presenting the findings of such research are necessary. Qualitative researchers in general and those engaged in doing qualitative research in schools and classrooms have been experimenting with different ways of writing up and presenting their research. These developments have partly been in response to a broad set of intellectual changes and movements over the last ten years. Of note here we would highlight the impact of feminism and post-structuralism and postmodernism. We unravel the meaning and significance of these ideas in connection with qualitative research briefly in the following chapters.

It is fair to say that whereas qualitative research techniques have received widespread discussion in the text books, the analysis of qualitative data has been given much less consideration. This is in part due to the variety of qualitative data and the complexities of handling and analysing such material. In Chapter 12 we add to the comments already made elsewhere in the book and attempt to formalize our view of qualitative data analysis identifying the ways in which this process can work. This viewpoint owes much to the work of two sociologists, Glaser and Strauss. We also spend some time looking directly at the analysis of natural language, and the use and analysis of photography in ethnographic case studies, an area which is often neglected.

Chapter 13 argues a case for the case study as the most appropriate framework for organizing and reporting small-scale school-based research.

Finally, Chapter 14 takes us into writing up qualitative research in what we hope will be a creative and exciting voyage into the possibilities and problems of conventions, narratives and stories. Again, each chapter contains suggestions for further reading though in the following chapter we have tried to make reference to more recent, and perhaps more experimental, research and discussions. Perhaps more than anywhere else in the book, Part III looks to the contemporary diversity of qualitative, naturalistic research. Increasingly, those engaged in research on schools and classrooms have been embracing these issues. At the same time we hope that the following chapters will provide some practical advice and a sense of security as the researcher moves into the challenging phase of analysing, presenting and writing up the products of their labour. It is fair to say that in the past qualitative research traditions have been less than explicit about the questions of analysis and writing up. We have tried to open up these issues and processes for researchers in this final part of the book.

12 Qualitative data analysis

INTRODUCTION

We have hinted at rather than directly approached the complex issue of qualitative data analysis so far. Whilst we have discussed data analysis as a stage in the research process and looked at the ways in which researchers have analysed their data and offered explanations, *the mechanics and nature* of qualitative data analysis have not been faced head on. We will remedy that in this chapter by drawing together what has been said about analysis so far and offering the reader an appreciation of the very different nature of qualitative data analysis, with some 'hands on' practical advice. It is important, therefore, to be clear about the ways in which the assumptions of qualitative research approaches influence data analysis, the nature of qualitative data analysis and the role of theory and concepts. Styles of qualitative data analysis, such as conversational analysis, thematic analysis and phenomenological analysis are explored, and, finally, the issues involved in looking at visual data are considered. The basic questions concern how it is possible to draw valid meaning from qualitative data. This leads on to an appreciation of the role of theory and concepts in qualitative data analysis.

SOME GENERAL CONSIDERATIONS

When we talk about analysis we are referring to the ways in which the researcher moves from a description of what is the case to an explanation of why what is the case is the case. Analysis involves discovering and deriving patterns in the data, looking for general orientations in the data and, in short, trying to sort out what the data are about, why and what kinds of things might be said about them. The distinction between petroleum engineers and explorers identified by Spradley, and which we alluded to in Chapter 2, is a useful starting point for identifying the special nature of analysis as an activity in qualitative research (Spradley 1979). Engineers know what they are looking for and make a clear distinction between collecting the various sorts of facts and analysing them in order to identify the likely site of oil. Explorers, on the other hand, tend not always to know what they are looking for and will interpret and make sense of information as it is received by them, as they go along. Engineers, Spradley likened to positivistic (quantitative) researchers, and explorers to naturalistic, interpretative (qualitative) researchers.

Naturalistic qualitative inquiry is concerned with the description and explanation of phenomena as they occur in routine, ordinary natural environments. In contrast to experimental design which seeks to control variables, qualitative research deals in words and meanings, seeking to maximize understanding of events and facilitating the interpretation of data. The very nature of qualitative data are such that they will require a different approach to the analysis of such data. The sheer variety, descriptive richness and, often, vast quantity of qualitative data mean that the researcher will approach the data in a different frame of mind. The purposes of qualitative research, with its emphasis upon *Verstehen* and the typically rich descriptive and subjective/introspective character of data produced using qualitative techniques, together make qualitative data analysis a very different enterprise than statistical analysis. Qualitative research produces large amounts of data in a vast variety of forms – from field notes, observations, conversations, life histories and unstructured interviews, to a range of records and documents. 'Analysis' in qualitative research means making sense of these kinds of data and, although debate continues as to the appropriateness of particular methods, there is general agreement that the principal task initially in looking at qualitative data is to try and make sense of those data. Lincoln and Guba (1985) outline the matter this way:

> What is at issue is the best means to 'make sense' of the data in ways that will facilitate the continuing unfolding of the inquiry, and, second, leads to a maximal understanding (in the sense of *Verstehen*) of the phenomena being studied.
>
> (Lincoln and Guba 1985: 224)

It is important to recognize, as we have stressed elsewhere, that data analysis is not altogether a separate process in qualitative research. Since the researcher herself is the funnel through which the data are received, some form of analysis will take place simultaneously with data collection. If the researcher has kept a diary then this, too, may be the source of analytical reflections. The qualitative researcher comes to the formal stage of data analysis having passed through much informal data analysis. This is quite important since it can provide the researcher with hunches, ideas and general lines of questioning to follow up. The more formal process will involve the researcher in breaking down the data where a fairly *inductive* approach is taken – data being explored in terms of both the general and particular units of meaning displayed within them. The qualitative researcher is looking for patterns, themes, consistencies and exceptions to the rule. Codes and categories can therefore emerge from the data and become formally identified by the researcher.

At this point it is worth reminding ourselves that qualitative research is not explicitly about the verification of existing theories and hypotheses, but rather with *discovery*. This has important implications for the role of hypotheses, theories and concepts. A distinction is often drawn between 'theoretical' hypotheses and 'empirical' hypotheses. Research geared up towards working with testing and evolving sets of theoretical hypotheses about the causal links and connections between phenomena is typical of the scientific paradigm. Empirical hypotheses and ideas about the workings of the social world can be viewed as sets of ideas that can help us to look at our data. These tend to feature more often in qualitative research and are at a different level to theoretical hypotheses.

Developments in the analysis of qualitative data are due, in part, to the extensive work of the symbolic interactionist sociologists and, in particular, to the ideas of Glaser and Strauss and their notions of *Grounded Theory* (Glaser and Strauss 1967). This approach argues for the detailed grounding of theory in the systematic and intensive analysis of empirical data in a microscopic detailed fashion. The researcher collects and compares data, codes the data and begins to organize ideas which emerge from the data. Working from this position, the analysis of qualitative data must recognize the complexity of the data, engage in microscopic familiarity with the data and be able to take into consideration the experience which the researcher brings to the data. Working through these aspects identifies a series of processes in the analysis of qualitative data. Once these stages have been completed then the researcher may make use of existing, or develop new, concepts and theories in a way which sensitizes issues rather than by imposing an order on to the data. It is in this way that the researcher moves from a description of what is the case to an explanation of why what is the case, is the case.

The process of analysis will also need to consider the question of validity identified earlier. In the analysis of the data, the researcher will be concerned to validate or verify the kinds of analysis made and explanations offered. That is concern over the explanatory validity of the claims made. This will mean constantly moving backwards and forwards between data and analysis, and between data and any theories and concepts developed, and between the data and other studies or literature. As we have said, qualitative data analysis moves in a fairly inductive fashion. Induction refers to the ways in which the researcher, finding a series of individual cases, begins to look for relationships between them. Once a series of relationships is observed, the researcher attempts to formulate a series of insights or hunches in the light of the relationships observed, into a theory which will cover and account for all the cases as far as possible. This is not unlike the way in which many social scientists proceed, but the important feature of the role of induction in qualitative analysis is the significance of the researcher's experience. The hunches and ideas are generated out of the interaction of the researcher's own personal and, in our case, professional, experience and the nature and content of the data. This is in part generated by the highly reactive nature of qualitative research. One of the ways of understanding this process is to refer to what has been described as 'theoretical sensitivity'.

THEORETICAL SENSITIVITY

Theoretical sensitivity is the ability to recognize what is important in data and to give it meaning. It helps to formulate theory that is faithful to the reality of the phenomena under study (Glaser 1978). Theoretical sensitivity has two sources. First, it comes from being well-grounded in the technical literature as well as from professional and personal experience. You bring this complex knowledge into the research situation. However, theoretical sensitivity is also acquired during the research process through continual interactions with the data – through your collection and analyses of the data. Whereas many of the analytic techniques that are used to develop theoretical sensitivity are creative and imaginative in character, it is important to keep a balance between that which is created by the researcher and the real. You can do so by:

> a Asking what is really going on here?
> b Maintaining an attitude of skepticism toward any categories or hypotheses brought to or arising early in the research, and validating them repeatedly with data themselves.
> c By following the data collection and analytic procedures as discussed in this book. Good science (good theory) is produced through this interplay of creativeness and the skills acquired through training.
>
> (Strauss and Corbin 1990: 47)

This quotation captures well the nature of qualitative analysis and shows us how we can move from description to explanation and to the development/generalization of concepts and theories. But, before we move on to questions of theory generation, let us consider some aspects of the 'nuts and bolts' of qualitative data analysis. Let us summarize what has been said so far. Key features of qualitative data analysis include:

- Qualitative data analysis is inductive, innovative, emergent, exploratory and creative.
- Qualitative data analysis involves re-working materials.
- Qualitative data analysis engages in re-writing field notes.
- Qualitative data analysis will involve the production of codes, from which categories can emerge.
- Qualitative data analysis will involve the comparison of events across time–space.
- Qualitative data analysis operates on a description–analysis–continuum.
- Qualitative data analysis deals with the classification of data and the creation of typologies.

CODING AND CATEGORIZING QUALITATIVE DATA

Qualitative data analysis involves making sense of the data. The task is initially one of sorting the data into manageable units. Qualitative research can generate huge amounts of data from different sources and when the analysis begins it is quite important to remember what went into the interview design, the nature of the field observations or whatever since this, too, will provide keys to the analysis of the materials. Obviously, this is greatly facilitated by the existence of a research diary. The researcher will seek to organize the data in such a way that will facilitate understanding of their meaning and significance. This will involve breaking the data down into units of meaning, topics or categories which the researcher can then subsume under a general heading bringing together diverse activities. The researcher's task is to put some kind of order on to the data without, of course, distortion. Here, recurrent topics and themes in the interview can be noted. There may be clusters or groups of topics which really may all be subsumed under one broad heading. Whilst engaged in this work, it is fundamental to keep in mind the distinction between categories, terms and ideas that are specifically referred to by the subject and those which are generated by the researcher. For example, an interview with a secondary-school pupil in an inner city context might generate a number of categories, including notions such as 'freedom', 'autonomy' and 'independence' although the pupil may have never actually used these terms in the conversation! Furthermore, the researcher may not treat all the categories as having the same status in the analysis. This will need to be made explicit.

The use of codes and categories in this way not only helps to break the data down into manageable pieces, it allows for the identification of relationships between units of meaning. This is likely to become a messy and overly complex activity unless the researcher introduces some order and structure into the proceedings. The use of colour coding with highlighter pens and the development of some form of card indexing will all help the retrieval and presentation of data for analysis. The important thing about coding is that it is itself a part of the process of analysis. Coding helps the researcher assign meaning to events and activities. As Miles and Huberman have commented:

> To review a set of fieldnotes, transcribed or synthesized, and to dissect them meaningfully, while keeping the relations between the parts intact, is the stuff of analysis. This part of analysis involves how you differentiate and combine the data you have retrieved and the reflections you make about this information.
>
> (Miles and Huberman 1994: 56)

The important issue here is maintaining a view of the data, however fragmentary, as being part of a broader whole, a wider picture. There are many examples and much advice on how to undertake coding in qualitative research. Strauss and Corbin (1990), for example, advocate a process whereby written data are reviewed on a line-by-line basis and below or alongside the data identifying categories or labels are given. Lofland (1971) suggested that it was useful to develop codes on a range of phenomena that moved from the micro, small-scale level to the large-scale macro level. This is discussed by Miles and Huberman (1994: 61):

1 Acts: action in a situation that is temporally brief, consuming only a few seconds, minutes, or hours.
2 Activities: actions in a setting of more major duration – days, weeks, months – constituting significant elements of people's involvement.
3 Meanings: the verbal productions of participants that define and direct action.
4 Participation: people's holistic involvement in or adaptation to a situation or setting under study.
5 Relationships: interrelationships among several persons considered simultaneously.
6 Settings: the entire setting under study conceived as the unit of analysis.

(Miles and Huberman 1994: 61)

Miles and Huberman also discuss Bogdan and Biklen's (1982) account of the application of qualitative methods to the study of education, which organizes codes along the following lines:

1 Setting/Context: general information on surroundings that allows you to put the study in a larger context.
2 Definition of the situation: how people understand, define, or perceive the setting or the topics on which the study bears.
3 Perspectives: ways of thinking about their setting shared by informants ('how things are done here').
4 Ways of thinking about people and objects: understandings of each other, of outsiders, of objects in their world (more detailed than above).
5 Process: sequence of events, flow, transitions, and turning points, changes over time.
6 Activities: regularly occurring kinds of behaviour.
7 Events: specific activities, especially ones occurring infrequently.
8 Strategies: ways of accomplishing things; people's tactics, methods, techniques for meeting their needs.
9 Relationships and social structure: unofficially defined patterns, such as cliques, coalitions, romances, friendships, enemies.
10 Methods: problems, joys, dilemmas of the research process – often in relation to comments by observers.

(Miles and Huberman 1994: 61)

The purpose of coding is to break down data, to identify meanings, discover relationships and to begin initial analysis. The major problem concerns the analytical relationship between the observer's generated order and the interactional in-use codes and categories generated by people themselves. Although qualitative research can make use of observer-generated codes and categories, these must at some point in the process, be related to the participant's codes and categories and more importantly their coding and categorizing system. In this way the qualitative researcher ensures a movement from description to explanation. Since qualitative studies are concerned to explore situations, investigations and analysis are not subsequently geared up to making predictions or looking for correlations. But they will be concerned with verifying their claims. The coding process will help to clarify what will subsequently be claimed, and the grounds for these claims.

The complexity of the coding and the categories generated will depend upon the nature of the study. However, there will always be a storage and retrieval problem. Clearly microcomputers can come to the rescue here. For example, Seidel and Clark (1984) have looked at *The Ethnograph* which is a program for the analysis of qualitative data. Since many teachers now have access to a personal computer, it is worth considering, especially if there are large quantities of data involved. The kind of help which computers can offer is highlighted by Rudestam and Newton (1992). However, a computer can never act as a substitute for the researcher's own insights. Consider the following comment:

> Qualitative data analysis can be greatly facilitated by the use of computer software. Qualitative analysis software, such as *The Ethnograph* for the IBM environment and *Qual Pro* for the Macintosh environment, allows the researcher to code segments of text and later retrieve all the text given any common code, or combinations of codes. For example, one of the authors recently completed a study of social workers' attitudes toward prepaid health care. Prior to any use of the computer, all interviews were coded by county, question number and job assignment. Interview text was then coded and recoded, individually and in group meetings, until a comprehensive coding system was developed. This code system was then used with *The Ethnograph* to code all interview transcripts. Only after this process had been completed was it possible to reorganize the text based on rules built into the coding system. Though *The Ethnograph* has the ability to reorganize text in multiple ways, the 'analysis' rest almost entirely on the sophistication of the code system built by the researcher. In qualitative analysis, the 'organizing framework' must be rebuilt by each analyst approaching a new body of textual material.
>
> (Rudestam and Newton 1992: 182)

The final remark is telling. Computers cannot do the analytical work of the researcher. What will help the researcher here are concepts and theories and in the next section we will explore the role of concepts and theories in qualitative data analysis.

USING AND DEVELOPING CONCEPTS AND THEORIES

We are all familiar with 'theory' in the work of education. Sets of ideas which underpin our philosophies of the curriculum, our pedagogy. Sets of ideas which are respected or contested, challenged and debated, created and recreated. Much of what passes for theory, however, turns out to be representations of commonsense thinking. Many contributions to in-service courses have, unfortunately, deteriorated to the level of the merely anecdotal, without any attempt to frame the anecdotal and personal knowledge in some broader theoretical or conceptual context.

In qualitative research generally we need to bear in mind two sets of interconnected questions when we approach theory. First, it is important to ask about the nature of qualitative ethnographic inquiry. Second, just exactly how are concepts and theories employed in qualitative research? That is, what are their roles? These questions all overlap with each other.

Ethnographic and qualitative research design differs from other models of research in a number of ways, as we indicated in Part I. One of these concerns the role of theory. Ethnography is about what Geertz (1973) described as 'thick description'. We have gone to some lengths to show how good quality, adequate descriptions of the world of teaching and learning can be made, but these descriptions are neither adequate on their own nor without some kind of initial guidance as to what to describe and how and why to describe it. The issue of the heavily descriptive nature of qualitative research and the kinds of criticisms made of it seem less strong today than they may have been in the past. For a long time, qualitative researchers have been welding their ethnographic descriptions to analyses of one kind or another. The main problem here concerns the extent to which analysis of often small-scale, single-case research can be generalized. The question of generalization is taken up in detail in the next chapter. However, Lutz, talking about ethnography puts his cards clearly on the table regarding this point:

> As description alone, it is knowledge alone, a body of data without analysis. It is the cognitive domaine of knowledge without understanding or synthesis. It cannot be generalized beyond the specific case. It is a useful picture of some culture or society, at some moment in time. It preserves something that may even be fascinating and interesting, but it is useless in helping others explain or even predict complex human behavior.
>
> (Lutz 1981: 62)

It is our view that, although getting the descriptions right is essential for qualitative research, it is vital to move from description to analysis. This will become a bit clearer if we consider the difference between qualitative research traditions and other traditions on these issues. Qualitative research traditions have been quick to point out the limitations of the dominant positivistic quantitative traditions which have taken an a priori stance to theory. That is, the theories or hypotheses are made in advance of their exploration in the empirical world. The theories or hypotheses are then tested against the results in a manner of confirmation or refutation. Obviously, the qualitative researcher does not enter the field in an empty-headed fashion, indeed, school-based teacher–researchers have to have some guiding ideas or notions. However, theory in qualitative research is not *prescriptive*, it is rather *creative* and *open-ended* and therefore operates in a different manner. Concepts and theories, then, can become crudely either sledge hammers which knock social reality into some kind of shape in a fairly overt and definite way or they can become loose clusters of ideas coming together in a single concept or group of concepts (theories) which sensitize the researcher to what is going on in the data. There are, of course, a number of potential sources of concepts and theories which the school-based researcher can draw upon and it may be helpful to elucidate these.

As we have highlighted, the teacher–researcher's own pool of personal knowledge and experience is a rich 'mine' which can be reflectively and critically worked to provide an important source of ideas for the generation of concepts and theories. The work of educational theory and practice, relying as it does so heavily on the human sciences, provides another important source of concepts, theories and controversies. There is plenty of substantive literature available for scrutiny here. The role of the literature review here may also help at this point. The underpinning knowledge of the social sciences has generally employed concepts such as class, gender, race and ethnicity but has also been responsible for developing debates in and around these concepts. For example, we could point to notions of underclass, double consciousness, the sexual division of labour, biculturalism, bilingualism and so on as debates within the debate over the concept of social class. All of these concepts and theories can be drawn upon by the qualitative researcher in the progression from description to explanation. Ultimately, what we are saying is that, despite the difficulties, the teacher–researcher can and should be able to draw from a broader body of educational and social science knowledge in however a limited fashion in order to make sense of and hence move towards the analysis of the data collected. There is certainly no point in re-inventing the wheel. Researchers have found the following concepts, theories and ideas helpful during qualitative data analysis: Labelling (Becker, Lemert); Ideal Types (Weber); Typification (Schutz); Alienation (Marx); Career (Becker); Stigma (Goffman); Presentation of Self (Goffman); Pupil/Teacher Culture (Hammersley and Woods); Coping Strategies (Pollard); Sub-Culture (Willis, Ball); Conversational Practices (Sacks, Schegloff, Sharrock and Anderson); Accounts (Lyman and Scott); Symbolic Reversal (Geertz); Ritual (Hall); Communicative Competence (Hymes); Code-Switching (Gumperz). This is a just a brief list of the sorts of concepts and theories which qualitative researchers have made use of and which the prospective researcher might find of value. Each has a wealth of research associated with it which can be followed up.

The qualitative researcher can also fall back on the concepts, ideas and kinds of analysis developed by particular philosophies and perspectives. Of major significance here are the ideas of phenomenologists whose work, which can be viewed as a 'bag of theoretical tricks', can be *raided* by the qualitative researcher. Schwartz and Jacobs (1979) point out some of the ideas which may be of use here:

1 The idea of eidetic science or a science of the possible.
2 Intentionality and intentional analysis.
3 Cognitive attitudes, their manipulation and significance.
4 Personal knowledge and the structure of intersubjective trust.
5 Distinguishing the act of awareness from the subject of awareness from the object of awareness.

(Schwartz and Jacobs 1979: 361)

It is worth considering briefly the ways in which concepts and theories have entered into two qualitative ethnographic studies of schooling. First, Dubberley's (1988) study of social class and the process of schooling in a Yorkshire comprehensive school during the time of the miners' strike and, second, Mac an Ghail's (1993a, b) natural history account of his use of qualitative methods in the study of black youths' schooling in England. Both these studies highlight the significance of concepts and theories to these qualitative ethnographic researchers. One the one hand, Dubberley (1988) is clear in his account about his own concepts, theories and orientations:

> As to myself, I have had a northern working class background and I was born and brought up in South Lancashire. The experiences of Grammar school and particularly University creates emotional and intellectual illusions in myself that sought resolution in an interest in politics and the theory of education. As a result of my experiences as a student and later as a teacher in a number of sectors in education, I believe one of the main effects of education is to perpetuate social class divisions.
>
> (Dubberley, 1988: 179)

In an attempt to re-introduce social class as a major variable in the process of schooling, Dubberley draws extensively on Marxist theoretical operations. Clearly, his attempt at the analysis of the materials is influenced by this. Some might say that this could be a source of bias. In this sense qualitative researchers need to take care about using such overarching theories and always come back to the data. Charges of bias and researcher influence might otherwise justifiably ensue.

Mac an Ghail (1993a, b), on the other hand, ably shows us how by the use of qualitative research methods a change in the initial focus of the research can be effected, generating what he hoped would be more grounded theory. Mac an Ghail enters a longstanding debate in social and educational research about the nature of 'problems'. He began his research by accepting that Asian and Afro-Caribbean students were a 'problem', that is the 'white-norm!' By rethinking this theory and by placing the students at the very heart of his study he was able, in a critical and reflective way to move effectively beyond the 'white-norm'. Whilst there is no space here to delve deeper into these two studies they clearly underscore some of the questions of theory and analysis we have raised and would repay further scrutiny. This leaves the question of the extent to which theory dictates method for a future debate.

Some of the most extended and elaborate forms of qualitative data analysis are contained in work described as conversational or phenomenological analysis. This is an important method of analysing everyday life, taking as it does a sharp focus upon language. We will consider this next.

THE SIGNIFICANCE OF NATURAL LANGUAGE: THE CONTRIBUTION OF CONVERSATIONAL ANALYSIS

As we have argued, there is a broad range of analytic traditions from which qualitative researchers can draw as they move from description to explanation. Indeed, one of the salient features of contemporary qualitative research endeavours is their diversity. One of the most elaborate and extended traditions here is that described as conversational analysis (CA). A focus upon naturally occurring talk for description, analysis and exploration treats natural language as the most significant source of data on the social world. Two eminent qualitative sociologists put the matter this way:

> Furthermore, as an activity, conversation seems to display the paradox of triviality. Its occurrence within daily life strikes us as remarkably unmomentous. Yet these millions of small verbal episodes may be the main vehicle for shaping what each of us become, know, and experience throughout our social life. Like the incessant sculpting of rocks by the sea, natural conversations may have more to do with shaping the nature of individuals and societies than wars, child-rearing practices, and political elections. Conventional wisdom already credits natural language with such properties as these.
>
> 1. It structures the thought process of those who use it.
> 2. It determines one's perception of the world and its meanings.
> 3. It is the main vehicle by which the man in the street receives, accumulates, and transmits beliefs and information.
> 4. It is one of the fundamental social skills which determines one's personal, economic, and social life chances.
>
> Any activity that does all these things to people's 'heads' and people's lives, day in and day out, in practically every known society, should be studied in detail. Conversational analysis is one way to do this.
>
> (Schwartz and Jacobs 1979: 341)

CA is the most elaborated and extended empirical work emerging from the sociological tradition known as ethnomethodology which we discussed earlier in Chapter 10. At this point it may be instructive to re-read the section on ethnomethodology in Chapter 10.

CA is nothing if not a highly technical and extraordinarily detailed approach. Some researchers are now working on the use of audio and video tape recordings. It follows that many of the early studies were done in specialized, institutional or interactional settings, for example, medical encounters, classrooms, courts of law, telephone conversations, etc. Benson and Hughes (1983) have argued that:

> Whatever the style or level of analysis involved in the study of naturally occurring conversation, there is always a link with the central concerns of ethnomethodology; namely, the description of the procedures which members use in the construction of the sense of social order. Its notion of social order is that produced by a local cohort of speakers and examines this order production through a description of naturally occurring phenomena.
>
> (Benson and Hughes 1983: 187)

The increasing body of research from conversational analysts has generated a series of useful concepts for the analysis of naturally occurring talk. These could be included in the broader theoretical analysis of qualitative materials. Schwartz and Jacobs (1979) have highlighted a number of these which have relevance for qualitative data analysis:

> **Interactional work**
>
> One can 'do' various activities, such as complaining, joking, or displaying one's status, through the use of talk. In fact, there are verbal activities which several people can co-operatively 'do' together through talk. Analysts have taken it as one of their tasks to identify the sorts of things that get done in and through talk, and to explore exactly how they are done.
>
> **Strategic interaction**
>
> Thus one can speak of people intending to do certain things, using various verbal tactics to get them done, and running into difficulties and opposition in the process. In short, one can study conversational 'tactics' together with the sense in which people 'win,' 'lose,' use 'ploys' or 'delaying strategies,' and so on.
>
> **'Conversational objects' and their functions**
>
> In and of themselves, talk and sequences of talk such as greeting pairs ('Hi,' 'Hi') or 'pre-invitations' ('Are you doing anything tonight?') 'do' certain interactional work. That is, they have standard functions. Speakers and listeners know of these functions and orient to them when using and responding to them. Because of this it is possible to speak of talk and sequences of talk as 'objects' and to examine their properties much

as chess commentary examines the properties of moves, independently of the motives or thoughts of players during actual games.

Conscious 'orientations'

One of the most important developments in conversational analysis has been the discovery of methods to retrieve what people are aware of by examining what they say and do not say. Here we need not interview them later to discover their 'point of view', but have ways of discovering what they notice, think about, and attend to in the very midst of their daily activity.

One of the key resources for doing this has been the fortunate fact that people are not merely cognizant of 'what's going on' but *deliberately display* this awareness to others through behavior. For example, listeners are often obliged to display that they understand a speaker by using a variety of conversational devices such as eye contact, gesture, listening noises, or replying.

(Schwartz and Jacobs 1979: 348)

Clearly, this kind of micro analysis can hold out considerable potential for the qualitative researcher. It may happen that during the general analysis of materials sections of data, for example, data from a staff meeting or other focused encounter, are worthy of analysis in this kind of way. The researcher may then move back to a more general level of analysis with other material. Nothing in this sense is ruled out in qualitative data analysis. As we argued, this approach is inductive rather than deductive, emergent, exploratory, innovative and individual. Miles and Huberman (1994: 8), summarize three general approaches to qualitative data analysis which subsume most of what we have been saying so far. These are: Interpretivism; Social Anthropology, and Collaborative Research. Finally, we need to highlight a technique which might be employed in the analysis of qualitative materials on teaching and learning: the focus upon *critical* incidents.

A critical incident is any happening which can be used as a focus or vehicle for looking at key aspects of a social or educational situation. This approach has its orgins in the anthropological concern with key happenings in a culture. These could include things such as status passages, unusual events, or otherwise remarkable happenings. In this way a particular event can be used as a way of reading aspects of a culture. A critical incident method is a way of identifying, describing, and analysing key events in a culture.

The application of critical incident approaches to teaching has been developed by Tripp (1993). He considers the way in which professional judgement develops from self-monitoring. He shows how a focus upon a critical incident and its analysis can help to draw out principles and ideas upon which to base future practice. Tripp shows us, via the use of extensive examples, how to go about *recognizing* and *analysing* a critical incident. In effect, Tripp is operating in a fairly inductive manner, working in much the same way to the qualitative researcher. Critical incident methods can offer the teacher–

researcher a particularly fruitful way of analysing data on schools and classrooms.

Now that we have a general understanding of what qualitative approaches to the analysis of data involves, we will focus on a less well-understood source of data.

QUALITATIVE DATA ANALYSIS AND VISUAL DATA SOURCES

Although we have underlined the general principles involved in qualitative data analysis, and offered suggestions as to ways into this process it is important to remember that different sorts of qualitative data, obtained by the use of different techniques will pose particular problems. We have looked at dealing with field notes, interview materials, documentary sources, classroom interaction data and data on the spatial organization of school and classroom life in the preceding chapters. We want to say something here about a little-used qualitative data source, that is visual representations and the issues involved in analysing visual data.

We live in a visually image saturated universe. Our lives are bound by, depicted in and largely lived through visual experiences of one sort or another (Becker 1975). Yet, the human sciences are largely disciplines of words. We have worked with many students who have collected visual materials, usually photographs or videos, but not known what to do with them. Here, we wish to explore briefly a number of interrelated questions and themes which might further the qualitative analysis of visual materials. These themes include:

- How is culture visually available?
- How is it possible to handle pictures in a discipline of words?
- How is our visual experience socially and culturally organized?
- What are the implications of treating pictures as documentary sources?
- What theoretical framework for analysing visual data exists?
- How can the analysis of visual data be represented?

The visual image has occupied a salient place in the discipline of social anthropology and sociology for considerable time. In particular, photographs as a form of data were extensively used by people such as Evans-Pritchard (1937), Bateson (1936) and, most notably, the famous photographic study of Balinese character by Bateson and Mead (1942). Photographs of people and artefacts appeared, too, in American sociology in the 1930s and 1940s and there is a strong trend of photographic journalism beginning around the 1890s with the tradition of US documentary photography and the work of Riis and continuing with the contribution of Walker Evans and Agee. Photographs were seen as important adjuncts to understanding culture. The photographs were for the most part taken as self-evidentiary, as unproblematically representing a reality. Culture, in this sense, was unproblematically visually available. Photographs, like artefacts to be found in a museum, were evidence to be included as part of the ethnographic report. But, the human sciences were not just disciplines of words, but disciplines of numbers and quantification. Graphs, statistical tables and so on far outweigh the inclusion of photographs even in those qualitative field-based sociological ethnographies of the 1940s and 1950s in the USA. Whilst recognizing that culture was visually available and could be recorded via the photograph, what the photograph said about the culture and, indeed, what was to be photographed by whom, when and how is clearly problematic. In this sense, the project undertaken by Evans and Agee (1975) was ahead of its time. One photograph simply shows a pair of working boots in the dust (Agee and Evans (1975); see also Fisher (1989)). These early attempts to incorporate photography into ethnography fit into what Van Maanen (1988) described as the 'realist tale' in his account of the different conventions used in reporting ethnographic research. Here, the researcher's scientific status is not questioned, the voice of the author and subject is kept separate and a photograph would as a consequence be regarded as a reflection of what happened, what was seen, rather than as a problematic interpretation of what was seen, and what happened.

It quickly becomes apparent that if photographs were to be used as a source of research data then the special methodological and analytical issues raised needed to be faced. Discussions of photographs as forms of data have been developed by Ball and Smith (1992) for anthropology, Becker (1975) for sociology, Bogdan and Biklen (1982) for education research, Harper (1987) for sociology, Templin (1982) for evaluation, and Wagner (1979). There is now a strong and vibrant tradition of ethnographic film stimulated by the Granada Television 'Disappearing Worlds' series of ethnographic films we referred to in Chapter 6. The visual image then is of significant value as a display of culture. A photograph of a 1930s British infants school showing separate entrances for girls and boys says an awful lot.

If we accept that it is possible to capture aspects of culture in a still photograph we are none the less left with considerable methodological and analytical problems. The human sciences are predominantly disciplines of words. Not only that, the prevailing orthodoxy has been quantification. The net result of this is that a discourse, vocabulary or philosophy for looking at pictures did not exist. Interpretative, qualitative naturalistic traditions, on the other hand, might be seen to be more favourably disposed to engaging in an encounter with the visual. The development of interactionist sociology and phenomenology brought an interesting focus upon visual materials and generated ways of exploring and analysing aspects of the social world through visual phenomena. These researchers began to see the use of audio-visual techniques, video tape, audio tape, film and still photographs as offering a clear potential, yet they recognized that whilst these approaches were on the surface non-reactive, they were in fact highly reactive. The paradox revealed was that whilst being able to capture more accurately more aspects of social life these methods were very much socially structured and that any subsequent analysis must take this into account. Seeing and hearing are always socially situated. Considerable doubt must be cast on the view that camera and tape recorder always capture reality accurately. They may, instead, capture one reality amongst many. What we see is always filtered by our own experience, our background, and our position in the world:

> Eyes are not cameras; they cannot zoom, nor can they pan. Ears are not microphones; they fail to hear high- and low-pitched sounds if these sounds are at low volumes (the Fletcher-Munsen effect).
>
> But even if an individual had microphones for ears and cameras for eyes, he is always 'situated' within a social environment at some time–space point. Depending on physical barriers, spacing patterns among those present, and his own patterns of locomotion, the same room can look and sound amazingly different to him than it does to them.
>
> (Schwartz and Jacobs 1979: 83)

Schwartz and Jacobs (1979) go even further here in highlighting the socially situated use of visual methods and the heavily localized and contextualized nature of the products:

> In sum, in no possible way can films and tapes directly 'recover' the visual auditory world experienced by different persons within an ongoing social scene. This point cannot be over emphasized, because we have been fed the physics model of reality and have been accustomed to regard a videotape as a direct record of 'what happened'. Yet if one wishes to know 'what happened' from the standpoint of those within the scene, it is necessary to make use of complex contextual information and cultural clues in order to 'make sense' of one's film or tape.
>
> (Schwartz and Jacobs 1979: 83)

Our visual experience, our perception, is structured by our culture, gender, age and ethnicity. In turn, what people see when they look at visual representations is coloured by the same factors. These observations have farreaching methodological and analytical consequences. One of the ways forward is to regard visual material and in particular, photographs, as *documentary sources*. In this connection it may be instructive to read or to re-read Chapter 9, on 'Using documents'.

Visual documents might be regarded in exactly the same way as written texts. They need to be interrogated and interpreted in order to reveal the meanings within them. Scott (1990: 188–91) uses the criteria of authenticity and credibility, meaning and literal meaning, interpretative understanding and representativeness to explore documents. These criteria will be applied variably in any qualitative ethnographic study making use of visual materials. In general, it is important to ask the 'Who', 'When', 'Where', 'What' and 'Why' questions levelled at documentary sources in general. The answers to these questions will prove fruitful and shape the kinds of analyses made and explanations offered. For example, when considering photographs it is essential to ask the following sorts of questions:

- Who took the photograph? (Identity, status, gender, class, race.)
- When was the photograph taken? (Time–space, chronology, history.)
- Where was the photograph taken? (Locale, context, boundaries, angle.)
- Why was the photograph taken? (Purpose, function, official, unofficial.)
- Of whom was the photograph taken? (Identity, status, gender, class, race.)

Such a focus begins to move us in the direction of the kinds of specific analyses which may be made of visual materials, thus raising a further set of issues including:

- The distinction between naturally occurring visual representations and researcher produced visual representations.
- First-order analysis (members analysis) and second-order analysis (researcher analysis).
- Ways of seeing, the role of perception and culture.

In coming to terms with the analysis of visual materials social scientists have made use of their varied epistemologies, perspectives and disciplines. Ball and Smith (1992) identify five major frameworks for the analysis of visual phenomena: content analysis; symbolism; structuralism; cognitive anthropology, and ethnomethodology.

We have offered some general guidelines on the analysis of qualitative data in this chapter and many of these points will apply to the analysis of visual data. However, as we hope to have shown visual data commands a different sort of gaze, a different sort of stance. This is still largely being worked out by researchers. We have simply tried to offer some guidelines towards making sense of a complex area. In all the theoretical approaches considered by Ball and Smith the role of theory differs. From a qualitative point of view, it is essential that the researcher understands the theory that guides the photography. Here, the extended account of content analysis, hermeneutic traditions, and semiotics in Chapter 9 will be helpful. We will conclude this section by looking at an example of the ways in which visual material, in this case still photography, can be incorporated into ethnographic qualitative research and analysis.

USE OF PHOTOGRAPHY IN ETHNOGRAPHIC CASE STUDIES

The use of still photography in ethnography is fairly underdeveloped. One of the reasons for this might be to do with the nature of photography and sociology. As Becker (1979) noted photography and sociology had about the same birth date, but sociology became more like science, photography became more like art. Prosser (1992) has bravely attempted to clarify the use of photography in an educational ethnographic case study. He argues, we believe quite rightly, for the need for greater methodological, theoretical and analytical sophistication. His account of the use and role of photography in the study of a newly formed comprehensive school argues for the need for theoretical and practical guidelines. Prosser identifies three phases from his own experience. These were indistinct and included acceptance of photography by school participants themselves, use of photography in ways acceptable to the research community, and exploration of the relationship between photographically derived data, and more visual ethnographically derived data and their impact on research questions.

These phases roughly parallel the ethnographic steps and stages we identified in Chapter 6. Clearly, Prosser sees the use of cameras to record aspects of school life as an exciting prospect but one which needs care. A major distinction exists between 'found photography' or 'found documents', such as those discovered in scrapbooks, old school photographs and so on, and those photographs which come into being as a direct result of the researcher's actions. Different analytic questions need to be addressed of these very different sorts of document. Prosser talks about basic illustrative photographs, some of which were posed, that is, they were taken in a considered context and situation which reflected the everyday work environment of the individual. Hence, we find photographs of 'the school caretaker', 'the Deputy head with a gun', etc.

Prosser begins to explore analytical issues in the so-called third phase of research. He describes the way in which photography was used to collect additional data and used to reflect emerging substantive issues in the research. But, most importantly, he suggests that photographs may be used to explore what he describes as 'taken-for-grantedness'. In this sense, a photograph can be interrogated in order to see what it reveals about the essentially accepted generic culture of schools. Clearly, the photographs taken by Prosser were seen to be carrying powerful, often highly sensitive messages. The role of qualitative analysis here would be to decode, to deconstruct and unravel exactly what these messages are and how the visual images in school life were received, interpreted and understood by participants themselves. Taking the lead from the pioneering work of Robert Frank, Prosser gives us an unusually clear insight into just what it was he was doing, trying to do and did, and he is worth quoting at some length:

> The object was to photograph everyday events, minor and major rituals and traditions, what Schutz (1964) calls 'the ready-made standardised scheme of cultural pattern handed down by ancestors' (p 238) – the essence of the generic culture of schools. A major problem throughout lay in recognising the limitations of my own skills which determined what I was capable of 'capturing' on film. Emphasis was placed on developing photographic skills, particularly how visually to communicate educa-

> tional issues and abstract concepts, rather than pre-defining the contribution of photography in this area.
>
> Initial attempts to photograph taken-for-grantedness failed, being trite and the result of reductionism. Applying the techniques of famous photographers helped, but experiments with Friedlander's and Winogrand's (both American photographers) 'snapshot aesthetic' (see Szarkowski, 1988) failed. More successful images were obtained by discarding empirical photography for ethnographic photography. This entailed perceiving phenomenologically, i.e. in a way that appears immediately to the consciousness, and from the school's participant's point of view. The work of Robert Frank illustrates this approach. Frank, being an outsider (Swiss) was able to treat the everyday as problematic and produced insightful images into the American culture (*The Americans*, 1955). Using Frank's approach as a model I treated taken-for-granted objects, places, traditions and events as exotic. *Fig. 4*, The Ritual of Knock and Wait, is typical of a taken-for-granted ritual. The setting, outside the headteacher's office, and activity, knocking-bending-ear to door, are commonplace in many schools. The image is made striking by freezing the act of bending, what Cartier-Bresson (1952) terms the 'decisive moment' and the inclusion of a visual clue (the big brother painting placed there by the art teacher), also a strategy employed by Cartier-Bresson (1987). Both are common photographic techniques each inviting the 'reader' to think, yet offering a visual example of taken-for-grantedness.
>
> (Prosser 1994: 407)

Prosser's study was essentially experimental and exploratory but it offers important insights into photography as a means of representing social reality and the kinds of analytical questions which are raised by visual materials. A clear potential exists. The requirements of qualitative research are clear here. There is no way of separating or distinguishing method from analysis, and both from underlying theoretical frameworks.

Given the contemporary diversity of qualitative approaches it is likely that visual materials will be explored in different ways. We have only been able to briefly open up what we hope will become an increasingly used source of data in educational research, one that ought to be used more extensively by teachers. The image is as important as the word and, indeed, may be a lot more imporant on some occasions.

> It is clear that visual representations help us learn ourselves; they help us to communicate to others; they help us teach our students to see and struggle through their own attempts at recording, analysing, and communicating. Most fundamentally, images allow us to make kinds of statements that cannot be made by words, thus images enlarge our consciousness and the possibilities for our sociology. Click!
>
> (Harper 1994: 411)

CONCLUSION

In this chapter we have attempted to open up the nature of qualitative data analysis. This is a complex area, but by this stage in the book it is imporant to try and summarize what the reader should be able to do. The teacher–researcher ought to be able to:

- Identify how qualitative data analysis is different from quantitative data analysis.
- Have an understanding of the basics of qualitative data analysis.
- Learn how to hear what the data are saying.
- Code and categorize data and search for themes and patterns.
- Have a knowledge of the role of theory and concepts in qualitative data analysis.
- Focus upon critical incidents as a way of analysing qualitative data on schools and classrooms.
- Collect, use and analyse visual materials in the course of naturalistic, qualitative research.

Qualitative data analysis is not closed, it is essentially open-ended, creative, emergent, and developmental. Listening to what your data are telling you and hearing what your data have to say is very important. We have tried to provide some baselines from which to begin the process of analysis. Collecting and analysing qualitative data on schools and classrooms poses its own problems. We hope to have broken the silence on this aspect of research. Our next concern is to explore appropriate frameworks for presenting qualitative teacher research and to consider some of the special questions posed for writing up qualitive research. These are the topics of Chapters 13 and 14. Certainly, qualitative data analysis is a complex affair. Yet it can be immensely enjoyable and rewarding. Where else can the researcher see analysis of the social world unfold in such an exciting manner?

SUGGESTED FURTHER READING

One of the most succinct accounts of the ways in which researchers go about developing their analysis and understanding of the data is given by a famous qualitative sociologist, Howard Becker, in 'How I learned what a crock was' (Becker 1993). The best overall and user-friendly accounts here are *Basics of Qualitative Research* (Strauss and Corbin 1990) and *Qualitative Analysis for Social Scientists* (Strauss 1987). Helpful guidelines are also given by 'Qualitative data as an attractive nuisance: the problem of analysis' (Miles 1979); *Qualitative Data Analysis: A Source Book of New Methods* (Miles and Huberman 1984) and 'The content analysis of qualitative research data: a dynamic approach' (Mostyn 1985) in *The Research Interview: Uses and Approaches* (Brenner, Brown and Canter 1985). Simple and practical guidance is given in *Getting the Most From Your Data* (Riley 1990).

Interpreting Qualitative Data (Silverman 1993) works through some examples. *Transforming Qualitative Data: Description, Analysis and Interpretation* (Wolcott 1994) deals extensively with the analysis of qualitative data dividing the process up into description, analysis and interpretation. Wolcott (1994) uses his own studies to illustrate. However, the collection and treatment of visual data, often in the past a central aspect of the anthropological ethnography, is problematic. Whilst we could not develop any extended discussion here the reader interested in making use of such data might consider some of the pointers in the Preface (Becker 1979) in *Images of Information: Still Photography in the Social Sciences* (Wagner 1979) and *Exploring Society Photographically* (Becker 1981). A recent monograph offers an excellent introduction to some of the issues here, see *Analyzing Visual Data*, (Ball and Smith 1992). The role which photography can play in educational research has been little considered in the past. Prosser highlights the need for a set of practical and theoretical guidelines for the application of photography in ethnographic research opening up many areas. 'Personal reflections on the use of photography in an ethnographic case study' (Prosser 1992). An extended discussion of visual documents as texts using particular criteria is contained in *A Matter of Record: Documentary Sources in Social Research* (Scott 1990). For us one of the most interesting and influential examples of the analysis of photographs is provided by *Gender Advertisements* (Goffman 1979), where more than 500 photographs are presented in order to analyse 'gender displays'. However, the most comprehensive recent overview of the current state of play is 'On the authority of the image, visual methods at the crossroads' (Harper 1994) in *Handbook of Qualitative Research* (Denzin and Lincoln 1994).

13 The case study

INTRODUCTION

This chapter aims to bring together some ideas about designing and writing up small-scale research into the teaching and learning process. We do this by arguing that the case study is in many ways the most appropriate format and orientation for school-based research. Of the many researchers who do case studies many call their work by some other name, for example, a small-scale study, an ethnography or even an ethnographic case study, and, given that some case studies are quantitative, the picture is somewhat confusing. We are predominantly concerned with case studies undertaken in a heavily qualitative mode, that is, where naturalistic everyday, cultural and interactional phenomena are studied in their own right and in their own territory. However, it is crucial to remember that what distinguishes a case study is principally the object which is to be explored, not the methodological orientation used in studying it (Stake 1994: 236). The 'case' in case study work is, therefore, paramount and it is this which we believe offers the teacher–researcher an important way forward in terms of both design and forms of writing. This contrasts markedly with what many assume to be the only way to conduct such enquiries, namely, via representative samples of a large kind. We will first provide a brief historical sketch of the development of case study research in the human sciences and then attempt to answer a series of questions and identify a number of problems, including the following:

- What exactly is a case and how is it identified?
- How are cases selected?
- What different types of case study exist?
- How is the triangulation of data collection achieved in case studies?
- What is the nature of validation in case studies?
- How might uniqueness versus generalization be managed in a case study?
- What are the most appropriate forms for writing and 'telling the tale' in case studies and qualitative research in general?

Obviously these issues will overlap and will feature to a greater or lesser extent in different kinds of case study. Let us start with some background information.

BACKGROUND TO THE DEVELOPMENT OF CASE STUDY RESEARCH

The case study approach has been very much a central feature of qualitative research over the past century. The case study has been widely used across a number of disciplines. As a consequence, the term has come to mean different things to different people. The major characteristic of a case study is the concentration upon a particular incident. The organizing principle involved is the isolation of a set of events and relationships which are appropriate to cases of that kind. Case studies evolve around the in-depth study of a single event or a series of linked cases over a defined period of time. The researcher tries to locate the 'story' of a certain aspect of social behaviour in a particular setting and the factors influencing the situation. In this way themes, topics and key variables may be isolated. The situation becomes the focus of attention. A case study is therefore likely to have the following characteristics:

- A concern with the rich and vivid description of events within the case.
- A chronological narrative of events within the case.
- An internal debate between the description of events and the analysis of events.
- A focus upon particular individual actors or groups of actors and their perceptions.
- A focus upon particular events within the case.
- The integral involvement of the researcher in the case.
- A way of presenting the case which is able to capture the richness of the situation.

The case study approach has a long history in the social sciences, indeed, the debate over the case study has an important place in the development of those disciplines. The debate in sociology in North America over this approach resulted in a row between 'statistical method' and 'case study' (Hammersley 1989: 92). In his scholarly account of the Chicago sociological tradition Hammersley locates the origins and nature of case study approaches:

> The concept of the case study seems to have arisen from a number of sources: the clinical methods of doctors; the case-work technique being developed by social workers; the methods of historians and anthropologists, plus the qualitative descriptions provided by primarily quantitative researchers. The diversity of models perhaps explains the variety of conception and practice to be found among advocates of the case study.
>
> In essence the term 'case study' referred to the collection and presentation of detailed, relatively unstructured information from a range of

> sources about a particular individual, group, or institution, usually including the accounts of the subjects themselves.
>
> (Hammersley 1989: 93)

Clearly, community studies, small-scale studies of organizations and even life-histories might all be regarded as belonging to the general category of case study. The development of case studies in Chicago sociology during the period 1920–1940 highlights the advantages of such an approach. Defenders of the approach argued that above all else it was capable of exploring a situation in depth, over time and in clearly bounded environments. In contrast to more quantitative approaches, such as the use of statistics, case studies were able to develop in-depth subjective understandings of people, situations and key episodes. However, in American sociology there followed a heated debate over the comparative value of case studies versus statistical methods. The decline of case study research during the post-war period was due to the dominance of quantitative methods in the social sciences stressing generalizabilty, probability, prediction and falsifiability criteria, coming together in the 'statistical method'. The main problem for many concerns the reliance on single cases and the subsequent problems regarding generalization.

From this research perspective, the main critique of qualitative case studies revolved around the question that if you are studying only one case it is difficult to maintain falsifiability criteria and generalization becomes impossible. This is the so-called N=I factor, namely that one case is too small a sample. What we were seeing in this debate was one more manifestation of the positivist versus the post-positivist position. In our view case study, even when it does make use of quantitative data, sits firmly in the post-positivist tradition. As Donmoyer puts it:

> The classic hypothesis/generation/verification distinction . . . ignores the fact that in fields such as education, social work and counselling – fields in which there is a concern with individual, not just aggregates – all research findings are tentative.
>
> (Donmoyer 1990: 183).

The problem for the qualitative researcher is that an alternative strategy and language has not been fully argued out (Donmoyer 1990: 182–86). Indeed, there is a continuum of positions between those using case study from some who wish to retain the criteria of validity, reliability and generalization but re-define them in line with qualitative aims of inquiry, and others who wish to abandon such criteria for the aims of qualitative inquiry.

WHAT IS A CASE AND HOW IS IT IDENTIFIED?

Cases may, indeed, be simple and straightforward, or they may be complex and extended. What is central, however, to all the people who have claimed to be carrying out case studies is a focus and emphasis upon the specific, the clearly bounded and unique. From anthropological case studies of small-scale societies to sociological case studies of organizations, the researcher will concentrate upon specifics in fairly clearly bounded settings that have some kind of internal coherence. Of course, part of the task will be the researcher's identification of boundaries for the case. In line with ethnographers, case study researchers will look for the common, widespread and general, but will also look for and attempt to identify the particular. As such, it is likely that case study researchers will collect a variety of data from a variety of sources, indeed, this will be the norm.

Whilst a case may literally be anything, a case study is certainly not any kind of research. The researcher will need to try to identify the boundaries, decide what is, in fact, inside 'the case' and concentrate the research questions appropriately. It is often very useful to attempt to identify diagramatically the boundaries of the case, breaking this down into 'key players', 'key situations' and sometimes to focus on what have been described as 'critical incidents' in the life of the case itself. Anthropologists, for example, often focus upon status passages, including birth, marriage or death in order to read aspects of wider attitudes. Such a critical moment in the life of a group will throw light on essential underlying factors. On the other hand, a case study of the introduction of new teaching strategies in a primary school would need to identify the scope and boundaries of the study. Would the nursery be included? Would any teaching in adjacent school buildings with their single classrooms be considered? Were all staff to be included in the research? And what would the researcher make of or do with the tragic consequences of the fire which destroyed half of the school, for example? Here, identification of a case, location of boundaries, identification of key players and key situations, with the concentration upon the impact of a critical incident would all need to be addressed. The major problem in defining a case surounds the notion of boundaries or territory. Researchers often have problems in exactly defining the scope of their case studies, deciding where their case ends or should begin. Miles and Huberman (1994: 25–7), discuss issues of boundaries in case studies. They argue that there is a focus, a heart of a case study, and a boundary which is often indeterminate, defining the edge of the case, this is not to be studied. This suggests that cases may be defined in terms of the following:

- Cases will have temporal characteristics which help to define their nature.
- Cases have geographical parameters allowing for their definition.
- Cases will have boundaries which allow for definition.
- Cases may be defined by an individual in a particular context, at a point in time.
- Cases may be defined by the characteristics of the group.
- Cases may be defined by role or function.
- Cases may be shaped by organizational or institutional arrangements.

CASE SELECTION

The decision to study any particular situation will be influenced by the nature of the research questions which have been formulated. In one respect then, case study design is a response to a set of theoretical, methodological and substantive questions. The researcher arrives at the case-selection stage, having worked through, in a fairly systematic fashion, a series of stages and questions. In this sense, case selection is not unlike the process of topic selection we identified in our guide to the research process. However, it may well be possible to look at more than one case in a single case-study. The case is not selected for its own intrinsic interest but for what it can tell the researcher in terms of the research questions posed and the questions which will emerge during the course of the research.

DIFFERENT TYPES OF CASE STUDY

It is important to realize that there is a distinction to be drawn between different approaches to undertaking a case study which arise from the original discipline which provided the model for the research design in the first place. A line may be drawn between the kind of case study which draws upon qualitative ways of collecting and analysing data, and the more specific use of the term 'Ethnographic Case Study'. In the latter instance, the case study is:

> More than an intensive, holistic description and analysis of a social unit or phenomenon. It is a sociocultural analysis of the unit of study. Concern with the cultural context is what sets this type of study apart.
>
> (Merriam 1988: 23)

Sociological and anthropological traditions have used the terms 'case study' and 'ethnography' differently (Hammersley and Atkinson 1983; Atkinson and Delamont 1985). It is important for teacher–researchers choosing to undertake a case study that they are clear from the start as to what kind of assumptions they are 'buying into' and this must be determined by what they hope to achieve. As Wolcott (1990) has pointed out, specific ethnographic techniques are available to anyone who wants to approach a setting descriptively. The anthropological concern for cultural context distinguishes ethnographic method from fieldwork techniques making ethnography distinct from other 'on-site' approaches. Hence, an ethnographic case study will use ethnographic techniques to provide descriptions and interpretations. The ethnographic focus upon sociocultural context, time and space, will therefore be crucial.

In the sense that we are using the term in this book, a case study can be considered as either the examination of a single instance in action or as the study of particular incidents and events over time or as the collection of information on the biography, personality, intentions and values of an individidual or group (Walker 1986). The essential point is that, in each instance, the individuality of the case is retained. In educational evaluation or research, a case study may study and portray the impact in a school of a particular curriculum, innovation, explore the experience of a staff development, trace the development of an idea through a number of social organizations, investigate the influence of a social and professional network, or portray a day in the life of a teacher, administrator or a pupil. These very different case studies have one thing in common – some commitment to the study and portrayal of the idiosyncratic and the particular as being legitimate forms of inquiry in themselves (Walker 1986: 189–91).

As Bromley (1986) has put it, by definition therefore, case study methods will get as close to the subject of interest as they possibly can, partly by their access to subjective factors (thoughts, feelings and desires). Case studies tend to spread the net for evidence much more widely than experiments and surveys which tend to have a specific focus (Bromley 1983: 23), but the question concerning the identification of the boundaries of the case remains. In contrast, surveys and experiments often use derivative data, for example, test results or official statistics. Clearly then there are different classifications of case study approaches. Yin (1984), for example, identifies three distinct types of case study differentiated in terms of their end product: 'exploratory', 'descriptive' and 'explanatory'. Drawing upon the rich heritage of past case studies, Yin (1984) argues that exploratory case studies have been used as 'pilots' before the research proper starts either to generate research questions or try out data collection methods or both. Descriptive case studies have aimed at giving a narrative account of life as it is in a social situation. These, Yin argues, have tended to be high in detail but low in theory. The explanatory case study, on the other hand, has tended to be used either to generate new theory or test an existing one (Yin 1984).

Merriam (1988) uses a slightly different but overlapping classification of descriptive, interpretative and evaluative case studies. The first, descriptive, are narratives of a sequence of events, rich in detail and atheoretical in the sense that basic description of the subject comes before hypothesizing or theory testing. The second, interpretative, although rich in detail, is used to develop conceptual categories or to illustrate, support or challenge existing assumptions which were held before the start of data collection. In this kind of case study, the method of analysis is essentially inductive and characterized by complexity, depth and theoretical orientation. The third, evaluative, combines, in addition to description and explanation, judgement which, it can be argued, is the essence of sound evaluation (Merriam 1988).

Considering the use of case study within education, Merriam cites four kinds of case study. The first is the ethnography case study, characterized by its socio-cultural interpretation, whatever its focus of study. The second is the historical case study, especially the historical organizational case study which focuses on a specific organization and traces its development. This kind of study is characterized by techniques common to historical research, in particular the use of primary data and the study of phenomena over a given period of time. The third is the psychological case study, with its focus upon the individual as a way to investigate human behaviour and drawing upon psychological concepts to inform studies not only of individuals but of events and processes. Fourth is the sociological case study, with its emphasis on the constructs of society (class, gender, ethnicity) and the importance of socialization in studying educational phenomena. A classic study in this tradition is still Colin Lacey's *Hightown Grammar: The School as a Social System* (Lacey 1970). Case studies of different types then have been widely used in educational research.

Finally Stake (1994) has distinguished between intrinsic case studies, an example of which he cites is the study of Macdonald, Adelman, Jushner and Walker (1982) on bilingual schooling in the USA; instrumental case studies of which the study of Becker, Geer, Hughes and Strauss (1961) of medical students is a good example, and collective case studies with Miles and Huberman's (1984) study of social impact, as an example. The first type is undertaken by the researcher in order to understand the particular case in question. The second is used when the researcher examines a particular case to gain insight into a certain issue or theory. The third example will involve the study of several cases (Stake 1994: 237–8). Certainly, all these classifications have much in common and the whole process is best seen as a continuum in which the researcher can draw on more than one model.

The term 'qualitative case study' has often been used therefore in a rather confusing way, to refer to several different types of activities simultaneously. Another problcm is that, whereas the method has been particularly associated with qualitative research, it is possible to do a case study whether or not the data is qualitative. All these different classifications of case study, indeed, highlight diversity. However, there are significant aspects which are shared in common to enable us speak in a generic sense about case study research.

WHEN TO USE A CASE STUDY

It has been argued that, in general, case studies are the preferred strategy when 'How' and 'Why' questions are being posed. When the investigator has little control over events or when the focus is on a contemporary phenomenon within some real-life context then it is here that the case study will come into its own.

It has also been pointed out that case studies can be of particular value where the research aims to provide practitioners with better or alternative ways of doing things. This partly accounts for the popularity of case study within management research and the whole area of managing change, for, as Gummesson argues, 'the change agent works with cases' (Gummesson 1991: 73), then, case study research is most appropriate.

We would like to argue that the qualitative or ethnographic case study is the research approach that offers most to teachers because its principal rationale is to reproduce social action in its natural setting, i.e. classrooms and workplaces, and that it can be used either to test existing theory or practice in an everyday environment, or it can be used to develop new theory or improve and evaluate existing professional practice. It also draws upon the data collection skills described in this book and the ways of analysing qualitative data which we have advocated.

However, different types of case study are genuine options that can reflect the different aims of school-based research, be they evaluation, inquiry, school development or how to manage change more effectively.

DATA COLLECTION IN CASE STUDIES AND TRIANGULATION

Obviously, studying the particular will require a certain methodological strategy. Since qualitative case studies have an underlying philosophy in common with qualitative research, the methods of qualitative research outlined and elaborated upon extensively in this book, apply here. If the major concern of the researcher is with the intrinsic interests of the case itself then it is likely that both a range of techniques will be used to obtain that data and different kinds of data will feature. Such triangulation can, in addition, also help the researcher to establish the validity of the findings by cross-referencing, for example, different perspectives obtained from different sources, or by identifying different ways the phenomena are being perceived. Triangulation is commonly used in social research but, clearly, case study researchers will inevitably become involved in the triangulation of data sources. However, this will be within-case triangulation, at least to begin with.

VALIDATING CASE STUDIES

As has already been indicated, the use of the case study in research has generated a good deal of debate over the past decade or so, largely concentrating on the issues of validity, reliability and generalization. Within educational research this has been reflected in a debate about the use of ethnographic or naturalistic research in schools and colleges. There are those who have argued for the need to bring case study research and especially ethnographic case study research more into line with quantitative research in areas such as generalization, validity and reliability (Hammersley 1992). Equally, there have been those who have argued that to avoid ethnographic and action research merely reproducing the status quo, there is a need to adopt a critical stance towards the values espoused by the subjects being studied and an imperative to place the case studies within a socio-political context (Atkinson and Delamont 1985). We will now look at some of these issues.

INTERNAL VALIDITY AND THE CASE STUDY

In dealing with issues of validity in relation to case study research, we will be drawing upon the material outlined earlier in the book. The section on access and ethics in conducting school-based research needs to be given careful consideration when undertaking case study research, as we highlighted in Chapter 3. We are also taking the view that 'since it is impossible to have internal validity without reliability, a demonstration of internal validity amounts to a simultaneous demonstration of reliability' (Guba and Lincoln 1981: 120). It should be stated at the outset that there is no sure way of assuring validity but that there are only 'notions of validity' (Ratcliffe 1988: 158). Data does not speak for itself but only through the interpreter. One cannot observe phenomena without changing it in some way and words and numbers are all 'abstract, symbolic representations of reality' (Ratcliffe 1988: 150). We identified some of the problems here in Chapter 5, and it might be helpful to re-read this at this point.

For the quantitative researcher, validity must be concerned with the degree to which findings capture the reality of the situation under investigation. However, underlying ethnographic–naturalistic data collection is the assumption that reality is 'holistic, multi-dimensional and ever-changing; it is not a single, fixed, objective phenomenon waiting to be discovered, observed and measured' (Merriam 1988: 167). We are dealing with people's constructions of the world and the researcher is trying to capture this, so what *seems* to be true for the subjects may be more imporant than what is true in the researcher's frame of reference.

The researcher can adopt a number of strategies in order to increase internal validity. Triangulation is one is one of these.

Triangulation

The researcher can undertake triangulation, which most writers on case study methodology have considered as vital to internal validity, especially those studies that seek explanatory outcomes. Denzin (1970) has argued that there are four types of triangulation used in research: 'data triangulation' which involves data that are collected over a period of time, from more than one location and from, or about, more than one person; 'investigator triangulation' which involves the use of more than one observer for the same object. This can also involve member checks. That means taking data and interpretations back to the subjects to ask them if the results are plausible (Guba and Lincoln 1981). Third, is 'theory triangulation' which involves the use of more than one kind of approach to generate categories of analysis. (Denzin can only give theoretical examples here which implies that this is difficult to achieve.) Fourth, 'methodological triangulation' which means the use, within a data collection format, of more than one method of obtaining information. For example, if questionnaires were used, the use of more than one type of question: fixed-choice alongside open-ended questions, or in interviewing, mixing structured with semi-structured interviews.

As well as triangulation the researcher can become engaged in a number of other processes. These may include the following suggestions:

- Undertake peer examination, which involves asking colleagues to comment upon the findings as they emerge.
- Adopt participatory modes of research which involve participants in all the phases of research from conceptualizing the study to writing up the findings.
- Be aware of your own biases as a researcher 'clarifying' your own 'assumptions, world view and theoretical orientation at the outset of the study' (Merriam 1988: 169–70).

UNIQUENESS VERSUS GENERALIZATION

We start from the premise that generalization is possible from case study research but that it must be defined in terms different from those applied to quantitative research.

As Eisner and Peshkin have pointed out, as humans 'we were generalizing animals well before the birth of inferential statistics' (Eisner and Peshkin 1990: 171). We generalize all the time from non-randomly selected real-life situations from which we learn a great deal. In addition, in education, much that we wish to understand is in a constant state of flux and replication of a qualitative study may not, in all circumstances, produce the same results. Generalization needs therefore to be considered in terms of degrees of generalization.

Robert Donmoyer (1990) has suggested three advantages of naturalistic case studies here. First, accessibility: the case study can take place where most of us would not have an opportunity to go. It can, in other words, widen our experience of education and training in different settings, institutions, cultures and countries. Second, these studies can help us to see reality through the eyes of others. In the process, we can see things that we might not normally see. Third, it can help prevent defensiveness and resistance to learning. As he points out, one of the weaknesses of the Piagetian theory of learning, for example, is that it assumes an automatic link between assimilation and accommodation, whereas in the real world, those with power, i.e. teachers, can make the world change to their conception rather than alter their cognitive structure to accommodate aspects that appear threatening and hostile. Such an example is the well-researched observation of the teacher's ability to socially construct self-fulfilling prophecies. We can all ignore such evidence but it is possible that we may accept such a possibility if we encounter it through reading rather than encountering it in our own experience which might allow us to ignore or justify it in some way (Donmoyer 1990: 192–7).

Donmoyer is quite prepared to argue, therefore, that the value of the naturalistic case study lies in its 'vicarious' properties and the method's ability to take into account teachers' practical knowledge which studies can reveal. These individual studies can produce valuable insights over time into the way teachers think and understand their classroom practice.

Another approach to this problem is to argue that it is possible to generalize from qualitative studies, provided one designs the research with this issue in mind (Schofield 1990). This position does suggest that a certain amount of generalization is possible in a case study. Certainly, as the case study becomes used more frequently in applied contexts then people may become more anxious that their research has a wider appeal and relevance to a wider range of situations. Schofield has pointed to several factors in explaining renewed interests in this question, pointing especially to the increasing use of qualitative studies in evaluation and policy-oriented research. She further argues that a consensus has emerged in recent years as to how qualitative researchers conceptualize generalization. This centres on the 'matter of the "fit" between the situation studied and others to which one might be interested in applying the concepts and conclusions of that studied' (Schofield 1990: 226). Schofield argues that there are three useful targets for generalization in qualitative research, namely: studying *what is the case* which refers to studying the typical, the common and the ordinary, for example, studying sites for typicality and/or multi-site studies. Studying *what may be* which refers to designing studies so that their fit with future trends and issues is maximized. Examples here could be studying sites and situations which may become more common with the passage of time and paying close attention to how such present instances of future practices are likely to differ from their future realization. Studying what could be, which refers to locating situations that we know or expect to be ideal or exceptional on some a priori basis, and studying them to see what is actually going on there (Schofield 1990: 226). What is common to the two positions outlined above is a regard for the primacy of the particular and the observable, the importance of first-hand experience and the need to see the situation from the actor's point of view.

Generalizations arising from qualitative research, therefore, will depend very heavily upon the richness and thickness of the data collected and, equally, on the context from which the generalizations arise. How useful the generalizations are will depend upon the motives of the research. Schofield's approach with its emphasis on maximizing generalizability is particularly useful for the evaluation and management of education policy, both locally and nationally. Here, case study is used as a means to better and more effective management or for an in-depth assessment of policy in action. Donmoyer's (1990) approach with its emphasis on naturalistic generalization may be nearer the position of the individual teacher–researcher either undertaking a qualitative ethnographic study of an aspect of their own or others' practice or attempting to evaluate the worth of other studies in this field.

It might be possible to increase the generalization of a case study by comparing similar case studies from education and allied areas of professional work. It has been argued that 'if studies are not explicitly developed into more general frameworks, then they will be doomed to remain isolated one-off affairs with no sense of cumulative knowledge or developing theoretical insight' (Atkinson and Delamont 1985: 249). It is also possible to undertake multi-site case study research or, alternatively, work in collaboration with colleagues in other schools by use of some networking agreement. By way of conclusion, it is instructive to consider some examples of case studies which highlight some of the questions we raise.

CONCLUSION

In this chapter we have tried to argue a case for case studies by highlighting different types of case study and exploring the problems and some possible solutions to these problems. We will try to pull some of these ideas together by looking at some examples. The question of the relationship of case study research to the generation of theory is a complex one but, initially, it is important to bear in mind the type of case study one is undertaking. A recent example from Canada will illustrate the point (Webber and Skaw 1993). This is a case study of a Canadian school system which sets out to investigate four aspects of school effectiveness, namely: school district culture; decision-making; leadership, and staff support (Webber and Skaw 1993: 21). This is a good example of the explanatory case study, where the researcher takes a body of current received academic wisdom and uses the case study to test it, producing some new explanatory concepts on how school organizations function.

Another example of the use of case studies and linking them to theory and practice is provided by *Reforming Education and Changing Schools* (Bowe, Ball and Gold 1992). This considers the impact of the 1988 *Education Act* on secondary schools in England and Wales through a series of empirical case studies to evaluate the effect of market forces on school policy. It moves to and fro between the macro level of national curriculum policy statements to the micro level of how they are being interpreted at the individual school level. It shows very well how one can widen case study research by placing it within an existing body of knowledge while allowing 'teachers' voices' to be heard. It is an attempt to use case study research as a way of linking the 'generation' of policy with the 'implementation' of policy and to look at the fit between the two, all deeply contexted and embedded in the everday world.

A case study is a rewarding way of conducting and presenting research evidence. We believe that the possibilities offered by this approach are great indeed and hope to have shown the teacher–researcher some possible directions here.

POSTCRIPT: WRITING CASE STUDIES AND TELLING THE STORY IN QUALITATIVE RESEARCH. A PROLOGUE TO CHAPTER 14 AND THE WRITING PROCESS

From what we have said so far it is clear that a number of opportunities are availabe for writing up and presenting case studies. Indeed, the whole question of writing up and presenting qualitative research is a complex one. Increasingly, writing as a process and the form a written report may take have become the subject of considerable debate. Many factors have been at work here. Writing and 'telling the story' in qualitative research in general is such an important issue that we will discuss it at length in the next chapter. As far as case studies are concerned 'telling the story' and describing the case are crucial features in establishing authenticity and credibility. Clearly, however, different types of case study, have different purposes and intentions and will result in different stylistic and presentational issues and forms. This may in part be due to the characteristics of the intended audience and to the kind of case study involved. Eventually, many more questions are asked about the actual ways case studies can be written. The prospect is undoubtedly an exciting one. But it will become clear on reading Chapter 14 that many cherished conventions are being broken. Increasingly, qualitative researchers are challenging conventional wisdom, new ways of writing about the worlds of teaching and learning are appearing, our discussion of case study is in many ways a preamble to this. We have tried to present a justification for the case study, in all its varieties, as offering qualitative teacher–researchers both a productive vehicle for their research, and a way of presenting their findings. The suggested reading at the end of this chapter will give an indication of these possibilities.

SUGGESTED FURTHER READING

Since cases and the single case feature so heavily in qualitative research it is crucial to be clear about what constitutes the case. *Qualitative Data Analysis: An Expanded Sourcebook* (Miles and Huberman 1994) provides a good account of case defining. *The Case Study Method in Psychology and Related Disciplines* (Bromley 1986); *Case Study Research in Education* (Merriam 1988) and *Case Study Research: Design and Methods* (Yin 1984) all provide coherent introductions to the design, scope and methodology of case study research. Critical appraisals can be found in 'Problems of sociological fieldwork: a review of the methodology of Hightown Grammar' (Lacey 1976), in *The Process of Schooling* (Hammersley and Woods) and 'Judging the quality of case study reports' (Lincoln and Guba 1990). In addition, it is worth considering the literature on educational evaluation in order to examine the ways in which case studies have been utilized in that design framework. Finally, it is valuable to explore some of the emerging literature from the field of *Nurse Training and Education* in order to see the role case studies play in that professional field.

14 Writing up: conventions, narratives and stories

INTRODUCTION

In this chapter we wish to return to a theme discussed earlier in Chapter 5, namely writing qualitative research. We pointed to the location of writing as a process in our attempt to provide a pathway through research. We looked, in a fairly mechanical way, at reports and report writing, the writing of dissertations and theses and some possible structures for these, the nature of writing in applied research, and made some brief comments on the writing process. We now wish to explore in more depth aspects of both the writing process and the very nature of writing qualitative, naturalistic research. The contemporary diversity of qualitative research has raised questions about the very character of writing about that research and presenting findings. Recent work (Van Maanen 1988) has highlighted the existence of distinct genres in writing up and presenting accounts of fieldwork. Action research and the collaborative inquiry it fosters will raise further questions about writing, namely who does it and who owns it. Whilst it is possible to speak in a very general way about writing up research, school-based practitioner research poses a number of unique problems. We are concerned with elaborating the significance of qualitative naturalistic research traditions for teachers and this too offers possibilities for breaking with conventional modes of writing. Our comments, then, can be broken down into two main areas: the practicalities of research writing for teachers and the implications of qualitative research traditions for writing qualitative research. We will organize our comments, which are intended to be a combination of practical advice and conceptual explorations of the nature of the writing process and product in qualitative research, under a series of headings: background considerations, practical considerations, narratives and stories.

BACKGROUND CONSIDERATIONS

It is useful to have a look at the factors which are likely to have an effect on writing up research. These can be highlighted in a general fashion and could include the following:

- The purpose of research.
- The nature of research.
- The characteristics of the researcher.
- The anticipated audience of the research.

It is well worth sitting down and asking how these factors are going to shape and constrain the writing up of the research. Research has many different sorts of focus, satisfying the requirements of a further degree; providing a document about the findings of a small-scale investigation for inclusion in a school development plan; or reporting the findings of an evaluation or action research enquiry, which will all shape the ways in which the research is written up. The role and characteristics of the researcher will also play their part in influencing writing as will the intended audience. Furthermore, different styles of research have generated different conventions for the presentation of research. Differing degrees of constraint will be placed upon the writing as a consequence. Journals, for example, often have very exacting 'Notes for authors' which must be followed to the letter in preparing manuscripts for consideration for publication. Clearly, some types of research may offer more scope or freedom for the author than others. Research conducted by teachers is likely to have a variety of purposes. As a result, it is possible to present it in a number of ways.

The researcher needs to ask what is the purpose of the research, what kind of research is it, how might personal attributes influence the research and who is the intended audience? The answers to these questions will, to a great extent, determine the nature of the final account. The character of school-based research by teachers poses some fairly basic considerations for the practice and style of writing. At this point it is worth making an initial distinction between writing that is aimed directly at a professional audience and that which is aimed at an academic audience (Walker 1985: 157). Walker has tried to draw out some of the differences here:

> If the kind of analysis you are working towards is one consisting of lists of issues, then these can be used as a means of organizing and selecting material. The pursuit of an issues analysis (which is common in applied research) makes for a different approach from that commonly taken in social science studies, where the pursuit is for generalizations which in turn leads the researcher towards statistical models (even in qualitative studies).
>
> (Walker 1985 : 157)

On the other hand, if the research is undertaken by use of an evaluation model or design as we pointed out in Chapter 2, the use of 'portrayal' of events may perhaps be the best way forward rather than extended analysis. Here, considerations include breadth in the writing up of a study rather than depth. The practical constraints of time and energy may go against the need for speedy feedback in evaluation studies. The need to disseminate the research findings quickly will be paramount. The means by which findings are cascaded to colleagues can be varied especially since evaluation is very often a group phenomenon. Stake and Gjerde in an evaluation of a summer school programme produced a written pamphlet in newspaper format which included student comments but no analysis (Stake and Gjerde 1974: 16–17). Another way to present evaluation findings is to use an adversarial format presenting alternative views, opinions and judgements, i.e. a dialogue between two or more positions. The means are therefore varied, the essential point being that the writing conveys the aims of the evaluation and provides an account of its results. Hopkins has argued that evaluation reports should normally be short and that the writer should decide in advance which debate they are trying to influence. The main determining factors should be the audience for whom you are writing and that feedback is essential. He does, however, make the point that case studies are by their very nature bound to be long if the full complexity of a situation is to be investigated. Here, he recommends that a summary should be provided, noting the main findings (Hopkins 1989: 47–8; 174–5). These are just some of the kind of background considerations which will need to be included when thinking about writing up research. The degree to which these issues feature in writing up of any particular study will, of course, vary. It is much better to anticipate likely problems and possibilities.

PRACTICAL CONSIDERATIONS

Everyone knows that writing requires discipline, dedication and hard work. The process can be made a bit easier by following some of the practical advice given by people such as Judith Bell. Bell (1987) has provided a checklist which is very helpful, she has drawn this from Barzan and Graff (1977):

1 Set deadlines.
2 Write regularly.
3 Create a rhythm of work.
4 Write up a section as soon as it is ready.
5 Stop at a point from which it is easy to resume writing.
6 Leave space for revision.
7 Publicise your plans.

(Bell 1987: 153)

These are all tried and tested ideas which can certainly ease the writing process. These practical considerations highlight the need for a methodical approach. One of the biggest troubles, of course, is getting started. The advice is write as you go along for the very process of writing will help clarify your thoughts. It may be possible to start with something on 'method' or with some incident that lends itself to a 'what happened' approach which will give the writer experience in mixing description with analysis. This last point is an important one for there is considerable debate about the mix of description and analysis in qualitative research traditions. However, it can be argued that in qualitative writing they should be kept separate because the strength of qualitative research lies in its rich, detailed description. Ethnographic adequacy and the production of 'thick descriptions' are seen as being goals of ethnographic research in their own right.

As the writing process begins some basic points need to be made so as to avoid time-consuming work later on. First, it is vital to keep records of references used, either by means of a good card index system, or on computer disc or both. Second, learn how to reference in the most appropriate way, including when to cite the whole book or article and when to give a more specific chapter or page reference. The main distinguishing points here revolve around whether you are aiming to give the gist of a whole book or article or are specifically referring to one or two ideas, examples or facts. Generally, sound advice is to make your references as specific as possible. Remember that the references you cite give an indication as to the range of a given field you have covered and it is important that you use at least the key research and books in the area.

It is normal practice these days to put any notes that accompany the written text at the end of each chapter or at the end of the text. Until a few years ago it was normal to see footnotes at the bottom of the page to which they referred, however, the economics of publishing and changes in fashion have relegated them to the back. This is now the accepted format even though the use of the word processor has reduced the cost and time involved. If you want to link text and notes more closely one way is to put in parentheses all references to data and secondary sources used within the text itself. Remember, however, to keep such references to a minimum.

One question often asked concerns the use of appendices. Our advice is to use them sparingly. The text is the place to communicate not the appendix. However, appendices can be useful for certain tasks. First, they can be a place for any relevant documentary sources, including interview transcripts, that need quoting in full. Second, they can be a useful place for diagrams, charts, maps or photographs though these are often better placed in the main text. Third, they can be a useful place to put specific details of case studies. Finally, they can be a useful place to put a glossary of key words or definitions. To some extent these questions will be resolved by the appropriate 'style' for the job in hand. Journals have rules about presentation, as do publishers and award-bearing diploma and degree courses. Try to find out as early as possible about the rules that apply. A useful guide to writers of research papers, theses and dissertations is still that provided by the revised edition of *A Manual for Writers of Research Papers, Theses and Dissertations* (Turabin 1980).

One of the main difficulties encountered in qualitative research is the large amounts of data which are collected. The qualitative researcher constantly needs to reassess the data and organize and file it. Here, some form of cross-referencing is necessary both to avoid unnecessary repetition and to capitalize on useful comparisons and contrasts. Constantly asking why a piece of information is used and how it fits into the general line of argument being developed is important. What is significant about this material and about this informant? How can the reality of the situation under discussion best be conveyed? Remember that one of the main functions of a first draft is to lose any surplus information as well as giving an opportunity to reflect on the data and their analysis. The researcher should try at this stage to look for ways of conflating data by use of diagrams and visual images if appropriate. Photographs can enliven a qualitative account both as a means of description and as a way of aiding analysis. We have explored some of these issues in Chapter 12.

It is useful to include a summary at the start of a chapter and a conclusion at the end of the whole study or project. Even if a 'chapter format' break up is not used in the text, the provision of periodic accounts of where the argument has got to so far keep the reader focused on the argument. Organize chapters around a single theme or topic as a means of further focusing the study. Look out in fieldnotes and data for striking incidents or encounters with key informants that can open up an area of the research. One of the main issues in writing up is how to link together diverse kinds of data. It is perfectly possible to link together qualitative data and also link qualitative with quantitative data and, indeed, there is much merit in doing so since qualitative data are often from a variety of sources, and comparative methods and triangulation are much used to increase validity (Fielding and Fielding 1986). It are less certain that one should mix qualitative analysis with quantitative analysis especially in evaluation as Kyriacou and Wan Chung have argued 'one of the most important features of a research study is that it should have a clear and coherent "thesis" (a sustained line or argument) to present to the reader' (Kyriacou and Wan Chung 1993: 19–20). Not only, they argue, does mixing two approaches dilute this objective, but qualitative approaches stem from a rejection of positivist epistemologies. This raises some important issues. Background questions and considerations are obviously very important in the writing process. But, perhaps of even greater importance is the nature of the research and the underpinning philosophy which informs it. Qualitative researchers are critical of other research traditions, claim to be engaged in a fundamentally different activity to conventional research and so, logically, are likely to employ different writing strategies.

NARRATIVE, STORIES AND QUALITATIVE RESEARCH

Qualitative, naturalistic-based research provides immense opportunities for breaking up the conventional mould of presenting and writing up research. The explosion of qualitative research and its increasing status as a distinct research tradition has meant that many researchers have been developing new ways of writing and presenting their research which is, as they see it, more in contact with the underlying aims and philosophy of qualitative research. Certainly, much early qualitative research was not overly concerned with such issues. Under the influence of broader trends in the human sciences qualitative researchers have clearly been presenting their accounts in different ways. Four main trends and developments have been largely responsible for this and it is important briefly to outline what these are in order to understand the contemporary situation.

To begin with 'Interpretivism' might be said to be the underlying theoretical and philosophical strand of qualitative research traditions. This approach encompasses the emergence of *Verstehen* style investigation in the German sociological tradition of Dilthey and later Weber, the philosophical critique of conventional positivistic views of science, the phenomenological writings of Husserl and Schutz up to American symbolic interactionism and ethnomethodology. These diverse trends have culminated in what has loosely beeen described as qualitative research traditions. Whilst this thinking might be foundational, three important positions need to be identified as crucial in shaping qualitative researchers' thinking about writing.

POSTSTRUCTURALISM, POSTMODERNISM AND FEMINISM

Postructuralism provides a focus upon the nature of varied discourses in 'art', 'science', 'literature', etc. in terms of the ways in which language, ideas and forms of representation function as systems of power and domination. This, in turn, has been transformed into deconstructionism following writers such as Derrida, Lacan, Lyotard and especially Foucault. Language, forms of social organization, cultural assumptions, subjectivity and power are all seen to be linked. Language is not a reflection of social reality but a construction of it. Language in this view is a medium of power. The implications for examining the ways in which a social or education situation is written about are obvious. Poststructuralists would direct our attention to this.

Postmodernism has been variously defined by different people. Writers across the fields of the human sciences, humanities, art, music, drama and popular culture have all made contributions to the debate over the idea of postmodernism. As we use the term it signifies a symbolic and political divide between modernity and after, but this is problematic since both what is 'modern' in modernity and what is 'post' about postmodernity are contested issues. Postmodernity therefore refers to a new social totality based upon its own organizing principles (which are frequently disorganized) in contrast to those of an earlier (modern) period. The idea of postmodern society seems to contain a focus upon the contemporary ways in which society seems to be organized. For example, traditional sets of allegiances seem to be changing, in political terms new social movements emerge, for example, the women's movement, environmental groups, increasing ethnic conflicts and so on. Inherent in the ideas of postmodernist thinkers is the general critique of overarching all embracing models or systems which have been relied on in the past so often as providing explanations of society. No single explanation for what is going on in the world is satisfactory since there are both linear and diffused influences, new sets of conflicts, fragmentation and rapid social change. Disciplinary boundaries in the human sciences no longer carry the weight they once did in academic circles and are frequently broken by multi- or interdisciplinary research. The most important feature of postmodernism for us here concerns the doubt some of these thinkers cast on the assumption that any one system of thought, one method or perspective, one genre or convention can make a universal claim to truth or being right (Jones 1992). In contrast, postmodernists frequently question claims to truth by asking what they are hiding, covering or passing for. As such, postmodernism is critical and sceptical of conventional modes of reporting research. Clearly, such a programme has far reaching implications and has been influential in social and educational research. Equally, it has not been without its critics. We simply wish to identify postmodernism as influencing the way in which some qualitative researchers have been writing and presenting their work.

Feminism implies a commitment to the development of a theory of gender relations and women's lives and the identification of the nature of women's oppression. We explored this position extensively in Chapter 4 and highlighted some of the implications of this view for carrying out and writing up research. It is worth stating at this point that we see some fundamental associations and similarity of purpose between postructuralism, postmodernism, feminism and the qualitative research traditions that we have been advocating in this book. There is no space to explore these issues here and not everyone would agree with us, not that that concerns us in any way, we simply wish to draw the reader's attention to this feature.

Taken together, these developments have had a profound impact on the human sciences generally. Most notably this has involved researchers becoming more critical about the ways in which writers have sanctioned their accounts as real and objective. The practice of research and the written products of research are no longer unproblematic but highly problematic affairs. The interpretivists' gaze upon the social constriction of reality has been turned on to the research process itself which is seen as a socially occasioned and organized affair. Fieldwork, for example, is seen as being a practical accomplishment which needs to be unravelled. The poststructuralists' concern with language, or more appropriately, forms of discourse suggests that a written research report is yet just one more 'text' which must be deconstructed in order to see how it is built up and achieves what it achieves. We discussed a number of related points in Chapter 9 when we considered the interpretation of documents, the hermeneutic tradition and semiotics. The idea of postmodernity and the theory of postmodernism highlights both the diversity and complexity of our lives in the twentieth century. New forms of political allegiance and action, a heightened concern with identity and so on are all aspects of this. Feminist scholarship as we saw in Chapter 4 has sharpened our awareness of the gendered nature of social and educational research in both its practices and in its products. As a whole these contemporary themes have had a major impact on the ways in which social and educational researchers write about their research. Some people have dubbed this as a 'turn to textuality' juxtaposing art and science. Indeed, the impact of postmodernist philosophy, feminism and literary turns in ethnography (Clifford and Marcus 1986; Jones 1992) have been and are increasingly embraced by those working in educational research. Self-consciously researchers are becoming more concerned with the 'art' of their work as much as or more than the 'science' of their endeavours. For example, the developments in life history research we explored in Chapter 8 raise important questions about the nature and form of cultural representations. Do life histories or ethnographies for that matter represent or construct social reality? Are not written texts social productions making use of a variety of genre conventions? Writing has therefore become a major source of debate. Nowhere is this more noticeable than in qualitative research traditions. One manifestation of this is with a concern over narrative qualities and the nature of stories in ethnographic fieldwork.

TALES OF THE FIELD?

One of the most approachable discussions of this area for our purposes is provided by Van Maanen (1988). *Tales of the Field* is a witty, subtle, far reaching account of the activities of field researchers and, in particular, their modes of writing. Clearly influenced by the developments we described earlier, Van Maanen's tales fall into three main categories of genre for telling field stories, each having its own distinct authorial voice. These are: realist, confessional and impressionist.

The most important aspect of Van Maanen's discussion of conventions for reporting qualitative studies concerns the crucial distinction he draws between the first two genres and the third. This revolves around the particular stance taken by the researcher towards the subjects of the research, how the data are to be presented and how much of the author's/researcher's voice appears. Van Maanen's discussion is complex, nevertheless, it raises very many important issues about the nature of writing and the kinds of messages which can be conveyed that are highly relevant for qualitative researchers. Qualitative researchers in general and teacher–researchers in particular ought not to avoid such issues on the grounds of their complexity. We will, therefore, outline Van Maanen's ideas here.

In *realist tales* the voice is that of a third person, the typical detached, so-called objective observer in the scientific framework. As Van Maanen argues the tale's authority is based upon the author's experience and is taken on trust, the author usually gliding through the text (Van Maanen 1988: 66). In the *confessional tale* the author reacts to criticisms of realist tales, that they fail to come clean about the underlying epistemological and methodological assumptions on which their claims are based. Confessional tales, therefore, abound with accounts of the fieldwork and contain details about how the study was 'brought off'. As a consequence there is a more apparent self-consciousness on the part of the researcher which functions to demystify the fieldwork or participant observation process showing how the techniques worked in the field. One effect of this, then, is that the confessional tale is characterized by a much more noticeable and high-profile authorial presence conscious of its own methodology. Finally, we have the *impressionist tale* which for Van Maanen and others capture most accurately the reality, or more appropriately, the realities of qualitative fieldwork research. From this view, the impressionist (postmodernist) tale will always be incomplete, highly localized, deeply contextualized, situational and partial. The aim is not to mask this but to celebrate it. The writers of impressionist tales, therefore, use an array of typically literary genres. They are out to startle their audience through the use of metaphor, multiple voices, collapsing time/chronology, the use of imagery, presenting stories within stories, and the expansive recall of fieldwork experience, using poetry amongst other devices. This results in a very different story, a very different way of reporting field research, but one which is striking, exciting, vibrant, richly descriptive and imaginative.

There is clearly a lot in the above discussion for the prospective writer of qualitative research. The researcher must make of this what she will. However, one basic question looms large here. Do we write our accounts in the third person or can we use the first person? In a fundamental sense this question poses the basic difference between scientific positivistic traditions and qualitative, naturalistic traditions. Traditionally, it has been expected that the reporting of research be conducted in the third person, 'the researcher, the investigator found', 'the subject recalled', or 'the respondent replied', etc. This, it was claimed, maintained objectivity, reduced bias and provided a sounder basis for judging any claims made. In sharp contrast many qualitative researchers, some of whom have been influenced by the developments we have unravelled, argue strongly for more use of the first person. The extent to which the prospective rèsearcher is able to achieve this is a moot point since the prevailing norm is to adhere to a neutral stance which will inevitably require the use of the third person. However, apart from being singularly unexciting this method of reporting research may, in fact, be distorting the very realities it is claiming to represent. Since qualitative researchers take the re-presentation and re-construction of social reality very seriously the use of first person narrative style may not only be justifiable, but essential. Here is how one commentator puts it:

> Because the researcher's role is ordinarily such an integral part of qualitative study, I write descriptive accounts in the first person, and I urge that others do (or, in some cases, be allowed to do) the same. I recognize that

> there are still academic editors on the loose who insist that research be reported in the third person. I recently had a journal submission edited into impersonal third-person language without my permission and without the editor informing me. I think the practice reveals a belief that impersonal language presupposes objective truth. Science may be better served by substituting *participants* for *we*, or *the observer* for *I*, but I have yet to be convinced that our highest calling is to serve science [see Wolcott 1990b]. Perhaps a more compelling case can be made on behalf of matching the formality of the writing with the formality of the approach. The more critical the observer's role and subjective assessment, the more important to have that role and presence acknowledged in the reporting.
>
> (Wolcott 1990a: 19)

Problems surrounding voice and styles of reporting qualitative research have been brought sharply into focus with recent developments in the use of biography and autobiography as a source of data in educational research. This has been most noticeable in life history research as we mentioned in Chapter 8. Decisions on how best to let subjects tell their own stories were critically explored in the interchange between P. Woods (1993) and P.J. Woods (1993). The increasing interest over recent years in the use of narrative and fictional approaches to professional development alongside life history approaches has meant that not only alternative ways of undertaking research have emerged, but different ways of writing also. We would simply encourage the teacher–researcher to explore and to take the preceding comments seriously (Bolton 1994: 55–68). One thing is clear though. It is not possible to put the clock back on these developments. Qualitative research traditions have been integrally bound up with these debates. Qualitative teacher research is therefore part of this. Teacher–researchers will have their own responses and their own distinctive contributions to make to the debate about the representation of the worlds of teaching and learning.

CONCLUSION

In this chapter we have tried to identify some background assumptions and practicalities about the writing process in qualitative research. Furthermore, we explored aspects of the debate over the ways in which qualitative research can be reported and written, identifying influential themes and debates. What is increasingly clear is the fact that 'writing' is firmly on the agenda in qualitative research traditions. Indeed, it is likely to become a highly contentious issue. Change is afoot. More and more educational research journals are accepting different styles of presenting research and its findings. There has been a large increase in the number of confessional tales in educational research and one of the major impacts of a focus upon gender and the contribution of feminist scholarship has been to open up ways of representing the gendered realities of schools and classrooms. Whilst all this might be seen as anxiety creation we believe it gets to the heart of some very important questions about the nature of research and the subsequent ownership of that knowledge, a challenge generated by the significant contributions of qualitative research. A challenge which we hope will be taken up by teacher–researchers in their attempts to explore, describe and understand the complexities of teaching and learning.

SUGGESTED FURTHER READING

The literature on writing up research and presenting research is increasing. Much of this literature provides sound practical advice and other works offer good insights into the particular problems of presenting and writing up qualitative research. *Use Your Head* (Buzan 1982) offers good examples of ways of improving note-taking skills, whereas *Read Better Read Faster* (DeLeeuw and DeLeeuw 1965) shows how reading techniques can be improved and the classic account of notetaking by Beatrice Webb can be found in *Field Research: A Sourcebook and Field Manual* (Burgess 1982); 'Keeping a research diary' (Burgess 1981) is also of value as an aid to the writing process, whereas *A Manual for Writers of Research* (Turabin 1980) remains indispensable. *The Good Study Guide* (Northedge 1990) contains two chapters on writing techniques. These sources all provide sound practical advice which should help the researcher during the writing up period. *Writing Up Qualitative Research* (Wolcott 1990a) provides one of the most accessible introductions to analysing and writing up qualitative data. Wolcott's highly personalized style goes a long way towards demystifying these processes in qualitative research and takes the reader through starting writing, keeping going, tightening up and finishing. One of the advantages of Wolcott's book is the way in which he draws examples from his own published educational ethnographies to illustrate his ideas. Another good article worth considering written by a key figure in the ethnography of education is 'New songs played skilfully: creativity and techniques in writing up qualitative research' (Woods 1985a) in *Issues in Educational Research: Qualitative Methods*. *Research Methods and Statistics in Psychology* (Codicon 1990) offers some useful guidelines on writing qualitative data reports drawing helpful distinctions between summaries of data, the analysis of data and interpretations. These guidelines might be read in conjuction with *Writing for Social Scientists: How to Start and Finish your Thesis, Book or Article* (Becker 1986). *Tales of the Field: On Writing Ethnography* (Van Maanen 1988) is to date the most sustained critique of writing conventions in ethnographic research. *Understanding Ethnographic Texts* (Atkinson 1992), Chapter 5, provides an excellent account of genres in ethnographic writing, why it is important to consider them, and what it is that different genres achieve. As yet we do not know of any discussion of ethnographies of schooling/education which have been conducted in this critical manner. No doubt these contributions will soon be arriving maybe even as we write.

References

Acker, J., Barry, K. and Esseveld, J. (1983) 'Objectivity and truth: problems in doing feminist research', *Women's Studies International Forum*, **6**, 4: 423–35.

Adams, C. and Arnot, M. (1986) *Investigating Gender in Secondary Schools*, London: Inner London Education Authority.

Adelman, C. (ed.) (1981) *Uttering, Muttering: Collecting, Using and Reporting Talk for Social and Educational Research*, London: Grant McIntyre.

Adler, S. (1991) 'The reflective practitioner and the curriculum of teacher education, *Journal of Education for Teaching*, **17 2**: 199–50.

Agar, M.H. (1986) *Speaking of Ethnography*, Qualitative Research Methods series Vol.2, Beverly Hills, CA: Sage.

Agee, J. and Walker Evans (1975) (Orig. 1939, 1940, 1941), *Three Tenant Families: Let Us Now Praise Famous Men*, London: Peter Owen.

Alexander, R. (1992) *Policy and Practice in Primary Education*, London: Routledge.

Allport, G.W. (1942) *The Use of Personal Documents in Psychological Science*, New York: Social Science Research Council, Bulletin No. 49.

Anderson, R.J., Hughes, J.A., and Sharrock, W.W. (1986) *Philosophy and the Human Sciences*, Beckenham: Croom Helm.

Archer, J. (1989) 'Childhood gender roles: structure and development', *The Psychologist*, **9**, 367–70.

Arnot, M. (1986) *Race and Gender: Equal Opportunities Policies in Education*, London: Pergamon Press.

Arnot, M. and Weiner, G. (eds) *Gender and the Politics of Schooling*, Milton Keynes: Open University Press.

Asher, R.E. *et al.* (eds) (1990) *The Encyclopedia of Language and Linguistics*, New York: Pergamon.

Atkinson, P. (1992) *Understanding Ethnographic Texts*, Newbury Park, CA: Sage.

Atkinson, P. and Delamont, S. (1985) 'A critique of "case-study" research in education', in M. Shipman (ed.) *Educational Research Principles, Policies and Practices*, Lewes: Falmer Press.

Atkinson, P., Delamont, S., and Hammersley, M. (1988) 'Qualitative research traditions: a British response', *Review of Educational Research*, **58, 1** 231–50.

Back, K.W. (1955) 'The well-informed informant', *Human Organization* **14, 4:** 30–3.

Bailey, K.D. (1982) *Methods of Social Research*, 2nd Edition, New York: Free Press.

Ball, M.S. and Smith, G.W.H. (1992) *Analyzing Visual Data*, Qualitative Research Method series No. 24, Newbury Park, CA: Sage.

Ball, S.J. (1985) 'Participant observation with pupils', in R.G. Burgess (ed.) *Strategies of Educational Research: Qualitative Methods*, Lewes: Falmer Press.

Ball, S.J. and Goodson, I.F. (eds) (1985) *Teachers' Lives and Careers*, Lewes: Falmer Press.
Barnes, D. (1969) 'Language in the secondary classroom', in D. Barnes, J. Britton and H. Rosen (eds), *Language, the Learner and School*, Harmondsworth: Penguin.
Barnes, J.A. (1971) *The Ethics of Inquiry in Social Science: Three Lectures*, Delhi: Oxford University Press.
Barnes, J.A. (1979) *Who Should Know What? Social Science, Privacy and Ethics*, Harmondsworth: Penguin.
Barnes, P. and Todd, F. (1984) *Communication and Learning in Small Groups*, London: Routledge.
Barnouw, E. (1983) *Documentary: A History of the Non-Fiction Film*, New York: Oxford University Press.
Barrow, R. (1984) 'The logic of systematic classroom research: the case of ORACLE', *Durham and Newcastle Research Review* **10, 53:** 182–8.
Barzan, J. and Goff, H.F. (1977) *The Modern Researcher*, New York: Harcourt Brace Jovanovich.
Bastiani, J. and Tolley, H. (1979) *Researching into the Curriculum*, Rediguide 16, Nottingham: University of Nottingham School of Education.
Bassey, M. (1990) 'On the nature of research in education', *BERA Research*, Parts 1–3.
Bateson, G. (1936) *Naven*, Cambridge: Cambridge University Press.
Bateson, G. and Mead, M. (1942) *Balinese Character: A Photographic Analysis*, Special Publications No. 2, New York: New York Academy of Sciences.
Bealing, D. (1972) 'The organization of junior school classrooms,' *Educational Research* **14, 3:** 231–5.
Becker, H.S. (1963) *The Outsiders*, New York: Free Press.
Becker, H.S. (1966) 'Introduction', in Show, C. *The Jack Roller*. Chicago: Chicago University Press.
Becker, H.S. (1967) 'Whose side are we on?', *Social Problems*, 14, 3: 239–48.
Becker, H.S. (1975) 'Photography and Sociology', *Afterimage*, **3**, May–June: 22–32, reprinted in H.S. Becker (1986) *Doing Things Together: Selected Papers*, Evanston, IL: Northwestern University Press.
Becker, H.S. (1979) 'Preface' in J. Wagner (ed.) *Images of Information: Still Photography in the Social Sciences*, Beverly Hills, CA: Sage.
Becker, H.S. (ed.) (1981) *Exploring Society Photographically*, Chicago: University of Chicago Press.
Becker, H.S. (1986) *Writing for Social Scientists: How to Start and Finish Your Thesis, Book or Article*, Chicago: University of Chicago Press.
Becker, H.S. (1993) 'How I learned what a crock was', *Journal of Contemporary Ethnography* **22, 1**, 28–35.
Becker, H.S. and Geer, B. (1982) 'Participant observation: the analysis of qualitative field data', in R.G. Burgess (ed.) *Field Research: A Source Book and Field Manual*, London: George Allen and Unwin.
Becker, H.S., Geer, B., Hughes, E.C. and Strauss, A.L. (1961) *Boys in White: Student Culture in Medical School*, Chicago: University of Chicago Press.
Bell, C. and Roberts, H. (eds) (1984) *Social Researching: Politics, Problems and Practice*, London: Routledge & Kegan Paul.
Bell, J. (1987) *Doing your Research Project: A Guide for First-Time Researchers in Education and Social Sciences*, Milton Keynes: Open University Press.
Bennett, J. (1981) *Oral History and Delinquency: The Rhetoric of Criminology*, Chicago, IL: University of Chicago Press.
Benson, D. and Hughes, J.A. (1983) *The Perspective of Ethnomethodology*, London: Longman.
Berelsen, B. (1952) *Content Analysis in Communication Research*, New York: Free Press.

Berlak, A.C., Berlak, H., Bagenstos, N.T. and Mikel, E.R. (1976) 'Teaching and learning in English primary schools', in M. Hammersley and P. Woods (eds) *The Process of Schooling: A Sociological Reader*, London: Routledge & Kegan Paul and Open University.

Bernstein, B. (ed.) (1971, 1972, 1975) *Class, Codes and Control*, Vols 1, 2 and 3, London: Routledge & Kegan Paul.

Bernstein, B. (1974) 'Open schools, open society?', *New Society*, 14 September.

Bertaux, D. (1981) *Biography and Society: The Life History Approach in the Social Sciences*, Beverly Hills, CA: Sage.

Bertaux, D. and Kohli, M. (1984) 'The life story approach: a continental view', *Annual Review of Sociology*, **10**, 215–37.

Best, R., Ribbins, P., Jarvis, C. and Oddy, D. (1983) *Education and Care*, London: Heinemann.

Beynon, J. (1984) ' "Sussing out" teachers: pupils as data gatherers', in M. Hammersley and P. Woods (eds) *Life in School: The Sociology of Pupil Culture*, Milton Keynes: Open University Press.

Beynon, J. (1985) 'Institutional change and career histories in a comprehensive school', in S.J. Ball and I.F. Goodson (eds), *Teachers' Lives and Careers*, Lewes: Falmer Press.

Blatchford, P. (1989) *Playtime in the Primary School: Problems and Improvements*, London: Routledge.

Blishen, E. (1969) *The School That I'd Like*, Harmondsworth: Penguin.

Blumer, H. (1969) *Symbolic Interactionism*, Englewood Cliffs, New Jersey: Prentice Hall.

Boehm, A.E. and Weinberg, R.A. (1977) *The Classroom Observer: A Guide for Developing Observation Skills*, New York: Teachers College Press.

Bogdan, R. and Biklen, S.K. (1982) *Qualitative Research for Education: An Introduction to Theory and Methods*, Boston, MA: Allyn & Bacon.

Bogdan, R. and Taylor, S.J. (1975) *Introduction to Qualitative Research Methods: A Phenomenological Approach to the Social Sciences*, New York: John Wiley.

Bolton, G. (1994) 'Fictional critical writing', *British Educational Research Journal*, **20, 1**, 55–68.

Borg, W.R. (1981) *Applying Educational Research: A Practical Guide for Teachers*, New York: Longman.

Bowe, R., Ball, S.J. with Gold, A. (1992) *Reforming Education and Changing Schools*, London: Routledge.

Bowles, G. and Duelli-Klein, R. (eds.) (1983) *Theories of Women's Studies*, London: Allen & Unwin.

Boydell, D. and Jasman, A. 'The pupil and teacher record', in *ORACLE Project: A Manual for Observers*, Leicester: University of Leicester School of Education.

Breakwell, G. (1990) *Interviewing*, London: Routledge/IBPS.

Brenner, M., Brown, J. and Canter, D. (1985) *The Research Interview: Uses and Approaches*, New York: Academic Press.

Brice-Heath, S. (1982) 'Questioning at home and at school: a comparative study', in G.D. Spindler (ed), *Doing the Ethnography of Schooling: Educational Anthropology in Action*, New York: Holt, Rinehart & Winston.

Brice-Heath, S. (1983) *Ways with Words: Language, Life and Work in Communities and Classroom*, Cambridge: Cambridge University Press.

Brice-Heath, S. and McLoughlin, M.W. (1994) 'Learning for anything every day', *Journal of Curriculum Studies*, **26**, 5: 471–89.

Briggs, C.L. (1986) *Learning How to Ask: A Sociolinguistic Appraisal of the Role of the Interview in Social Science Research*, Cambridge: Cambridge University Press.

British Sociological Association (1973) *Statement of Ethical Principles and their*

Application to Sociological Practice, London: BSA; copies available from British Sociological Association, 10 Portugal Street, London, WC2A 2HU.
Bromley, D.B. (1986) *The Case Study Method in Psychology and Related Disciplines*, London: Wiley.
Browne, N. and France, P. (1985) 'Only cissies wear dresses', in G. Weiner (ed.) *Just a Bunch of Girls*, Milton Keynes: Open University Press.
Browne, N. and France, P. (1986) *Untying the Apron Strings: Anti-Sexist Provision for the Under Fives*, Milton Keynes: Open University Press.
Bruner, J. (1992) *Acts of Meaning*, Cambridge, MA: Harvard University Press.
Bulmer, M. (1980) 'Comment on "the ethics of covert methods"', *British Journal of Sociology*, **31, 1**: 59–65.
Bulmer, M. (ed.) (1982) *Social Research Ethics: An Examination of the Merits of Covert Participant Observation*, London: Macmillan.
Bulmer, M. (1983) '"The Polish peasant in Europe and America": a neglected classic', *New Community*, **10**, 3: 470–6.
Burgess, R.G. (1980) 'Some fieldwork problems in teacher-based research', *British Educational Research Journal* **6, 2**: 165–73.
Burgess, R.G. (1981) 'Keeping a research diary', *Cambridge Journal of Education*, **11, 2**: 75–83.
Burgess, R.G. (1982a) 'The unstructured interview as a conversation', in R.G. Burgess (ed.) *Field Research: A Sourcebook and Field Manual*, London: Allen & Unwin.
Burgess, R.G. (ed.) (1982b) *Field Research: A Sourcebook and Field Manual*, London: Allen & Unwin.
Burgess, R.G. (1983) *Experiencing Comprehensive Education*, London: Methuen.
Burgess, R.G. (1984a) *In the Field: An Introduction to Field Research*, London: Allen & Unwin.
Burgess, R.G. (1984b) *Field Methods in the Study of Education*, Lewes: Falmer Press.
Burgess, R.G. (1984c) *The Research Process in Educational Settings: Ten Case Studies*, London: Falmer Press.
Burgess, R.G. (ed.) (1985a) *Strategies of Educational Research: Qualitative Methods*, Lewes: Falmer Press.
Burgess, R.G. (ed.) (1985b) *Issues in Educational Research: Qualitative Methods*, Lewes: Falmer Press.
Burgess, R.G. (ed.) (1989) *The Ethics of Educational Research*, Lewes: Falmer Press.
Burke, V. (1971) *Teachers in Turmoil*, Harmondsworth: Penguin.
Buzan, T. (1982) *Use your Head*, revised edn, London: BBC Ariel Books.
Carley, K. (1990) 'Content analysis', in R.E. Asher *et al.* (eds), *The Encyclopedia of Language and Linguistics*, New York: Pergamon.
Carr, W. and Kemmis, S. (1986) *Becoming Critical: Education, Knowledge and Action Research*, London: Falmer Press.
Cazden, D., John, V. and Hymes, D. (eds) *Functions of Language in the Classroom*, Columbia and London: Teachers College Press.
Champion, J. and James, J. (1980) *Critical Incidents in Management*, Homewood, IL: Irwin.
Chisholm, L. (1990) 'Action research: some methodological and political considerations', *British Educational Research Journal*, **16, 3**: 249–57.
Chodorow, N. (1978) *The Reproduction of Mothering: Psychoanalysis and the Sociology of Gender*, Berkeley: University of California Press.
Cicourel, A.V. (1964) *Method and Measurement in Sociology*, New York: Free Press.
Cicourel, A.V. (1973) *Theory and Method in the Study of Argentine Fertility*, New York: Wiley.
Cicourel, A.V., Jennings, K., Jennings, S., Leiter, K., Mackay, R., Mehan, H. and Roth, D. (1974) *Language Use and School Performance*, New York: Academic Press.
Clarricoates, K. (1978) 'Dinosaurs in the classroom: a re-examination of some aspects

of the "hidden" curriculum in primary schools', *Women's Studies International Quarterly* **1**: 353–64.

Clarricoates, K. (1980) 'The importance of being Ernest . . . Emma . . . Tom . . . Jane: the perception and categorization of gender conformity and gender deviation in primary schools', in R. Deem (ed.) *Schooling for Women's Work*, London: Routledge & Kegan Paul.

Clifford, J. and Marcus, G.E. (1986) *Writing Culture: The Poetics and Politics of Ethnography*, Berkeley: University of California Press.

Codicon, H. (1990) *Research Methods and Statistics in Psychology*, London: Hodder & Stoughton.

Cohen, L. and Manion, L. (1986) *Research Methods in Education*, 2nd edn, Beckenham: Croom Helm.

Connelly, F.M. and Clandinin, D.J. (1986) 'On narrative method, personal philosophy and narrative unity', *Journal of Research in Science Teaching*, **23, 4**: 293–310.

Connelly, F.M., and Clandinin, D.J. (1990) 'Stories of experience and narrative inquiry', *Educational Researcher*, **19, 5**: 2–14.

Cooper, H.M. (1982) 'Scientific guidelines for conducting integrative research reviews', *Review of Educational Research* **52**: 291–302.

Cooper, H.M. (1984) *The Integrative Research Review: A Systematic Approach*, Newbury Park, CA: Sage.

Cooper, H.M. (1989) *Integrating Research: A Guide for Literature Reviews*, Newbury Park, CA, Sage.

Corsaro, W.A. (1979) ' "We're friends right": children's use of access rituals in a nursery school', *Language in Society*, **8**, 315–36.

Corsaro, W.A. (1981) 'Entering the child's world: research strategies for field entry and data collection in a pre-school setting', in J.L. Green and C. Wallat (eds) *Ethnography and Language in Educational Settings*, Norwood, NJ: Ablex.

Cottle, T.J. (1972) 'Matilda Rutherford: she's what you would call a whore', *Antioch Review* **31, 4**: 519–43.

Cottle, T.J. (1973) 'The life study: on mutual recognition and the subjective inquiry', *Urban Life and Culture* **2, 3**: 344–60; reprinted in R.G. Burgess (ed.) (1982) *Field Research: A Sourcebook and Field Manual*, London: Allen & Unwin.

Cottle, T.J. (1978) *Black Testimony: The Voice of Britain's West Indians*, London: Wildwood House.

Crawford, P. and Turton, P. (eds) (1992) *Film as Ethnography*, Manchester: Manchester University Press.

Croll, P. (1986) *Systematic Classroom Observation*, London: Falmer Press.

Croll, P. and Galton, M. (1986) 'A comment on "Questioning ORACLE" by John Scarth and Martyn Hammersley', *Educational Research*, **28, 3**: 185–9.

Cullingford, C. (1993) 'Children's views of gender issues in school', *British Journal of Educational Research*, **19, 5**, 355–63.

Davies, B. (1979) 'Children's perceptions of social interaction in school', *Collected Original Resources in Education* **3**, 1.

Davies, B. (1982) *Life in Classroom and Playground: The Accounts of Primary School Children*, London: Routledge & Kegan Paul.

Day, C., Pope, M. and Denicolo (eds) (1990) *Insights into Teachers' Thinking and Practice*, London: Falmer Press.

Dearden, R. (1971) 'What is the integrated day?', in J. Walton (ed.) *The Integrated Day in Theory and Practice*, London: Ward Lock Educational.

Deem, R. (ed.) (1980) *Schooling for Women's Work*, London: Routledge & Kegan Paul.

Delamont, S. (1976) 'Beyond Flanders fields', in M. Stubbs, and S. Delamont (eds) *Explorations in Classroom Observation*, Chichester: John Wiley.

Delamont, S. (1980) *Sex Roles and the School*, London: Methuen.

Delamont, S. (1983a) *Interaction in the Classroom*, 2nd edn, London: Methuen.

Delamont, S. (1983b) *Readings in Interaction in the Classroom*, London: Methuen.
Delamont, S. and Atkinson, P. (1980) 'The two traditions of educational ethnography: sociology and anthropology compared', *British Journal of Sociology of Education* **1, 2**: 139–52.
DeLeeuw, E. and DeLeeuw, M. (1965) *Read Better, Read Faster*, Harmondsworth: Penguin.
Delphy, C. (1984) *Close to Home*, London: Hutchinson.
Denzin, N. (1970) *The Research Act in Sociology*, Chicago: Aldine.
Denzin, N. (ed.) (1978) *Sociological Methods: A Source Book*, London: Butterworth.
Denzin, N.K. (1988) *Interpretive Biography*, Beverly Hills, CA: Sage Publications.
Denzin, N.K. and Lincoln, Y.S. (eds) (1994) *Handbook of Qualitative Research*, Thousand Oaks, CA: Sage.
Department of Education and Science (1992) *Curriculum Organization and Practice in Primary Schools*, London: HMSO.
Dewey, J. (1933) *How We Think: A Restatement of the Relation of Reflective Thinking to the Educative Process*, Chicago: Regnery.
Dobbert, M.L. (1982) *Ethnographic Research: Theory and Application for Modern Schools and Societies*, New York: Praeger.
Donmoyer, R. (1990) 'Generalizability and the single case study', in E. Eisner and A. Peshkin (eds), *Qualitative Inquiry in Education: The Continuing Debate*, New York: Teachers College Press.
Douglas, J.D. (1976) *Investigative Social Research*, Beverly Hills, CA: Sage.
Draper, J. (1992) 'We're back with Gobbo: the re-establishment of gender relations following a school merger', in P. Woods and M. Hammersley (eds) *Gender and Ethnicity in Schools: Ethnographic Accounts*, London: Routledge.
Dubberley, W.S. (1988) 'Social class and the process of schooling', in A. Green and S. Ball (eds) *Progress and Inequality in Comprehensive Education*, London: Routledge & Kegan Paul.
Dumont, R. and Wax, M. (1969) 'Cherokee society and the intercultural classroom', *Human Organization*, **28, 3**: 217–26.
Durkheim, E. (1952) *Suicide*, London: Routledge & Kegan Paul.
Dyehouse, C. (1977) 'Good Wives and Little Mothers: social anxieties and the schoolgirls curriculum 1890–1920', *Oxford Review of Education*, **3, 1**, 21–35.
Edwards, A.D. (1979) *The West Indian Language Issue in British Schools*, London: Routledge & Kegan Paul.
Edwards, A.D. (1983) *Language in Multi-Cultural Classrooms*, London: Batsford.
Edwards, A.D. and Westgate, D. (1986) *Investigating Classroom Language*, London: Falmer Press.
Eichler, M. (1987) *Non-Sexist Research Methods*, London: Allen & Unwin.
Eisner, E. and Peshkin, A. (eds) (1990) *Qualitative Inquiry: The Continuing Debate*, New York: Teachers College Press.
Elliott, G. and Crossley, M. (1994) 'Qualitative research, educational management and the incorporation of the further education sector', *Educational Management and Administration*, **22**, 3, 188–97.
Elliott, J. (1986) Democratic evaluation as social criticism: or putting the judgement back into evaluation, in M. Hammersley, (ed.) *Controversies in Classroom Research*, Milton Keynes: Open University Press.
Ely, M. (ed.) (1990) *Doing Qualitative Research: Circles within Circles*, London: Falmer Press.
Erickson, E.H. (1953) *Young Man Luther*, London, Random House.
Erickson, F. (1987) 'Qualitative methods for research on teaching', in M. Wittrock (ed.) (3rd edition) *Handbook of Research on Teaching*, New York: Macmillan.
Erikson, K.J. (1967) 'A comment on disguised observation in sociology', *Social Problems*, **14, 4**: 366–73.

Equal Opportunities Commission (1982) 'Gender and the secondary school curriculum', *Research Bulletin No. 6*, Spring.
Evans, K. (1974a) 'The spatial organization of infant schools', *Journal of Architectural Research*, **13 1**: January.
Evans, K. (1974b) 'The head and his territory', *New Society*, 24 October.
Evans-Pritchard, E.E. (1937) *Witchcraft, Oracles and Magic Among the Agenda*, Oxford: Oxford University Press.
Faraday, A. and Plummer, K. (1979) 'Doing life histories', *Sociological Review*, **27, 4**: 73–98.
Festinger, L., Riecken, H.W. and Schochter, S. (1956) *When Prophesy Fails*, Minneapolis: Minnesota University Press.
Fielding, N. (1982) 'Observations of research on the National Front', in M. Bulmer, (ed.), *Social Research Ethics*, London: Macmillan.
Fielding, N.G. and Fielding, J.L. (1986) *Linking Data*, London: Sage.
Finch, J. (1984) '"It's great to have someone to talk to": the ethics and politics of interviewing women', in C. Bell and H. Roberts (eds) *Social Researching: Politics, Problems and Practices*, London: Routledge & Kegan Paul.
Fine, G.A. and Glassner, B. (1979) 'Participant observation with children: promise and problems', *Urban Life*, **8, 2**: 153–74.
Fine, G.A. and Sandstrom, K.L. (1988) *Knowing Children: Participant Observation with Minors*, Qualitative Research Methods series No.15. Newbury Park, CA: Sage.
Fink, A. (1993) *Evaluation Fundamentals: Guiding Health Programs, Research and Policy*, Newbury Park, CA: Sage Publications.
Fisher, A. (1989) *Let Us Now Praise Famous Women: Women Photographers for the U.S. Government 1935–1944*, Pandora Press: London.
Fishman, P. (1983) 'Interaction: the work women do'. In: B. Thorne, C. Kramaroe and N. Henley (eds), *Language, Gender and Society*, New York: Newbury House.
Flanders, N.A. (1960) *Interaction Analysis in the Classroom: A Manual for Observers*, Ann Arbor: University of Michigan Press.
Flanders, N.A. (1970) *Analyzing Teacher Behaviour*, Reading, MA: Addison Wesley.
Fonow, M.M. and Cook, J.A. (eds) (1991) *Beyond Methodology: Feminist Scholarship as Lived Experience*, Bloomington: Indiana University Press.
Fontana, A. and Frey, J.H. (1994) 'Interviewing: the art of science'. In: N.K. Denzin and Y.S. Lincoln (eds) *Handbook of Qualitative Research*. Thousand Oaks, CA: Sage Publications.
Foster, P. (1990) 'Cases not proven: an evaluation of two studies of teacher racism', *British Educational Research Journal*, **16, 4**: 334–49.
Foster, P. (1991) 'Case still not proven: a reply to Cecile Wright', *British Educational Research Journal*, **17, 2**: 165–70.
Frake, C.O. (1962) 'The ethnographic study of cognitive systems', in T.Gladwin and W.C. Sturtevant (eds), *Anthropology and Human Behavior*, Washington, DC: Anthropological Society of Washington.
Frank, G. (1979) 'Finding the common denominator: a phenomenological critique of life history', *Ethnos* (i), 69–94.
Frank, G. (1981) 'Mercy's children', *Anthropology and Humanism Quarterly*, **6**: 4–7.
Frank, G. (1984) 'Life history model of adaptation to disability: the case of a congenital amputee', *Social Science and Medicine*, **19, 6**: 639–45.
Frank, G. (1985) '"Becoming the Other": empathy and biographical interpretation', *Biography* **8, 3**: 189–210.
Frank, G. (1988) 'Beyond Stigman: disability and self-empowerment of persons with congenital limb deficiencies', *Journal of Social Issues*, **44, 1**: 95–115.
Frank, G. and Vanderburgh, R.M. (1986) 'Cross cultural use of life history methods in gerontology', in C.L. Fry and J. Keith (eds) *New Methods for Old-Age Research: Strategies for Studying Diversity*, Massachusetts: Bergin & Garvey.

French, P. and French, J. (1984) 'Gender imbalances in the primary classroom: an interactional account', *Educational Research*, **26, 2**: 127–36.
Frielich. M. (ed.) (1970) *Marginal Natives: Anthropologists at Work*, New York: Harper & Row.
Fullan, M. (1982) *The Meaning of Educational Change*, New York: Teachers College Press.
Fuller, M. (1980) 'Black girls in a London comprehensive', in R. Deem (ed.) *Schooling for Women's Work*, London: Routledge & Kegan Paul.
Fry, C.L., and Keith, J. (eds) (1986) *New Methods for Old Age Research: Strategies for Studying Diversity*, Mass: Bergin & Garvey.
Galton, M. (1981) 'Differential treatment of boys and girls during science lessons', in A. Kelly (ed.) *The Missing Half*, Manchester: Manchester University Press.
Galton, M. and Simon, B. (eds) (1980) *Progress and Performance in the Primary School*, London: Routledge & Kegan Paul.
Galton, M., Simon, B. and Croll, P. (1980) *Inside the Primary School*, London: Routledge & Kegan Paul.
Garfinkel, H. (1967) *Studies in Ethnomethodology*, Englewood Cliffs, NJ: Prentice Hall.
Geertz, C. (1973) *The Interpretation of Cultures*, New York: Basic Books.
Geiger, S.N. (1986) 'Women's life histories: method and content,' *Signs* **11, 2**, 334–51.
Giddens, A. (1978) 'Positivism and its critics', in T. Bottomore and R. Nisbet (eds) *A History of Sociological Analysis*, London: Heinemann.
Giddens, A. (1979) *Central Problems of Social Theory*, London: Macmillan.
Gilbert, N. (ed.) (1993) *Researching Social Life*, London: Sage.
Gilmore, P. and Glathorn, A.A. (eds) (1982) *Children In and Out of School: Ethnography and Education*, Washington, DC: Center for Applied Linguistics.
Gittins, D. (1979) 'Oral history, reliability and recollection', in L. Moss and H. Goldstein (eds) *The Recall Method in Social Surveys*, studies in education 9, London: University of London Institute of Education.
Glaser, B. (1978) *Theoretical Sensitivity: Advances in the Methodology of Grounded Theory*, Mill Valley, CA: Sociology Press.
Glaser, B.G. and Strauss, A.L. (1967) *The Discovery of Grounded Theory: Strategies for Qualitative Research*, Chicago, IL: Aldine.
Goetz, G.L. and LeCompte, M.D. (eds) (1984) *Ethnography and Qualitative Design in Educational Research*, New York: Academic Press.
Goffman, E. (1971) *The Presentation of Self in Everyday Life*, Harmondsworth: Penguin.
Goffman, E. (1979) *Gender Advertisements*, London: Macmillan.
Goldthorpe, J. (1983) 'Women and class analysis: in defence of the conventional view', *Sociology*, **17**.
Goodson, I.F. (1980) 'Life histories and the study of schooling', *Interchange*, **11, 4**: 62–76.
Goodson, I.F. (1982) *School Subjects and Curriculum Change*, London: Croom Helm.
Goodson, I.F. (1983) 'The use of life histories in the study of teaching', in M. Hammersley (ed.) *The Ethnography of Schooling: Methodological Issues*, Studies in Education Limited, Driffield: Nafferton Books.
Goodson, I.F. (1985) 'History, context and qualitative methods in the study of the curriculum' in R.G. Burgess (ed.) *Strategies of Educational Research: Qualitative Methods*, Lewes: Falmer Press.
Goodson, I.F. (ed.) (1990) *Studying Teachers' Lives*, London: Routledge.
Goodson, I.F. (1991) 'Sponsoring the teachers' voice: teachers' lives and development'. *Cambridge Journal of Education*, **21, 1**: 35–45.
Gouldner, A. (1968) 'The sociologist as partisan', *American Sociologist* 103–16, reprinted in A. Gouldner (1973) *For Sociology: Renewal and Critique in Sociology Today*, London: Allen Lane.

Graddol, D., Cheshire, J. and Swann, J. (1987) *Describing Language*, Milton Keynes: Open University Press.

Graham, H. (1983) 'Do her answers fit his questions? 'Women and the survey method', in F. Germarnikow, D. Morgan, J. Purvis, and D. Taylorson (eds) *The Public and the Private*, London: Heinemann.

Graham, H. (1984) 'Surveying through stories', In C. Bell, and H. Roberts *Social Researching Politics, Problems and Possibilities*, London: Routledge & Kegan Paul.

Green, J.L. and Wallat, C. (eds) (1981) *Ethnography and Language in Educational Settings*, Norwood, NJ: Ablex Publishing.

Grele, R. (ed.) (1975) *Envelopes of Sound: Six Practitioners Discuss the Method, Theory and Practice of Oral History and Oral Testimony*, Chicago, IL: Precedent Publishing.

Griffin, C. (1988) 'Qualitative methods and cultural analysis: young women and the transition from school to un/employment' in R.G. Burgess (ed.) *Field Methods in the Study of Education*, London: Falmer.

Griffiths, M. and Davies, C. (1993) 'Learning to learn: action research for an equal opportunities perspective in a junior school?', *British Educational Research Journal* 19, 1: 43–76.

Grugeon, E. (1992) 'Gender implications of children's playground culture', in P. Woods and M. Hammersley (eds) *Gender and Ethnicity in Schools*, London: Routledge.

Guba, E.G. (1981) 'Criteria for assessing the trustworthiness of naturalistic inquiries, ERIC/ECTJ annual review papers', *Educational Communications and Technology Journal*, **29**, 75–91.

Guba, E.G. and Lincoln, Y.S. (1981) *Effective Education*, San Francisco: Jossey Bass.

Gummesson, E. (1991) *Qualitative Methods in Management Research*, Newbury Park, CA: Sage.

Hall, E.T. (1969) *The Hidden Dimension*, London: The Bodley Head.

Hamilton, D. (1977) *In Search of Structure: Essays from a New Scottish Open-Plan Primary School*, Scottish Council for Research in Education, Publication No. 68, London: Hodder & Stoughton.

Hamilton, D. and Delamont, S. (1974) 'Classroom research: a cautionary tale', *Research in Education* **11**: 1–15.

Hammersley, M. (ed.) (1983) *The Ethnography of Schooling: Methodological Issues*, Studies in Education, Driffield, Nafferton Books.

Hammersley, M. (ed.) (1986a) *Controversies in Classroom Research*, Milton Keynes: Open University Press.

Hammersley, M. (ed.) (1986b) *Case Studies in Classroom Research*, Milton Keynes: Open University Press.

Hammersley, M. (1986c) 'Measurement in ethnography: the case of Pollard on teaching style', in M. Hammersley (ed.) *Case Studies in Classroom Research*, Milton Keynes: Open University Press.

Hammersley, M. (1986d) 'Revisiting Hamilton and Delamont: a cautionary note on the relationship between "systematic observation" and ethnography', in M. Hammersley (ed.) *Case Studies in Classroom Research*, Milton Keynes: Open University Press.

Hammersley, M. (1989) *The Dilemma of Qualitative Method: Herbert Blumer and The Chicago Tradition*, London: Routledge.

Hammersley, M. (1990) 'An evaluation of two studies of gender imbalance in primary classrooms', *British Educational Research Journal*, **11, 2**: 125–43.

Hammersley, M. (1992) *What's Wrong With Ethnography?*, London: Routledge.

Hammersley, M. (ed.) (1993) *Social Research: Philosophy, Politics and Practice*, London: Sage.

Hammersley, M. and Atkinson, P. (1983) *Ethnography: Principles and Practices*, London: Tavistock.

Hammersley, M. and Scarth, J. (1993) 'Beware of Wise Men bearing gifts: a case study in the misuse of educational research', *British Journal of Educational Research*, **19, 5**: 489–98.

Hammersley, M. and Woods, P. (eds) (1976) *The Process of Schooling: A Sociological Reader*, London: Routledge & Kegan Paul and Open University.

Hammersley, M. and Woods. P. (1987) 'Methodology debate: ethnography', *British Education Research Journal*, **13**(3), 283–317.

Harding, S. (ed.) (1988) *Feminism and Methodology*, Milton Keynes: Open University Press.

Hargreaves, D. (1967) *Social Relations in a Secondary School*, London: Routledge & Kegan Paul.

Hargreaves, D., Hestor, S.K. and Mellor, F.J. (1975) *Deviance in the Classroom*, London: Routledge & Kegan Paul.

Harper, D. (1987) 'The visual ethnographic narrative', *Visual Anthropology*, 1, 1: 1–19.

Harper, D. (1994) 'On the authority of the image: visual methods at the crossroads', in N.K. Denzin and Y.S. Lincoln (eds) *Handbook of Qualitative Research*, Thousand Oaks, California: Sage Publications.

Hartnett, A. (ed.) (1982) *The Social Sciences in Educational Studies: A Selective Guide to the Literature*, London: Heinemann.

Hexter, J.H. (1972) *Doing History*, London: Allen & Unwin.

Hitchcock, G. (1979) 'Preliminary notes on the doing of fieldwork and ethnography', *Urban Review*, **11, 4**: 203–14.

Hitchcock, G. (1980) *Social Interaction in an Organization Setting: The Analysis of the Social Organization of a School*, unpublished Ph.D. Thesis, University of Manchester, England.

Hitchcock, G. (1982) 'The social organization of space and place in an urban open-plan primary school', in G.C.F. Payne and E.C. Cuff (eds) *Doing Teaching: The Practical Management of Classrooms*, London: Batsford.

Hitchcock, G. (1983a) 'What might INSET programmes and educational research expect from the sociologist?', *British Journal of In Service Education*, **10, 1**: 18–31.

Hitchcock, G. (1983b) 'Fieldwork as practical activity: reflections on fieldwork and the social organization of an urban open-plan primary school', in M. Hammersley (ed.) *The Ethnography of Schooling: Methodological Issues*, Studies in Education, Driffield, Nafferton Books.

Hitchcock, G. (1992) 'Book review', W. Louden, *Understanding Teaching: Continuity and Change in Teachers' Knowledge*, *Educational Review*, **44, 2**: 223–24.

Hitchcock, G. and Hughes, D. (1989) *Research and the Teacher: A Qualitative Introduction to School-based Research*, London: Routledge.

Hodder, I. (1994) 'The interpretation of documents and material culture' in N.K. Denzin and Y.S. Lincoln (eds) *Handbook of Qualitative Research*, Thousand Oaks, CA: Sage.

Holdoway, S. (1992) '"An inside job": a case study of covert research on the police', in M. Bulmer (ed.) *Social Research Ethics*, London: Macmillan.

Holly, P. (1984) 'The institutionalisation of action-research in schools', *Cambridge Journal of Education*, **14**, 2.

Holly, P. (1986) 'Soaring like turkeys', *School Organization*, **6**, 1: 321–26.

Hopkins, D. (1985) *A Teacher's Guide to Classroom Research*, Milton Keynes: Open University Press.

Hopkins, D. (1989) *Evaluation for School Development*, Milton Keynes: Open University Press.

Hoskins, J.A. (1985) 'A life history from both sides: the changing poetics of personal experience', *Journal of Anthropological Research*, **41, 2**: 141–69.

Horowitz, I.L. (ed.) (1967) *The Rise and Fall of Project Camelot: Studies in the Relationship between Social Science and Practical Politics*, Cambridge, Mass: MIT Press.

Howard, K. and Sharp, J.A. (1983) *The Management of a Student Research Project*, London: Gower Press.

Hoyles, C. and Sutherland R. (1989) *Logo Mathematics in the Classroom*, London: Routledge.

Huberman, A.M. and Miles, M.B. (1984) *Innovation Up Close: How School Improvement Works*, New York: Plenum.

Hughes, P., Ribbins, P. and Thomas, H. (1987) *Managing Education: The System and the Institution*, London: Cassell.

Humphreys, L. (1970) *Tearoom Trade*, London: Duckworth.

Humphries, S. (1984) *The Handbook of Oral History: Recording Life Stories*, London: Inter-Action Trust Limited.

Husserl, E. (1965) *Phenomenology and the Crisis of Philosophy*, New York: Harper.

Hustler, D., Cassidy, T. and Cuff, E.C. (eds) (1986) *Action Research in Classrooms*, London: Allen & Unwin.

Hycner, R.H. (1985) 'Some guidelines for the phenomenological analysis of interview data', *Human Studies* **8**: 279–303.

Hymes, D. (1962) 'The ethnography of speaking', in T. Galdwin and W.C. Sturtevant (eds) *Anthropology and Human Behavior*, Washington, DC: Anthropological Society of Washington.

Jacob, E. (1987) 'Qualitative research traditions: a review', *Review of Educational Research*, **57, 1**: 1–50.

Joffe, C. (1971) 'Sex-role socialisation and the nursery school: or the living is bent'. *Journal of Marriage and the Family*, August: 467–75.

Joiner, D. (1976) 'Social ritual and architectural space', in H.M. Proshansky, W.H. Ittleson and G. Rivlin (eds) *Environmental Psychology: People and Their Physical Settings*, 2nd. edn., New York: Holt, Rinehart & Winston.

Jones, G.R. (1983) 'Life history methodology', in G. Morgan (ed.) *Beyond Method Strategies for Social Research*, Beverly Hills, CA: Sage.

Jones, P. (1992) 'Post-Modernism', *Social Science Teacher*, **21, 3**: 20–2.

Jupp, V. and Norris, C. (1993) 'Traditions in documentary analysis', in M. Hammersley (ed.) *Social Research: Philosophy, Politics and Practice*, London: Sage.

Isaacson, Z. (1988) 'The marginalisation of girls in mathematics: some causes and some remedies', in D. Pimm (ed.), *Mathematics, Teachers and Children*, Sevenoaks: Hodder & Stoughton.

Keddie, N. (1973) '*Tinker, Tailor . . . The Myth of Cultural Deprivation*, Harmondsworth: Penguin.

Kelly, A. (1978) 'Feminism and research', *Women's Studies International Quarterly*, 225–32.

Kelly, A. and Shaikh, S. (1989) To mix or not mix: Pakistani girls in British schools', *British Journal of Sociology of Education*, **2**: 193–204.

Kemmis, S. and Henry, C. (1984) *A Point by Point Guide to Action Research for Teachers*, Geelong, Australia: Deakin University Press.

Kemmis, S. and McTaggert, R. (1982) *The Action Research Planner*, Geelong, Australia: Deakin University Press.

Kincheloe, J.L. (1991) *Teachers as Researchers: Qualitative Enquiry as a Path to Empowerment*, London: Falmer.

King, R.A. (1978) *All Things Bright and Beautiful? A Sociological Study of Infant Classrooms*, Chichester: Wiley.

King, R.A. (1987) 'No best method: qualitative and quantitative research in the sociology of education', in G. Walford (ed.) *Doing Sociology of Education*, Lewes: Falmer Press.

Kirk, J. and Miller, M.L. (1986) *Reliability and Validity in Qualitative Research*, Qualitative Research Methods Series No.1, Newbury Park, CA: Sage.

Krippendorf, K. (1980) *Contents Analysis: An Introduction to Its Methodology*, Beverly Hills, CA: Sage.

Kuhn, T.S. (1970) *The Structure of Scientific Revolutions*, Chicago: University of Chicago Press.

Kvale, S. (1983) 'The phenomenological research interview: a phenemonological and hermeneutic mode of understanding', *Journal of Phenomenological Psychology*, **14**: 171–96.

Kyriacou, C. and Wan Chung, I. (1993) 'Mixing different types of data and approaches to evaluating a curriculum package', *British Educational Research Association Newsletter*, Summer 1993.

Labov, W. (1973) 'The logic of non-standard English', in N. Keddie (ed.) *Tinker, Tailor . . . the Myth of Cultural Deprivation*, Harmondsworth: Penguin.

Lacey, C. (1970) *Hightown Grammar: The School as a Social System*, Manchester: Manchester University Press.

Lacey, C. (1976) 'Problems of sociological fieldwork: a review of the methodology of Hightown Grammar', in M. Hammersley and P. Woods (eds) *The Process of Schooling*, London: Routledge.

Langlois, C.V. and Seignobes, C. (1908) *Introduction to the Study of History*, London: Duckworth.

Langness, L.L. and Frank, G. (1981) *Lives: An Anthropological Approach to Biography*, CA: Chandler & Sharp.

Lee, A.A. (1991) 'Integrating positivist and interpretive approaches to organizational research', *Organization Science*, **2(4)**: 342–65.

Lewin, K. (1946) 'Action research and minority problems', *Journal of Social Issues*, 2: 34–6.

Lewin, K. (1952) *Field Theory in Social Science*, London: Tavistock.

Lewis, A. (1992) 'Group child interviews as a research tool', *British Educational Research Journal*, **18, 4**: 413–21.

Lewis, L. (1970) *Culture and Social Interaction in the Classroom: An Ethnographic Report*, Working Paper 38, Berkeley, Calif: Language Behavior Research Laboratory, University of California.

LeCompte, M. and Goetze, J. (1992) 'Problems of validity and reliability in ethnographic research', *Review of Educational Research*, **52, 1**, 31–61.

Light, R.J., Singer, J.D. and Willett, T.B. (1990) *By Design: Planning Research on Higher Education*, Cambridge, MA: Harvard University Press.

Lincoln, Y.S. and Guba, E.G. (1985) *Naturalistic Inquiry*, Beverly Hills, CA: Sage.

Lincoln, Y.S. and Guba, E.G. (1990) 'Judging the quality of case study reports', *Qualitative Studies in Education*, **3**: 53–9.

Lloyd, B. and Duveen, G. (1992) *Gender Identities and Education: The Impact of Starting School*, London: Harvester Wheatsheaf.

Lofland, J. (1971) *Analyzing Social Settings*, New York: Wadsworth.

Lofland, J. and Lofland, L. (1984) *Analyzing Social Settings: A Guide to Qualitative Observations and Research*, Belmont, CA: Wadsworth.

Loizos, P. (1993) *Innovation in Ethnographic Film*, Manchester: Manchester University Press.

Lomax, P. (Ed.) (1989) *The Management of Change: Increasing School Effectiveness and Facilitating Staff Development Through Action Research*, Clevedon: Multilingual Matters.

Louden, W. (1991) *Understanding Teaching: Continuity and Change in Teachers' Knowledge*, London: Cassell Educational.

Lubeck, S. (1985) *Sandbox Society: Early Education in Black and White America – A Comparative Ethnography*, London: Falmer Press.

Lutz, F. (1981) 'The holistic approach to understanding schooling', in Green, J.L. and Wallat, C. (eds) *Ethnography and Language in Educational Settings*, Norwood, NJ: Ablex Publishing.

Mac an Ghail, M. (1993a) 'Beyond the white norm: the use of qualitative methods in the study of black youths' schooling in England', *International Journal of Qualitative Studies in Education*, **2, 3**, 175–89.

Mac an Ghail, M. (1993b) 'Beyond the white norm: the use of qualitative methods in the study of black youths' schooling in England', in P. Woods and M. Hammersley (eds) (1993) *Gender and Ethnicity in Schools: Ethnographic Accounts*, London: Routledge.

McCall, G.J. and Simmons, J.L. (eds) (1968) *Issues in Participant Observation: A Text and Reader*, New York: Addison Wesley.

McCracken, G. (1988) *The Long Interview*, Qualitative Research Methods series No. 13, Newbury Park, CA: Sage.

MacCrossan, L. (1984) *A Handbook for Interviewers*, London: HMSO.

McDermott, R.P. (1974) 'Achieving school failure', in G.D. Spindler (ed.) *Education and Cultural Process*, New York: Holt, Rinehart & Winston.

McDermott, R.P. (1977) 'Social relations as contexts for learning in school', *Harvard Education Review*, **47, 2**: 198–213.

McDermott, R.P. (1978) 'Relating and learning: an analysis of two classroom reading groups', in R. Shuy (ed.) *Linguistics and Reading*, Rawley, MA: Newbury House.

MacDonald, B. (1974) 'Evolution and the control of education', in D. Towney, (ed.), *Curriculum Evaluation Today: Trends and Implications*, London: Macmillan.

MacDonald, B. and Sanger, J. (1982) 'Just for the record? Notes towards a theory of interviewing in evaluation', in E. House (ed.) *Evaluation Review Studies Annual*, Beverly Hills, CA: Sage.

MacDonald, B. and Walker, R. (eds) (1974) *Innovation, Educational Research and the Problem of Control*, Norwich: University of East Anglia, Centre for Applied Research in Education.

MacDonald, B. and Walker, R. (1975) 'Case study and the social philosophy of educational research', *Cambridge Journal of Education*, **15, 1**: 2–11.

MacDonald, B., Adelman, C., Jushner, S. and Walker, R. (1982) *Bread and Dreams: A Case Study of Bilingual Schooling in the USA*, Norwich: University of East Anglia, Centre for Applied Research in Education.

MacDonald, K. and Tipton, C. (1993) 'Using documents', in N. Gilbert (ed.) *Researching Social Life*, London: Sage.

MacFarlane Smith, J. (1972) *Interviewing in Market and Social Research*, London: Routledge.

McIntyre, D.I. (1980) 'Systematic observation of classroom activities', *Educational Analysis*, **2, 2**: 30.

McIntyre, D.I. and Macleod, G. (1979) 'The characteristics and uses of systematic classroom observation', in R. McAleese and D. Hamilton (eds) *Understanding Classroom Life*, London: NFER.

Malinowski, B. (1922) *Argonauts of the Western Pacific*, London: Routledge & Kegan Paul.

Mandelbaum, D.G. (1973) 'The study of life history: Gandhi', *Current Anthropology*, **14, 3**: 177–96, reprinted in R.G. Burgess (ed.) (1982) *Field Research: A Sourcebook and Field Manual*, London: Allen & Unwin.

Marwick, A. (1977) *An Introduction to History*, Milton Keynes: Open University.

Matza, D. (1964) *Delinquency and Drift*, Chichester: Wiley.

May, N. and Ruddock, J. (1983) *Sex Stereotyping and the Early Years of* Schooling, Norwich: University of East Anglia, Centre of Applied Research in Education.

Mead, G.H. (1934) *Mind, Self and Society*, Chicago: University of Chicago Press.

Mead, G.H. (1971) *Coming of Age in Samoa: A Study of Adolescence and Sex in Primitive Societies*, Harmondsworth: Penguin.

Measor, L. (1985) 'Interviewing: a strategy in qualitative research', in R. G. Burgess (ed.) *Strategies of Educational Research: Qualitative Methods*, Lewes: Falmer Press.

Measor, L, and Sykes, P.J. (1990) 'Ethics and methodology in life history', in I.F. Goodson, (ed.) *Studying Teachers' Lives*, London: Routledge.

Measor, L. and Woods, P. (1983) 'The interpretation of pupil myths', in M. Hammersley (ed.) *The Ethnography of Schooling: Methodological Issues*, Studies in Education, Driffield: Nafferton Books.

Measor, L. and Woods, P. (1984) *Changing Schools*, Milton Keynes: Open University Press.

Mehan, H. (1973) 'Assessing children's language-using abilities: methodological and cross cultural implications', in M. Armer and A.D. Grimshaw (eds) *Comparative Social Research: Methodological Problems and Strategies*, New York: Wiley.

Merriam, S.B. (1988) *Case Study Research in Education*, San Francisco: Jossey Bass.

Miles, M.B. (1979) 'Qualitative data as an attractive nuisance: the problem of analysis', *Administrative Science Quarterly*, 24 Dec: 590–601.

Miles, M.B. and Huberman, A.M. (1984) *Qualitative Data Analysis: A Sourcebook of New Methods*, Beverly Hills, CA: Sage.

Miles, M.B. and Huberman, A.M. (1994) *Qualitative Data Analysis: An Expanded Sourcebook*, Thousand Oaks, CA: Sage.

Milgram, S. (1974) *Obedience to Authority*, London: Tavistock.

Milroy, L. (1987) *Observing and Analysing Natural Language: A Critical Account of Sociolinguistic Method*, Oxford: Blackwell.

Mishler, E. (1986) *Research Interviewing: Context and Narrative*, London: Harvard University Press.

Mishler, E. (1990) 'Validation in inquiry guided research', *Harvard Educational Review*, **60, 4**: 414–42.

Mostyn, B. (1985) 'The content analysis of qualitative research data: a dynamic approach' in M. Brenner, J. Brown, and D. Canter, (eds) *The Research Interview: Uses and Approaches*, London: Academic Press.

Murphy, R.J.L. and Torrance, H. (eds) (1987) *Evaluating Education: Issues and Methods*, London: Harper & Row/Open University Press.

Myerhoff, B. (1978) *Number our Days*, New York: Dutton.

Myerhoff, B. and Tufte, V. (1974) 'Life history as integration: an essay on experiential model', *The Gerontologist*, December: 541–43.

NATFHE (1993) March. *An Equal Opportunities Guide to Language*, London: National Association of Teachers in Further and Higher Education.

Nebraska Feminist Collective (C. Trainor, B. Hartung, J.C. Ollenburger, H.A. Moore, M.J. Deeger) (1983) 'A feminist ethic for social science research', *Women's Studies International Forum*, **6, 5**: 534–43.

Newman, O. (1973) *Defensible Space: People and Design in the Violent City*, London: Architectural Press.

Nias, J. and Groundwater-Smith, S. (1988) *The Enquiring Teacher: Supporting and Sustaining Teacher Research*, London: Falmer Press.

Nisbet, J. and Entwhistle, N.J. (1970) *Educational Research Methods*, London: University of London Press.

Nisbet, J. and Entwhistle, N.J. (1984) 'Writing the report', in J. Bell *et al.*, *Conducting Small-scale Investigations in Educational Management*, London: Harper & Row.

Nixon, J. (ed.) (1981) *A Teacher's Guide to Action Research*, London: Grant McIntyre.

Northedge, A. (1990) *The Good Study Guide*, Milton Keynes: Open University Press.

Oakley, A. (1974) *The Sociology of Housework*, London: Martin Robertson.

Oakley, A. (1981) 'Interviewing women: a contradiction in terms', in H. Roberts (ed.) *Doing Feminist Research*, London: Routledge.

Olesen, V. (1994) 'Feminisms and models of qualitative research', in N.K. Denzin and Y.S. Lincoln (eds), *Handbook of Qualitative Research*, Thousand Oaks, CA: Sage.

Open University (1993) *An Equal Opportunities Guide to Language and Image*, Milton Keynes: Open University Press.

Osmond, H. (1959) 'The historical and sociological development of mental hospitals', in C. Gasken (ed.) *Psychiatric Architecture*, Washington, DC: American Psychiatric Association.

Outhwaite, W. (1975) *Understanding Social Life: The Method Called Verstehen*, London: Allen & Unwin.

Palmer, V.M. (1928) *Field Studies in Sociology: A Student's Manual*, Chicago, IL: University of Chicago Press.

Parsons, T. (1959) 'The social structure of the family' in R. Anshen (ed.) *The Family: Its Functions and Destiny*, New York: Harper & Row.

Patton, M. (1980) *Qualitative Evaluation Methods*, London: Sage.

Payne, G.C.F. and Cuff, E.C. (1982) *Doing Teaching: The Practical Management of Classrooms*, London: Batsford.

Perera, K. (1984) *Children's Writing and Reading: Analysing Classroom Language*, Oxford: Blackwell.

Phillips, S.U. (1972) 'Participant structures and communicative competence: Warm Springs children in community and classroom', in C.B. Cazden, D.H. Hymes and V.P. John (eds) *Functions of Language in the Classroom*, New York: Teachers College Press.

Pitt, D.C. (1972) *Using Historical Sources in Anthropology and Sociology*, New York: Holt, Rinehart & Winston.

Platt, J. (1981a) 'Evidence and proof in documentary research: some specific problems of documentary research', *Sociological Review*, **29, 1**: 31–52.

Platt, J. (1981b) 'Evidence and proof in documentary research: some shared problems of documentary research', *Sociological Review*, **29, 1**: 53–66.

Platt, J. (1981c) 'On interviewing one's peers', *British Journal of Sociology* **32, 1**: 75–91.

Platt, J. (1988) 'What can case studies do?', *Studies in Qualitative Methodology*, **1**: 1–23.

Plowden Report (1967) *Children and Their Primary Schools*, Report of the Central Advisory Council for Education, London: HMSO.

Plummer, K. (1983) *Documents of Life: An Introduction to the Problems and Literature of a Humanistic Method*, London: Allen & Unwin.

Pollard, A. (1984) 'Coping strategies and the multiplication of differentiation in infant classrooms', *British Educational Research Journal*, **10, 1**: 33–48.

Pollard, A. (1985a) 'Opportunities and difficulties of a teacher–ethnographer: a personal account', in R.G. Burgess (ed.) *Field Methods in the Study of Education: Issues and Problems*, Lewes: Falmer Press.

Pollard, A. (1985b) *The Social World of the Primary School*, London: Holt, Rinehart & Winston.

Pollard, A. (1987) 'Studying children's perspectives: a collaborative approach', in G. Walford (ed.) (1987) *Doing Sociology of Education*, London: Falmer Press.

Pollard, A. and Tann, S. (1993) *Reflective Teaching in the Primary School: A Handbook for the Classroom*, 2nd edition, London: Cassell.

Popper, K. (1959) *The Logic of Scientific Discovery*, London: Routledge & Kegan Paul.

Powdermaker, H. (1966) *Stranger and Friend: The Way of an Anthropologist*, New York: Norton.

Powney, J. and Watts, M.D. (1984) 'Reporting interviews: a code of good practice', *Research Intelligence*, September.

Powney, J. and Watts, M.D. (1987) *Interviewing in Educational Research*, London: Routledge & Kegan Paul.

Prosser, J. (1992) 'Personal reflections on the use of photography in an ethnographic case study', *British Educational Research Journal*, **18, 4**: 397–412.

Punch, M. (1994) 'Politics and ethics in qualitative research' in N.K. Denzin and Y. Lincoln, (eds) *Handbook of Qualitative Research*, Thousand Oaks, CA: Sage.
Rabinger, M. (1992) *Directing the Documentary*, Boston, MA: Focal Press.
Ramazanoglu, C. (1989) *Feminism and the Contradictions of Oppression*, London: Routledge.
Randall, G. (1987) 'Gender differences in pupil–teacher interaction in workshops and laboratories', in G. Weiner, and M. Arnot (eds) *Gender and the Politics of Schooling*. London: Unwin Hyam.
Ratcliffe, S.W. (1988) 'Notional validity in qualitative reseach', *Knowledge Creation Diffusion and Illustration*, **52**: 147–67.
Reid, W. (1986) 'Curriculum theory and curriculum change: what can we learn from history?', *Journal of Curriculum Studies*, **18, 2**: 159–66.
Reinharz, S. (1992) *Feminist Methods in Social Research*, New York: Oxford University Press.
Rhode, D. (ed.) (1990) *Theoretical Perspectives on Sexual Difference*, New Haven, CT: Yale University Press.
Ribbens, J. (1989) 'Interviewing – An "Unnatural Situation"?', *Women's Studies International Forum*, **12, 6**: 579–92.
Ribbins, P. and Thomas, H. (1981) *Research in Educational Management and Administration*, Coombe Lodge: BEMAS.
Richards, T.J. and Richards, L. (1994) 'Using computers in qualitative research', in N.K. Denzin and Y. Lincoln (eds) *Handbook of Qualitative Research*, Thousand Oaks, CA: Sage.
Riis, J.A. (1971) (Orig. 1890) *How the Other Half Lives*, New York: Dover.
Riley, J. (1990) *Getting The Most From Your Data*, Bristol: Technical and Educational Services.
Rintoul, K. and Thorne, K. (1975) *Open-Plan Organisation in the Primary School*, London: Ward Lock Educational.
Rist, R.C. (1970) 'Student social class and teacher expectations: the self-fulfilling prophecy in ghetto education', *Harvard Education Review*, **40, 3**: 411–51, reprinted in M. Hammersley (ed.) (1986) *Case Studies in Classroom Research*, Milton Keynes: Open University Press.
Rist, R.C. (1972) 'Social distance and social inequality in a ghetto kindergarten classroom', *Urban Education*, **7, 3**: 241–60.
Rist, R.C. (1973) *The Urban School: A Factory for Failure*, Cambridge, MA: MIT Press.
Rivlin, L.G. and Rothenberg, M. (1976) 'The use of space in open classrooms', in H. Proshansky, G. Rivlin and W. Ittleson (eds) *Environmental Psychology: People in Their Physical Settings*, New York: Holt, Rinehart & Winston.
Rock, P. (1979) *The Making of Symbolic Interactionism*, London: Macmillan.
Roberts, H. (ed.) (1981) *Doing Feminist Research*, London: Routledge.
Rosen, H. (1985) 'The voices of communities and language in classrooms', *Harvard Education Review*, SS, No. 4: 448–56.
Rosenthal, R. and Jacobson, L. (1968) *Pygmalion in the Classroom*, New York: Holt, Rinehart & Winston.
Rubin, Z. (1980) *Children's Friendships*, London: Fontana.
Rudestam, K.E. and Newton, R.M. (1992) *Surviving Your Dissertation: A Comprehensive Guide to Content and Process*, Newbury Park, CA: Sage.
Runyan, W.M. (1982) *Life Histories and Psychobiography: Explorations in Theory and Method*, New York: Oxford University Press.
Rynkiewich, M.A. and Spradley, J.P. (eds) (1976) *Ethics and Anthropology: Dilemmas in Fieldwork*, New York: Wiley.
Saran, R. (1985) 'The use of archives and interviews in research on educational policy,' in R.G. Burgess (ed.) *Issues in Educational Research*, London: Falmer Press.

Scarth, J. and Hammersley, M. (1986) 'Questioning ORACLE: an assessment of ORACLE's analysis of teachers' questions', *Educational Research*, **28, 3**: 174–84.

Scarth, J. and Hammersley, M. (1987) 'More questioning of ORACLE: a reply to Croll and Galton', *Educational Research*, **29**, 1.

Scheflen, A.E. (1972) *Communication Structure*, Bloomington: Indiana University Press.

Schofield, J.W. (1990) 'Increasing the generalizability of qualitative research' in E. Eisner and A. Peshkin (eds) *Qualitative Inquiry in Education: The Continuing Debate*, New York: Teachers College Press.

Schofield, M. (1968) *The Sexual Behaviour of Young People*, Harmondsworth: Penguin.

Schon, P.A. (1983) *The Reflective Practitioner: How Professionals Think in Action*, New York: Basic Books.

Schon, P.A. (1987) *Educating The Reflective Practitioner: Toward a New Design for Teaching and Learning in the Profession*, San Francisco: Jossey-Bass.

Schostak, J.F. (1982) 'The revelation of the world of pupils', *Cambridge Journal of Education*, **12, 3**: 175–85.

Schwartz, H., and Jacobs, J. (1979) *Qualitative Sociology: A Method to the Madness*, New York: Free Press.

Scott, J. (1990) *A Matter of Record: Documentary Sources in Social Research*, Cambridge: Polity Press.

Scriven, M. (1987) 'The methodology of evolution', in B.R. Worthen and J.R. Sanders, (eds), *Educational Evaluation: Theory and Practice*, CA: Wadsworth.

Seabourne, M. and Lowe, R. (1977) *The English School: Its Architecture and Organisation, 1870–1970*, London: Routledge & Kegan Paul.

Seidel, J.V., and Clark, J.A. (1984) 'The Ethnograph: a computer program for the analysis of qualitative data', *Qualitative Sociology*, **7,** 110–25.

Sharma, U. and Meighan, R. (1980) 'Schooling and sex roles: the case of GCE's level mathematics, *British Journal of Sociology of Education*, **1, 2**: 193–206.

Sharpe, R. and Green, A. (1975) *Education and Social Control*, London: Routledge & Kegan Paul.

Sharrock, W.W. and Anderson, R.G. (1982) 'Teaching and talking: reflective comments on in-classroom activities', in G.C.F. Payne and E.C. Cuff (eds) *Doing Teaching: The Practical Management of Classrooms*, London: Batsford.

Shostak, M. (1981) *NISA: The Life and Words of A! Kung Woman*, Cambridge, MA: Harvard University Press.

Sikes, P., Measor, L. and Woods, P. (1985) *Teacher Careers: Crises and Continuities*, Lewes: Falmer Press.

Silverman, D. (1985) *Qualitative Methodology and Sociology*, London: Gower.

Silverman, D. (1993) *Interpreting Qualitative Data: Methods for Analysing Talk, Text and Interaction*, London, Routledge.

Simon, A. and Boyer, E.G. (1967) *Mirrors for Behavior: An Anthology of Classroom Observation Instruments*, Philadelphia: Research for Better Schools Inc.

Simons, H. (ed.) (1980) *Towards a Science of the Singular*, CARE Occasional Publications 19, Norwich: University of East Anglia, Centre for Applied Research in Education.

Simons, H. (1981) 'Conversation piece: the practice of interviewing in case study research', in C. Adelman (ed.) *Uttering, Muttering: Collecting, Using and Reporting Talk for Social and Educational Research*, London: Grant McIntyre.

Simons, H. (1982) 'Suggestions for a school self-evaluation based on democratic principles', in R. McCormick (ed.) *Calling Education to Account*, London: Open University Press and Heinemann Educational Books.

Sinclair, J. McL. and Coulthard, C.M. (1975) *Towards an Analysis of Discourse*, London: Oxford University Press.

Skeggs, B. (1992) 'Confessions of a feminist researcher', *Sociology Review*, September, 14–17.
Slocum, S. (1975) 'Woman the gatherer: male bias in anthropology', in R. Reiter (ed.) *Toward an Anthropology of Women*, New York: Monthly Review Press.
Sluckin, A. (1981) *Growing Up in the Playground*, London: Routledge.
Smith, D. (1974) 'Women's perspective as a radical critique of sociology', *Sociological Inquiry*, **44**, 1, 7–13.
Smith, D. (1989) *The Everyday World as Problematic*, Milton Keynes: Open University Press.
Smith, L.M. (1994) 'Biographical method', in: N.K. Denzin and Y.S. Lincoln (eds), *Handbook of Qualitative Research*, Thousand Oaks, CA: Sage.
Smith, L. and Geoffrey, G. (1968) *Complexities of an Urban Classroom*, New York: Holt, Rinehart & Winston.
Smith, L. and Keith, P. (1971) *Anatomy of an Educational Innovation*, New York: John Wiley.
Smythe, J. (ed.) (1987) *Educating Teachers: Changing the Nature of Professional Knowledge*, Lewes: Falmer.
Soltis, J.F. (1989) 'The ethics of qualitative research', *Qualitative Studies in Education*, **2, 2**: 123–30.
Sommer, R. (1967) 'Classroom ecology', *Journal of Applied Behavioral Science*, **3**: 489–503.
Sommer, R. (1969) *Personal Space*, Englewood Cliffs, NJ: Prentice-Hall.
Spindler, G.D. (ed.) (1982) *Doing the Ethnography of Schooling*, New York: Holt, Rinehart & Winston.
Spradley, J.P. (ed.) (1979) *The Ethnographic Interview*, New York: Holt, Rinehart & Winston.
Spradley, J.P. (ed.) (1980) *Participant Observation*, New York: Holt, Rinehart & Winston.
Stake, R. (1980) 'The case study method in social inquiry', in H. Simons (ed.) *Towards a Science of the Singular*, Norwich: University of East Anglia Centre for Applied Research in Education.
Stake, R. (1981) 'Case study research in social inquiry', *Educational Researcher*, **7**: 5–8.
Stake, R. (1994) 'Case studies', in N.K. Denzin and Y.S. Lincoln (eds) *Handbook of Qualitative Research*, Thousand Oaks, CA: Sage.
Stake, R. and Gjerder (1974) 'An evolution of TCITY, The Turin City Institute for Talented Youth', in Kroft, R. *et al.* (eds) *Four Evolution Examples: Anthropological, Economic, Narrative and Portrayal*, AERA Monograph Series on Curriculum Evaluation, Chicago: Rand McNally.
Stanley, J. (1992) 'Sex and the quiet schoolgirl', in P. Woods and M. Hammersley (eds) *Gender and Ethnicity in Schools: Ethnographic Accounts*, London: Routledge.
Stanley, L. and Wise, S. (1983) *Breaking Out: Feminist Consciousness and Feminist Research*, London: Routledge.
Stanworth, M. (1981) *Gender and Schooling: A Study of Sexual Division in the Classroom*, London: Hutchinson.
Stanworth, M. (1984) 'Women and class analysis': a reply to Goldthorpe', *Sociology*, **18**, 2, 159–70.
Steedman, C. (1987) *The Tidy House*, London: Virago.
Stenhouse, L. (1975) *An Introduction to Curriculum Research and Development*, London: Heinemann.
Stenhouse, L. (1981) 'Library access, library use and user education in academic sixth forms: an autobiographical acount', in R.G. Burgess (ed.) *The Research Process in Educational Settings*, Lewes: Falmer Press.
Stenhouse, L. (1987) 'The conduct, analysis and reporting of case study in educational research and evaluation', in R. Murphy and H. Torrance (eds) *Evaluating Education: Issues and Methods*, London: Harper & Row.

Strauss, A.L. (1987) *Qualitative Analysis for Social Scientists*, Cambridge: Cambridge University Press.
Strauss, A.L. and Corbin, J. (1990) *Basics of Qualitative Research*. Newbury Park, CA: Sage.
Stubbs, M. (1983a) *Language, Schools and Classrooms*, 2nd edn, London: Methuen.
Stubbs, M. (1983b) *Disclosure Analysis: The Sociolinguistic Analysis of Natural Language*, Oxford: Blackwell.
Swann, J. (1992) *Girls, Boys and Language*. London: Blackwell.
Swann Report (1985) The 'education for all: report of the Committee of Inquiry into the education of children from ethnic minority groups,' HMSO Cmnd 9453, March.
Templin, P.A. (1982) 'Still photography in evaluation' in N.L. Smith (ed.) *Communication Strategies in Evaluation*, Beverly Hills, CA: Sage.
Terkel, S. (1970) *Hard Times: An Oral History of the Great Depression*, London: Allen Lane.
Terkel, S. (1977) *Working*, Harmondsworth: Penguin.
Thomas, D. (1993) 'Empirical authors, texts and model readers: a response to "managing marginality"', *British Educational Research Journal*, **19, 5**, 467–74.
Thomas, W.I. and Znaniecki, F. (1958) *The Polish Peasant in Europe and America*, (Orig. 1918–1920), New York: Dover Publications.
Tosh, C. (1991) *The Pursuit of History*, London: Longman.
Tripp, D. (1993) *Critical Incidents in Teaching*, London: Routledge.
Trudgill, P. (1974) *Sociolinguistics: An Introduction*, Harmondworth: Penguin.
Turabin, K.L. (1980) *A Manual for Writers of Research Papers, Theses and Dissertations*, London: Heinemann.
Turner, G. (1982) 'The distribution of classroom interactions', *Research in Education* **27**: 41–8.
Underwood, G., McCaffrey, M. and Underwood, J. (1992) 'Gender differences in a co-operative computer-based language task', *Educational Review*, **32**(1), 44–49.
Van Maanen, J. (1988) *Tales of the Field: On Writing Ethnography*, Chicago: University of Chicago Press.
Vierra, A., Boehm, C., and Meely, S. (1982) 'Anthropology and educational studies', in A. Hartnett (ed.) *The Social Sciences in Educational Studies: A Selective Guide to the Literature*, London: Heinemann.
Wagner, J. (ed.) (1979) *Images of Information: Still Photography in the Social Sciences*, Beverly Hills, CA: Sage.
Wakeman, B. (1986) 'Action research for staff development', in C. Day and R. Moore (eds) *Staff Development in the Secondary School*, London: Croom Helm.
Waksler, F. (1986) 'Studying children: phenomenological insights', *Human Studies*, **9**, 71–82.
Walford, G. (ed.) (1987) *Doing Sociology of Education*, Lewes: Falmer Press.
Walker, R. (1980) 'The conduct of educational case studies: ethics, theory and procedures', in B. Dockrell and B. Hamilton (eds) *Re-thinking Educational* Research, London: Hodder & Stoughton; reprinted in M. Hammersley (ed.) (1986) *Controversies in Classroom Research*, Milton Keynes: Open University Press.
Walker, R. (1985) *Doing Research: A Handbook for Teachers*, London: Methuen.
Walker, R. (1986) 'The conduct of educational case studies', in M. Hammersley (ed.) *Controversies in Classroom Research*, Milton Keynes: Open University Press.
Walker, R. and Adelman, C. (1975) 'Interaction analysis in informal classrooms: a critical comment on the Flanders system', *British Journal of Educational Psychology* **4, 1** :73–6; reprinted in M. Hammersley (ed.) (1986) *Controversies in Classroom Research*, Milton Keynes: Open University Press.
Wardhaugh, R. (1986) *An Introduction to Sociolinguistics*, Oxford: Blackwell.

Warnock Report, The (1978) 'Special education needs: report of the Committee of Inquiry into the education of handicapped children and young people', HMSO Cmnd 7212.

Warren, C. (1988) *Gender Issues in Field Research*, Newbury Park, CA: Sage.

Warren, C. and Rasmussen, P.K. (1977) 'Sex and gender in field research', *Urban Life and Culture*, **6**: 349–69.

Watson, L.C. (1976) 'Understanding a life history as a subjective document: hermeneutical and phenomenological perspectives', *Ethos*, **4**: 95–131.

Watson, L.C. and Watson-Franke, M.B. (1985) *Interpreting Life Histories*, New Brunswick: Rutgers.

Wax, M.L. and Wax, R.H. (1971) 'Cultural deprivation as an educational ideology', in E.B. Leacock (ed.) *The Culture of Poverty: A Critique*, New York: Simon & Schuster.

Wax, R.H. (1971) *Doing Anthropology: Warnings and Advice*, Chicago, IL: University of Chicago Press.

Webb, B. (1926) 'The art of note-taking,' in B. Webb, *My Apprenticeship*, London: Longmans' Green.

Webb, R. (1990) *Practical Research in the Primary School*, Lewes: Falmer Press.

Webb, S. (1985) 'Feminist research and qualitative methods', in R.G. Burgess (ed.) *Issues in Educational Research: Qualitative Methods*, London: Falmer Press.

Weber, L. (1971) *The English Infant School and Informal Education*, New York: Prentice-Hall.

Weber, M. (1949) *The Methodology of the Social Sciences*, New York: Free Press. (English translation).

Webber, C.F., and Skau, K.G. (1993) 'Seeking school district effectiveness', *Studies in Educational Administration*, **58**: 15–22.

Whyte, W.F. (1955) *Street Corner Society*, Chicago: University of Chicago Press, 2nd edition.

Whyte, W.F. (1982) 'Interviewing in field research,' in R.G. Burgess (ed.) *Field Research: A Sourcebook and Field Manual*, London: Falmer Press.

Whyte, W.F. (1988) *Learning from the Field: A Guide from Experience*, London: Sage.

Willis, P. (1977) *Learning to Labour: How Working-Class Kids Get Working-Class Jobs*, Farnborough: Saxon House.

Wilson, S. (1977) 'The use of ethnographic techniques in educational research', *Review of Educational Research*, **47, 1**: 245–65.

Windass, A. (1989) 'Classroom practices and organization', in C. Skelton (ed.), *Whatever Happens to Little Women?*, Milton Keynes: Open University Press.

Wittrock, M. (ed.) (1987) *Handbook of Research on Teaching*, New York: Macmillan.

Wolcott, H. (1973) *The Man in the Principal's Office: An Ethnography*, New York: Holt, Rinehart & Winston.

Wolcott, H.F. (1990a) *Writing Up Qualitative Research*, London: Sage.

Wolcott, H.F. (1990b) 'On seeking – and rejecting validity in qualitative research', in E.W. Eisner and A. Peshkin (eds) *A Qualitative Inquiry in Education: The Continuing Debate*, New York: Teachers College Press.

Wolcott, H.F. (1994) *Transforming Qualitative Data: Description, Analysis and Interpretation*, Newbury Park, CA: Sage.

Woods, P. (ed.) (1980) *Pupil Strategies: Explorations in the Sociology of the School*, London: Croom Helm.

Woods, P. (1985a) 'New songs played skilfully: Creativity and technique in writing up qualitative research' in R.G. Burgess (ed.) *Issues in Educational Research: Qualitative Methods*, Lewes: Falmer Press.

Woods, P. (ed.) (1985b) 'Conversations with teachers: some aspects of life history method', *British Educational Research Journal*, **11, 1**: 13–26.

Woods, P. (ed.) (1986) *Inside Schools: Ethnography in Educational Research*, London: Routledge & Kegan Paul.
Woods, P. (1987) 'Life histories and teacher knowledge' in J. Smyth (ed.) *Educating Teachers: Changing the Nature of Pedagogical Knowledge*, Lewes: Falmer Press.
Woods, P. (1993) 'Managing marginality: teacher development through grounded life history', *British Educational Research Journal*, **19, 5**: 447–65.
Woods, P.J. (1993) 'Keys to the Past — and to the future: the empirical author replies', *British Educational Research Journal*, **19, 5**: 475–98.
Woods, P. and Hammersley, M. (eds) (1993) *Gender and Ethnicity in Schools: Ethnographic Accounts*, London: Routledge.
Woods, P. and Sykes, P.J. (1987) 'The use of teacher biographies in professional self-development, in F. Todd, (ed.) *Planning Continuing Professional Development*, London: Croom Helm.
Woodhead, M., Light, P. and Carr, R. (eds) *Growing Up in a Changing Society*, London: Routledge.
Worthen, B. and Sanders, J. (1987) *Educational Evaluation: Alternative Approaches and Practical Guidelines*, London: Longman.
Wragg, T. (1984) 'Conducting and analysing interviews', in J. Bell *et al.* (eds) *Conducting Small-scale Investigations in Educational Management*, London: Harper & Row.
Wright, C. (1986) 'School processes: an ethnographic study', in J. Eggleston, D. Dunn, M. Antali (eds) *Education For Some*, Stoke on Trent: Trentham Books.
Wright, C. (1987) 'The relations between teachers and Afro-Caribbean pupils: observing multi-racial classrooms', in G. Weiner, and M. Arnor, (eds) (1987) *Gender and the Politics of Schooling*, London: Unwin Hyman.
Wright, C. (1990) 'Comments in reply to the article by P. Foster', *British Educational Research Journal*, **16, 4**: 351–55.
Yin, R.K. (1984) *Case Study Research: Design and Methods*, Newbury Park, CA: Sage.
Zimmerman, D.H. and Wieder, D.C. (1977) 'The diary–diary–interview method', *Urban Life*, **5, 4**: 479–98.
Zuber-Skerritt, O. (1992) *Action Research in Higher Education*, London: Kogan Page.

Author index

Subject index